BAL MAIDENS

Joyce, showing Bal Maiden Costume
Courtesy of Paddy Bradley

BAL MAIDENS

Lynne Mayers

Blaize Bailey Books
2008

First published in 2004 by
THE HYPATIA TRUST

Second Edition
4th Revision
Published by
BLAIZE BAILEY BOOKS
2008

© Lynne Mayers

Front cover: Bal maidens spalling and wagoning copper ore at Carn Brea 1881, from Harper's New Monthly Magazine No. 378 Vol 63 p. 806

Back cover: Working model of a racking frame, King Edward Mine Museum (courtesy of KEM)
Sculptures of clay workers, Wheal Martyn China Clay Museum (courtesy of China Clay Country Park Mining and Heritage Centre)

All rights reserved. No part of this publication may be reproduced, stored in a retrieval system or transmitted in any form by any means, electronic, mechanical, photocopying, recording or otherwise, without the written consent of the publisher.

CONTENTS

Chap 1.	Bal Maidens - Their History	Page 1
Chap 2.	Bal Maidens at Work	25
Chap 3.	Bal Maidens at Home	53
Chap 4.	Bal Maidens at the Copper Mines	73
Chap 5.	Bal Maidens at the Tin Mines and Smelters	91
Chap 6.	The 'Clay' Maidens	115
Chap 7.	Bal Maidens and Other Minerals	131
Chap 8.	The Counthouse Women	151
Chap 9.	Bal Maidens - the Cost	167
Chap 10.	Mine Closures - the End of the Road or a New Life?	195
Chap 11.	Myth and Reality	217
Chap 12.	Bal Maidens – the Real People	239
Glossary		263
References:	Books, journals etc.	266
	Cost Books	269
	Newspaper reports & Mining Journal	270
General Index		271
Mine Index		275
Bal Maiden Index		278

ILLUSTRATIONS

Fig No.	Title	Page
	Joyce, showing Bal Maiden Costume	Frontispiece
1	Map Showing Employment of Bal Maidens by Parish	3
2	Dressing Floor at Dolcoath c. 1831	9
3	Dressing Floors of Tin Mine 1858	11
4	Proportion of Women and Children Employed at Mines	14
5	Number of Bal Maidens by Census Year	21
6	Age Distribution of Bal Maidens	28
7	One Penny Mining Tokens (1811 and 1812)	40
8	St. Ives Consols 1863	45
9	Spalling Women at Mitchell's Shaft, East Pool	47
10	Tin Framing at Dolcoath c. 1890	50
11	Mine Housing at Wheal Josiah, Tavistock	54
12	Frog Street in Bere Alston	55
13	Cornish Bal Maidens (Simonin 1867)	59
14	Bal Maiden in Work Dress and Sunday Best	63
15	Dolcoath Bal Maidens	64
16	Iron Shod Shoes	65
17	Bal Maiden Meeting her Sweetheart after Work	69
18	Typical Copper Dressing Procedures	76
19	Bal Maidens Tools of the Trade	78
20.	Bal Maidens Spalling (Henderson c. 1858)	79
21.	Bal Maidens Washing and Picking (Henderson c. 1858)	80
22.	Bal Maidens Cobbing (Henderson c. 1858)	82
23.	Bal Maidens Bucking, Barrowing and Riddling (Henderson c. 1858)	83
24.	Bal Maidens Jigging (Henderson c. 1858)	85
25.	Typical Tin Dressing Procedures	96
26	Tincroft Spallers	100
27	Tincroft Spallers	100
28	Serving the Buddles, Wheal Basset	102
29	Tozing and Packing Tin	103
30	Bal Maidens at Racking Frames (Henderson c. 1858)	105
31	Bal Maidens at Racking Frames, South Wheal Frances	106
32	Bal Maidens Barrowing, West Wheal Seaton	107
33	Women at Geevor Picking Belt	113
34	Cleaning Clay Blocks under Reeders	118
35	Women Operating Hand Pumps at Clay Works	119
36	Great Treverbyn Mill Women Workers	120
37	Women Clay Dressers with Scraping Tools	120
38	Seasonality of Female Employment at Clay Works	121
39	Number of Females Employed at Clay Works	123

Fig No.	Title	Page
40	Lower Ninestones Clay Works Cost Book	124
41	Polpuff Dressing Tables	127
42	Women Orthoclase Dressers at Polpuff Mine	128
43	Bal Maiden at Brunton's Calciner	133
44	Girls Picking Lead from a Rotating Trommel	137
45	Bal Maidens at Silverbrook Lead Mine	139
46	Morwhellam Quay showing Manganese Mill	143
47	Women and Girls Dressing Wolfram	144
48	Women Employees, Great Rock Iron Mine	145
49	Woman Employee at Mill, Great Rock Iron Mine	145
50	Botallack Counthouse	152
51	Counthouse Woman	153
52	Cameo Sketch of Counthouse Woman	154
53	Botallack Counthouse Pewter Dinner Service	157
54	Named Counthouse Women	159
55	Counthouse Staff (S. Condurrow?)	163
56	Spalling Floor, Pednandrea	172
57	Percentage of Female Deaths by Age	182
58	Gravestone for Ellen Vincent	188
59	Spalling and Loading Copper Ore-Stuff	189
60	Ex-Bal Maiden Marah Goninan	200
61	Mountain Mine Engine House, Allihies	203
62	Cornish Village and Counthouse, Allihies	204
63	Zealous Gold Diggers, Bendigo 1852 (S. T. Gill)	207
64	Ex-Bal Maiden Ann Gribble	209
65	Ex-Bal Maiden Susan Dunn	209
66	Ex-Bal Maiden Mary Bennetts Harry	211
67	Ex-Bal Maiden Caroline Adams	212
68	Ex-Bal Maiden Caroline Rodda	212
69	'The Three Graces'	219
70	Frontispiece from 'Norah Lang, the Mine Girl'	228
71	Dolcoath Bal Maidens	230
72	Women Clay Dressers, Carloggas	231
73	Grace Briney, c. 75 yrs	240
74	Susan Robins on her 100th Birthday	247
75	Loretta Wilton with Husband Thomas	249
76	Sidwell Kruge with Husband Henry	253
77	Gravestone for Sidwell Kruge	253
78	May and Jane Davis at Rocks Clay Works	256
79	Women Working at the Monitors at Rocks Clay Works	257
80	The Late Phyllis Lockett, Geevor	258
81	Minnie Andrews 1967	260

ABBREVIATIONS USED IN TEXT

CB	Cost Book (Mine Accounts)
CEC	Children's Employment Commission: report by Charles Barham on the Employment of Children And Young people in the Mines of Cornwall and Devonshire, and on the State, Condition and Treatment of such Children and Young Persons 1842 (page numbers relate to the transcript by Ian Winstanley, PICs Publishing 1999)
CFHS	Cornish Family History Society
CMHRC	Coal Mining History Resource Centre www.cmhrc.co.uk
CSL	Cornish Studies Library, Cornish Studies Centre, Redruth
CRO	Cornish Records Office, Truro
CT	Cornish Telegraph
MJ	Mining Journal
NMRS	Northern Mines Research Society
PDMHS	Peak District Mining History Society
PDRO	Plymouth & Devon Record Office
RCG	Royal Cornwall Gazette
RIC	Royal Institution of Cornwall, Truro
TNA	The National Archives, Kew
WB	West Briton
WM	China Clay Country Park Mining and Heritage Centre Archives, Wheal Martyn
WMN	Western Morning News

UNITS OF MONEY AND WEIGHT

The following Imperial Units are used in the text, as found in the original documents:

Money (£ .s. d.)

£1 = 20s (shillings) 1s = 12d (pence), 1d = 2 halfpence or 4 farthings

Weight (Ton, cwt, lb, oz.)

1 Ton = 20 cwt (hundredweight), 1 cwt = 112 lbs (pounds), 1 lb = 16 oz (ounces)
(Metric equivalent: 1 kg = approx 2.25 lbs)

REFERENCES AND FOOTNOTES

Footnotes appear at the end of each chapter, and give an abbreviated form of the references listed alphabetically at the end of the book. Please note that mine cost book and newspaper references are recorded as separate lists in the reference section, entered alphabetically by mine name. There is also a Mine Index, giving the parish in which they are located, at the end of the book.

PREFACE TO THE SECOND EDITION

Since the publication of the first edition of *Balmaidens*, new information has continued to come to light about the lives of the women and girls who worked at the mines of Devon and Cornwall. As a result, the most significant change has been to extend the geographical area covered in the book. This edition includes Dartmoor, and the Teign and Exe Valleys, for the first time. This gives us some very special new insights into the role of women in the early Dartmoor tin trading, and late 18th century manganese mining in the Exe Valley, as well as glimpses of women's duties at Great Rock Iron Mine in the mid 20th century. Other important additional material has been a more extensive use of the 1952 Scrapbook compiled by the Troon Women's Institute, and the '*Day and Night Book*' of two captains at Dolcoath written in 1822 and 1823. The Troon document has furnished additional 'cameos' of the lives of individual women or girls associated with mine work (for the final chapter) and contributed to a much fuller treatment of the late 19th century tin streams. The two documents together give us new glimpses into everyday life at the dressing floor, counthouse and sampling room, at Dolcoath, in particular.

Finding an appropriate referencing system has continued to be a challenge. With so much of the information discovered almost a sentence at a time, from disparate sources, it was always a choice between referencing only those which are quoted most regularly (which for the most part are already in the public domain) or enabling the reader to find documentation which may be hidden in some unexpected corner. In this edition we have continued to choose the latter, which leaves the problem of the bulk of footnotes created. As a result, we have moved to a double system of referencing in order to reduce the impact on each chapter. Firstly, reference numbers in the text continue to refer to footnotes (now at the end of the chapter, rather than at the back of the book). Secondly, at the end of longer quotations, references are given either in full, or as part-references which can be traced in the bibliography at the back of the book. In addition, where information for a named mine comes from a newspaper or mine cost book, the source is listed alphabetically by mine under two additional lists in the reference section already mentioned. This is still far from ideal, but hopefully slightly less cumbersome.

Finally, this edition uses the terminology '*bal maiden*' throughout, in preference to '*balmaiden*' (as in the first edition). This is following the advice of Prof. Charles Thomas, that the former is probably the more authentic usage.

PREFACE

The Cornwall and West Devon metal mines and smelters of the 18th and 19th century formed a unique and quite separate part of the mining heritage of these islands. It was here that much of our nation's mineral wealth was created, based in no small part on the labour of girls (from the age of eight or nine years old) and young or widowed women. No other metal mining district was so extensive, nor used women and girls in such abundance. Unlike the coalmining districts of the Scotland, the North East, Lancashire and parts of Wales, however, there was no history of women and girls working underground in Cornwall or Devon during this time; they were employed on the dressing floors only. They continued to be employed in this way even after 1842, when increasing public concern about the 'moral welfare' of women and children brought legislation to limit their employment in the factories and collieries. The last bal maidens were dismissed during the first two decades of the 20th century.

Comparatively little contemporary writing has been found about these women and girls. The only 'first-hand' accounts found, so far, come from just come four sources: five interviews, recorded in 1952 by the Women's Institute, of women who had worked in the mines and tin streams of Troon some fifty years previously; about eight interviews conducted in the 1970s with women who had worked at the Polpuff 'Glass' Mine in St. Dennis during the First World War; an interview of the *'last bal-maiden'* (Minnie Andrews) made in her ninetieth year in 1967; and a personal recollection from one of the women who worked on the picking belt at Geevor during the Second World War. The next 'nearest' first-hand accounts are from twenty-one interviews conducted for the 1842 Royal Commission researching into the conditions of employment of young people at the mines, and a tiny book entitled *'Patty Tremellin - written by herself'*. No journals or diaries of bal maidens appear to have survived, but this story of Martha (Patty) Tremelling, although written after her death, and published in 1841, seems to be based on her journal, and written by someone who had a first-hand knowledge of her life. Despite it not being actually written by Patty first-hand, it gives a startling insight into the world of the bal maiden in the St. Austell area in the 1820s and 1830s.

As well as there being so few contemporary documents relating to the life and work of these bal maidens, it has been equally difficult to find surviving relatives who may have archival material or anecdotal stories to tell. About twelve relatives have been kind enough to contribute information about their forebears but, even here, sadly, much of the information is very limited, and, with exception of a few photos, no artefacts or written documents have survived. It is now about ninety years since the last bal maidens went to work at the mine, and these stories are almost lost, as they pass from the communal memory.

Most other writing and observations about these women and girls in the Victorian era comes from middle or upper-class observers; some travellers passing through, artists or writers, or mine surgeons or adventurers with an interest in the business. Generally, they were far more interested in describing the activities surrounding the underground tasks of mining, or the events at the counthouse, than about what went on at surface on the dressing floors. The best descriptions of the work that the bal maidens carried out during this period have come from mining engineers writing about the dressing operations for their peer group. The most notable of these are William Pryce (published in 1778), William Henwood (1832), James Henderson (1858), and John Darlington (1878). The amount of space devoted to the dressing tasks, compared with the amount of information given on the other aspects of the mining operation, is also very sparse in much of the 20th century literature. Most has been written from the perspective of the major mining engineering and technological achievements, as an overview of the economic production and management, as a social study of the underground miner, or out of a concern and interest in the surviving industrial archaeology. While all of these are important and worthy subjects, the contribution and work of women and children at surface of the mines has either received no attention at all or, at best, very limited mention 'in passing'. The place of the bal maiden in the mining economy has only occasionally been seriously discussed, most notably by Gill Burke, Stephany Norwood, and Sharron Schwartz, all during the last decade of the 20th century.

In contrast to the lack of documents written by bal maidens, or of focused studies, there is much brief evidence of the work of these bal maidens scattered about in different places (often only a sentence at a time); in old mining documents, early travelogues, parish and census records, letters, periodicals and newspapers. Because references are hard to find, or in some cases incomplete (leaving many gaps, especially with regards to the finer detail of the dressing processes), it was only by visiting actual mining heritage sites, seeing what is left of the dressing floors, and imagining how they might have been that any really coherent understanding began to emerge of the jobs that these women and children had to do. This involved handling tools, and watching replica or re-installed equipment at work (asking numerous questions of their present-day operators) in order to try and assess what the everyday problems and challenges were, and to begin to understand the level of skill and strength required for each process.

So, this book is an effort to redress the dearth of record, and to write something from the perspective of the women and children at the mines. The first chapter sets the historical scene of mining and quarrying in West Devon and Cornwall, and the place of the women and children in it. It also tries to give a numerical overview of the numbers of bal maidens employed over the years. The next two chapters look at the general life of the bal maidens, at work as well as at home. The subsequent five chapters deal with the tasks allocated to women at the different types of metal mines and smelters, clay pits and quarries. Two more chapters look at the costs of working at the mine (in terms of health, education and accidents) and what happened to the bal maidens when the mines closed. The final chapters look at some of the myths and ideas about bal maidens that have built up over the years, and compare that with the real people. This includes cameos of fifteen women and girls whose stories have survived and who, together, illustrate many different aspects of their lives.

It has been almost impossible to separate the history of the mines in Cornwall from those in West Devon (especially on the east bank of the Tamar). A few records for this area have found their way into the wrong county, and others appear to be in the wrong county due to changes in the county boundary over the years. Mine management and personnel did not necessarily observe county boundaries in their work, and certainly the policies for employment of females was the same, so it seems appropriate to include both geographical areas in the book.

Many of the areas in West Devon and Cornwall also show a complex array of mining and extractive activities (for instance, in the St. Austell area) where women and girls may be involved in a range of employments, and even possibly move between one and another, or, at very least, with members of the same family sometimes working in different industries (such as the copper mines and clay works). The scope of this book, therefore, goes beyond just the metalliferous mines (copper, tin, lead etc.) and includes those women and girls who also worked at the manganese mines, clay works and slate quarries.

Neither is the book restricted just to bal maidens (to ore or stone dressers), but it also extends to other women and children who were involved at the mines. For instance, there were women employed for domestic duties (the counthouse women). Girls sometimes were responsible for the ponies or horses operating machinery at surface, and others were waggoners. Some operated pumps, and some made or repaired dressing equipment. Occasionally, there were women who were mine or clay pit managers. During the World Wars, some women were employed to carry out tasks which the men had previously done (such as hosing out clay from the clay pits). There is also emerging evidence that women and girls worked at the tin and lead smelters. This book includes any females who received economic benefit directly from working at or for the mine. It does not, however, include women adventurers who had bought 'shares' in a mine, or inherited their husband's interest in a mine at their death, unless they were actively involved in the management. (For instance, nineteen women held shares in Wheal Agar in 1893 (Wheal Agar Cost Book TL 96) but so far there is no evidence that they were active in the managing decisions of the mine, or that they attended any of the business meetings). Also, this book does not include the very small number of women who may have worked at the surviving tin mines in Cornwall, since the introduction of Equal Opportunities Legislation in the 20th century.

If this book has moved us to feel for the women and children who worked at the mines of Cornwall and Devon, sometimes under appalling conditions, I hope we will also be moved to consider the plight of today's child miners (or indeed, any women and men who continue to labour in mines where there is no adequate provision for their health and safety). Despite international agreements abhorring and outlawing child labour at the mines, there are still hundreds (and possibly thousands) of children working underground or in health-threatening working conditions at surface. Work is continuing among communities in the Philippines and Burkina Faso to relieve the abject poverty which drives families to send their children into the mines. Authorities in Vietnam are yet to find out how many children are still working in illegally operated gold mines in the remote Bac Kan Province. In May 2003, seventy-two children were discovered working under terrible conditions, carrying baskets of earth and rocks through water up to their waists, for up to 14 hours a day. The youngest was ten years old. In some cases, their parents had sold them in desperation to the mine owners, others had been abandoned; others had run away to the mines, lured by the tales of wealth and regular wages. Looking at the history of women in mining in Cornwall, it has always been the poorest of this world who have been the most vulnerable to exploitation and danger, with little redress should things go wrong. We still have much to do to wipe out inhuman and life-threatening forms of labour, especially for children, even today.

Finally, I have envisaged this book as only a first tentative step in unravelling the history of the many thousands of women and girls who laboured at the mines in the South West. I hope it will have sparked discussion and stimulated memories so that more accurate information will come to light. I am conscious that there will be many errors in this text, either from mistaken transcription or from inaccurate assumption. I would be very grateful for any comments, corrections or additional information which will continue to carry the subject forward.

ACKNOWLEDGEMENTS

I wish to thank all those who have helped and encouraged me in the writing of this book. When I first mentioned the possibility of writing a book on the subject of bal maidens, I was warned, from several quarters, that there was not enough documentation and that it would not be possible. Thankfully, there are many other people who have proved this assumption wrong, and have been very willing to share whatever information they have so that this book could be created. Without them, this book would not exist.

Very special thanks go to Jan Gendall, John Tonkin, and John Symons who have given unstintingly of their time, both in sharing ideas, knowledge and resources, and who have also been kind enough to comment on the texts relating to their particular expertise. I must also acknowledge the late Justin Brooke for his transcript of an interview with Minnie Andrews in 1967 (reputedly the last surviving 'old style' bal maiden), and allowing me to quote freely from it. Also, I am indebted to the late Mrs. Phyllis Lockett for her first hand account of working on the picking belt at Geevor Mine during the Second World War.

A very big thank you must also go to those descendants and relatives of women who worked at the mines and clay pits who were kind enough to respond to my various public requests for information, and have shared their family research, photographs or oral history with me, allowing me to publish what has sometimes been very personal detail. These include Ian Argall, Peter Benbow, Bev. Bennie, Adele Casbolt, Edna Collins, Jenny Elliston, Val Flint-Johnson, Ian Gribble, Judith Hellyar, Jean Henry, Wendy Hicks, Sylvia Hodson, the late Frank Houghton, Daphne Hughes, Arthur Jacob, Isabel Jamson, Gillian Johns, Sharon Kay Jones, Lesley Morton, John Saunders, Alison Shaw, Norma Smitian, Anne Stephens, Kate Symons, Harry Trembath, Tom Tremellen, and Helen Webster.

I am indebted to the many institutions, heritage sites and voluntary organisations who have allowed me access to their archives, and to their willing and helpful staff, many of whom have gone out of their way to find elusive and rare material. Among these, I mention the Blue Hills Tin Streams (Collin Wills), Bodmin Museum (Margaret Tooze), British Geological Survey (Tim Colman), Carnglaze Slate Caverns (Caroline Richards), Cornish Family History Society (Pat Fawcett and volunteers), Cornish Studies Library (Kim Cooper and Neil Williams), Cornwall Federaton of Women's Institutes, Cornwall Record Office, the Courtney Library and the Royal Institution of Cornwall (Angela Broom and Rob Cook), Delabole Local History Society (Brenda Burnard and Wesley Mills), Delabole Slate Co. (Pamela Free), Exeter Local Studies Library (Ian Maxted), Family Records Centre in Central London, Geevor Tin Mine Heritage Centre (Ben Beckwith, Jo Warburton), Helston Museum (Mrs. Spargo), Institute of Mining and Metallurgy Library, Morwellham Quay Museum (Antony Power), Morab Library, National Trust (Cornwall), Northern Mines Research Society (Sally Bassam), Redruth Old Cornwall Society (Terry Knight and Ron Opie), St. Ives Archive Study Centre (Janet Axten), The National Archives, Wayside Folk Museum, Zennor (Sara and Bob Priddle), Wheal Martyn Museum (Lis Chard, Brian Strathen, Derek Giles), The Wellcome Library, and The Women's Library, London. Also, I thank the many members of the on-line Mining History Mailing list for their patience with a continual stream of abstruse questions, and especially to those who have been able to answer them, including Tony Brooks, Peter Claughton, Bryan Earl, Martin Roe, and Jan

Wegner. There has also been a network of people around the world who have helped with information on aspects of migration, including Roger Bradford, Kelly Dixon, Richard Francaviglia, Heather Hobbis, Ron James, Vivian Martin, Sylvia Pettem, Daryl Povey, Dieter Retz, Sally Zanjani, Christine Teale, and Mark and Karen Vendl.

Various other authors and researchers have also offered help and encouragement, and in some cases extensive access to their research: Tony Brooks, Caroline Cudmore, Bryan Earl, Tom Greeves, Alan Kent, David Langsworthy, Catherine Lorigan, Geof Purcell, Sharron Schwartz, and Prof. Charles Thomas.

The sources of poems, photographs and illustrations are acknowledged in the text, but special thanks go to Paddy Bradley for his help and encouragement, and allowing us to use photos from his extensive collection. We have tried to ensure that copyright permissions have been sought and are correct, and apologise for any omissions or errors.

There are many who have made it physically possible to visit the various archives and heritage sites in Cornwall. During the preparation of the first edition of this book, the late David Jenkin and his wife Juliet offered hospitality, encouragement, access to their archive resources and helpful comments on the script. I am so very grateful for all that they contributed in many different ways. My husband, Peter Boorman, has acted as chauffeur for many hundreds of miles and over some unforgiving terrain, has had to endure hours of 'mining' conversations, transcribed pages of hardly legible records, been dragged down mines, through hedgerows and to just about every mining heritage site in the UK. He has been the IT specialist, invaluably retrieving lost information in moments of computer crisis, and has also acted as proof reader. He, and my sons Kieren and Marcus, have been unstinting in their encouragement and patient in the extreme, while our lives have been taken over by this project. I am greatly in their debt.

For the second edition, I also thank Ian Boorman for his painstaking proof reading, and Ann and Nick Round for their invaluable advice on editorial matters. Since the publishing of the first edition, various people have been very kind in providing additional information, or correcting points raised in the original text. I am also indebted to them.

Finally, my thanks also go to Philip Budden and to Melissa Hardy of the Hypatia Trust, for enabling the first edition to be published, without which the second would not exist.

'A mine spreads out its vast machinery.
Here engines, with their huts and smokey stacks,
Cranks, wheels, and rods, boilers and hissing steam,
Pressed up the water from the depths below.
Here fire-whims ran till almost out of breath,
And chains cried sharply, strained with fiery force.
Here blacksmiths hammered by the sooty forge,
And there a crusher crashed the copper ore.
Here girls were cobbing under roofs of straw,
And there were giggers at the oaken hutch.
Here a man-engine glided up and down,
A blessing and a boon to mining men:
And near the spot where, many years before,
Turned round and round the rude old water-wheel,
A huge fire-stamps was working evermore,
And slimey boys were swarming at the trunks.
The noisy lander by the trap-door bawled
With pincers in his hand; and troops of maids
With heavy hammers brake the mineral stones.
The cart-man cried, and shook his broken whip;
And on the steps of the account-house stood
The active agent, with his eye on all'.

From 'Labyrinths' by John Harris, 1820-84

Chapter 1

BAL MAIDENS - THEIR HISTORY

INTRODUCTION

The majority of women and girls employed at the mines and clay works of Cornwall and West Devon were involved in the various stages of ore or clay dressing, and were colloquially known as 'bal maidens'. The term 'bal maiden' can be found in accounts of Victorian travel writers and various governmental reports from the middle of the 19th century onwards. In the 18th century, Pryce does not seem to have heard of the term (1778), and females working at the mines tend to be referred to as maidens (maid'ns) in the 18th century cost books. The earliest references to 'Ball Maidens' come from the West Briton in 1819 and 1823 respectively.[1] 'Bal' is Old Cornish for 'mining place', but was widely replaced, from the 18th century, with the word 'Huel' and then 'Wheal'. The word 'bal' was sometimes incorporated into the name of a mine, such as Balmynheer, and has occasionally been retained as the name of a hamlet or village, as at Higher Bal (St Agnes) and Baldhu. Bal maiden, or variably written balmaiden and bal-maiden, then, was a term often used to describe young women who worked at the Cornish mines, or sometimes, more loosely, to describe all females working 'at surface' at the bal. By the end of the 19th century, it seems it was a general term used for all females working on the dressing floors, regardless of age or status, as Muriel Sara remembered from her childhood in the 1890s: *'Women of all ages, married or mere girls, they were all known by that name.'* [2]

How far the term 'bal maiden' was used over the border into Devon, is unclear. With continual interchange of mining personnel between Cornwall and West Devon, it is no surprise to discover *'ball maidens'* [sic] recorded in the *1851 Census* for Sydenham Damarel. Whether the term was used more generally, across Dartmoor and to the Teign and Exe valleys, is not known.

Other terms have been used for female ore dressers, over the centuries, some of them being given to both male and females performing the same tasks. William Pryce, in his description of tin streaming in Cornwall, published in 1778, describes ore dressers as lappiors:

'Leavings from the stamping mills which are carried by the rivers to lower grounds; and after some years of lying and collecting there, yield some money to the laborious dressers, who they distinguish by the name of Lappiors, I suppose from the Cornish word Lappior, which signifying a Dancer, is applied to them, in this from the boys and girls employed in work, and moving up and down in the buddles, to separate the Tin from the refuse, with naked feet like to the ancient Dancers.' (Pryce 1778 p.136)

However, 'Lappior' is not a term that frequently appears in the literature. The women and girls were also sometimes referred to by the specific task assigned to them, such as 'cobbing girls', 'bucking women' or 'spalling maidens', or more generally, 'mine girls'. The term 'bal maiden' does not appear in the census returns, as the enumerators were instructed not to use local terminology. Instead, they tended to use terms which were rather functional; such as variations on miner, mine girl, maid or labourer, ore dresser or cleaner, or labourer or worker at mine. The occasional 'working at bal' also can be found. There are the same restrictions on the use of words placed on district registrars, so similar phraseology appears on marriage and baptismal certificates. For instance, Lavinia Terrill, an ore dresser, was described as a 'miner' at her marriage at Camborne Parish Church in 1845. The women and girls who worked at the slate quarries were referred to in the census records as 'quarry girls' or 'quarry women'.

There were small numbers of women and girls who were employed at the mines and clay works who were not involved in the dressing operations, but undertook various other tasks. Probably the largest of these other groups were the counthouse women who were employed to do housekeeping duties at the mine office, as most of the larger mines would employ one such person and, in some cases, as many as three or four. Sometimes girls or women were employed to look after animals at the mine, or were actually responsible for 'drawing kibbles' (raising ore at the horse whim). Older women were sometimes involved in the transport of ore, slate, coal, oil or machinery, either as donkey drivers or wagoners. Children were paid for simple casual tasks, such as collecting moss to line the clay pans, or weeding. Females were also employed in making or mending equipment for the mines, sewing ore sacks and punching holes in copper sieves, for example. Occasionally, they prepared building materials, such as cleaning bricks. A few women and girls assisted the mine assayer in the sample room.

There are also records of women carrying out what would normally be deemed as 'men's jobs', such as kibble (bucket) landing and working the pumps. During the World Wars, it was not unusual for women and older girls to be drafted in to undertake some of the processes which had previously been the preserve of men, such as the women who worked hosing out clay in some of the clay works bottoms in the First World War, and those who worked on the tin picking belts in the Second. There are also a few accounts of women who actually became managers of clay works or mines.

Not only were women and girls to be found fulfilling a variety of tasks, they were also employed at mines or clay works right across Cornwall, and to a lesser extent into Devon. They were not confined just to the major mining areas, but bal maidens have so far been found recorded in eighty-three parishes in Cornwall and thirty-eight in Devon, at some point in their mining history. Employment in Devon (with the exception of Tavistock, Beer Ferris, Beer Alston and Mary Tavy) was always in low numbers. However, in Cornwall, eighteen of the parishes had employed over 100 bal maidens, and thirty-nine parishes had employed between 10 and 99 (Fig. 1).

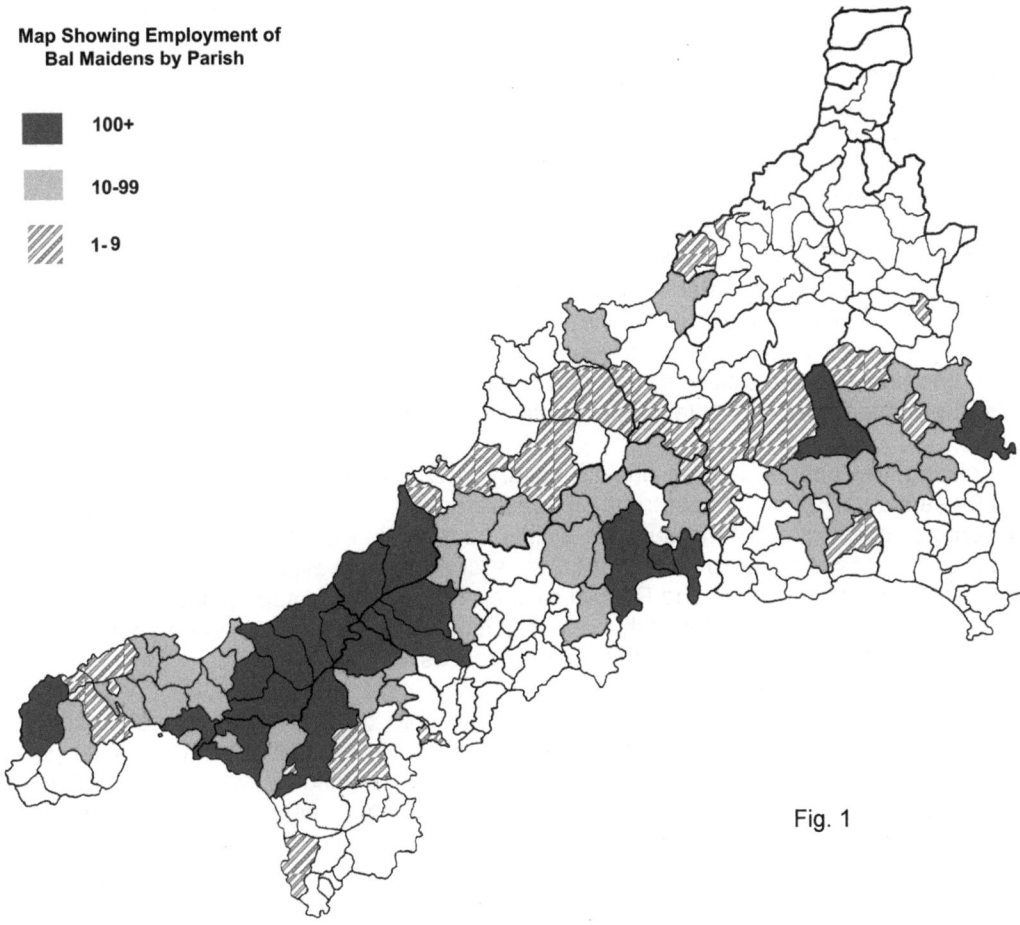

Fig. 1

BAL MAIDENS - THE HISTORY

Women and children were probably involved in mining activities in Cornwall from the days of antiquity, but earliest written records of females working at the tin mines and lead smelters date from the 14th century; for copper, from the beginning of the 18th century. In all of these records, the work done by the women and girls was at the surface. In Cornwall, there seems to have been a long standing tradition that it was unlucky for women to go below ground, and so there is no record of them having been employed as hauliers or carriers below surface, as they were at the collieries in Wales and the North.[3]

Mining in the days of antiquity

Copper was mined in Cornwall from the Bronze Age. Unfortunately, women and female children do not usually leave identifiable archaeological evidence for their presence in the workforce, so it is not proven that they worked underground. It is assumed that these copy mines were developed by small communities of extended family units, with distributions of tasks probably by age and gender. The Bronze Age copper mines recently uncovered on Great Orme in North Wales, for instance, have such small underground tunnels and caverns that only children or very small adults could have worked them. However, mining has traditionally been a woman's task in areas of America and Africa, before colonial settlement. In Wisconsin, some of the mine leases of the 19th century, when first issued, were given to native American women. Their method, known as fire-setting, involved drift mining, and kindling fires at the rock face, then applying cold water to fracture the ore. These women then smelted the ore in make-shift furnaces, and apparently extracted a greater concentration of lead than the early settlers.[4] So, although evidence and documentation is lacking, it is possible that women were involved in copper mining processes in Cornwall at a very early stage and, as in other cultures, may even have had prime responsibility for this part of the family economy. However, it seems that, after the Bronze Age, very little copper mining took place in Cornwall until the 16th century.

Tin mining, like copper, has an ancient history in Cornwall, probably dating from at least 3000 years ago. For many centuries, ore was retrieved from where it was washed out into streams or outcropped at the surface. Unlike copper, tin extraction seems to have been more or less continuous, from ancient times. Archaeological evidence suggests continued low-level production through the Roman period and beyond, to supply both the British and European market. As with the early copper mining in Cornwall, we can only speculate as to the involvement of women and girls in this process.

The first surviving written documents that confirm that tin was being mined in Cornwall and Devon are from the 12th Century, and relate to the transfer of administrative power from the King to the Stannaries. Suggestions of early mining activity in Cornwall come from Thomas Beare, the Bailiff for the Blackmore Stannary when he writes in the latter half of the 16th Century. He says:

'It appeereth [sic} by working of our Tinners in Cornwall that the Saxons being heathen people... were skillful workers of and sercers [searchers] for black tyn, which in thos aunciente dayes wrought not with spades and working tooles made of Iron as we have now in our tyme, but all of the hart of oake...for prooff where of diverse workers of our tyme have fownd their shovells spades and mattox made all of oke and holme.' (Beare 1586 p.1)

Mining from 1200 to 1690

It is during this period that there are enough surviving documents to give a fairly clear picture of mining in Cornwall and Devon, especially with regards to tin mining. At this time, all the mines in England were owned by the Crown, and most of our information comes from the court records relating to the setting up and workings of the Stannaries. These documents occasionally mention women in the workforce, but references are few and far between. The earliest recorded involvement of women in the tin mining industry is of a few tin traders in the Dartmoor area, during the early 14th century. By the mid 14th century, there are also records of females working at tin works on Bodmin, and in the Redruth and Marazion areas. Records also survive of a few women trading tin and leasing blowing mills on Dartmoor in the 16th century. When Thomas Beare wrote about tin mining (around 1550), he did not mention women or girls, whereas he did mention the employment of boys in the ore dressing process. Similarly, other 17th century accounts describe tin being dressed by boys, but not women or girls.[5]

Tin extraction at this time was generally from stream works, the sea, drift mining (following lodes into the hillside), or at its most complex, sinking shallow shafts. Generally, we imagine the men and older boys would be involved in the heavy work of digging, constructing water leats, and heaving and barrowing the heaviest loads of rock and ore. The women, girls, if employed, and younger boys would presumably be involved in washing, panning, sorting ore from rubble and breaking down rock-bearing ore. Initially, this was done with mortar and pestle, or the equivalent of small hand corn mill. By the 16th century, water stamps were being used to break down the larger pieces of tin-bearing rock, prior to manually breaking the smaller pieces.

Although day-to-day management of the tin mines had long since been handed over to the Vice Wardens of the Stannaries, other mines remained under control of the Crown up until the end of the 16th century. Another very early reference to females working in the mining industry comes from surviving accounts for the silver-lead mines at Calstock and Bere Ferris, which had been opened up by the Crown at the end of the 13th century. These exchequer rolls indicate that about seven hundred people may have been employed at this time, including women washing ore at the lead smelters. It is in these records that we find the earliest named bal maidens. Later, in 1480, some of the men employed at Bere Alston were paid for dressing ore as well as mining, possibly suggesting that they had brought a team of people to carry out both processes. These teams would almost certainly include women and children. Mining at this time was a very well paid activity compared with other artisan trades or unskilled labouring.[6]

An uncertain 16th century record of a woman tin dresser comes from a stained-glass window. The discovery of surviving drawings of an early 16th century window at St Neot's Church (which was sadly replaced in the mid 19th century) has led to a discussion as to whether the depiction was of a tinner and his bal maiden wife.[7] However, the case is not proven, and the woman looks to be in a costume that could have been worn by most women of the time. The elegant gloves in her hands perhaps indicate a woman of some standing. The figures may be of a mason and his wife, rather than a miner and bal maiden.

Copper mines in Britain were still under the control of the Mines Royal in Elizabethan times. When the value of copper was realised, in the production of brass for armaments, German mining experts were encouraged to come to England with their skills. They brought many workers with them, including ore dressers, smelters and smiths, who then lived in barracks or lofts on site. At the Cumbrian copper mines, this certainly included their own male ore dressers.

Eventually, between 1568 and 1605, the Company of Mines Royal started to release control of the mines by giving leases out to individuals to set up mining operations. It was at this time that Customer Thomas Smythe was given a lease by the Crown to mine copper in the Illogan, St Just, St Ives, St Agnes, and Perranzabuloe areas of Cornwall. Letters survive relating to some of these ventures. It seems that only a handful of men were employed at each mine and from the itemised pay lists they also appear to be mostly German. Again, there is no mention of women or girls. These small mines closed when the main shareholders died, and no more copper was worked in Cornwall for about 100 years.

Contemporary descriptions, by Georgius Agricola, of mining operations on the continent in the 16th century indicate that it was quite normal for women and boys, but not girls, to be involved in the copper dressing processes. Here are descriptions of some of the processes in southern Germany:

'The work of sorting the crude metal or the best ore is done not only by men, but also by boys and women. They throw the mixed material upon a long table, beside which they sit for almost the whole day, and they sort out the ore; when it has been sorted out, they collect it in trays, and when collected they throw it into tubs, which are carried to the works in which they are to be smelted.' (Agricola 1556 p. 269)

'Into this sieve a boy throughs [sic] the material to be washed, and a woman shakes it up and down, turning it alternately to the right and to the left.' (p. 293)

There is also evidence of women being involved in the silver dressing operations at Kutna Hora, about 70 km east of Prague, in the late 15th century. A wonderful colour illustration of the working silver mine survives, showing several women at work on the dressing floors. One is washing ore in a large vat, others carrying ore between the different processes on platters or in baskets, and one who looks as if she is being subjected to a mouth search![8]

The scarcity of records does not necessarily mean absence of women and girls in the workforce during this period. It may just be that they were not recorded. Even in the 19th and 20th century, women workers are not always mentioned in the ledgers and cost books, even when present in large numbers in the workforce. They sometimes remained 'invisible', either recorded as an ore dressing cost, or as a total amount of money paid to the surface captain or tributor responsible for dressing. However, times were about to change, not only in the more detailed keeping of mine records and in the total numbers of females employed, but in the number of surviving records of their work.

Mining from 1690-1860

A major development in the dressing and smelting of ores, at the beginning of the 18th century, was the introduction of the reverberatory furnace. When ore had been traditionally smelted at a 'bole' or ore hearth, the very finest particles were usually lost, so there was no point in trying to extract this portion from the parent material. In the reverbatory furnace, a gentler draught was used for reaching the high temperatures required for smelting. It was found that very fine ore particles were not destroyed but could be smelted and recovered for the first time. This resulted in far more attention being paid to the 'slimes' (the fine-grained residues from the washing sieves and buddles). Consequently, from about 1710, more complex dressing operations were introduced. In these more extensive dressing operations, with the slimes being collected and rewashed countless times, there was a significant increase in the numbers employed on the dressing floors.

Descriptions of mining in Cornwall at this time come mostly from several generations of well-to-do travellers who recorded their journeys, historians, or professional miners. When Celia Fiennes travelled into Cornwall in 1695, she described passing close to twenty tin mines in the St Austell area, and about another hundred (probably meaning the number of shafts rather than mines) between Truro and Redruth. Her attention was caught by the great number of men and boys working at the pumps on a continuous rota, in order to keep the mines clear of water, but she did not mention the activities on the dressing floors, nor any women or girls at work:

'There was at least 20 mines all in sight which employs a great many people at work, almost day and night, but constantly all and every day including the Lord's day which they are forced to, to prevent their mines being overflowed with water; more than 1000 men are taken up about them; few mines but had then almost 20 men and boys attending it.' (Fiennes 1699)

By 1700, the Mines Royal had ceased to operate as such, and had allowed private landowners to lease out all the mining rights to private adventurers. In these early days (before about 1720), all the mining concerns in Cornwall and Devon were relatively simple, due to lack of technological development. Once free of the Mines Royal, stream or sea tinning, or mining for tin where the lodes outcropped near the surface, could be done by the extended family unit, or small companies.

An early record of named women working at the mines or smelters was in cost and receipt books for the Newham Smelter. With the introduction of the first coal fired reverbatory furnaces in Cornwall, women were paid to barrow coal from ships on the shoreline to the smelters. They were also employed to sieve the coal, culm and cinders. Between three and twelve women were employed at Newham from 1704 to 1707, of whom nine were named.

From 1718, with the introduction of mechanical pumps, ore could be more easily won from below the water table. Installation of horse whims and, later, winding engines also meant that ore could be raised more efficiently and safely. At the same time, the new techniques were developed for ore dressing. These improvements required far more investment and a greater labour force, so these larger and deeper mines were financed by groups of adventurers, and increasingly, from 1750 onwards, by mining companies. One of Carew's manuscripts from the second half of the 17th century indicates just how extensive some mines and tin streams were at that time, with about 1,000 people employed at St Agnes Bal and Trevaunance Valley: *'Continuously great numbers of Boyes and humane youths are employed about washing, vanning or cleansing tin.'* [9]

It was at this time, too, that the real value of copper was recognised, and there was a rush into investment in copper mines, in preference to tin. It is not known how many women and girls were working at the mines prior to the introduction of these new technologies, but with the improved capability of bringing ore 'to grass' came the need for a cheap workforce to process the ore as quickly as it was raised. So, from about 1720, it seems that women and children were drafted in numbers not seen before, as they had the necessary skill and dexterity to process the ores, and were cheaper to hire than men. One of the earliest records of women and girls working at the copper mines comes from the *Pool Adit Cost Book*, where there were about twenty-five named female dressers recorded between 1729 and 1731. In 1736, the vicar of Ludgvan laments the difficulty in obtaining house servants, as so many of the young women were *'employed about copper'*.[10] In March 1742, twenty-seven bal maidens were employed at Wheal Dudnance.

By 1750, when Dr. Pococke (Bishop of Neath) was travelling through central Cornwall, women and girls seem to be a well-established part of the commercial mining workforce. This is his description of a mine in Chacewater:

'A succession of men are always at the mine, except on Sundays. They work eight hours, from six until two, and from two until ten, and then again from ten until six. When they come up, they call it 'coming to grass'. When the ore is brought up, women and children are employed in breaking it, and separating the 'country' [waste] from the ore, and the tin from the copper.' (Pococke 1750 p. 191)

Similarly, the implication from the travel writings of Swedish 'industrial spy' R. R. Angerstein, in 1754, is of widespread employment of females in Cornish mining by that time:

'In Cornwall, most men are miners, and children and young women are occupied in the stream-works and on the dressing-floors.' [11]

The new technologies transformed Cornish tin and copper mining at an amazing rate during the 18th century. It is from the second half of the 18th century that we begin to find accounts of women and girls at the mines in considerable numbers for the first time. William Pryce wrote about mining in Cornwall in the 1770s and gives one of the earliest and most detailed accounts of the work of women or girls at the copper mines in sorting, cobbing and bucking the ore. He goes on to compare this with the tasks performed by women and girls at the tin and lead mines. By the time he wrote, he took the presence of women and girls on the dressing floor for granted:

'Copper...being placed in the more interior strata of the earth and requires greater skill in hydraulics and mechanicks. The expense of coal, candles, timber, leather, ropes, gunpowder, and various other materials, added to the labour of men, women, children and horses, occasion such a vast monthly charge, as will not easily be credited by those who are unacquainted with Mining.' (Pryce 1778 p. intro d.)

There is some suggestion that when the quality of copper ore raised was poor and copper prices low, such as during the 1770s, women and children actually replaced male workers on the dressing floors, to keep costs low. (Similar tactics were sometimes used a century later at the tin mines, for the same reason.)[12] In 1794, a visitor to 'Trevigho' (probably Trevigro) in the St Austell area was delighted to see women and children employed at the tin works there:

'I was pleased to see so many women and boys engaged in the latter parts of this work, as I always am with any manufactory that gives employment to the female sex whose province is too often intruded on by the other'. [13]

Mining in Devon was never to compete with that in Cornwall, in terms of scale. Up until the mid 18th century, it was mostly confined to the extensive and widespread tin works on Dartmoor. Women were also working at the simple shallow manganese mines in Upton Pyne and Newton St Cyres (on the east side of Dartmoor) by 1800. The development of deep mining tended to happen later in Devon, but by the end of the 18th century, a few copper and lead mines had been developed around the Tamar and Teign. For some, such as Wheal Friendship and Wheal Jewell, records survive of female employment on the dressing floors at this time.

Eventually, over 200 mines were worked in Devon during the 19th century, many of which are recorded as employing female dressers. The most important of them were around the Tamar and on the Bere Ferris peninsular (copper or silver-lead). Smaller mines were also found in the Lifton area (manganese), on the north boundary of Dartmoor (copper) and in the Teign valley (lead and iron).

Fig. 2 Dressing Floor at Dolcoath c. 1831
Allom

A number of statistics of women and children working in or at the mines in Cornwall and South West Devon were published during the 19th century, as a public concern developed about their working conditions and moral welfare. This concern became expressed in a Government decision to establish a Royal Commission to investigate the conditions under which children and young people worked in the mines in England, Scotland and Wales. The Commission gathered evidence during 1841, and their report was before parliament in 1842. Despite this growing concern about the effects of the bal maidens' work on their well-being, the legislation which was enacted as a result was only applied to coal mines. No change was made to employment practice at surface or underground in the metalliferous mines at this stage.

Post Industrial Revolution: Women or Technology? (1860-1920)

There was always a direct connection between the market value of the minerals mined, and the amount of dressing that made extraction economic. Thus, in times of high prices, it was worth extracting from low-grade ore which required more extensive labour. Conversely, when prices were low, only the best-grade ores would be worth processing, with the low-grade ore being cast aside and surface workers laid off. As early as 1826, Henwood succinctly describes this relationship, with regards to tin:

'We reject portions that will not repay the cost of dressing.' (Henwood W. J. 1826 p.145)

With increased technology, machinery could be used to extract ore at less cost, and this was particularly true when applied to the extraction of the poorer ores:

'Every time the tin stuff is handled, be it by boy or girl, the cost of the dressing of the ore is increased. By automatic machinery this might be avoided, and considerable saving secured. All that has been said in reference to the dressing of tin applies equally to copper and lead ores.' (Hunt 1887 p. 713)

The 18th century mines were heavily dependent on the labour of women and children, and by the turn of the 19th century, it seems they constituted about half of the workforce (in the copper mines at least). However, from then on, they were gradually replaced. It is probable that the first significant step in this decline began when John Taylor introduced the first copper and lead crushing machine at Wheal Crowndale, in 1804. In 1836, the total proportion of women and children in the workforce at the tin mines and copper mines in Cornwall had dropped to 38% and 41% respectively, or 43% in those mines extracting both tin and copper.[14] In 1839, De La Beche commented that:

'In most of the principal mines the process of breaking the best ores by bucking is discontinued and the same work is accomplished better and at much less cost by means of crushing machines.' [15]

One of the next processes to be mechanised was one of the other most demanding tasks on the dressing floor: that of hand jigging. Semi-automated machines were introduced from about 1830. Hunt summarised the local feelings towards this innovation:

'It was anticipated that all persons engaged in [hand] *jigging the ores would be thrown out of employment and starved, and it was a matter of some difficulty to convince people of the inefficiency of the old method and that a great deal of valuable stuff was lost through it's use'.* (Hunt 1887 p. 694)

Certainly, by about 1850, technology and public opinion together had begun to spell out the last days of young women and girls working at the mines. While for the time being the total number employed was still increasing due to the continued expansion of the industry, their presence in the workforce (as a proportion) was definitely declining.

By 1858, despite technological 'improvements' in dressing copper, many mining captains believed that copper dressing was still far too labour intensive. By now, though, the economic tide had turned, and as copper mining was considered to be *'past its zenith'* very little new equipment was installed. After 1860, only a few mines introduced new rock crushers, picking tables and power jigs, while most continued with existing methods until their closure.

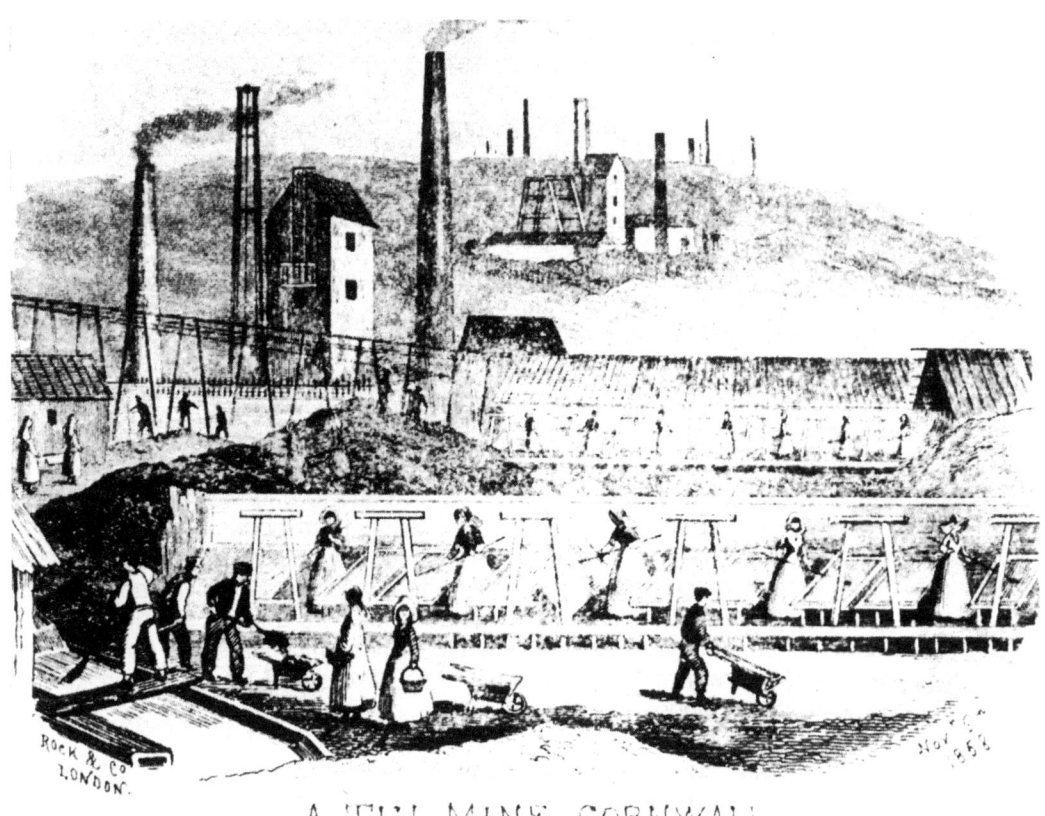

Fig. 3 Sketch of Dressing Floors of Tin Mine 1858
Courtesy of the Cornwall Centre Collection

In contrast, in the tin mining industry, new technologies were adopted more quickly, as a longer future was anticipated. At Condurrow in 1858, for instance, new equipment was installed when there was a so called *'shortage of available labour'* to dress a backlog of tin. With these newly installed 'self-acting frames', one girl could do the work of twelve:

'At Condurrow Mine, having a large quantity of tin remaining in the stamps leavings, and being unable to get hands to dress it, and which with manual labour would be attended with heavy expense, they are preparing to erect 10 or 12 self-acting frames, to be set in motion by a water wheel on the mill floor. Those at work in the north east floor (10 of them) and attended by one girl, are effecting more work than 12 girls in the ordinary way.' (MJ 20th Feb 1858 p. 128)

Schwartz makes the point that, when mechanical crushers were installed for breaking down copper ore-stuff, to replace the arduous and costly task done by the female buckers, not only did many girls lose their jobs, but the new machinery was invariably operated by boys or men. So, throughout Cornwall and West Devon, nearly all female buckers had been replaced by 1858, except for a few small mines which still employed girls to do this task, and generally the new crushers were now overseen by boys.[16] In the same way, when mechanised frames were installed at St Day United Mines in 1858, one boy replaced between 20 and 30 girls. Similarly, with each step of technological development, tasks previously done by women were generally handed over to men and their machinery.

The world demand for minerals, and the copper and tin economy, had always affected the amount of employment available at the mines in the South West. Concurrent with the technological changes, there was a dramatic fall in the price of copper from about 1866, so that many Cornish copper mines began to close. By 1870, due to the 'improved' technology and the slump in copper prices, the number of women and girls employed, officially, at the mines had fallen by about 50% to 4450. Another blow to the industry came in 1873 when tin prices also plummeted, having been very high in 1871 and 1872, due to new discoveries in Australia. More mines closed, leaving only 307 open. During the 1870s, lead production also began to drop in the South West, as mines were exhausted, throwing more out of work, especially in the Perranzabuloe and Newlyn East area.

Some mines discovered rich tin lodes at depth, and changed from copper to tin production, which sometimes required less labour on the ore dressing floors, again affecting the number of females employed. This change from copper to tin, however, needed considerable investment, so some mines chose to continue with a cheaper labour intensive system, rather than paying for expensive new machinery. For instance, it was 1879 before the old square buddles and rectangular frames were replaced, at Botallack, with round buddles and rotary frames. As a result, sixty-eight of the one hundred and twelve girls, who had formally worked on these floors, were laid off. Dolcoath did not replace the last of its square buddles until 1892.[17]

Meanwhile, significant changes were taking place with regards to employment practice. In the 1872 *Metalliferous Mines Regulation Act,* legislation was introduced for the first time to restrict employment of women and children at the metalliferous mines. Employment of any child under the age of 12, either above ground, or below, became illegal. Regulations were also brought in about the safe use of machinery.

By 1876, the various *Elementary Education Acts* were also in place, providing a network of schools throughout the country, and legislating for compulsory education for children up to the age of 10 years old. This was followed in 1878 by the *Factory and Workshop Act,* forbidding employment of any children under 10 years of age, and restricting children between the ages of 10 and 14 to working no more than thirty hours per week. These Acts effectively removed many young bal maidens from the workforce, and placed them, for the first time, in full-time education. Many others would only be employed part-time, if at all, potentially changing the age structure of the women and girls engaged on the dressing floors. Even so, in 1890, the Chief Inspector of Factories complained that Cornish Mines still *'swarmed with children of insufficient age'*.[18]

Whereas there had been a considerable migration of miners from Cornwall, from the 1840s onwards, both to other parts of the UK and overseas, the combined events of the mid-1870s led to mass migration, on a scale not seen before, of able-bodied men and women from the South West. Those mines that stayed open restructured from the cost book system, which discouraged sensible investment, to limited liability companies, and continued to become increasingly mechanised. It is suggested that more men were sacked than women or children at this stage, as they were the more expensive to employ.

An example of this was the proposed replacement of the *'burning house man'* (calciner) by a woman or child, at Penhalls Mine in 1879.[19]

Of 307 mines remaining open in 1873, only 23 were still open in 1895, and all had become limited companies. In the early 1880s, there was an attempt by the government to ban all female labour at the mines throughout Britain. In 1886, a sizeable delegation of pit brow lasses travelled to London from the Lancashire collieries to lobby MPs, and the move was also opposed vigorously by the mining companies in Cornwall:

'To prevent the employment of 'bal girls', under present conditions in most of our Cornish mines would be to render the struggle which is being so gallantly fought against adverse circumstances in many cases practically hopeless. From the other point of view it would mean an enormous amount of suffering and distress by reducing the already low family wage fund. It can, we believe, be said with truth that at the present day there is nothing necessarily demoralising or degrading, or injurious to health in the surface work of women and girls at any well regulated mine in the West of England.' (MJ 23rd Apr 1892 p. 455)

The bill was defeated, and females continued to work at surface in the various collieries and mines in Britain. By 1881, the tin mines employed just over 1,200 women (now only 10% of the workforce). This had fallen to just under 300 by 1902 (5% of the workforce).[20]

In Cornwall, with new equipment designed for crushing and separating, and then the introduction of electric power, there was redesigning or rebuilding of most of the remaining dressing floors, with subsequent job losses for the ore dressers. The introduction of Frue Vanners and shaking tables (for separating the ore) meant that nearly all job losses between 1896 and 1900 in Cornwall were women surface workers. This further move to mechanize seemed to be accompanied by either a real or imagined reluctance of men and women to continue to work manually on the dressing floor, as implied in this comment from the manager of West Wheal Basset in 1900:

'I do not recommend to work any more of the old buddles (at West Basset stamps) as the time is past for us to get labour of this class of work....I suggest we erect Frue Vanners to deal with the sand, and flat and round fames to deal with the slimes.'[21]

Similarly, fewer spallers at Dolcoath were needed when electrical powered stone breakers were installed in about 1907. The last women at Tincroft were dismissed in 1914, when stone crushers were installed there. A correspondent in the Mining Journal made this final lament:

'The latest innovation is the doing away with the spalling maidens and their attendant knights, with a consequent lessened cost of some £400 per annum, the work previously so done being more efficiently executed by the existing stone breakers and an ingeniously arranged system of sliding shoot, hoppers, sampling tables and drop doors, by means of which the ore from tributers and sampling is despatched to the stamps with no handling whatever.' (MJ 23rd May 1914 p. 493)

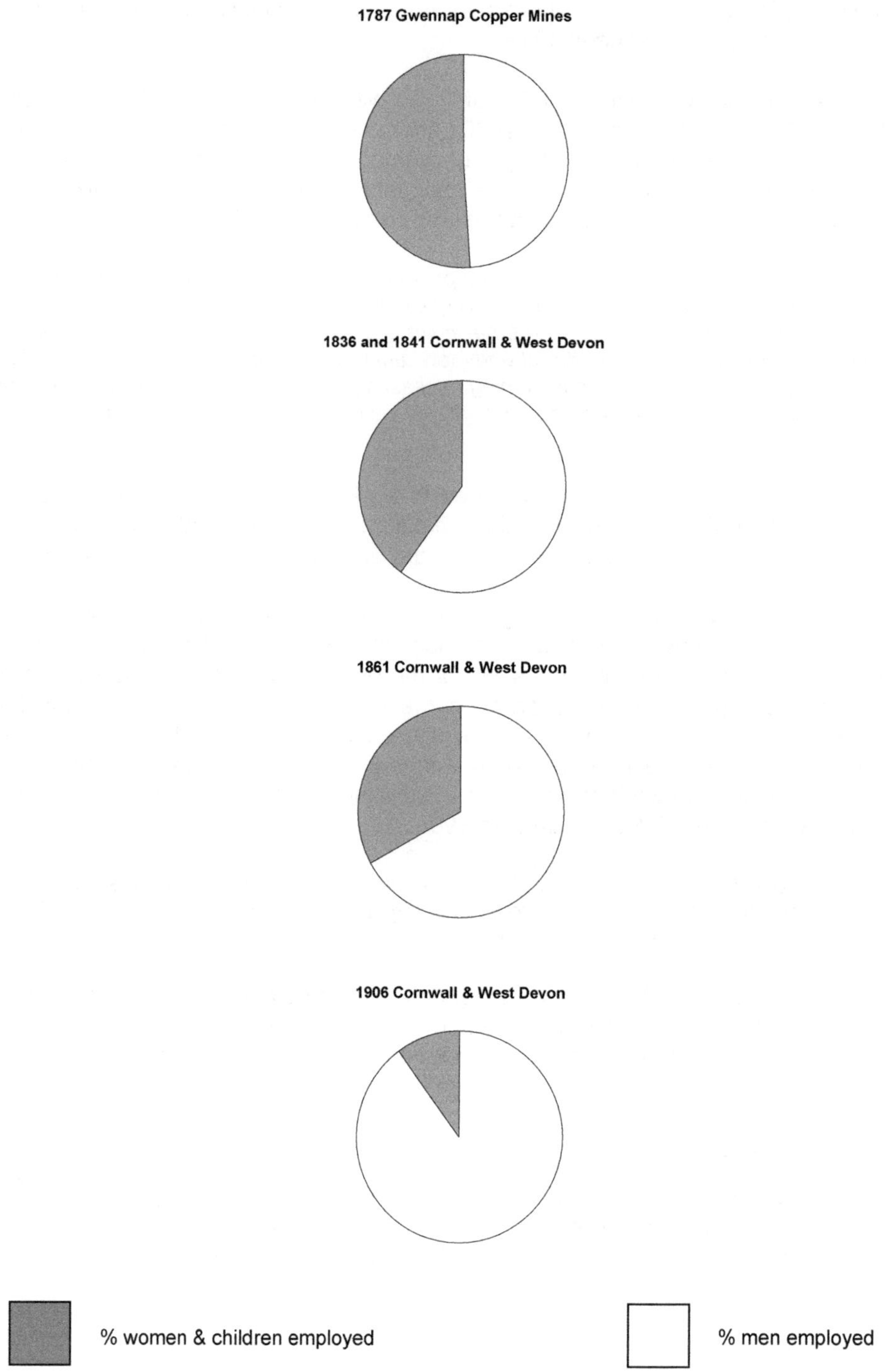

1787 Gwennap Copper Mines

1836 and 1841 Cornwall & West Devon

1861 Cornwall & West Devon

1906 Cornwall & West Devon

% women & children employed   % men employed

Fig. 4 The Proportion of Women and Children Employed at the mines 1787-1908

(expressed as a % of the total workforce)

The gradual but unrelenting replacement of female labour by machinery with male overseers is illustrated by some statistics from Devon Great Consols. In 1849, almost 50% of the 275 surface workers were female. The figure steadily declined until, in 1900, the total had been almost halved, of which only about 4% were female. A few women continued to work at the tin streams during the beginning of the First World War, but seem to have finished altogether by 1922. Only a handful of mines remained open in Cornwall and Devon beyond 1918. Dolcoath was probably one of the last to continue to employ females, with a few spalling women still working until it closed in 1921.[22] This was the end of an era.

Wartime Jobs for Women

During both World Wars, mining was a reserved occupation, so miners and clay workers were not normally called up into the armed forces; but, inevitably, some men volunteered for active service and left their jobs. In March 1915, there was a special appeal for women to register for war work, to help fill some of these important vacancies. In the clay industry, with no available men to replace them, young women were sometimes called on to do their very heavy manual work in the clay pits, extracting clay.

With trade blockades in operation and new requirements for minerals, a potash felspar mine was re-opened in the St Austell area during the First World War, in order to meet an increased demand in the glassmaking process. Young women were called to work there to dress the mineral. Similarly, women were employed at Wheal Mary Ann in Menheniot to re-dress the waste heaps for wolfram. In Devon, they also worked in the wolfram concentration plant and mills at Hemerdon Mine, and re-dressed the waste heaps for arsenic at Wheal Friendship. [23, 24]

During the Second World War, some mines re-opened in the South West to meet a desperate requirement for home-produced ores. Government inspectors looked at tin mines in Cornwall, with a view to re-opening for war work, but very few were thought viable. Generally, those mines which were already working were encouraged to increase production. Geevor was one of these, and women were employed to sort ore on the picking belts, also replacing men who had left for war service. Similarly, women were brought in to dress iron ore at Great Rock Mine in Devon.[25] At Great Treverbyn China Clay Mill in St Austell, and Treamble Iron Mine in Perranzabuloe, women were also employed to pack clay and Fuller's earth, respectively. It took some years for the normal economy to function again after both wars, so it was not unusual for these women to remain in work for some years after the end of hostilities.

BAL MAIDENS – THE STATISTICS

Studying the statistics of the number of women and girls working at the mines in Cornwall and Devon is fraught with difficulty. Only occasional regional collations of numbers were made of those at the metal mines, and those that survive used different criteria. Some totals included the West Devon mines, some were for Cornwall only; some counted all surface labourers together, some separated out the numbers of male and female workers. Some recorded the numbers of women and children, and others just the total number of employees above and below ground. Some totals distinguished the number of employees at the copper, tin and lead mines, some were overall totals for workers at all the mines, and others were totals for just copper or tin. No overall figures are available for employees at the clay works or the slate quarries, independent of the census material.

The earliest detailed and extensive source of employment figures for the mines comes from Sir Charles Lemon for the year 1836 to 1837. He collected information about the main tin, copper and lead mines in Cornwall and West Devon.[26] Of the 160 mines he listed, only 108 distinguished the numbers of women and children employed from the total. These statistics were then reviewed and expanded by William Henwood in 1838, although it is unclear how many of Lemon's figures were actually updated.[27] Here again, the information was in the same mixed format, and a few significant mine returns were still absent.

Some of the most detailed statistical information comes from the *1842 Royal Commission of the Employment of Women and Children at the Non-Metalliferous Mines*, but even here the author reports that a proportion of mines never sent in their returns. Even for those received there were occasional discrepancies and contradictions in the figures, or parts missing. The author believed that there was an under-reporting of the number of boys at the mines, for fear of the information being used for conscripting them for military service, but he makes no comments on the accuracy of the number of women and girls.

In 1864, Thomas Spargo published a prospectus of Cornish mines, which gave numbers of females employed in 1861. Once again, the information is not consistent in format, and for some mines it is missing altogether. Spargo also published similar summaries in 1865 and 1868, both of which appear to be more complete for Cornwall, and with the mines of South and West Devon being included, for the first time, in the latter. Unfortunately, it is not clear to which years of operation these later publications relate.[28]

These various mining statistics were presumably based on official reports, returns and inspections, but even the accuracy of these figures needs to be treated with a little caution. There may be many reasons why mine managers might not give accurate employment figures for women and children. For instance, after 1874, under-reporting may have been quite common where managers had been employing children illegally.

A further source of statistics for women and girls working at the mine, independent of mine reports, is the general population census. As employment details were only collected from the *1841 Census* onwards, this source gives us no insight into the first century of 'industrial' employment of women and girls at the mines. From the years available there seems to be considerable variation as to how much information was given, both between different censuses, and between different enumerators in any one year. However, an even greater problem with the census material seems to be the probable under-reporting of female employment in general. This may be illustrated by the case of Martha Buckingham, one of the bal maidens interviewed by the *1842 Commission*. The Commission records her working at Consolidated Mines on 15th May 1841 and for the previous four years. However, she was not recorded as having any occupation at all just three weeks later, in the census of 5th June. This was also true of her sister Mary who, according to the same evidence, was also an ore dresser. In contrast, Martha's two brothers *were* recorded as tin miners in the same census return, indicating a possible gender bias in the recording of that enumeration district.[29]

On a larger scale, the *1841 Census* for Cornwall and West Devon seems to show an under-reported total of 3,300 bal maidens, compared with the 5,500 estimated for the same year by the *1842 Royal Commission*. It is not possible to make comparisons in subsequent census years as parallel figures are not available, with the exception of 1861. In this case, there is a reasonable correlation between the census results and some of the other mining records. On the other hand, a significant proportion of bal maidens appearing in Cost Books in the same month in which the census was taken have not been found under the same name in the census. Under-recording may be partly due to instructions to the enumerators not to include part-time work, or work where wages were not paid directly to the individual. For instance, many clay workers were not working full-time, and certainly some bal maidens did not have wages paid to themselves, but to their father or older siblings.

Parish Registers are not very useful in indicating overall numbers of bal maidens. They give very limited information about employment; only giving the occupation in marriages registered from 1837, or at burial, if the death is work-related.

Following the employment history of any one mine is just as difficult. Many mine records are missing, or were never made. Those that survive are rarely consistent in their presentation. Cost Books (showing general mine income and expenditure) sometimes have pay lists giving names of the individual bal maidens working each month. In others, only a total sum for the women's and girls' pay appears, or as a total for all the surface labourers, especially where the dressing floor operations were contracted out, and so may include the boys and men as well. Day Books (details of work done by individual employees) are usually the best sources of information about females, as they may give names, numbers of hours worked for each day in the month, the pay calculations, as well as the tributer or tributers for whom they dressed ore. Unfortunately, far fewer of these seem to have survived.

The Proportion of Females at the Mines

The greatest concentrations of females working at the mines in Cornwall during the 18th century were probably in the Breage and Crowan area and also around Gwennap. By the end of the century, this was to change, with a rapid development of a concentration of mines in what became known as the central mining area, around Carn Brea. Subsequently, this area was to continue to be the main centre of female mine employment for the rest of the 19th century, and the only area to continue to employ females into the 20th century, in any numbers. Figures taken from the census records show that, even from 1841 and 1881, between 30 and 35% of all the bal maidens in Cornwall were resident in the Carn Brea parishes of Camborne, Illogan and Redruth. This figure had risen to 77% by 1891, and to over 90% in 1901 (see Fig 5).

Richard Lanyon collated the number of women and girls working at the mines in Camborne, using the *1841 Census* information. He found 222 female mine workers recorded as living in Camborne, and 527 in the rural parts, totalling 749 for the parish. This constituted 9% of the female population in Camborne itself, 18% of those living outside, and 14% on average. This is interesting as it implies that most of the mining communities were based outside of Camborne itself, rather than in the town.[30] In the parishes of St Agnes and Perranzabuloe in 1841, 297 and 31 bal maidens were recorded in 1841, being 56% and 34% of the employed females respectively and 8.5% and 3% of the female population.

In the parish of Lanner, in 1851, as many as 31% of women in work were employed in mining (although this had been reduced to about 11% by 1891). Deacon found that the percentages of females working at the clay works from the 'clay' parishes of Roche, St Stephens, and St Dennis, were very low in comparison at 1.5% in 1871, and 0.1% in 1881.[31]

The *1861 Census* for Cornwall shows that the parish with the highest total number of females employed at the mines was Camborne, with approximately 900. Of these, more than a third were recorded as dressing tin, a third dressing copper, with the rest unspecified. The parishes of Gwennap, Redruth, Illogan, and St Just, reported the next highest totals, each with between 350 and 500 bal maidens. The highest figure recorded for any one parish between 1841 and 1901 was 1000 for Camborne, in 1871.

The Main Employers

With such incomplete documentation there are many mines for which no records have survived, and probably just as many who never recorded detailed employment figures to start with. However, the largest mines tend to be the ones for which records are still available. Employment figures for the 18th century are particularly sparse. The largest tin mines of the time appear to have been Godolphin and Wheal Vor (Breage), possibly along with Polgooth (St Austell) which, in 1794, was described as *'the richest and largest tin mine in Cornwall'*.[32] Dolcoath was the largest copper mine. Each of these mines was employing a total workforce of several hundred in the second half of the 18th century. None give separate figures for the number of women or children, but we can only surmise that they would be there in considerable numbers. For two other fairly large employers at this time, we do have more detailed figures. In 1777, Consolidated Copper Mines in Gwennap (comprising Wheal Virgin, West Wheal Virgin, Wheal Maiden and Caharrack) employed 316 females (constituting 30% of the total workforce).[33] The other is Crenver Tin Mine (Crowan), where 193 women and children were employed in 1787.

Dolcoath Copper Mine was still one of the largest employers, if not the largest, in the early 19th century. The number of females engaged was certainly in the hundreds, and it was possibly more than 400 at its height. But by 1836, with 290 women and children employed, it no longer featured at the top of the list. It had been overtaken by Consols and United Mines (the renamed consortium of mines in Gwennap) which together employed an impressive 869 women and 597 children. The next largest copper mines were Fowey Consols & Lanescot with 308 women and 315 children, and East Wheal Crofty with 404 women and 144 children. Cook's Kitchen and Tincroft were probably employing in large numbers too, but separate totals for female workers were not given.

By 1841, the major copper employers were still the Consolidated Mines and Fowey Consols, with 334 and 342 females respectively. United Mines (now recorded separately) and Tresavean were also employing similar numbers; 370 and 326, respectively. By 1864, the picture had changed radically, with many of these large copper mines having closed, or having changed over to mining tin. The days of the Cornish copper mines with huge payrolls were gone, with none employing more than about 50 women and children. Only those which were mining both copper and tin still employed in large numbers, such as Wheal Seton, which employed 260 children.

It seems that tin dressing floors were less intensive of labour in the 18th and early 19th century than their copper mining counterparts. Christopher Wallis, of Helston, wrote in his journal of 1810: *'The surface tasks connected with the preparation of copper ores were much more intensive of child and female labour than were those connected with the dressing of tin ores.'* [34] The earliest figures we have for female employment at individual tin mines are for 1836. The largest were Wheal Vor, with 327 women and 255 children; Great Works Consol with 40 women and 74 children; Godolphin with 70 women and 40 children; and Wheal Kitty with 52 women and 88 children. By 1841, Wheal Vor was probably still the largest, with 154 girls employed under the age of 18 years (but no figures given for women over 18). Most other tin mines record less than 40 females at this time.[35] By 1856, Great Wheal Vor had diversified and built copper dressing floors in addition to its large tin dressing areas, and was employing 236 females. In 1863, it was still a key player, with a total of 374 surface workers.[36] However, in 1864, the largest tin mine was Dolcoath with 383 children. There were also a few tin mines which now employed more than 100 women and children.

Although the major mines employed a significant proportion of the female workers between them, the experience of many women and girls would have been of small operations. In 1836, 42% of the mines employed less that 20 women and children, and a further 15% employed between 20 and 49. Only six mines employed more than 250. By 1864, the percentage of mines employing less than 50 women and children had risen to 86%, with only one mine employing more than 250.

With the exception of Devon Great Consols, none of the mines in Devon employed females in great numbers. Some of the larger mines in the Tamar basin (such as Lady Bertha and Wheal Friendship) employed around 50 at maximum, but generally totals were low. In the mining communities around the periphery of Dartmoor, it was noticeable that women and girls (including those from mining families) were often employed at the numerous woollen mills. The ore dressing work at the mines seems to have been done mainly by men and boys instead. This was particularly true at Ashburton and Buckfastleigh, for instance. Similarly, in the Teign Valley, large numbers of women and girls were employed at the potteries (especially in the Bovey Tracey area) rather than at the mines. In contrast, Devon Great Consols was employing 199 and 174 bal maidens in June and July 1859 respectively. This had increased to 217 by 1864.

Total Numbers of Bal Maidens

Owing to the scarcity of statistical material, and because it is almost impossible to compare like with like, it very difficult to assess the total number of girls and women who may have worked at the mines in Cornwall and Devon. Only informed guesses may be made. The starting point must be the overall figures available, from various sources, inconsistent and sketchy though they are.

Although it seems that women and girls were first employed on a more commercial scale at the tin and copper mines from about 1720, the first available estimate of the total number of bal maidens at work comes from 1787, with '*2,648 women and children*' working at the copper mines in Cornwall. Certainly, there were over 2,000 women and children working just at those copper mines which had installed Boulton & Watt steam engines (mostly in Gwennap) in that year. By 1799, Vyvian considered that between four and five thousand women and children were employed. [37, 38] This probably translates to at least 2,500 females.

Lemon, quoting statistics for 1836-37, records totals of 3,855 women and 3,641 children at eighty-seven mines. He listed a further twenty-one mines which only gave total employment figures (amounting to 3,455). Henwood's expanded figures of 1838 gave more detail, and included more mines in Devon. His totals were 4,639 women and 4,648 children at one hundred and ten mines. This still left twenty-three mines not detailing female employment (with a total workforce of 4,368). As Lemon had calculated that about 40% of the workforce at this time were women and children, we can project an approximate number of women and children, for Henwood's 'missing' twenty-three mines. This would give us an overall total of approximately 10,500 women and children (with roughly equal numbers in each category).

By 1841, there are several sources of statistics available. The most detailed were those collected for the *1842 Royal Commission*, when 4,136 females were reported to be employed by the sixty-eight mines in Cornwall and West Devon which sent in returns. Of these, 2,700 bal maidens were over the age of eighteen, 1,740 were between the ages of thirteen and eighteen years old, and 696 were under the age of thirteen. Barham estimated that there was a general under-reportage of about one third, thus making projected figures of approximately 5,500 females in total (3,600, 2,320 and 730, in each of those age groups, respectively).[39] In the same year, Watson, not stating his sources, estimates that as many as 60,000 people were employed at one hundred and twelve copper mines, and another 12,000 at the tin mines.[40] This is over twice the number reported in the *1842 Royal Commission*. Based on his figures, even allowing for only 20% of the workforce being female, this would indicate a total greatly in excess of the Commission estimates.

In contrast, studying the microfilms of the *1841 Census* gave a figure of about 3,200 bal maidens for Cornwall, plus just a handful for Devon (mostly in the Tavistock, Beer Ferris and Mary Tavy areas). This total is somewhat higher than those quoted by Spackman, from the same census, in 1847. He recorded totals of 2,276 females working in the mines of Cornwall compared with fourteen in West Devon. Of these, he notes just over 2,000 at the copper mines, 135 at the tin mines, 20 at the lead mines and 5 at the manganese mines.[41] These figures compare reasonably well with those found by studying the census microfilms, of about 2,500 at the copper mines (if most of those not ascribed are added to this group), 27 at the lead mines and 8 at the manganese mines. However, Spackman's figures for those at the tin mines seem to be too low, compared with about 500 found on the microfilm. Both the microfilm study and Spackman's totals from the *1841 Census* for Cornwall suggest an under-recording of bal maidens, when compared to the *1842 Commission* figures for the same year.

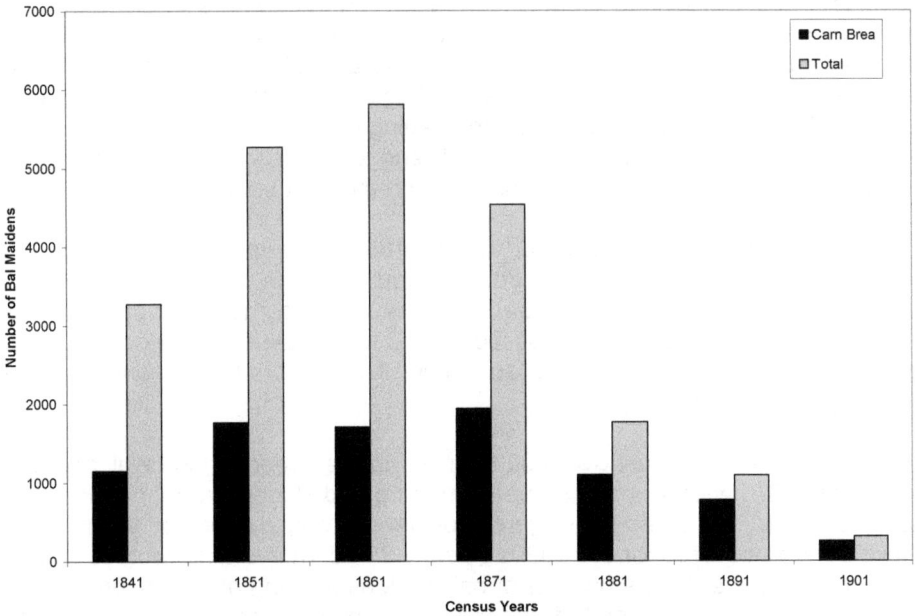

Fig. 5 Number of Bal Maidens by Census Year

Comparing the Carn Brea Area (Camborne, Illogan and Redruth) with the total for Cornwall

When Leifchild was writing in 1855, he quoted a 'Cornish friend' suggesting that 7,000 females were working in 1854. A figure of about 5,000 women and 2,500 girls seems to emerge as estimated employment figures for the 1850s, and is slightly higher than the *1851 Census* totals of about 5,300 bal maidens in Cornwall and 250 in Devon.

Barton quotes total figures of the mining workforce for Cornwall and Devon in 1861, as being 40,000, with an estimate that one third (13,000) were probably women and children.[42] Williams described 50,000 people being employed at 340 mines in Cornwall and West Devon in 1862 indicating a possible minimum of 7,500 females, if the proportion of females in the work force had fallen to about 15% of the total.

The *1861 Census* gives a total of about 5,700 women and girls for Cornwall plus another 175 in South and West Devon. Another source of employment figures for 1861 comes from Spargo. He records only 2,763 females (but with information from significant mines missing). His undated figures, published in 1865, give a more complete view with a total of about 5,000 (with an adjusted total of 5,500 allowing for missing mines). By 1866, as mines began to close, Rowe reports 18,000 miners in the Cornish mines, one sixth (3,000) of whom were estimated to be female.[43]

By the time of the *1871 Census*, 1,544 children between the ages of 13 and 18, plus 4,450 women were reported as working at the mines of Cornwall, making a probable total for the female workforce of about 5,000. From the microfilms, just over 4,500 females were found, plus 54 bal maidens in West Devon, and 7 on the south side of Dartmoor at Buckfasleigh and Hennock.[44] The inspector of mines recorded 3,225 females employed in Cornwall and just over 200 in Devon in 1874, and 2,859 and 250, respectively, in 1875.[45] Comparing these figures with the 1871 returns, we begin to see the effect of the multiple mine closures in Cornwall in the early 1870s. Interestingly, the relatively high numbers of females recorded for Devon, compared with 1871, suggest a serious under-recording in the census, plus a more stable employment situation on the east bank of the Tamar.

The total number of bal maidens recorded in the *1881 Census* was about 1,800 for Cornwall and just 15 for Devon. This dropped to about 1,100 in the 1891, nearly all of whom were employed in the Carn Brea area. Only one was recorded east of the Tamar. This tallies quite well for a national statistic of 1,035 females employed at all the metalliferous mines in the UK in 1893 (when Cornwall was probably the only surviving region which employed any females).

In the *1901 Census* there were just over 300 bal maidens recorded in Cornwall and none for Devon. Of these, 270 were working in the Camborne and Illogan area, and most were working at tin streams. No other total figures for female employment at the mines in Cornwall have been discovered for the 1890s or early 20th century. Mine records suggest that, from about 1900 onwards, the number of bal maidens working at the mines was only in the hundreds. In 1906, it was reported that the total number of people employed at the mines in Cornwall and Devon had dropped to about 6,500, of whom 600 were boys and 'only a few girls'.[46] The last record of women being employed as conventional ore dressers (other than during the two World Wars) was in 1921.

In Conclusion

The main period of commercial employment of women at the mines in Cornwall and Devon seems to be for a period of approximately 200 years, from 1720-1920. The statistics indicate something under 2,000 being employed by the end of the 18th century, rising to between 5,000 and 7,000 by the mid 19th century, or possibly as high as 14,000 (depending on the sources). The proportion of women and girls in the total workforce seems to be generally higher in the first half of the 19th century, possibly as high as 40%. With improved technology, and men or boys being employed to supervise machinery, the proportion of females in the workforce decreased rapidly in the latter half of the 19th century. It is generally considered that the number of women and girls working at these mines in Devon and Cornwall peaked around 1860.

There are no clear figures available for women and girls working at the lead or manganese mines, slate quarries or clay pits. It seems that their commercial employment in these enterprises extended for a much shorter period of time than at the tin and copper mines. It probably did not exceed 100 years, and, in the case of manganese, not more than 20 or 30 years. Estimating the numbers of women and girls who worked in these quarries, mines, and pits, is very difficult. Maximum numbers employed at each place seem rarely to exceed twenty or thirty, so the indications are that together they would total only a few hundred at the peak of their employment, probably prior to about 1850.

So how many bal maidens were there? It is impossible to even hazard a guess at how many worked at the mines, stream works, and quarries, prior to about 1720. For the period of commercial employment of women and girls, which lasted for approximately 200 years (between 1720 and 1920), the total number can only be vaguely estimated, based loosely on the available statistics.

Taking the metalliferous mines only, we could assume a minimum of between 1,000 and 2,000 females were employed (at any one time) in the first 80 years up to 1800. This may be understated, bearing in mind Angerstein's observation that *'most men are miners, and children and young women are occupied in the stream-works and on the dressing-floors'*. With a rapid increase in mining technology, and the concurrent development of the extensive dressing floors, there appears to have been a massive increase in the number of bal maidens over the next 60 years, peaking in the early 1860s, probably at a minimum of 7,000. This was followed by a decline to about 5,000 by 1870, and to 500 by 1900.

Even taking an average 'working life-span' of a bal maiden of 10 years before 1870, and 5 years after 1870, a very rough total number of bal maidens can be projected at 55,000 individuals. This figure does not include the non-metalliferous mines, works and quarries for which we might add another 500 per decade of their economic life, over a period of about 100 years, totalling another 5,000. This brings us to a very rough total of 60,000 women and girls employed at the mines, quarries and clay works in Cornwall and Devon during the 200 years of commercial production between 1720 and 1920. As each of the component figures of the calculation is based on the most conservative figures available, it is almost certain that the real figure would be in excess of this amount, and perhaps considerably so. In addition, these figures do not take into account those who were employed before 1720.

FOOTNOTES

1. WB 5th February 1819, 16th May 1823.
2. Sara (1970) p. 43.
3. Although it was considered unlucky for women to go underground, it seems that female members of the Royal Family (commencing with Queen Victoria at Polberro Mine in 1846) set a precedent. The wife of mine photographer Burrows assisted him when he took the first photos underground in the 1890s.
4. Todd (1967) p. 47.
5. Phil. Trans. (1678) p. 949.
6. Accts Excheq. K. R. bundle 263 No. 17.
7. Mattingly, Joanna; et al. 'A Tin Miner and a Bal Maiden – Further Research in the St Neot Windows' *RIC Jour.* (2001) pp. 96-100.
8. Ford, Trevor '15th Cent. Mining as shown In the Kuttenberger Kanzionale' *PDMHS Bull.* Vol. 12 No. 3 (1994) pp. 81-2.
9. Carew (CRO: BM Add. Mss 29762).
10. Borlase (CRO). Mss
11. Berg, Torsten; Berg, Peter (Ed.). *R. R. Angerstein's Illustrated Travel Diary, 1753-1755* (Science Museum 2001) p. 120.
12. Rowe (1993) p. 70.
13. Tour into Cornwall to the Land's End, Letter from James Forbes to Anne Graves Oct 17th 1794 *RIC Jour.* Vol. 9 1983 pp.146-206.
14. Review of Copper Mines Using Boulton & Watt Boilers (CRO: AD/1683/11/68), Taylor (1831), Lemon (1838) pp. 70-75.
15. Michell, F. B. 'The Development of the Copper Mining Industry in Cornwall and the Industrial Revolution' *Camborne School of Mines Jour.* (1980) p. 58.
16. Schwartz (2000) p. 87.
17. Morrison (1983) p. 49.
18. Report of the Chief Inspector of Factories & Workshops 1889 (TNA: PP 1890, XX Cmd. 6060).
19. Penhalls and Blue Hills Minutes (CRO; STA/191).
20. Annual Reports of the Inspector of Metalliferous Mines 31st Dec. 1889 (TNA: PP 1889 XXIV, C5779 and 1903 XV Cd. 2119).
21. Palmer, Marilyn; Neverson, Peter 'The Basset Mines; Their History & Archeology' *British Mining* No. 32 (1987) p. 35.
22. Troon WI (1952) p. 12.
23. Terrell, Ernest (1920) p. 86.
24. Greeves (2006) p. 9.
25. Brookes (2004) p. 111.
26. Lemon (1838) pp. 70-75.
27. Henwood, W. J. (1838; 1843).
28. Spargo (1864); (1865); (1868).
29. 1841 Census Kea 147/0/1/31.
30. Lanyon (1841) p. 117.
31. Deacon, Bernard Paper read to China Clay History Soc, Sept 2002.
32. Maton, William George *Observations and Antiquities of the Western Counties of England 1794-6* Vol. 1 (Easton 1797).
33. Review of Copper Mines, op. cit.
34. Rule, John G. 'Some Social Aspects of the Cornish Industrial Revolution' in Burt, R. (Ed.) *Industry and Society in the South West* (Univ. of Exeter 1970).
35. CEC Tables 11-14.
36. Barton (1989) p. 103; MJ 21st March 1868.
37. Rowe (1993) p. 8.
38. Review of Copper Mines, op. cit.
39. CEC (1842) p. 42.
40. Watson (1843) p. 3.
41. Spackman, William Frederick: *Analysis of the Occupations of People of the United Kingdom of Great Britain* (London 1847)
42. Barton (1989) p. 240.
43. Rowe (1993) p. 157.
44. General Census of England and Wales Census (1871) p. 253 (TNA: PP111).
45. Le Neve, Dr. C. Report Part 2 Mines Classed Under the Coal Mines Reg. Act Summary of Stats 1875 (CRO: CA/B43/26).
46. Barton (1989) p. 240

Chapter 2

BAL MAIDENS AT WORK

EMPLOYMENT PRACTICES

In the early days of small mining concerns, women and girls would have constituted part of the extended family or community working unit, and would probably not have had any negotiated employment rights or wages as such. It was only as the mines became larger that they would have received wages in their own right.

In Cornwall, however, there was an intermediate stage, where the women and girls were part of a 'tribute' team, which was contracted out to extract and dress ore from an agreed part of the mine. The 'tribute' system is thought to originate, in part, from the need for flexibility in working patterns. Miners often needed to supplement their income with other seasonal occupations such as cultivating smallholdings or fishing. A tribute team was not employed by the mine adventurers as such, but agreed a kind of sub-contract for the task in hand. On 'setting day', each tribute team would bid for a given area to be mined during the subsequent two months, at a pre-set rate for dressed ore extracted. Fines could be imposed if the team did not work their pitch, and the risk factor was transferred (very largely) to the tribute teams. Deducted from their earnings were various costs for candles, explosives, work done by the blacksmith, carpenter etc. In the early days, the tribute team included the ore dressers, and, as ore was landed from the shaft (by their own landers) it would be brought to their own dressers and kept quite separate from ore dressed by any other tribute teams. Depending on the relationships within the tribute team, the women and girls may have received a direct wage from the chief tributer, be given 'pocket money', or received nothing other than their 'board and lodging' if the money went into the communal family purse. At most of the larger mines, there were two types of miners - tutworkers and tribute workers. The tutworkers were paid at a flat rate for sinking shafts, and driving levels. They did not need to employ surface dressers, as their task was primarily to open up new areas in the mine for ore extraction.

Tribute teams often could not afford the labour or the time to dress the poorer grades of ore, especially when the price of tin or copper was low. This ore was often cast aside into waste heaps. As a result, at some mines, other groups of tributers or ore dressers were paid to dress this waste, quite separately from the tribute teams, because they:

'...cannot often afford to dress the coarser parts of what they raise, they reject it. It is let to others who stamp and clean it, having a proportional price likewise.' [1]

As mines began to extract greater quantities of ore, and in some cases, more than one type, the organisation of separate teams of ore dressers at surface became more and more complicated. It became the norm that, by about 1820, and certainly by 1840, a combined workforce of ore dressers was employed and paid for by the mine managers, and each tribute team charged a sum for dressing depending on the amount raised. For instance, William Cullum & Co., a tribute team at Fowey Consols, was charged 5s for dressing ores in December 1841. Some Mine Day Books (compared to Cost Books) recorded the amount of ore dressed for each tributer, so that these costs could then be calculated. For example, at East Wheal Russell (between 1856 and 1859), the women and girls were recorded as dressing ore for up to four or five tributers, as well as for the mine owners, in any one month.

In some mines, the whole dressing floor operation was taken over by one or more enterprising tributers, who would agree to prepare so many tons of ore ready for smelting in a given time, in return for a percentage of the market value. John Taylor suggested this was the norm in 1814: *'Dressing is set in bargains, and generally each to one man who employs the women and boys who assist him.'* [2]

In 1841, between fifty and sixty boys and girls were employed independently in this way at Charlestown Mines, as were all the dressers at Balleswidden. Around the same time, Billy Bray (founder of Bible Christian Movement) became a 'captain-dresser' in the Twelveheads area, when he was no longer fit enough to work underground. There, he employed his own team of boys and girls to dress copper ore. A similar arrangement operated where tin was taken to be dressed at independently owned stamps. The women and girls would then be employed by those who held the agreement or lease. William Sincock employed about thirty-five females at the 'stamps and burning house' at Wheal Agar between 1893 and 1894, and was paid accordingly. (These women were accounted for quite separately in the cost book from the spalling women, who carried out the initial preparation of the ore for the stamps, and who were paid directly by the mine manager). A similar practice of paying a subcontractor for organising female workers sometimes occurred at the clay works, where small groups were involved in carrying the clay blocks out to dry on the hillsides.

Recruitment

When mines first opened, it would be many months before material was brought to the surface ready for dressing. Even then, the numbers of females required on the dressing floor would be small. Gradually, as operations were rationalised and production got under way, the numbers employed in dressing would increase. In the larger mines, responsibility for the surface workers, including recruitment, was with the surface captain. In smaller mines, it was with the purser or mine agent.

Different mines, or, more accurately, different mine captains, sometimes had different views on employing girls and women. For example, at South Caradon, and probably at Wheal Mary and Wheal Trelawney, Captain Peter Clymo Jnr. would willingly employ women, as well as very young children from 7 or 8 years old. Similarly, at Carn Entral in 1861, of twenty females recorded as working at the mines, fourteen were 16 years old or under, one being 7 years old. In contrast, Captain Thomas Trevillion, of Herodsfoot Mine, preferred to employ only males for surface dressing, as he believed they *'worked better'*.[3]

From about 1780 to 1870, there was almost continuous poverty and under-employment in Cornwall, so that recruitment of ore dressers was rarely a problem. Parents would present their children to the Surface Captain for work, as they reached the appropriate age. Sharron Schwartz has discovered information that suggests that there was a policy in place for giving preferential employment to wives and children of those miners who had either died or were unable to work. Certainly the census records seem to indicate that, in some parishes, up to a third of girls at the mines came from families that fell into these categories. In Gwennap, the Guardians of the Poor were concerned that the new Poor Laws of 1834 (which abolished outdoor relief) would result in mining families, who previously relied on earnings of the children, needing to be taken into the Workhouse and become a 'burden' on the parish.[4] After 1834, it seems that desperate mining widows sometimes presented children for this preferential appointment when they were still under-age. For instance, in 1841, the Mine Captains sometimes complained that undue pressure was placed on them by desperate families to take children 'too young', at between 5 and 7 years of age. The mine agent at Tresavean remarked that children were being brought earlier because of *'difficulty in obtaining relief under the new Poor Law'* and that children *'are brought by their mothers who complain they cannot get bread for them'*. In the same year, the Poor Rate Collector for Redruth observed the following: *'Girls seldom go to the mine whilst their father is alive.'*

In the Marystowe area in 1851, of twenty-five girls and women who were recorded as working at the manganese mines, over half were either supporting widowed mothers or were widowed themselves. A similar pattern was observed among the women and children working at Delabole Quarry in the same year. In 1861, 13 year-old Mary Hannah Reynolds and her two brothers, of Polwheveral near Constantine, were working at the mine (probably Wheal Vyvian) in order to support themselves, their grandmother and mother.[5] Similarly, girls were often working at the mine because their father was abroad, as were Eliza, Hannah and Jane Jeffery of Illogan, and Ann and Grace Richards of Camborne in 1861. Young people not only had to support widowed mothers or young siblings, but sometimes disabled members of the family as well. For example, Jane, Fanny, and Henry Remfry, (all in their early twenties) who lived in Blackwater, were all working at the mine in 1841, to support their mother, an *'infirmed'* 15 year-old sister and a baby sister.

Girls were also sent to the mines from the workhouse. For instance, Gracey Briney was taken from the workhouse at a very young age to drive the horse at the horse whim at a mine in Redruth in the 1780s, and Mary Ann Roscorle [sic], at 12 years old, had been sent to Tresavean Mine by 1841. In 1829, J. T. Austen, the manager of Fowey Consols, wrote to the overseers of Fowey Parish suggesting that some of those on 'outside' parish relief should be sent to work at his mines:

'Much work may no doubt be done with advantage to the parish within the walls of the Parish House, but if you have any paupers able to get their living out of doors, I think it necessary to say that I will find employment, at good wages, for any number of boys, girls or women at the mines'. [6]

It is not known how many bal maidens may have been recruited in this way. Although some were recorded as *'parish paupers'* in the census records, this probably indicates that they were out of work and in receipt of parish relief, rather than having been placed by the parish overseers at the mines.

Another factor that seemed to affect the age at which girls were brought to the mine, was the actual employment pressure on a parish. For instance, there was an almost insatiable 'hunger' for cheap labour for surface dressing in the parishes of Camborne, Illogan and Redruth (something in excess of 1000 at the peak of production). Consequently, between 1841 and 1871, not only were these the parishes with greatest number of bal maidens employed, but were also those which tended to record both the youngest and oldest bal maidens in the South West.

Although there is little information, it has been implied that, in the 18th century, girls may have started work at the mines around the age of 8 years old. The main sources of later information about the ages of girls and women at the mines, quarries or clay pits in the mid 19th century are the *1842 Commission on Employment* [CEC], and the population censuses. When Richard Lanyon reported to the *Commission* about the age at which children began work at the mine, he suggested that there had been a recent decrease: *'…about seven years very commonly. Girls begin at the same age. They are put to work earlier than formerly.'* This tallies fairly well with the ages found in the *1841 Census*, with the very youngest being 6 year-olds Eliza Waters of Illogan and Christian Butson of Kenwyn. Interestingly, one of the youngest employed in the St Agnes area during the 1840s, 6 year-old Susan Wills, must have also been one of the most long-lived bal maidens, celebrating her 100th and 101st birthday in the 1930s.[7] In contrast, the 1841 mine employment returns submitted to the *1842 Commission* told a different story, with the youngest recorded at 8 years old.

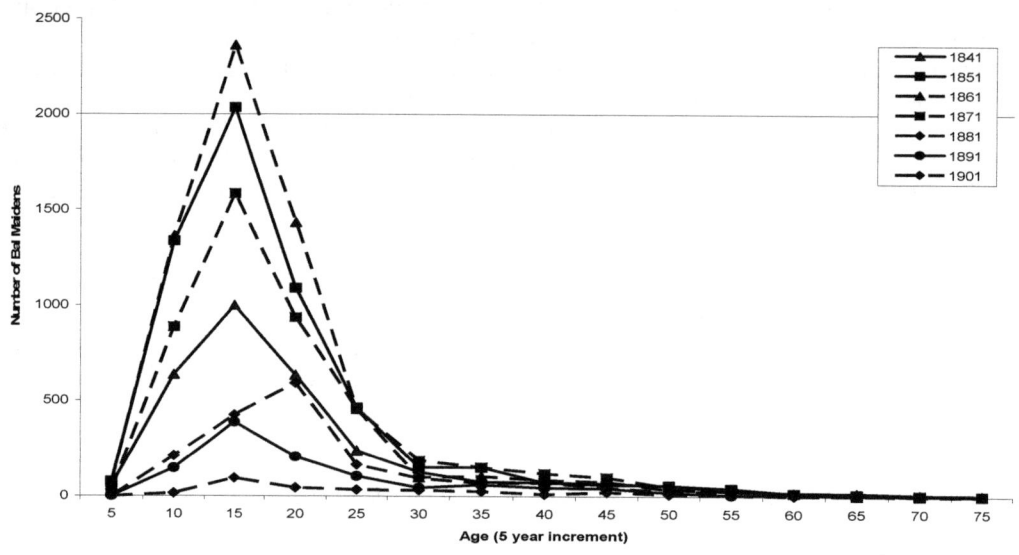

Fig. 6 Age Distribution of Bal Maidens (from Census Records)

While we might expect the average age of employment to have risen significantly after the 'Shaftesbury era', when there was such a public hue and cry about child exploitation, between 1841 and 1871, the age range of bal maidens (as taken from the census returns) remained almost identical. In 1851, the youngest were; 6 year-olds Amelia Launder of Redruth, and Grace Bawden of Breage. There were even younger bal maidens in 1861; 5 year-olds Matilda Michell of Connor Downs and Mary Roberts of St Just. It is impossible to tell whether these are recording errors, or whether these children were truly working at the mines at this age. In Devon, the age of recruitment during these years appeared to be generally higher than in Cornwall, but among the youngest (in 1861) was 6 year-old Charlotte Northcott of North Dimson. Although employment might have started very young, or continued into old age, by far the majority of bal maidens fell into the 15 to 19 year-old age bracket throughout this time (Fig. 6).

Even when the *Metalliferous Mines Regulation Act 1872* made employment of children under ten years old illegal, the *Inspector of Mines Employment Returns* for 1874 showed that 9% of bal maidens in Cornwall were only eleven or twelve years old, but by 1875 it had dropped slightly to 7%. In Devon, for those two years, the proportion of eleven or twelve year-olds was even higher, at 14% and 13% respectively. This indicates how keen the mines were to continue to exploit the youngest (and presumably the cheapest) labour they could find.[8] The *Education Acts* of 1876, together with the *Factory and Workshops Act 1878*, should have meant a complete removal of children from the mine workforce by 1880. Certainly the age range recorded in the census of 1881 began to reflect this, for the first time showing a considerable shift to older employment. By 1891 though, the situation seems to have reverted, with young children still employed. In fact, it was well known in the late 1880s and early 1890s that many mines and tin streams in Cornwall were openly flouting the legislation and continuing to employ children who were under age. Captain Bennetts described the scene in a tin stream works in Camborne at this time:

'*As soon as an Inspector appeared under Brea Arch, word would be passed along, and all the children under age would be sent to hide in the houses, or out into the fields to play. If there wasn't time to send them out of the way, a bit of dry cloth would be placed on the ground for one or two to sit on, and a kieve turned upside down over them, with a bit of wood about an inch thick pushed under, for air.*

Very soon the cab drivers at Camborne station all got to know those inspectors, and the cabbies would arrive on the 'streams' or mines twirling a whip over their heads [as signals]. *As soon as the inspector was sighted a man would stand on a bank with his right hand behind his back. This signal would pass up and down ten miles of valley in a few minutes.*' (Troon WI 1952 p. 4a)

It was not unheard of for women or girls with some sort of disability to be employed at the mines. Mary Hendra, born in 1839, who had been deaf from birth, worked at a tin mine in the Gwinnear area in 1861, 1871 and 1881. (By 1891 she appears to be an inmate at the Redruth Union Workhouse). Similarly, other young bal maidens who were recorded as deaf were 16 year-old Catherine Peeps of Liskeard (1861), 25 year-old Elizabeth Maynard (Devon Great Consols 1861), Martha Rowe of Illogan (1861 and 1871), 12 year-old Susan Scollar of Sithney (1871), and 21 year-old Mary Ann Trezise of Perranzabuloe (1871). In 1881, 21 year-old Anne Maria Harris, who had been partially deaf for five years, was working at a mine in Roskear. In contrast, a blind woman was employed as an ore dresser in the St Columb Major area in 1861. She was 62 year-old Betsy Miner. Nor was it uncommon for young girls or women with special needs to be employed at the mines.

Inmates at the Truro Union Workhouse, Mary Ann Harris and Ann Nancarrow, were ex-bal maidens but also described as *'imbecile from birth'* in the 1851 and 1881 census respectively. Similarly, Sarah Jane Allen was described in the same way when she was an inmate of Redruth Union Workhouse in 1871, having been *'at the copper mines'* in 1861 when she was 12 years old. Sadly, she was still in the Workhouse thirty years later.

Sometimes all the girls of eligible age of one family would be working together, as with six sisters of the Craze and Heathorne families (of Camborne) in 1851, and six members of the Jennings family (of Illogan) in 1871. On occasion it seems that groups of women presented themselves for work together, with one person receiving payment for the whole group on pay day. This certainly seemed to have been the case of the barrow women at Newham Smelter in the first few years of operation in the early 18th century, and possibly with women laying out the clay at the clay works in the early 19th century.

The girls would usually continue to work at the mine until they were married, on average at about 19 years old, and only a very small proportion left to seek alternative employment, as long as there was work to be found at the mines. Although married women were generally discouraged, it was not uncommon for widows of all ages to ask for work, on the death of their husbands. This must have been the case with Harriet Knuckey whose husband, Philip, died on 23rd December 1849 at Wheal Trehane. She was left with an infant son, and gave birth to a second child 6 months after his death. By March 1851, she was lodging in a house in Menheniot with her children, and working at the mine.[9] Similarly, Mary Webster, who was killed in a boiler explosion at the unfortunately-named Boiling Well Mine in 1858, appears to have gone to the mine to work to support herself after her husband, too, had been killed in a mining accident. The women with young children, who returned to the mines after being widowed or abandoned, were often in difficulty. If they were lucky, they might leave children or babies with family, or an older child. For instance, 22 year-old widow, Hannah Gliddon, who was working at a manganese mine in Stowford in 1861, presumably left her 3 year-old son with her 72 year-old mother (with whom she was living). Sometimes mothers just had to leave their children in the care of other very young children or even on their own, as with a suicidal mother at Wheal Basset.[10] One of the most famous widowed bal maidens must have been Dolly Trebble. For many years, she lived with her husband in a cottage way off the beaten track between Brimps and Yar Tor. When Dolly was widowed, she took up work at Hexworthy Tin Mine, where a shaft was named after her.[11]

Women who had never married often continued to work at the mines, sometimes into their old age. Among the oldest bal maidens, in 1841, were 80 year-old Blanch Coombe and 85 year-old Mary Ivey. In Cornwall in 1861, there were eighteen women working over the age of 60 years, and seven over the age of 75 years. By 1871, these figures had increased to an incredible twenty seven and ten, respectively. Even in 1881 elderly women were still being employed, and in 1891, the very oldest appears to be 93 year-old Mary Thomas of St Agnes, who was recorded as a tin miner. At the time, she was living with a 63 year-old widowed daughter and two granddaughters, in Illogan. The story of the elderly unmarried woman working at Carn Brea in about 1880 (see Chapter 12) graphically illustrates the great fear people had of the workhouse, being perceived, by many, as the only alternative to toiling at the mine. Some mines seem to have had a policy of giving preferential employment to older single or widowed women, and this appears to have been the case in the Crowan area in 1861, when thirty-six of the ninety-five females employed were over the age of 50. Some women were still working at the mine to a considerable age in order to support aged parents, such as 59 year-old Mary Bastin of Twelveheads, supporting her 86 year-old mother, in 1861.

The length of time which girls and women remained employed at the mine depended very much on personal circumstances, as well as on the local mining economy. For single women, work at the mine often became their life. Many worked there for 20 or 30 years. Where there were daughters in a widowed family, the prospects of marriage could be poor, as a prospective husband might feel unable to support the mother and sisters, as well as his wife. As a result, it was often groups of sisters who remained working at the mine the longest, even after their widowed mother had died. For instance, Harriet and Jane Pidwell of Tregajorran were recorded as working at the mine in census records spanning 30 and 40 years respectively, Similarly, the four Cadwell sisters of Pengigan were each recorded over three or four decades. Two Chapple sisters of Carn Brea were recorded over three decades, while a third worked over a period of 50 years. Another woman whose career as a bal maiden spanned 40 years of census records was Sarah Chellow of Ludgvan,

Very often, the girls were no strangers to the mine and, well before they were due to start work, would be sent with dinner for other members of their family. Minnie Andrews remembered '*I was five years old when I first took father's crowst across to Carn Camborne.*' [12] This meant they became familiar with the layout, the different processes, and the language of the dressing floors from an early age. Their lack of awareness of the dangers, however, sometimes led to tragic accidents, such as with 9 year-old Mary Dale, in October 1893, and 8 year-old Ada Harris, in December 1896, both of whom died after falling through arsenic flues at Botallack and East Pool, respectively.[13]

Job Security

Surface workers and labourers were expected to give between two and four weeks' notice, and this was probably enforced by the threat of withholding wages for that period. This was quite possible with the workforce being paid either one or two months in arrears. However, it seems that there were no written agreements, and arrangements could be very fluid on both sides. There was no job security, as workers could be, and often were, laid off with no notice. When mines ran into difficulty, wages were frequently reduced, and sometimes no payment was made at all. When bad weather made it impossible for the dressing floors to operate, there was no system of retainment pay. In 1872, when mine workers held out for the abolition of the 'five week month', and an impassioned plea was made for fairness by a Mr. Bassett on this issue of notice and dismissal:

'Surface hands should be entitled to receive the same notice which they give; they were often discharged at a moment's notice, whilst if about to leave of their own accord, they are obliged to give a fortnight's notice.' (RCG 27th Jan 1872)

On the other hand, non-attendance at work, without adequate reason, was a frequent complaint heard from the mine agents. It seems that sometimes women and girls were poached away from one mine or clay works to another when more attractive pay or working conditions were offered. Minnie Andrews, the '*last bal maiden*', worked in a number of different mines, and commented: *'We go the places where we gather most money, see?'* [14] In order to encourage loyalty of the workforce, some mines offered monthly bonuses for continuous attendance. At Wheal Vor, in 1841, the older women and girls were given an additional 1s, and the younger girls 6d if they had attended the dressing floors all month.

Employment on the dressing floors was not necessarily continuous, even when mines were in full production. Although ore stuff could continue to be raised from underground independently of weather conditions (with the exception of severe flooding), the processes on the dressing floor could be adversely affected. Although the women and children normally continued to work through appalling weather conditions, only taking shelter in extremes, there were occasions when work had to stop completely.

Cost Books for the late 18th century indicate fewer bal maidens working in the winter months than in the summer. When George Skerry wrote about the Chiverton Mines in 1799 he described female surface workers only being employed in the summer.[15] At Wheal Cocke, during 1822 and 1823, twice as many women were employed between April and November as from December to March. In February 1841, work had to stop at many mines when the dressing floors and apparatus were covered in snow. Again in February 1855, which was described as the worst weather for fifty years, the only tin stamps still working in the parish of St Just were at Wheal Owles and Boscean. All the other surface workers in the parish were thrown out of work. Similarly, in January 1881, all manual work stopped in St Austell area clay works, due to deep snow and bad weather. Continuous work was most difficult in the remote moorland areas, and this was especially true of the mines on Dartmoor. For example, the water leats at Birch Tor regularly froze over.

Conversely, those women and girls working at water-powered stamps could not work when the water supply was insufficient, often from May to September. Two months of drought seriously affected dressing at Boswidden in the summer of 1868.[16] Similarly, there was little stamping done at Drakewalls in Calstock in August 1887, and again from July to November during 1893. At Levant, the dressing floors were short of water in June 1892, and the bal maidens sent home until the dressing floors were operating again. Some mines were able to make use of temporary solutions to water shortages, as at Spearn Consols in 1870:

'Messrs Holman and Son of St Just have just come to the rescue of the idle 'heads' [stamps] and unoccupied boys and girls. They have a travelling steam engine which rolls alongside the disused stamps, buckles itself to the axles.'

Occasionally, work also stopped at the dressing floors when underground accidents or damage to machinery prevented ore from being raised to the surface. For instance, after a shaft was damaged at Dolcoath in 1823, the captains hoped for a speedy repair so that *'we may draw as soon as possible to keep the maidens going'*.[17]

Hours of Work and Holidays

During the late 18th century and most of the 19th century the bal maidens' working day at the metalliferous mines started at 7 a.m. in summer, and at dawn in winter, except at 'sampling', for about two weeks in every eight, when they started at 6 a.m. In winter it would be a daunting task for young children to leave home in the dark and to walk across country to work. Frank Booker describes the scene in the Tamar Valley:

'At night and on dark winter mornings, lanes near the mine were full of bobbing lanterns as the shifts returned or went to work; and many younger children were often carried on their parent's backs.' [18]

Mrs. Dalley, of Troon, remembered her daily childhood journey to Dolcoath quite clearly:

'I used to leave Carwinnen at six o'clock in the mornings. It was alright in the summer, but in the winter mornings I was afraid of the dark. When I got to Troon the children used to come along from Black Rock and Bolenowe. We used to lead hands and sing to keep our spirits up.'

At the other end of the day, the bal maidens normally finished at 5 p.m. in summer and dusk in winter. Some tasks, such as bucking, sometimes continued for a short while in candlelight during winter, but in general it was not efficient or effective to try to separate ore in poor light. Breaks were allowed during the day with half an hour or an hour for dinner, and sometimes a short break mid-morning. No time allowances were made for age, so even the youngest girls, of 8 or 9 years old, would be expected to work these hours from the outset.

The hours worked by the women and girls at the clay works, however, were slightly different. Up until 1853, the normal hours of work were 8 hours per day, but with many working 'days and quarter' or 'days and half', making 10 or 12 hours, and for which they were paid accordingly. In 1853, however, when workers asked for an increase in pay, it was only given in return for extending the standard working day to 10 hours. A confusingly persuasive broadsheet was published by the 'clay masters' to counter the complaints of the workers, and the longer working day was adopted.[19]

Some girls or women were employed by the 'task', at an agreed price, and their working day would finish when the task was completed. At 'sampling' the surface workers, having started an hour early, still might not finish work until 8 p.m. The normal working week was from Monday to Saturday lunchtime, with a half day on the monthly pay-day. This meant that in an average week, the number of hours worked by the women and girls was at least 50 in summer, and 45 hours in winter. At sampling this could rise to between 55 and 65 hours.

Depending on the amount of dressing required, there were a few females employed at the mines who were part time. In Carharrack in 1871, Mary Rickard was described as working *'at the mine or in the fields'*, and Mary Bray *'dresses ore occasionally'*. Widow Matilda Williams, of Lanner, was both *'mine girl and charwoman'*. As described in more detail in Chapter 6, work at the clay works tended to be more seasonal, with full-time employment over a few dry weeks in the summer, but part-time for most of the year.

Apart from sampling, overtime was occasionally required when large amounts of un-dressed ore had accumulated. For instance, this seemed to be the case at Dolcoath, in July 1823, when the Night Captain reported that *'There has been a pretty good number of maidens working out of core tonight.'* [20]

By 1841, generally, no work was undertaken on Sundays. The exception to this would be where water-powered tin stamps were in operation in areas where water supply was at a premium. In these cases, stamping continued around the clock, 7 days a week. Women and girls were then sometimes required to take their turn at the stamps on Sundays. In 1867, there was an attempt to introduce Sunday working on the dressing floors at Condurrow. The surface workers threatened to strike, and the managers withdrew the suggestion. At some mines, women were also employed to watch over the calciners on Sundays. Ann Gribben was paid 1s per day for this work at Wheal Coates in 1882.

The women and girls did not usually do shift work as dressing at surface normally only took place during daylight hours. However, there were exceptions to this. Girls and women were employed on day and night shifts during the peak of copper production in 1845 at Devon Great Consols, to keep a constant supply of dressed ore ready for shipping from Morwellham Quay. Girls were also working shifts there in 1854. It is not clear whether this shift system was the norm, whether it was the 'Devon Great Consols' equivalent of 'sampling', or their method of coping with occasional back-logs. Three shifts per day were also worked at the Manganese Mills at Morwellham at this time. Later in the century, there were also some tin steam operations on the Red River which are reported as having continual shifts working day and night.[21]

In the 18th and early to mid-19th century, Christmas Day and Good Friday were the only regular holidays during the year, but at some mines Whit Monday or the Parish Feast Day were celebrated as a holiday as well. If these were not official holidays, the women and girls very often used to take unpaid leave, or work in lieu, in order to take part in the celebrations. In some parishes, the feast day was an extended holiday, as at St Just. Here, in the 1840s, Monday to Wednesday were taken off for the carnival, and attendance at the mine was very low on the subsequent Thursday and Friday.[22]

Midsummer's Day was a special day at the mines, when normal work was suspended and there was a general clean-up and repair, both below ground and above. One of the tasks was to deck headgear or one of the engine houses with a new flag, or greenery. When all was completed, the workers were given a bonus, and allowed to go early to the local Midsummer Fair. The women and girls received 6d, the men received 1s.

There were also other, less regular, celebrations at the mines. The occasion of the christening of a new engine, or the opening of a new mine, was, in effect, another feast day. A grand parade would be arranged through the nearby neighbourhoods, with local bands playing music, and local inhabitants joining the procession to the mine. Mine workers in the procession took their customary order of precedence, with the managers and clerks first, followed by the underground workers, the male surface labourers, and then the women and children. Local dignitaries would also be invited. After the engine was 'christened' and started up, the special guests were entertained to a feast at the counthouse, and the workers provided with a roast ox, and plenty of beer and cider. The rest of the day would be spent celebrating, with games and competitions.

The china clay parishes held an additional annual holiday, usually in the summer months, as described in the West Briton in 1859:

'It is the practice on some day of this season of the year for those employed in the clay works to enjoy a holiday to commemorate the first discovery of clay in the locality; and on Saturday last the persons employed under Mr. John Lovering, working on the lands of Mr. Thomas Gill, walked into the town of St Austell in procession, headed by a band of music, and after paying a visit to the residence of their employer, they halted outside the Globe Hotel, where the lord of the manor is staying, and gave three hearty cheers for him, when Mr. Gill, with his usual liberality, presented them with a donation, to add to their day's enjoyment.' (8th July 1859)

Major national events were also celebrated. During national peace celebrations in June 1798, William Jenkin gave a mug of ale to each of his 300 employees at Tincroft.[23] At the end of the long protracted war with the French, celebrations were held at many mines in July of 1814. For instance, at Dolcoath:

'Tables and benches were prepared for 1500 under the windows of the counting house, where some of the principal adventurers and their friends met to celebrate together with their men, the return of peace. Flags of all nations were displayed throughout the mine, which with innumerable triumphal arches, added much to the gaiety of the scene, and the whole was rendered under a completely cloudless sky. On a signal given by a cannon, the captains marched their companies of men, women and children, preceded by a band of music to their appointed tables: half a loaf, two pounds of beef, and three pints of porter were allotted to each individual.' (WB 1st July 1814)

Similarly, in June 1856, the end of the Crimean War was celebrated at Wheal Owles with a parade, followed by a huge dinner of beef served outside the Counting House, for all the boys and girls under the age of 15, all *'provided by the purser'*. (WB 20th June 1856)

Rates of Pay and Methods of Payment

The rates of pay for the women and girls at the mines did not change significantly over many years. Levels of pay were never high, compared to the cost of living, and mining families nearly always had to supplement their earnings with other income. If the earnings of the men were low, the bal maidens were consistently paid less, not unusually half of the amount paid to their male counterparts on the dressing floor.

As mentioned before, in the early 'family' mining operations, or where the females were part of the tribute team, it is probable that the majority never received wages, as such. But, once employed by the mine management, they were paid an agreed rate. They were paid either for the number of barrows dressed, at a set rate per day, or for a particular task.

The earliest recorded pay found for females in the mining industry in Cornwall was for women and children washing ore or slag at the silver-lead smelters in Calstock in the early 14th century. The adults were paid between 4d and 6d per week, and their 'assistants' 2d or 3d per week. The next earliest entries were for the barrow women employed at the Newham Smelter between 1704 and 1707. They were paid about 2d per ton for carrying coal from the shore to the yard, or 6d per day for barrowing and sifting cinders at the smelter. The frequency of pay varied, but in these early operations they seem to have been paid every one or two weeks.

In the early part of the 18th century, most female workers at the mines, despite their age or task, appear to have been paid at a standard rate of 4d per day. This was true at Pool Adit in 1731, where all twenty-one girls or women on the payroll were paid the same. This is consistent with Borlase reporting that girl and boy pickers at the copper mines were paid 4d per day in 1759.

Subsequently, it appears that the women and girls began to be paid different rates, as at Cook's Kitchen in 1766. Girls working there in October were earning either 4d or 5d per day. Similarly, at Wheal Towan in 1772, they were paid between 4d and 6d per day, whereas women breaking ore at Wheal Uny in 1773 were all being paid 5d per day.

Increasingly, the rates at which the women and girls were paid depended on their age, and the task they were carrying out. At Fowey Consols in 1836, for instance, girls under 12 years old were paid 8s per month, 12 and 13 year-olds 12s, 14 to 17 year-olds 15s, and those 18 years and over 18s.[24] Minnie Andrews described being paid according to her age; 16s at 16, 18s at 18 etc. but up to a maximum of 22s. One of the lowest paid appears to be Susan Wills who was given *'two pence ha'penny a day'* when she first started work in the early 1840s, at the age of 6 years old.[25] This graduated scale of 'wages by age' was also observed by a French visitor in 1858. Those over 17 years were paid between £1 and £1 5s, girls from 14 to 17 years old were paid 14s, and girls under 14 years were paid 10s. (This was cited as per day, but should surely be the monthly wage.)[26] Some women and girls were paid by the number of barrows dressed, or were set a daily task of dressing so many barrows in a day. A traveller passing through the Carn Brea area, in 1788, recorded the following:

'Women work by task, earn from four-pence to eight-pence a day, and are paid by measure according to the quantity they can buck; girls and boys earn from two-pence to four-pence a day, some more; thus there is a constant employment of both sexes and all ages from five to sixty years old.' [27]

Some form of tally system must have been used to record the amount dressed in a day. Up until about 1870, so few of the women and girls were able to write, or perhaps even add up, that a system of notching tally sticks was probably used, as described by a traveller in 1824:

'The ore...when raised form the mine, is divided into...shares; these shares are measured by barrows, an account of which is kept by a person who notches a stick for that purpose.' [28]

The system used was probably the same as that used in the coal mines, where each person delivering a wagon or barrow would carry a stick which was notched for each full wagon or barrow delivered. At the end of a shift the tally stick would be split lengthways, the barrower and the tally clerk both keeping similarly marked portions as their 'tally' for the day.

Conditions of payment could even vary between pay-days. At Wheal Cocke in 1822, bucking maidens received two different rates for bucking; 12d for either 4.5 or 7 barrows -

presumably depending on the quality of the ore to be dressed. Some of the same women were also paid at a daily rate, in the same month, as well as by the barrow.

The wages paid reflected the prices that could be obtained at market for the dressed ore, and, in the course of the late 18th century and throughout the 19th century, there were great fluctuations in the prices of copper, tin, and lead. It was not unusual, therefore for employees to have their rates of pay reduced. For instance, at Tresavean in 1841, the amount that the bucking girls were paid went down from 1s for six barrows dressed, to 1s for eight barrows.

Overtime was sometimes available for the girls and women, depending on the backlog of ore waiting to be dressed. It was not normally compulsory, but it was commonly feared that a bal maiden *'might lose her place'* if she were to turn it down out of hand. It was not unusual for the older girls to stay on after 5 p.m. for another two hours or so, to buck or cob an extra one or two barrows. For those women who were paid by the day, extra time was paid for by the day. For instance, at Wheal Agar in 1893, the spallers regularly worked up to a total 25 days per month. In August 1833, Elizabeth Grose, who worked at Ninestones Clay Pit, was paid for a total of 31 days. There was overtime available at Consolidated Mines during 1841. Extra work at sampling was not considered overtime, and it was not usual for extra wages to be paid for this. Where overtime was paid, the girls were sometimes allowed to keep it by the family, as pocket money.

Wage levels for the women and girls also varied according to the region, and the overall availability of labour. In 1837, the average wage for surface workers in the Penzance area was 42s per month, and in the Camborne-Redruth area it was 41s, compared with the St Austell area at 45s. In the 1840s, the wages had increased slightly across the board, but the same pattern could be observed, with the lowest wages paid in the Camborne, Redruth, and St Agnes area, at 12s per week, compared with 13s in the St Just area and 14s in East Cornwall and Devon. The most well-paid women and girls (in 1841) were in Wendron and Kea, where the average weekly wage was 18s. It was estimated that 6d per day, or 15s per month, was the amount needed to feed and clothe a young person at this time.

By the 1850s, the youngest girls coming to the mines were still being paid 2d or 3d per day while they learnt their trade. It was then increased to 3d or 4d per day. This was little more than the women and girls had been earning one century before.[29] For example, the manganese dressers at Coryton Mine were only being paid 4d per day in 1858.[30]

At East Wheal Russell in 1857, riddlers were paid 11 or 12d per day, compared to pickers at 6 or 7d. These wages reflected the different ages of the women and girls at the different operations. The bal maidens who alternated between cobbing and bucking however, were paid 8d and 12d respectively for each task, possibly indicating the number of hours worked at each. Even in 1864, when the Kinnaird Commission was investigating conditions at the mines in Cornwall, they discovered that the women were paid between 8d and 1s per day, and the girls were still receiving between 4d and 6d. The rates paid at the lead-silver mines seem to have been roughly similar, with the bal maidens at Carn Vivian being paid between 5d and 12d for dressing or 15d for bucking between 1856 and 1862, 15d per day North Porthilly in 1862, and between 6 and 12d per day at New Trelawney Mine in 1867.

Wages at the clay works tended to be kept at roughly the same level as at the tin and copper mines in the same area, in order to prevent losing employees to the mines. There is evidence from the clay works that different groups of women were paid in different ways and at different rates. At any one time, there could be women being paid a daily rate, usually 6d to 8d per day in 1830s, whilst other women were being paid a price per ton that they had cleaned varying between 4d and 5d. Those who were involved in carrying clay out to dry on the hillsides seem to have been paid indirectly by a sub-contractor who in turn received '*1d per yard*'.

In 1873, there was a sudden drop in the price of tin, and by October of that year wages had declined by 20%. In 1880, when tin prices had recovered, it was only after the mine employees in the Camborne area vociferously demanded an increase that wages were raised again. In 1893, bal maidens at Dolcoath were being paid 1s to 1s 2d per day for spalling or 4d or 6d per ton. Minnie Andrews remembers being paid between 18s and £1 per month when she was working in the 1890s. In 1893, at Dolcoath, the spalling girls were paid between 3d and 5d per ton, depending on the hardness of the rock, and could break 3 to 5 tons per day. This could earn them 25s to 40s per month, a maximum of under 2s per day. The highest wage paid to bal maidens appears to be £2 per week at Dolcoath (in 1920), followed (in early 1921) by £4 per week. However, this only lasted for two or three weeks before the mine closed.

Using '*comparative purchasing power*' statistics, the highest-paid bal maidens during the 18th and first half of the 19th centuries seem to have received about the equivalent of £12 per week (at 2005 prices). This gives us some indication of how far short their wages fell of a realistic living wage. This would have bought them just a little more than a loaf of bread per day! Their wages subsequently increased to the present day equivalent of about £30 per week by the 1890s, and to £60 for the last Dolcoath bal maidens (briefly) in 1921.

From as early as 1720, full-time male employees of a mine were encouraged to pay into the Sick Club, and possibly for a surgeon as well, from their wages. For female employees, paying into the Sick Club or for a surgeon was either optional or just not on offer. It was considered by the management, and often by the women and girls themselves, as not viable due to their employment not being 'long term', and that the benefits derived would be limited. Although the funds paid into the Sick Club were used, in part, to pay a Mine Surgeon, the conditions under which the doctors could treat injured or sick employees, whether at the mine or at home, were often appalling. As early as the 1770s, Pryce was recommending that all employees, including the women and children, should contribute 3d per week into a county-wide fund. This would provide £4,500 per annum for specially designated doctors based at a miners' hospital, probably to be based in Redruth. This suggestion was not taken up. From 1794, however, local mine adventurers had been subscribing to the Truro Infirmary, where most of the patients were either injured or sick miners. There was no particular provision for bal maidens but it is possible that some bal maidens were treated there, but on the basis of being 'deserving poor', rather than employees of the mine who had paid into a sick club.

Although it was not the norm, women and girls did pay into a Sick Club at Dolcoath in the early 1840s, but the managers reported that the scheme '*had failed*'. However, at Fowey Consols, at about the same time, the bal maidens paid 1d from every 5s earned, up to a maximum of 5d. From this subscription, they could claim 12s per month if they were ill. At

South Exmouth Mine, in 1863, the females paid 3d per month for the doctor, but nothing for the Sick Club. This was also the amount paid by spallers at Pednandrea between 1883 and 1887. Those paid *'per stem'* (piece work) at Pednandrea did not seem to make this payment. In 1864, bal maidens at South Caradon Mine were paying 2d per month *'for the doctor'*.[31] Bal maidens at Wheal Uny paid the same amount, between 1877 and 1883 if they earned less than 1s per day; otherwise they paid 3d. Tin dressers at Wheal Coates also paid 3d per month between 1882 and 1884. At Wheal Agar, in 1893, all the spalling women paid 6d per month into the *'club'*. A hospital for miners was eventually set up in Redruth in 1863, but there were no facilities for women or girls until 1890. Perhaps those women spallers at Wheal Agar, who were paying 6d per week for the Sick Club, may have been entitled to go there.

Another deduction that could be made from the bal maidens wages was a *'spale'* or fine. This might be levied for general misbehaviour, using bad language, absenteeism or damage of mine property. Only three references have been found of bal maidens possibly being fined. In 1823, when the night captains at Dolcoath discovered a group from Roskear stealing equipment, a letter was to be sent to the mine agents at Roskear, asking for the girls to be spaled. In the same year, Jenny Stone was also fined 5s for inaccurate recording of the bal maidens hours.[32] In later years, Susan Robins recalled that she would be deducted *'a quarter'* from her wages for arriving late, or for not working hard enough.

In the earliest accounts for the Calstock Smelters, from 1302 to 1309, surprisingly, the women and their assistants who were washing black slag were paid very regularly. They were paid weekly in arrears, either on a Saturday or a Sunday. This was not to be the subsequent pattern in the South West.

Prior to the keeping of regular cost books (accounts) it is quite possible that mine workers would work for many months without being paid, but sometimes being given loans against their earnings until the mine came into profit. Certainly, the early 18th century cost books do not necessarily record wages being paid every month. Sometimes there is a gap of a month or more. Even after proper accounting records began to be made, mine employees may not have been paid regularly. Between 1816 and 1821, workers at Botallack seem to have been paid only every 3 months. At Wheal Comfort, St Ives, between 1832 and 1834, a woman was paid 6s for a total of 11 months work of washing and mending an agent's clothes.[33] This was a long time to wait to be paid! At Carn Vivian, in 1861, the workers were usually paid two months in arrears anyway, but had to wait until November, not just for their September pay, but for July and August as well.

General payment of wages was always at least one month in arrears. In some mines employees were required to work for two complete months before payment, and then continued to be paid two months in arrears. In 1872, an experiment was tried at West Wheal Basset to pay the surface workers weekly, but the outcome of that is not known. By 1890, there are indications in the Cost Books that wages were paid once every two weeks almost as a matter of course. In 1893, all the spallers at Wheal Agar were applying for their 10s subsist on a regular basis, as a way of being paid fortnightly rather than monthly. Payment every two weeks certainly seems to have been the policy at Dolcoath by 1899.[34]

The first Saturday in the month was traditionally thought of as payday, and the subsequent Monday described as 'Mad' or 'Maze' Monday because of the perceived over-indulgence.

However, the Cornwall and Devon Mining Directory for 1862 shows that the only consistent thing about pay-day was that it was monthly! In the Perranzabuloe area alone, at East Wheal Golden payday was *'the Saturday after the first Friday'*, at Great Retallack *'the Friday before the first Saturday,'* and at Wheal Hope *'the Friday before the second Saturday'*! It seems pay day could be Friday or Saturday, and fall at any time of the month. In some mines, such as Wheal Vor, the women and children were paid on the Friday evening and the men were paid on the following Saturday morning.

No pension schemes ever seem to have been implemented in the South West mines during the working life of any bal maiden. It was not as if the ideas were not around, nor was there a lack of awareness of the advantages that came with a loyalty generated by genuine care of employees. William Waller recognised such issues as early as 1698. In a paper to the adventurers of the lead mines in Pembroke, he wrote:

'One thing more to offer to your consideration…that the poor may have some small share with you in so rich a treasure, especially the poor miners and labourers. That when they have spent their lives to make you rich, and are grown impotent, and unable to work, either though age or accident, they may have a comfortable subsistence provided for them….And this will tend to no small advantage…every miner will have an interest in the work…as if they were his own. Your works will never be in want of able miners, or in danger of being lost either by neglect or treachery.' [35]

Sadly, the wisdom of these words was not heeded in Cornwall and West Devon, any more than they were in West Wales, until it was far too late for the humble bal maiden.

Fig. 7 One Penny Tokens (1811 & 1812) Issued by Scorrier House & Devon Copper Mines

Payment of wages was usually made by the mine purser (book-keeper) at the Count House. There was a prescribed hierarchy in the order of payment. It was usual for the tutworkers and tributers to be paid first, followed by the male labourers, then the older women and girls, followed by the children. In the case of the children, they would not normally receive their own pay if there was an older relative working at the same mine. The names of the employees would be recorded on a ledger, and the recipient asked to sign for it, if capable, or to mark with a cross. Most pay ledgers are now lost, but sometimes the names and marks of individual employees appear in the Mine Cost Books. Interestingly, the cost book ledger for Wheal Agar from 1893 to 1898 does not just record the names of the employees, but has printed columns for a cumulative total of the numbers of 'girls', boys and men employed in each month.

It was well-known throughout the mining industry that the women and girls did not receive equal pay for equal work, when compared to the older boys or men. It seems to have been the case as early as the 1300s when women were paid 5d for washing black slag, and men paid 6d. In 1810, Sarah Davies was only paid 1s per stem for watching the burning house at Wheal Union (Devon) whereas Henry Davis was paid 2s for the same work. Even later in the century, female ore dressers were generally paid between one half and two thirds of the wages of the male surface labourers. In 1858, a French visitor noticed that girls and boys under twelve years of age both earned the same amount, but that between twelve and fourteen years girls earned 14s, compared with 15s for the boys, and at fourteen years to seventeen years they earned 16s compared with £1.[36] Similarly, at Wheal Agar women were paid half that of the male surface labourers between 1855 and 1859. Even in 1893, the women observed that they often broke more ore than the men they worked alongside, but they still only earned 1s 3d per day compared with the 2s 6d that the men were paid.

Various dubious practices took place in the methods of pay. These were often extended to the women and children, and, in some cases, purposely directed at them. Some mines paid in credit notes or tokens that could only be cashed at the mine shop or the counthouse, removing the option of buying cheaper goods elsewhere. Tokens were in use, in particular, between 1811 and 1818. Due to the high price of copper, many of the general currency cartwheel pennies had been taken out of circulation and melted down, leading to a severe shortage of coinage. Some mines began to mint their own pennies, the most notable were those owned by John Williams in the Gwennap area, Dolcoath Mine, West Wheal Fortune in Ludgvan, and the Tamar copper mines (Fig. 7). With rumour that the issuing houses were not redeeming the value of their own coins because of claims that some were forged, all coins of this type were taken out of circulation from 1813. What financial difficulties these tokens may have caused in households dependent on their meagre value is hard to imagine. Particularly vulnerable would have been the lowest paid, i.e. the girls and boys. The 'Truck System', whereby employees were forced to purchase goods at the mine shop at inflated prices (by the use of credit notes or tokens) was outlawed by the *Truck Act of 1831*. However, it was almost impossible to police, and it seems that these abuses continued well beyond that date.

At some mines early on, workers were paid, or given 'subsist', by credit at the mine shop, which again meant they were they were having to pay over the odds for their goods. Once in debt at the mine shop, it made it increasingly difficult for them to leave the employment of the mine, and many families were never free of this debt.

Another example of sharp practice was the payment of groups of children together using a large currency note, so that they needed to go to the shop to buy something, in order to obtain change to separate out each child's wages. At Levant in 1841, groups of 5 or 6 children were paid together with a five pound note plus change, necessitating the note to be exchanged at the shop in this way. In contrast, however, at East Wheal Crofty and at Consolidated Mines it was reported that *'each child was paid the exact sum due to them'*.

In some mines, employees might be vulnerable to under-payment. For instance, in the Carn Vivian Cost Books (1860-1863), there appear to be some inconsistencies, including a few apparent underpayments to bal maidens. With little auditing of mine accounts, it was easy for genuine mistakes to be made or deliberate fraud to occur. With the majority of bal maidens having few numeracy skills it would be difficult for them to know if they had been exploited in this way.

Most mines recognised that their employees could be in strained financial circumstances, and operated the system of 'subsist' or 'sist'. This was an advance made on the wages, in cases of severe need. The women and girls were allowed to apply for subsist, and could apply for up to half their wages. This, of course, was deducted from the subsequent wages, and could be applied for from about half way through the month.

Sometimes workers were not paid at all! The earliest record of this was in 1357, when 'Abraham the Tinner' failed to pay his three hundred men, women and children working at his four enterprises at Crukbargis. Much later, when two men from Illogan took over a lease for water stamps near South Condurrow in 1878, they employed several children to help with the tin dressing. However, once the ore was dressed the men took it to be sold, and were never seen again! Needless to say the children remained unpaid. When mines were failing, it was not uncommon for the wages not to arrive from the bank. This often happened with no warning to the workers, or sometimes even the Purser. This left mine employees being owed one month's wages, or sometimes two, with no means of redress. Sometimes, the mine captains or pursers found a token amount of money from their own pockets for those most in need. When work at Boscaswell Downs suddenly stopped in 1874, three hundred employees including *'men and women, girls and boys drawn from every strata of the hierarchy from the chief ore dresser...to the count house cleaners were left with two months wages due.'* As the mine was probably already mortgaged, little hope was held out that any of the workers would gain any compensation. Although under Stannary Law, the mine employees had first priority for payment, in practice mortgages and loans were usually honoured first. These employees were all severely affected by the loss of two months' wages.

'From what has now transpired it would seem that the mine must have been for some time getting into difficulties and it is stated that the plant has been heavily mortgaged...when Saturday week came, which was pay day, the unfortunate employees found there was no money forthcoming to pay them. According to the usual system of paying monthly and holding a month's wages in hand, they were minus each two months pay.' (WMN 21st Sept. 1879)

A similar situation arose with the closure of Pednandrea and Wheal Prussia a few months later:

'Distress in the Redruth Area: The fact that the men and girls not having been paid on the regular pay day, has also added to the evil, there being two months kept in hand at the mines.'

In desperation, when it became obvious that a mine was in difficulties, some mine employees filed petitions to the Vice-Warden of the Stannaries for the winding up of the mines for which they worked, in the hope, presumably of gaining some recompense. This was the course of action taken by the men and women of Boscaswell Downs:

'And so on Monday, the resumption of work under such circumstances being out of the question, something like 200 of them - men and women, girls and boys - came into Penzance, a distance of six miles, in a body, and applied for summonses. Meantime the case is one of extreme hardship. The loss of two months wages will leave nearly the whole of those who sought aid of the law on Thursday practically penniless.' (RCG 11th April 1874)

In a similar case in April 1874, involving Budnick Mining Consols, of the fifteen petitioners to the Stannary Court, four were women employed at the mine: Catherine Warne, Grace

Penna, Ellen Higgins and Frances Trebilicock. The first three were owed between £1 3s and £4 respectively, for non-payment of wages between June and August 1873. It is unlikely that any of these ever received any compensation.[37]

INDUSTRIAL RELATIONS

With the advent of mining unions elsewhere in the UK during the mid and late 1860s, Cornwall was to remain steadfastly 'un-unionised' until the mid-1870s. The tribute system, which was competitive, between groups of miners, as to who would take work for the lowest price, tended to mitigate against corporate action. This meant that the Cornish workforce were entirely dependent on the goodwill of the managers and adventurers in terms of working conditions and pay. They rarely had any realistic power to influence decisions, with others always being ready to take their places should they be dismissed.

On several occasions in the late 1840s, disputes had arisen between the management and the women and children working on the dressing floors of Devon Great Consols, Devon's largest copper mine, with regards to wage levels. Wages paid to the pickers had remained at 10d per day during 1847, despite desperate food shortages, due to failure of the potato and turnip crop, and massive increases in the price of wheat, from 10s to 30s per cwt. Eventually, the mine owners agreed to increase the pay by 2d, to 1s per day. However, as wheat prices dropped in 1849, they reduced the pay to the original 10d, and then, in January 1850, threatened to reduce the wages again to 9d. John Henry Murchison described the response of the surface workers:

'I had scarcely arrived at my first visit (January 1850) than 200 of these youngsters of both sexes came clamouring to the counting house complaining that their wages had been 'cut' and that they could not live on 10s 6d a week.'

The 200 pickers working on the dressing floor walked out and went home in protest. When they arrived at the mine the following morning, the gates were locked and they were told they were no longer needed. Murchison describes the scene the following morning:

'On the second day they presented themselves and offered to resume work on any terms. They were, in fact, engaged at 1d/day less than was given to the strangers and those who had not mis-conducted [sic] themselves.' (MJ 26th Oct 1850 p. 586)

So despite their efforts, the women and children ended up worse off, rather than better, as a result of their actions. In December 1857, the surface workers at Balleswidden went out on strike when the adventurers tried to cut all wages by one fifth, owing to the mine working at a loss. The outcome of this action is unknown. As the Cornish miners became more politicised, there were increasing number of strikes recorded from the 1870s. Even after the establishment of unions in the county in the mid 1870s, it seems that the membership lay with the men, and little was done by way of protecting the employment rights of the women workers. Particular causes of dissatisfaction among the female workers were the ore prices rising without subsequent increase in wages, or male surface workers being paid significantly more for similar work. The women and girls working at Dolcoath went on strike for higher wages in September 1871. The girls at surface at Wheal Basset Mines also went on strike in January 1872 for an increase in pay from 9d to

11d per day, as tin prices rose to unprecedented heights. In the same year, girls at Pendeen struck for more wages, but soon resumed work. In the following June, surface workers at Ding Dong Mine went out on strike over working hours. In 1877, there was also trouble at West Seton when management wanted to increase working hours for the same pay:

'The executive at West Seton resolved that the girls employed in dressing copper should work half an hour longer per day, and not leave off until half-past five, instead of five o'clock as before. The management say that the girls cannot work a full day in winter and therefore, they should be willing to work a little longer in summer. The new rule was to begin on Monday last, but the girls left precisely at five o'clock as before. On Friday morning two or three were turned off for leaving before time on Thursday, and because of this all the rest, numbering nearly a hundred, struck and walked to Camborne, singing Sankey's hymns, and otherwise amusing themselves. On Saturday most of the pickers (the younger girls) went to work again, but the older ones, numbering about fifty, remain out on strike. The girls employed in the tin-yard have always worked until half-past five.' (WB 9th Apr 1877)

The situation was not resolved in the bal maidens favour in this case either. Married women returned to their original hours, but for reduced pay. The single women had to work the extra half-hour for the same pay. In 1878, there was trouble again at Devon Great Consols, when all employees went out on strike for two months after a reduction in wages on re-introducing the five-week month.

When tin ore prices were again improved in 1880, there was a series of strikes at the Camborne mines by the surface workers, asking for their share in the increased profit. Mr. M. G. Penrose, one of the adventurers at Dolcoath, tried to persuade the management to increase the wages of the women and girls. As an act of goodwill, he actually gave the bal maidens, over one hundred of them, an extra 1s out of his private purse. The strike had started at Dolcoath, and spread to Cook's Kitchen, Tincroft, and some of the other mines, resulting in a march through Camborne. A subsequent increase in pay was granted by the adventurers, and this was one of the few occasions when striking workers were able to negotiate better working conditions.

In August 1882, there was another rare success for striking workers. At Phoenix United, a mine inspector had discovered that the young people were working too many hours on Saturday afternoons, thereby contravening the *Employment Acts*. The management subsequently reduced the Saturday working hours, expecting them to work the extra hours during the week for the same pay. As the mine had always closed early on pay day, every four weeks, the young people were effectively being asked to work two and a half hours more in the pay day week than previously, for the same money. It was at this point that 170 boys and girls (all under the age of 18) walked out. The young people lost two days pay while out on strike, but, before they returned to work, the management offered payment for the extra hours.

While lack of unionisation had always left the bal maidens vulnerable in any dispute with the managers, increased unionisation did not always work in the bal maidens favour either. By 1919, miners (via the Worker's Union) were asking for pay rises across the board in Cornwall, including a minimum of 30s per week for women. At Dolcoath, the women only benefitted from the resulting pay increases for a few weeks before they lost their jobs entirely, as Mrs. Simms of Troon remembered:

'I went to work at Dolcoath in 1899. Women only got £2 per month. In 1920 when the Workers Union was formed they put up the wages. In 1921 I got £4 a week for two or three weeks. Then the mine closed down, and we were out of work.'

THE WORKING ENVIRONMENT

Both from the descriptions of earlier years, and the photos of later years, it is clear that the working environment on the mine dressing floors was noisy, dirty, dangerous and chaotic. A visit to a present day quarry or workings gives us some idea of what it may have been like, only on a lesser scale. Dressing floors were never tidy or clean places, and, in the days of the bal maiden, rarely purpose-built. They would have developed in a haphazard fashion, according to requirements, water supply and general topography in a very 'Heath Robinson' sort of way, but with some degree of logic and intuitive ergonomics.

Fig. 8 St Ives Consols, 1863
Courtesy of Paddy Bradley

All of the surviving photographs of bal maidens at work show the very crude working environment, but none more so than the one of the dressing floor of St Ives Consols taken in the mid 1860s. From the picture, (Fig. 8) it can be seen that the surface workers have to pick their way through mud and slippery surfaces, with only narrow walkways, between hazardous pools, tanks and piles of ore and waste. The bal maidens themselves seem to perch precariously on the narrow planks between their racking frames, some three to six feet above the ground.

This following 'word' picture, penned circa 1853, gives us a flavour of the environment:

'Looking around we…see vast heaps of rubbish, interspersed with clusters of wooden sheds, among which streams of water are flowing in nearly all directions. Men and boys may also be dressing ores; but the most conspicuous of the persons there engaged are young women and girls'. [38]

Nothing much had changed when Elihu Burritt walked from London to Land's End via Carn Brea in 1865:

'The whole region is disembowelled, and the surface is piled thick and high with mounds of the earth's vitals, still red and reeking. The entire district is studded with shafts, looking like the grain elevators at Chicago or Buffalo. The clatter and chatter and hammering of machines, pumping water, drawing up ore, pounding it to dust, and the squashy, splashy sound of the washing, all unite to make it an area of the roughest and noisiest industry.' (Burritt 1865 p. 325)

John Gurney captures something of the combination of the red-stained environment of the tin mine, and the bal maidens place in it, in his poem *'Bal-Maidens'*:

> *'spalling at the dull blood-coloured ore*
> *with hessian hands, and*
> *fragments of a song.'* [39]

Provision of shelter for the surface workers was rarely adequate. Some mines provided nothing at all, while expecting men, women and children to continue to work in all but the very worst of weather. The best they might hope for would be hessian sacks for putting over their heads and shoulders. In other cases, very primitive 'sheds' just consisting of piece of roofing was provided, and sometimes proper sheds were built. When the Rev. John Swete visited a copper mine in the Callington area, in 1792, the cobbing and bucking 'girls' were working under cover.[40] In contrast, the engraving of Dolcoath Mine by Allom, dated about 1831, shows picking, spalling, cobbing and bucking all being carried out in the open air (Fig. 2).

Practice also changed, depending on the equipment used. For instance, in the 1850s and 1860s, framing seems to have been carried out under open-fronted sheds. From the 1870s onwards, when racking frames were built in much larger blocks, the women often worked in the open air. Conditions did not necessarily improve with time, nor with the size or profitability of the mine. *The Kinnaird Report* of 1864 still commented on many large mines not providing even the basic necessities in terms of shelter for work:

'Where the comforts of those employed are attended to, the women and children work under cover of wooden sheds with glass let into the roof, but with many, even in the large mines, they are needlessly exposed to the inclemency of the weather'. (Kinnaird 1864 p. 122)

Spalling women almost always worked outside, with some mines providing crude shelters over the spalling floors later in the 19th century. A photo of Mitchell's shaft, taken about this time, shows a real apology for a shelter, with timber hanging off at precarious angles, threatening to fall at any time (Fig. 9). However, a visitor to Dolcoath's tin streams in 1877 described good shelter for the framers:

'This place in beautifully provided with wood sheds over all the frames, so that the employees can work irrespective of weather.' (RCG 12th Oct 1877 p. 7)

Fig. 9 Spalling Women at Mitchell's Shaft, East Pool c. 1890
Courtesy of Paddy Bradley

Muriel Sara remembered how bal maidens working at the tin streams in the late 1890s would only be allowed to take shelter in the dinner shed if it rained heavily:

'*If there was an extremely heavy shower or it was croust time, then the maidens gathered in a big long shed to sit around the fire in a corner, drinking strong tea out of terrible old cracked mugs, almost as brown as their tea.*' (p. 43)

Certainly the picture of the Dolcoath frames (probably taken in the 1890s) shows no shelter anywhere near (Fig. 10). At least one 20th century writer noticed that the machinery and engines were afforded more shelter and protection than the workers:

'*There may have been something picturesque and romantic about quaintly dressed bal maidens, accompanied by the lusty youths who did the more laborious part of the work in the dressing floors, scattered about the moors and valleys of Cornwall, but the life was hard, the pay small, and in winter exposure to the storms in the open air meant, all too often, suffering and hardship. The engines and boilers were housed, the stamps and buddles were in the open; the burning house and tin house were the only other parts covered in. What would be expected in the way of efficiency when working under conditions of such exposure?*' [41]

Bal maidens were usually expected to keep working even under extreme conditions. On both the occasions when bal maidens were killed in boiler explosions (see Chapter 9), they were sheltering from extremely cold weather in the engine house. Minnie Andrews '*the last bal maiden*' remembered '*I been dying with the cold, my hands.*' when she cleared the channels to the frames. Similarly, Mrs. Dalley of Troon remembered her time at Dolcoath:

'Sometimes when we got to the bal the water was frozen over. I have cried scores of times with wonders in my fingers and toes'. Up on Dartmoor, it was an even worse place to be in winter: *'The women are wrapped against the wind and rain and the children do cry of the cold. They spend most of their time at turf fires and in erecting windbreaks of timbers and cloth'.* [42]

Working conditions were slightly different at the tin streams. Nestled in valleys, they were not usually as subject to the extremes of weather as those mines out on the moors or cliff sides. Nevertheless, they could still be cold, damp places in winter and indescribably hot in summer. With most of the machinery water powered, they must have been a much quieter working environment, but without the comfort of a warm engine house on a cold day. George Henwood describes the Carnon Tin Streams, in about 1816. Although he does not mention the work of the women and girls, he gives a graphic account of the working environment:

'A Machine in a desert of red sand, heaped into vast piles and hollows, the only herbage visible being a few tufts of the sea daisy, while here and there in the trenches might be seen the tinners working knee deep in water, and a few squalid half-clad boys wheeling the tin ore to the stream head in barrows.' (Henwood, W. J. 1826 p.5)

Bal maidens were not issued with any uniform or clothes for work and would be expected to provide their own. However, they were provided with tools and equipment. The initial cost of these would be charged to the tributers, including any repairs or sharpening. The girls would be expected to report to the tool house on arrival at the mine, to be issued with the tools they might need - bucking or cobbing hammer, barrow, rake, fork, shovel or sieve. They would then have to return them at the end of the working day.

Noon was the traditional time for dinner at the mines. It was usually half an hour, and at some mines this was extended to one hour in the summer. Most surface workers ate their mid-day meal (crib) at the mine; it was not usual for employees to go home, even if they lived close by. An exception to this was Wheal Friendship, Devon in 1864 where the mine agent reported *'the principal part of the girls reside very near the mine, and generally go home for their meals'*. Food was not provided at the mines for the many who stayed; the workers would bring their own. In the early days, the mines did not even provide a place of shelter (crib or dinner house) for the surface workers to eat, or provide any drinking water. In cold or wet weather, they would find what warmth and shelter they could around the dressing floors, in the engine house, the dry (where underground workers' clothes were dried) or the smithy.

By 1841, some mines were allowing the women and children to warm their food in the dry, and providing a small barrel of water, as at Consolidated Mines. At Carnon Mines, there were two small sheds where the workers could eat. Pasties could be warmed in an oven attached to the furnace, and they could also heat water to make tea. At Dolcoath, dinner sheds had been provided for all the surface workers by 1864:

'We have four establishments with a large enough oven in each of them to contain 200 pasties or hoggins. Then we have benches around a long room where they can sit down, and hot water is always prepared by dinner time'.

It was reported that some mines made a charge for the use of these ovens, as at Fowey Consols, where 1d per week was deducted from the surface workers' pay! Later in 1864, the Kinnaird Commission was particularly impressed with arrangements for eating at North Roskear Mine:

'There are six dining houses on the floors. This prevents a large number congregating together. These houses have in them an open fire, and also an oven with shelves in it for warming the dinners. Half an hour before the bell rings for the hands to leave work, one of the girls for each house goes in, prepares the fire, boils the kettle, makes the tea, puts the pasties in the oven etc, so that when the bell rings and the dressers go in, they can sit down to a warm meal at once.'

Interestingly, at East Caradon, no provision for dinner sheds was made 'on purpose' - implying that this would encourage time-wasting. It was also reported that there was no special provision for warming dinners at the lead mines in Menheniot where the surface workers used the engine house. The discomfort of eating cold food in the open air on a cold or wet day was noted:

'At some of the larger mines sheds are provided for young people to dine in, also small ovens in which to warm the pasties. Otherwise they dine in the open air, and when the weather is chilly and their dinners consist of cold fish or vegetable pasties, their lot is anything but enviable.'

In 1877, one of the tin streams was highly praised for its dinner sheds:

'We see here the best kept dinner houses we have ever seen in our rambles through Cornwall and Devon, exceeding as much as possible the dinner house at Balleswidden when in her splendour.' (RCG 12th Oct 1877 p. 7)

Although the Commissioners of 1864 strongly recommended the provision of dinner sheds, concern for the conditions under which the mine workers laboured was still being expressed two decades later. This letter appeared in the West Briton in 1887:

'Sir, It has occurred to me that if some hot refreshment were served out on the mines at suitable times to the miners and also to the women and girls, who now work so cheerfully and uncomplainingly at the drudgery (and in all kinds of weather), that it will do more good to them than one can first imagine, and no doubt prolong their lives very considerably indeed. The miners, who have to leave their homes in the early hours of the morning, and then walk some of them four or five miles to work, should be able to obtain their cups of coffee, cocoa, milk or soup on the mine, at a very small charge when they desire it, before they go to or return from their work.' (WB 29th Sept 1887)

It is not known that any mine made this provision, other than between 1836 and 1841 at Dolcoath, when soup was provided for the underground workers only.

A senior girl or woman was responsible for going to the sheds to prepare the tea and warm food which the others had brought. Mixing of the women and girls with the boys and men at crowst or lunch time was not encouraged, so different dinner sheds were built for the different groups. Minnie Andrews was one of the women who was given the task of making preparations for the dinner. Similarly, when the women were brought in to work on the picking belt at Geevor during the Second World War, they could make their own tea in the tea shed, but had to make their own arrangements for a mid-day meal.

Fig. 10 Tin Framing at Dolcoath, c. 1890
Courtesy of Paddy Bradley

No reference has yet been found to the provision of appropriate private toilet facilities for the women and girls. It was accepted that the men and boys below ground just used any abandoned corner. In later days, a latrine, colloquially referred to as 'the parson's house', was erected for the male surface workers. For the most part, presumably, the women and girls had to 'make do' as best they could.

In general, although self-interest was a major motivation for the mine adventurers, there were also occasions where philanthropic concerns surfaced. For example, the mine managers sometimes provided emergency supplies in times of desperate need, and widowed women and their children often seem to have been a priority for employment. During the food shortages of the 'hungry' 1840s, and later in 1867, some mine captains obtained wheat flour or bread in bulk, which they sold on to their employees at reduced prices. Some required repayment by the miners when times improved, others absorbed the shortfall in cost themselves.[43] However, despite some charitable actions on behalf of the mine owners and managers, the provision for the comfort, safety and well-being of the mine employees tended to be minimal.

FOOTNOTES

1. Information throughout this chapter is drawn from material gathered in 1841 for the *1842 Royal Commission on the Employment of Women and Young People* [CEC] especially pp. 27, 43,102, 109, 119,132, Evidence Nos. 18, 21, 50, 56, 75, 85, 86, 93, 98, and Tables 11-16, 20.
2. Taylor (1814).
3. Bartlett (1994) p. 77.
4. Personal correspondence (SS/LM 2008).
5. Personal correspondence (I J/LM 2002).
6. Lewis (1997) p. 56.
7. WB 31st Oct 1935 p. 6 + 29th Oct 1936
8. Le Neve, Dr. C. Report Part 2...Mines Classed Under Metalliferous Mines Reg. Act (CRO: CA/B43/26)
9. Bartlett (1994) p. 85.
10. Payton (1984) p. 200.
11. Baring Gould, Sabine (1900) *A Book of Dartmoor* (Methuen).
12. Cornishman 6th Apr 1967.
13. CMHRC: Women's Mining Accidents.
14. Brooke (1967).
15. Rowe (1993) p. 8.
16. Noall (1973) p. 74.
17. Buckley (2007) p. 56.
18. Booker (1971) p. 24.
19. Barton. R. (1966) p. 94.
20. Buckley (2007) p. 56, Lowenac MS F.146 (A. L. Thomas Collection, Camborne School of Mines).
21. Barton (1971) p. 71; Nash (1933) p. 58; Toll (1958) pp. 17-19.
22. Razzelle (1973) p. 29.
23. Hamilton Jenkin (1951) p. 5824.
24. Lemon (1838) p. 64; Lewis (1997) p. 70, 83.
25. WB 29th Oct 1936.
26. Moissenet, M. L. *Préparation Mécanique du Minerai d'Etain dans le Cornwall* (Dalmont & Dunod 1858) p. 15.
27. Shaw, Rev. Stebbing *A Tour to the West of England in 1788* (Robson & Clarke 1789) p. 403.
28. Stockdale, F. W. L. *Excursions Through Cornwall 1824* (facs. Bradford Barton 1972) p. 23.
29. Leifchild (1855) pp. 227, 282.
30. Newman (1940) p. 111.
31. Kinnaird (1864) p. xxv.
32. Buckley (2007) p. 32, Lowenac MS F.146 (A. L. Thomas Collection, Camborne School of Mines).
33. Noall (1982) p. 6.
34. Troon WI, (1952) p. 33.
35. Waller (1698) p. 52-3.
36. Moissenet, op. cit. p. 43.
37. Budnick Consols Tin Mining Co. Ltd (CRO: STA/26 Part 2).
38. Honor (1869) pp. 37, 55.
39. Gurney, John *Bal-Maidens Cornish Review* (Summer 1972) no. 21 p. 8.
40. Swete Rev. John *Travels in Georgian Devon* Vol. 1 (Devon Books 1997) p. 133.
41. Furze (1936) p. 22.
42. Greeves (2006) p 8.
43. Rowe (1993) p. 160.

Chapter 3

BAL MAIDENS AT HOME

Bal maidens' lives were set within the context of the mining communities, where the daily routine, outlook and attitudes revolved almost entirely around the mine. This description from the early 19th century gives the feel of one such village:

'Early in the morning the scene becomes animated. From the scattered cottages, as far as the eye can reach, men, women and children of all ages, begin to creep out; and it is curious to observe them all converging like bees towards the small hole at which they are to enter the mine. On their arrival, the women and children, whose duty it is to dress, or clean the ore, repair to the rough sheds under which they work. (In the evening...as soon as the men come to grass they repair to the engine house to wash...and put on their clothes. By this time the maidens and little boys have also washed their faces, and the whole party migrates across the fields in groups, and in different directions to their respective homes'. [1]

The way in which the mine impinged on their daily consciousness is also captured in these words about Gunnislake, in the Tamar Valley:

'The bell from the count house on the mine opposite [the Devon bank] *provided a timepiece for the workers in the field, for those men waiting to go on core. For all of these the counthouse bell spaced out the day and the night.'* [2]

HOUSING CONDITIONS AND THE FAMILY ECONOMY

The majority of bal maidens lived at home with their families. The very youngest, of course, were still dependent on the support of their parents, and even for older girls it was not the custom to live independently before marriage. Bal maidens who did not marry, and continued to work at the mine, also usually continued to live at home. Bal maidens who were part of an 'orphaned' family also tended to remain with their siblings until marriage, sharing the financial support and care. Generally, only those who were married or widowed might be living independently in their own homes. There were also a small number, however, such as Mary Ann Roscorle [sic] at Tresavean Mine, who had no supporting family and who lived in lodgings.[3]

In Cornwall and Devon, it was not usually the practice for mining companies to provide housing or communal lodging houses for their employees, as it was in other parts of the country. This was probably due, in part, to the short term contractual nature of the tribute system, which meant that individual miners were only tied to a particular mine for two months at a time. It may also be because the miners often needed to supplement their income through other seasonal employments, which at certain times of the year took them away from mine employment. As miners' wages were so low and unpredictable, many families cultivated a smallholding, or took part in the local fishing industry. In 1841, one in ten of the miners in the St Just area, for instance, had a part-interest in a seining team. Both fishing and agriculture required seasonal input of labour, and Cornish miners were well known for arranging their mine work around their land and sea harvests. This pattern of work was not conducive to mining companies providing housing for their workforce. An exception to this was when the Duke of Bedford built 250 cottages in Tavistock, Gulworthy and Morwhellham for his workers at Devon Great Consols, between 1850 and 1860 (Fig 11). This was after public protests at the terrible overcrowding and squalor in these communities. The rent for these cottages was 1s 3d per week, plus '*1d for a stove*'.[4]

Fig.11 Mine Housing at Wheal Josiah, Tavistock

Generally, however, mining families had to build their own homes where they could. In the early days, when mining concerns were small, the head of a mining household would usually build some simple dwelling within the confines of the tin or copper bound that had been leased. As the mines grew larger and required more hands, local families came to work from their existing homes, or new workers migrated from the rural parishes. Before the *Enclosure Acts* of the end of 18th century and beginning of 19th century, new families moving into an area had the right to build a home on common land if they could build it overnight. In practice, this meant erecting a temporary shack, and having a fire burning in its chimney before dawn. The cottage could then be built properly with time. These were called 'sun-rising houses'. After the *Enclosure Acts*, families would negotiate a lease of a non-productive corner of land from a landowner, in order to build. These early cottages were usually cob built with thatched roofs, and often only had one room, with a 'talfat', a platform reached by a ladder for beds or storage.

Fig. 12 Frog Street, Bere Alston, home to many bal maidens in the 19th Century

Some of these dwellings might have rights to 'turfuel' (permission to cut peat turf or gorse); a bonus, indeed, when any source of fuel was rare. A traveller passing through the Zelah to Blackwater area in 1797 commented on the barrenness of the environment and the poverty of the fuel supply:

'From Zelah…we came into the Mining Country: All here is barrenness in the extreme. The miner's cottages are scattered up and down…The ground everywhere is covered with heath, which they cut for fuel. A sad substitute for more substantial materials.' [5]

Later, from about 1840, miners began to build more substantial and larger stone houses, some with two rooms downstairs, and two rooms upstairs. However, these often accommodated more than one family. The lease with the landowner was generally for 'three lives', sometimes with the option to buy additional 'lives' at the time of signing the agreement. Three named persons would be recorded on the lease, and it was valid for their lifetime. It was not until about the 1880s that the mining families, began to have the luxury of more than about four rooms for their accommodation.

The plots of land on which the early miners' cottages were built were usually of one acre or more, with the intention that it could be brought into cultivation. Clearing these rocky, and often steep, corners was a mammoth task in itself. The whole family would be involved in maximising the production from this smallholding, each with his or her own particular tasks. The main crops were potatoes, both for human consumption and for feeding livestock, with wheat or barley and 'neaps' (turnips). Land left uncultivated was sometimes used to keep a cow or a pony, the latter to be rented to the mine for transporting ore, and most families planted a few apple or plum trees. Normally, a family would hope to raise a pig to supply ham and bacon at Christmas time, with some salted down in a bussa (a large earthenware pot for salting fish or meat) for the rest of the year. Some of the meat would usually be sold to buy a replacement pig for the following year. It was said that the Cornish found a use for every part of the pig except its squeal! Many villages had a Pig Club so that miners could buy and sell pigs co-operatively. If a family was able to raise two pigs in a year, the extra income made a great difference to the economy of that family:

'The miner was thus always secure of a good supply of potatoes and other vegetables. The quantity of potatoes which he produced was frequently not only sufficient for the consumption of his family but also for the feeding of one or two pigs. When he killed his pig generally at Christmas, he would sell enough of it to enable him to buy another young pig or two. If he killed two pigs he would sell enough to enable him to pay the rent for his plot of ground for the year. The chief advantage was that in many cases it enabled the parents to send the children for some part of the day to school'. [6]

Where these miners' plots were situated on very poor land, cultivation would be extremely difficult. The families might resort to growing pillas, a small-grained naked oat which would grow in very poor soils, and perhaps keep goats or sheep. Throughout Cornwall, pillas was commonly grown on small patches of land that were too poor to grow wheat or barley, up until the 20th century.

Seining for pilchards, would also have a significant effect on the economy of the household. In a good year, a share in a seining team would provide a high protein winter food, cheap 'train' (pilchard) oil for rush lights, and, hopefully, extra income from the surplus.

Unlike other mining communities, where housing was offered along with work, once a Cornish miner had invested money and effort in building a home and clearing a plot for cultivation, it was unlikely that a family would want to leave. This meant that the whole family was dependent on the availability of local employment, and, if the local mines failed, mine employees would usually choose to travel considerable distances for work, rather than move. It was not uncommon for bal maidens to walk up to six miles to work and back, although most walked about three or four miles each day.

Not all mining families, however, lived in a rural situation. From the mid-18th century, mining towns began to develop around the chief mining centres, with more limited opportunities for food production, and with all the attendant health hazards of industrial areas. These are words from a traveller, in June 1795:

'Redruth is a long town, near a mile long, in a Vale in the center [sic] of the mines, so that it is in a Cloud of Smoak [sic], which is the reason we did not breakfast...Camborne to Penzance: The country is filled with smoke from the number of steam engines. The whole country in these parts consists of Tin, Lead and Copper Mines, with few trees, no fruit trees nor vines, and very little corn, but a great number of goats.' [7]

With six to twelve children per family being normal during the 19th century, mining households must have been very crowded and busy. These households often had lodgers, in-laws, or married children, living with them as well. Where possible, a 'linney' or lean-to was added to the house to give extra accommodation. Even so, how these tiny cottages and houses accommodated so many is hard to imagine. The situation would have been eased slightly where the men and underground boys were working different 'cores' (shifts), so that they would not all be home at the same time. There were three or four cores in a day, and for those working in the same tribute team, there would be family members taking over from each other at each shift. Those on early shift would be sleeping overnight, and home for the main family meal in the evening. Those on the afternoon shift would also be sleeping overnight, but those on night shift would be taking over the vacated beds of the early shift workers when they came home in the morning. So there was a saying in Cornwall that *'in mining parishes beds were never cold'*. As one group of men and boys left for work, another would be returning. Bal maidens, however, did not normally work shift patterns in this way, so all the female ore dressers in one household would almost certainly be working the same hours, 7 a.m. until 5 p.m., unless at sampling.

In these crowded and busy households, privacy for these young girls and women must have been at a premium. It would be a very exceptional home for a bal maiden to have a bed of her own, let alone a bedroom of her own. At best, most would be sharing beds with their sisters, or other female members of the household, in a room set aside for them. At worst, they may have been sharing the same sleeping space as parents or members of the opposite sex, including lodgers, as reported in the *1842 Royal Commission*:

'The houses are too small to admit proper separation of sleeping rooms and it often happens...that men come from a distance and lodge with families, in which case they frequently sleep in the same room with the females.'

Households of eight or ten were commonplace, but some exceeded that number. In 1861, teen-aged bal maidens Elizabeth and Mary Warren (of Higher Trewellard) lived in a household of thirteen, which included two other bal maidens who were boarders with the family. Even as late as 1881, there is evidence of severe overcrowding in the mining communities. For instance, in the small house where bal maidens Angelina, Mary, and Elizabeth Taylor lived in North Terrace, St Cleer there were also thirteen individuals recorded as resident (ten members of one nuclear family, plus three cousins).

There was no internal sanitation or water supply to these miners' cottages. Once the water supplies of the area were being drawn off and paid for by the mines, it seems that water supply for domestic use was often a problem. Sometimes the younger members of the household had to walk many miles to obtain water, as one of their evening tasks. The lamentable lack of water supply to each household was noted even as late as 1864:

'The absence in most instances of a good supply of water owing to its being drawn off at the low levels by the pumping engines at the mines is a drawback to sanitary improvements.'

All the members of the household would have to wash at the stone sink in the kitchen, or outside near the well or pump, if there was one. Hot water was a luxury, usually just for bath time once a week, if they were lucky. Prior to about 1780, there was probably no privy at all, with the family having to make do with a system of buckets to be emptied in a piece of the land set aside for such purposes. Subsequently, there might be a shed down the garden somewhere. Clothes were washed by hand in the linney or outside, or at the warm water outlet from the engines at the mine. They would then be laid out on the ground or on bushes to bleach and dry. A water supply to the house, and a flushing outside toilet, were probably luxuries not experienced by most bal maidens until late in the 19th century, if then.

The bal maiden, however old or young, would contribute a vital part of the household economy. Her earnings were a crucial element in the survival of the family. Her role of worker was important, and would take her away from the home from early in the morning until mid-evening, and yet she would also have domestic duties at home, as a female member of the household. In 1841, some of the bal maidens described having such duties at home as needlework, preparing food, and collecting water. Patty Tremellin told how she, as a young girl, had to prepare food and clean the house, as well as carry out nursing duties, on her return from the mine.[8] Bal maidens' tasks would also include childcare, and assisting with cultivation of crops or tending animals on the family smallholding.

Just as the boys were 'groomed' for a life at the mines from an early age, being given toy mining tools and encouraged to play mining games or solve mining puzzles with their elders, it is very likely that girls were prepared in the same way too.

THE DAILY ROUTINE

Bal maidens, regardless of age, usually started work at 7 a.m. Most would have to get up by 6 a.m., and those who lived three or four miles or more from the mine would have to get up even earlier, some as early as 4 a.m. During sampling, the women and girls started work an hour earlier still, which would require a 3 a.m. start for some. Because of the long walk and the strenuous working day ahead of them, the girls would try to have breakfast before leaving. In reality, however, it was usually a very basic affair, consisting of some barley bread or pillas with water, or, if they were lucky, some milk. Pillas would be set to sprout and was toasted and then ground to make a porridge. In times of real hardship, they would leave home without having had anything to eat at all. One widowed woman, left with small children to support, who took up work at Wheal Bassett, spoke of sometimes leaving the house and children with no food at all in the morning, only buying food after a day's work and having claimed 'subsist'.[9] Even in the 1870s, breakfast was still a very frugal affair, such as bread and treacle for 9 year-old Alice Head, before she left for work at Brook Mine in Buckfastleigh.[10] Susan Robins (née Wills) recalled her extraordinary income-earning duties at home, even before she left for the mine:

'We were not allowed to waste our time so the whole family used to sit around the kitchen table at four in the morning knitting striped stockings which nearly everyone used to wear. We worked by the light of a candle and were paid a penny for every ounce of wool we knitted.' [11]

The bal maidens would also need to prepare the food that they would take to the mine, unless they lived sufficiently nearby that food could be brought by younger brothers or sisters later in the day. If taking their own food, it would invariably be either a pasty or a hoggan. The hoggan was probably a good poverty indicator over the years, re-appearing when wheat prices were high, to be replaced by the more favoured pasty when times were not so hard. The hoggan was made of unleavened barley bread, with a little green pork or potato set in it. The sweet version of this was the fuggan, made with dried fruit (called figs). It was generally very indigestible and very poor fare. In 1841, one mine agent described hoggans as *'hard as street tiles'*! The pasty, which was much more nutritious and easier to eat, had its outer pastry made from wheat flour, would certainly contain potato and turnip, and, with luck, a little pork, ham, or even mutton. Grace Bowden and Martha Williams both took pasties with them for their dinner at Trethellan Mine. The bal maidens would pack their pasty or hoggan in a white linen 'flour bag' tied with a piece of string, known as a 'crib-bag', 'hoggan bag' or 'frail'. Inside their crib-bag, they would usually slip a smaller one containing some dried mugwort or pennyroyal for their tea; then, they would tie the bag around their waist or under their skirts. At some mines, the tea making was done communally, so that each bal maiden would need to provide her own cup, make a contribution towards the cost of a kettle, and take it in turns to provide 'tea' for the group. Those that could not afford this drank hot water.

Fig. 13 Cornish Bal Maidens
(Simonin, 1867)

Going to work in summer, the women and girls would wear a light calf-length dress, covered with their best apron, plus a gook or bonnet, and what was, usually, their only pair of shoes. In winter, they would wear a heavier, warmer dress covered with a shawl, a felt bonnet, and boots, if they had any. They would also carry with them their food for the day, their change of apron, if they had one, and protective gloves or leg bands to put on at the mine. In addition, they probably had a handkerchief and some knitting or crochet tucked into a pocket. They would have to walk up to six miles to the mine, in all weathers, normally walking in family groups, and collecting friends on the way. Even the youngest sometimes walked long distances, such as seven year-old Susan Wills of St Agnes who walked six miles a day.[12] Many of the mines in Cornwall were in wild, exposed places - either on remote moors, or out on headlands or cliffs. This made spectacular walking in good weather, and atrocious, sometimes dangerous, conditions in bad weather. These groups of bal maidens were renowned for their singing, as they made their way to and from the mine.

Once at the mine, the bal maiden's working hours were regulated by the mine bell, which marked the beginning and ends of shifts, crowst and dinner time. Some mines allowed a short break during the morning around ten o'clock, but their main dinner break was at mid-day. For those who lived close to the mine, this was the time for meeting up with the sisters or brothers who had brought their food. They may well have been brought a hot meal of fish or potato stew and were probably the envy of those who had to eat cold hoggans or pasties. Where more than one member of a family was working at a mine, it was usual for them to gather together for their meal. Otherwise, the surface workers were strictly segregated by gender at this time.

After eating, there was usually time for recreation. The youngest girls would play various games together, if they had the energy. This was the time when some of the most serious accidents occurred on the dressing floor, with young people 'off their guard' and forgetting the dangers of moving machinery. The older girls and women would bring their needlework, and chat. It was also a good opportunity to try to talk to the men and the boys, although this was generally discouraged by the management.

In a few mines, bal maidens who lived close to 'the bal' went home for dinner. This was particularly the case at Wheal Friendship, Devon, when, in the Kinnaird Report of 1864, it was reported that so many went home that no special provision was made for people to stay.

There was no afternoon break, and most of the bal maidens finished work around 5 p.m., unless it was sampling time. Working at surface was always a very dirty job, with dust in dry weather and mud in winter. The tin ore, especially, left its unique red-orange stain on clothes and skin alike. The girls and women would do their best to clean up before leaving the mine, finding some source of relatively clean water in which to wash their hands and faces. They would change from their working 'towsers' into their best aprons, before leaving, and then carry their working aprons home, over their arm.

On arrival home, usually their mother or an older sister would have prepared the main meal for the day. Seated around the family table in the evening would be the men, women, boys and girls who had just come home from the mine, plus those boys and men about to go out the night shift. The meal would be basic, based on the few home-grown vegetables and fruit, and meat or fish as available. Potatoes, boiled or roasted, were the mainstay, with parsnips or turnips, served with 'tea' made from mugwort. In season, there might be apples or plums from their own small orchard. In the coastal areas, especially if the family had an interest in a seining team, there would be salted pilchards to see them through the winter. Alternatively, dried Newfoundland cod was sometimes bought for the main meal, and served as 'niflin' or 'towrag'. In season, there might also be fresh fish; usually conger, pilchards or mackerel. Susan Robins (née Wills) of St Agnes remembered that as a child in the 1830s and 1840s bread and swedes constituted their main diet. As a treat, they sometimes had pilchards too, when they were able to pick up the fish that fell of the farmers carts as they were taking the surplus for manure.[13] After this simple communal supper, the bal maidens would then have their own domestic duties to complete before bedtime. Depending on their age, they would go to bed between 7 p.m. and 10 p.m. Working clothes were not washed during the week, as the women and girls normally only had one set. If wet, they would be hung up around the fire to dry overnight, as best they may. Often they were still damp when the girls came to wear them the following morning.

THE BAL MAIDEN AND HER EARNINGS

Some bal maidens never saw their earnings, either because they were not paid individually, their wages forming part of the total earning of the tribute team, or because their wages were collected by the adults in their family. In these cases, they may have been given pocket money to spend. Other bal maidens collected their wages for themselves, but would usually hand the total amount over to their parents or parent, out of which, again, they may have been given some money to spend. In some families, depending on their economic circumstances, girls were allowed to keep their overtime pay.

However, around the age of 18 or 19, they would usually come to an agreement with their parents over an amount to pay for board and lodging, and then be allowed to keep the rest. The average amount for board and lodging in 1841 was about 14s per month from earnings of about 18s. Some bal maidens, of course, were independent of their families. When Grace Bowden was working at Trethellan in 1841, she was paying 6d per day for her board and lodgings in Lanher from her earnings of 9d per day. These older girls and women who were able to keep more than just 'pocket money' usually started saving for their marriage.

On pay day, the girls often treated themselves to some small luxury out of their pocket money, if they had any. Sometimes the pursers at the mine did not pay the girls separately but as a group, so they had to go to the mine shop to buy something first, before they could share out their wages. If they were wise, however, they would resist buying at the mine shop as items could be up to 25% more expensive than at the market or village shop. Pay day was usually market day, and, at some mines, the market was set up in the immediate vicinity, with stalls selling food, clothes, household items and trinkets. Invariably, the packman, 'Johnny Fortnight' or 'Johnny-go-Fortnight', would also turn up on pay day, and regularly in between. This travelling salesman would not ask for cash payment for an expensive item, but entice the girls to buy, allowing them to pay by fortnightly or monthly instalments. Some bal maidens, of course, were lured into agreements that they could not fulfil, ending up in court, not having understood the nature of the debt they had taken on. This was noted in the Kinnaird Report of 1864:

'*They* [the packmen] *go around with the packs and exhibit their finery and coax women to take it, telling them they may pay 6d or 1s a month, when once the goods are received they have them entirely under their power, and summon them by a dozen at a time to the County Court.*'

However, the girls and women would mostly buy small items such as handkerchiefs, ribbons, brooches, or earrings. Bal maidens also treated themselves in other ways. Minnie Andrews described how on pay day, she and her friends would '*call at Brea Inn for a penny glass of porter*'.[14] As an alternative to getting into debt with Johnny Packman, the young girls sometimes took the initiative and formed a 'Dress Club' enabling them to buy special clothes, which they then took turns in wearing, much to the disapproval of the local clergy!

Dressed for the Occasion

It seems that bal maidens made little additions to their working clothes as a mark of their individuality, but when eventually released from their working environment at the week-end, liked to make rather bolder fashion statements. Victorian commentators certainly had much to say about the way in which bal maidens spent their earnings on clothes. Simonin, visiting from France and writing in 1867, makes the following rather strange observations and, as the text is accompanied by an illustration of Cornish ore dressers, one assumes he is referring to the bal maidens. Some of his meaning appears to have been lost in the translation:

'In England, the women and girls either do not sing, or if they do, they often sing out of tune. To make up for this however, they are dressed coquettishly like regular ladies, wearing on their hair the cornette, or the net, and elegant and well fitting boots on their feet.'[15]

Many Victorian commentators remarked on how well-dressed the miners, and especially the mining women were on Sundays or holidays, with the inevitable insinuation that they were dressed 'above their station', and beyond their means. This description comes from the pen of R.M. Ballantyne in his novel *'Deep Down'* and is more neutral in its attitude:

'No one who entered the Wesleyan Chapel of St Just that morning for the first time could have imagined that a large proportion of the well-dressed people who filled the pews were miners and bal maidens. Some of the latter were elegantly - we might say - gorgeously attired, insomuch that, but for their hands and speech, they might almost have passed for ladies of fashion. The very latest thing in bonnets, and the newest mantles, were to be seen on their pretty heads and shapely shoulders'. (Ballantyne 1897 p. 16)

One traveller, on his journey to Land's End in 1865, also noticed the fashion consciousness of the bal maidens as he travelled through:

'Many of the young women were dressed a la mode, with ringlets furled and clewed under a band, ready for being shaken out upon the breeze when their work was done.' (Burritt 1865 p. 320)

Seymour has left us with a wonderful glimpse of this transformation, from working days to weekend, in his cartoons of 1877 entitled *'Bal maiden Friday'* and *'Bal maiden Saturday'*. These should possibly read *'Bal Maiden Saturday'* and *'Bal Maiden Sunday'*, as are the L. Adams watercolours of the same drawings held by the RIC (Fig 14). Apart from possibly owning a 'best' dress for Saturdays or Sundays, and their working clothes, in the 'good times' bal maidens might also have a second best for wearing to church meetings and other activities during the week. Money was always at a premium, but the women and girls made sure that the pennies spent on jewellery, ribbons or lace were creatively invested.

Dressed for Work

Although many Victorian commentators remark on the neatness and cleanliness of the women and girls working at the mines, their tasks could not possibly have kept them clean. Working with ores, wet or dry, is a messy business. Workers with tin ore, for example, became covered with a russet dust or deposit, which stained badly. In most of the earliest photographs, the bal maidens all look very clean, but are posing in their clean 'walking out' aprons, without their protective leg, arm or hand coverings. Only in post-1890 photographs (Figs. 27 + 28) do we begin to see them as they really were at work, in their grubby hessian 'towsers' (work aprons).

We may conclude that items of clothing worn to the mine would be long past first or even second-best, and were probably hand-me-downs. It was considered lucky for boys going underground for the first time to have a new duck suit to wear, but it is unlikely that new clothes were made in the same way for the boys or girls working at surface. They would presumably wear old everyday clothes, modified for wearing at the mine. A visitor to Dolcoath mine in 1893 describes the bal maidens' clothes in this way:

'The bal maidens had not the white sunbonnets and almost spotless apron which they sometimes wear at their work; for here they work in the open and had to cope with the drenching rain. But their faded dresses, of varied hues, which at one time were smart 'Sunday best clothes' and their coarser sack aprons and padded home made cloth gloves (to prevent their hands from being galled by the hammers with which they spalled the stone) were an admirable match for our white 'cappen's [Mine Captain] *suits.'* (Cornishman 5th Jan 1893)

Fig. 14 Bal Maiden in Work Dress and Sunday Best
(Seymour, c. 1870) *Courtesy of Mining Communications Ltd*

An early Victorian traveller and writer, describing women at the Cornish mines, in the Penny Magazine of 1835, suggests that the bal maidens were not always adequately dressed for the prevailing weather conditions, and then makes a quite extraordinary observation:

'The large pieces or blocks are broken with hammers by women, called bal maidens, many of whom are very good-looking; but they seem to require warmer clothing, and must find their occupation painful and tiresome; they were all without stays.' (Penny Magazine 5th September 1835)

Unfortunately, there are no records of what the younger girls wore. The only picture is from Henderson, who drew a group of girls at the picking table. It is difficult to see exactly what they are wearing, but presumably relatively short frocks. The older girls and women all seem to have worn either mid-calf, rather than ankle-length, dresses or skirts as their one concession to the working conditions. Scandal seems to have been averted, as the potentially exposed legs and ankles were covered with protective bands or coverings. The dresses, or cotton blouses and cotton or linsey skirts, worn over numerous petticoats as was the style, served basically as an outer coat. In addition, in cold weather, a long-sleeved bodice (Garribaldi, or in dialect a 'gollibolder') or shawl was worn. By the 1880s, fashions began to change and the women wore coats instead of the Garribaldi and layers of petticoats. Muriel Sara remembers the costume of bal maidens towards the end of the 19th century:

'*In the summer they wore cotton or print dresses and big coloured print bonnets. In the winter they needed old coats and shawls, with perhaps their heads wrapped in flannel beneath their bonnets, as it was very cold work.*' (Sara 1970 p. 43)

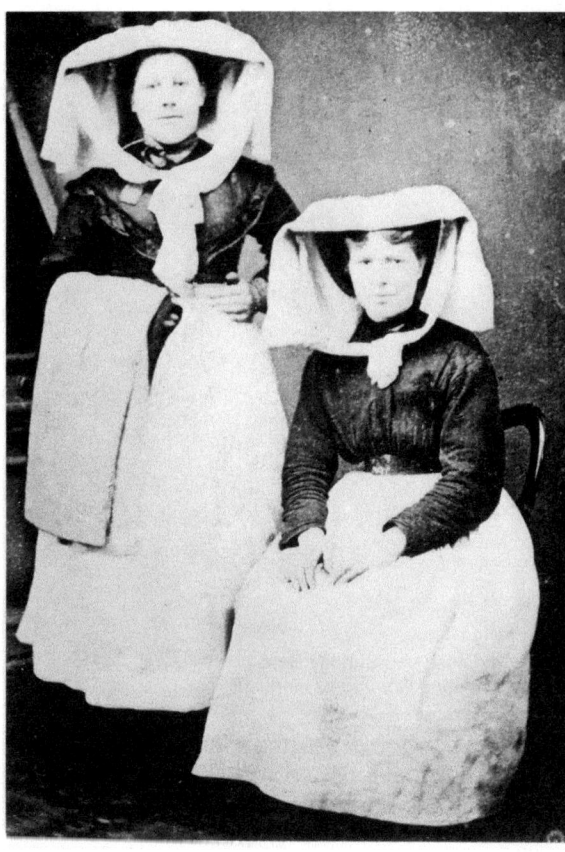

Fig.15 Dolcoath Bal Maidens
Courtesy of the Cornwall Centre Collection

Protection of the arms and legs from the weather, and from cuts and bruises, was very important. Some women or girls wore removable over-sleeves, usually of hessian, to protect the dress or blouse. The legs were wrapped in cotton bands, in summer, and wool or flannel bands in winter. These were a vital protection from flying shards, and from the cold and damp wet ore and waste that often accumulated around the feet and lower legs, and this was especially important for those women and girls who were cobbing or bucking. In 1858, Henderson describes bucking girls as putting on *'kitty bags'* when they reached the mine. These were waterproofed leg protectors probably made from canvas, proofed with a mixture of resin, tallow and pitch (kit). Similar protectors may also have been made from hand-made ropes of straw, which were worn more generally and were called 'thumblebinds' or 'thumblebeans'.[16] By the turn of the 19th century, when cobbing and bucking was rarely done by hand, it seems that bands and kitty bags had been replaced by thick woollen stockings.

The bal maiden's apron appears to be almost a badge of office. For those who could afford it, ideally two aprons were required: a best white apron, and a coarser hessian one for work (Fig. 15). The best one was probably made from herden, flour bag material of coarse hemp and flax, which could wash very white, and was to wear to and from the mine as well as for photographs or special occasions at the mine itself. Once at the mine, the girls would change into the hessian one, called a towser, for work. These were usually waist length, and occasionally had a bib. As well as ties at the waistband, they might also have ties around the hips in order to give better protection. There is no evidence of this custom in Cornwall, but in some European countries an apron tied at the hip indicated a married woman, loose hip ties indicated a single woman.[17] Minnie Andrews described how it was a great matter of honour to have a clean apron, at least at the beginning of the week, and described how much time and effort she put into washing hers white again.[18]

Suitable shoes were a problem for the bal maidens, as so many families could not afford more than one pair per person, and sometimes not even that. In the *1842 Royal Commission Report*, it seems that some wore ankle-high boots or stout shoes giving good protection, but others had flimsy or unsuitable shoes for the work. A pair of undated bal maiden's shoes may be seen in Bodmin Museum (Fig 16). They have wooden soles and irons, leather uppers and ankle straps, and iron toecaps. Also in Fig. 16, a much more modest pair of shoes can be seen, which, although less strongly built, have been iron shod. These, no doubt, were more likely to double as everyday shoes as well as work shoes. Towards the end of the 19th century, it seems some women and girls wore clogs. Others wore hobnailed boots. Phyllis Lockett, who worked at Geevor in the Second World War, described how the women working there often preferred to wear clogs, as they lasted longer.

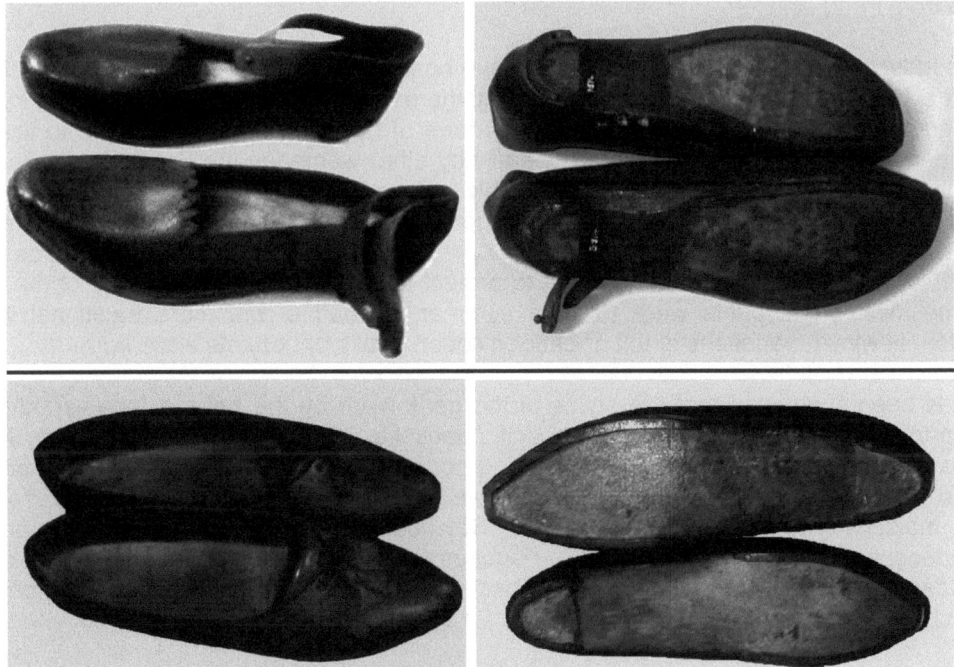

Fig. 16 Iron-Shod Shoes
Courtesy of (above) Bodmin Museum, (below) Jan Gendall

By the very nature of their work, bal maidens' hands were particularly vulnerable to damp and cold, as well as to bruises and cuts. Sharon Schwartz describes the cobbing and bucking girls as wearing short pieces of India rubber piping on the fingers of their left hand to protect themselves from the blows of the hammer. (Women working on the dressing floors in Anglesey protected their fingers by binding on iron rings, but it is not known whether Cornish women did the same).[19] As the girls and women were continually handling wet or dirty ore stuff, in winter they protected their hands with old warm stockings made into a sort of padded mitten or cloth bands. Francis Richards, a bal maiden at Devon Consuls in the 1860s, described to her daughter how they used to bind the palms of their hands with these dry rags. When they became wet they hung them up to dry on the hot water pipe in the miners' dry.[20] Similarly, a sister of a Troon bal maiden recalled how they used to make mittens out of old stockings:

'She also wore hand-cloths which were made out of white stockings, wrapped round and round the hand and stitched together. The stockings were not worn as long as they are today, so they made a thumb-piece out of a piece of calico'. [21]

By about 1880, these cut-up stockings or bandages appear to have been replaced with proper gloves.

The head-covering was a crucial part of the protective clothing, for those working outside in particular. Their heads and necks needed protection from cold, wind and wet in winter, and sunburn in summer. In addition, they needed protection from excessive noise levels, and from flying splinters.

The most common headgear appears to have been the gook, the traditional loose bonnet with a wide brim over the eyes and ears, gathered at the neck and under the chin, but falling loose again over the shoulders. This form of headwear was not unique to the bal maidens in Cornwall, but was worn generally by other women in the South West, as well. Simple white cotton versions were commonly worn in the summer, and some had a loop under the chin so that the ends of the gook could be drawn through to give extra protection to the face and throat (Fig. 13). Some women pinned the gook right across the face, leaving only the eyes uncovered, to protect themselves from the effects of the sun. Sometimes, bright prints were used in summer, instead of the more traditional white cotton. In winter, variations of felt or padded cotton gooks or bonnets were worn.

It has been suggested that the styles of the gook worn by the bal maidens varied from area to area, some being unique to specific parishes. Although sketches drawn by Mary Mills indicate variation, there is no surviving corroborative evidence.[22] A rather elaborate style was the 'yard of cardboard'. A diminutive form of this seems to be worn by the two bal maidens photographed at Dolcoath. Seymour, in his charming sketches of bal maidens, caricatures the style (Fig. 68). Esquiros described the headwear worn by the bal maidens at Botallack, and Paynter described the tin streamers at St Ives Consols, both of which seem to describe this type:

'A pasteboard foundation covered with a piece of gaudy calico fastened on the head by means of ribbons, while large wings fall and float around the face. Such an apparatus serves at once as bonnet, cap and veil - it admirably protects the face from the sun; and the mining girls are very anxious to retain their ruddy complexion.' (Esquiros 1865 p 65)

'They [bal maidens] used to wear a picturesque headdress, something like a sun bonnet. The top part was flat, stiffened with cardboard and covered with print, and from this a frill hung over the ears and back of the head. It was tied firmly under the chin, and effectively protected the wearer from the sun.' [23]

The alternative summer headwear was the straw bonnet, again making its appearance in a variety of colours and styles. These bonnets were made from bent grass (bents) or sea grass (finny grass).[24] By the turn of the 20th century, it seems that they had largely replaced the gook. A Miss Carvolth, working at Tobias Uren's Tin Streams in Gilbert's Coombe, Redruth, was probably one of the last bal maidens to wear the traditional gook in about 1920, and still changed from her work towser to her white apron to go home.[25] A description of women working at tin streams in Redruth after 1900 describes the gook going out of fashion: *'They wore a towser in work and a white apron going to and fro. They didn't wear the gooks then, just a bonnet with a hat pin stuck in it.'*

It seems that the work dress of the bal maiden remained very similar for over a century. However, by the start of the 20th century, there were significant changes in clothing in general, and also a comparative improvement in the financial condition of most mining families. Eventually, some bal maidens began wearing long white jackets (presumably similar to the male surface workers) during the 1890s.[26]

By the time women were being employed at the mines and clay works during the First World War, the typical full skirts with layers of petticoats, and gook or straw bonnet had been replaced by more practical shorter and slimmer-fitting dresses and skirts. These were worn with knee boots, belted coats, and fur or woollen hats in winter, and cotton pinafores in summer. Those women who were called into work at the mines during the Second World War, were often dressed in dungarees and boots, like their male counterparts. The bal maiden's image had been given a make over!

SOCIAL ACTIVITIES

The main social life in these mining communities, of course, happened informally amongst neighbours; chatting together on doorsteps in fine weather, popping into each others houses for a chat in cold weather, and by 'walking out' with friends to the market or fair. The more organised activities revolved around the chapels and pubs. As it was not acceptable for women or children to go to the taverns, their formal socialising took place at the church or chapel. Although the women and girls would be precluded from the business meetings there, and neither could they usually hold any significant office, there were plenty of activities in which they were involved. Apart from Sunday worship, in the morning and evening, they were encouraged to attend class meetings, Bible studies, or belong to the choir. They were also encouraged to teach in the Sunday School if they could read and write, or attend, if they could not, as well as to visit the sick and needy. There were also social groups, such as the sewing circles. Most nights of the week, there would be some chapel-related activities, if the bal maidens had the time or energy, after their long working day. Most of Sunday would be taken up with attending various services, Bible Studies and Sunday Schools. For instance, 17 year-old Fanny Francis, working at United Consols in 1841, was helping as a Sunday School teacher at the local Bryanite Chapel.

However, it was more usual that bal maidens were the pupils, rather than the teachers, at Sunday School, often attending until they were 17 or 18 years old. Unfortunately, bal maidens from the poorest families often felt excluded from these activities, as they only had their working clothes to wear. In most mining communities, from about 1840, there were evening classes, set up for young people from the mines, in reading and writing, and in some cases to teach basic mining skills, but girls seem to have been largely excluded from these as well.

Most bal maidens were working at the mine on a Saturday morning, and sometimes into the afternoon, but it was common practice, when they had finished, to go to the local market, sometimes known as *'Giglet* [young girl] *Fairs'*. Most major towns had a Saturday market, and the one at Redruth was among the largest. Even in 1778, four or five thousand people would attend each week, and apparently the most available commodities for sale were shoes and boots. These Saturday markets were, apparently, the time for *'miners to treat their bal maiden sweethearts to a bowl of soup'*.[27] For those without a 'sweetheart', this was a time to band together with their friends from the mine, to have a good time. Contemporary writers describe how these groups of mine girls were readily identifiable on market day. A change in style of dress worn by the bal maidens, between the earlier years and the middle years of the 19th century is rather patronisingly described in this newspaper account of a Whitsuntide Fair, in 1844:

'Formerly it was a rich sight of itself to see the mine girls in their ill-assorted dresses, in which every variety of gaudy colour - the stronger the contrast the better - was called into active service. If the day was wet, the treat was much the greater, for then the white muslin frocks, the green boots, the yellow bonnets and the red and glowing cheeks of the distressed maidens, were seen to greater advantage. But the times are changed, and those who come to a Cornish fair must expect to see the country girls clad in the same attire as their sex of the towns - the only difference being perhaps the want of a nice discrimination in the choice of colours that harmonise and blend, and in the love, if that be possible, of greater finery.' (WB 31st May 1844)

It seems that there were other social opportunities for bal maidens that were not so openly accepted. Patty Tremellin describes attending 'dance floors' or 'rooms' in Truro, in the late 1820s or early 1830s, with other girls from the mines.[28] These 'floors' were, apparently, sometimes built in or over the trunks of oak trees, such as the Meavy Oak (between Plymouth and Tavistock), and the Trebursey Oak at Launceston.[29] Such dance floors were associated with 'loose morals' and were definitely frowned upon by the chapel communities.

Cornwall has been well known for its choirs, especially those based in the mining communities, and bal maidens grew up in this tradition of music. The men and boys sang as they made their way down into the mine at the beginning of the day, and also at the end if they had breath. It was a way of 'not being alone' in the dark, and a way to keep up the rhythm of climbing, while making the long journey up the ladders to the surface. Commentators described the wonderful harmonies resounding around the caverns of the mine, when the men sang. The bal maidens seem to have formed spontaneous singing groups too, either travelling to and from the mine, or at work. The impression is certainly given that they were told to sing hymns when visitors were around on the dressing floor in order to create a good impression. One visitor, in 1855, wrote *'How well the girls take their parts.'* [30] This comment appeared in the Cornubian in 1887:

'It is the custom for the female employees at the various mines in Cornwall to sing on returning from their daily labours. Some of these 'lasses' have wondrous voices.' (Cornubian 7th Jan 1887)

The same admirer then went on to publish a long poem entitled 'The Cornish Mine Girls' Song' which begins:

Eve minstrels! Oft I've heard ye sing,
Have marvelled much how ye could fling
Such liquid notes that richly ring,
And thrill us ere they die:

Across the Tamar, at Devon Great Consols, music seemed just as much part of life on the dressing floor, as in Cornwall:

'*The girls at the dressing floors are very fond of singing psalms and hymns whilst at work, and their vocal efforts really have a very pleasing effect.*' (Tavistock Gazette 23rd Dec. 1864)

Apart from singing at work, bal maidens would be part of the 'family' chorus and probably also the chapel choir. In the novel '*Norah Lang, Mine Girl*', the heroine is described as going twice a week to choir practice at the chapel, and being selected as one of their soloists for church services and concerts.

There is no clear evidence as to whether the bal maidens used music in order to create a working beat, on the dressing floors. In 1878, Darlington, when describing the work of the bucking girls, remarked that '*in Cornwall it is customary to keep time with the blows*'. Visitors often remarked that the women and girls sang spontaneously while they worked:

'*The females select the best portions of ore and occasionally relieve their labours with low, soft, and melodious choruses which surprise the stranger.*' [31]

Fig.17 Bal Maiden Meeting her Sweetheart After Work
(Seymour 1880)
Courtesy of Mining Communications Ltd

On the dressing floors of the mines, such singing must have happened in the quieter corners or the quieter moments; certainly not adjacent to any stamps or crushers. However, tin streams presented a quieter environment. The sound of the massed choirs of the Red River tin stream works, in the 1880s, must have been truly memorable:

'*The women and children were happy enough. They would start at seven in the mornings and before half past seven somebody would begin to sing a hymn or song. The singing would be taken up all the ten miles of the valley and it was grand.*' [32]

It would appear then, that the bal maidens may have worked in unison and used music to provide a regular beat. While it is quite possible to use hymns to work to in this way, they may also have sung other work-songs which have not been recorded or handed down.

Up until the 20th century, there were no long holidays in the mining communities, but the few festivals and feast days were occasions of great celebration. Special 'mining' celebrations included St Piran's Day (5th March) and Chegwidden Day (or White Thursday, the day on which St Pirran was believed to have first smelted tin), which was held on a Thursday before Christmas. On Whit Monday, Midsummer's Day and the Parish Feast Day, there were also special markets, parades, competitions and games. In 1844, one such fair at Truro was described as follows:

'*The Whitsuntide Pleasure Fair had about the average number of shows, which are stationed in High Cross, the Market Place, and Boscawen Street, and these all proved very attractive to the miners and the bal-girls, who on these occasions have been accustomed to pour into the town in large numbers from time immemorial.*' (WB 31st May 1844)

These fairs and feast days were great occasions for bal maidens to be seen with their 'intended', or to find one. The expectation was that bal maidens would eventually marry, and, although they were usually free to choose their husbands, there were unwritten expectations about marrying within the mining community and within 'one's status'. It was not usual for a bal maiden to marry one of the mine officers, for instance (this was made clear in the novel '*Norah Lang – The Mine Girl*'). It was very common for cousins to marry, or for a marriage to take place within the extended family. Most bal maidens married between the ages of 19 and 24 years old, and usually to local miners. As there were so few holidays, Christmas Day or Boxing Day were popular days for getting married. Once married, a bal maiden was not expected to continue to work at the mine, but to take on the responsibility of running the new household.

FOOTNOTES

1. Watson (1843) p. 11.
2. Doyle, J. and T. *Tamar Valley Traveller* (Cornish Safari, 1978) p. 21.
3. Information throughout this chapter is drawn from material gathered in 1841 for the *1842 Royal Commission on the Employment of Women and Young People* [CEC] especially pp. 119, 131 and Evidence Nos. 6, 7, 18, 46. and also the *Kinnaird Commission of 1864*, especially pp. xxv, 122, 439.
4. Barton (1971) p. 77.
5. Skinner, John *West Country Tour; Diary of an Excursion through Somerset, Devon and Cornwall in 1797* (Ex Libris 1985) p. 50.
6. Razzelle (1973) pp. 28-9.
7. Spreadbury, I. D. (Ed.) *Impressions of the Old Duchy; Book 1 Through Cornwall by Coach 1795* (Kingston Publications 1971) p. 12.
8. Tremellin (1841).
9. Payton (1984) p. 200.
10. Greeves (2006) p. 8.
11. WB 31st Oct 1935 p. 6 + 29th Oct 1936.
12. Ibid.
13. Ibid.
14. WB 7th March 1968.
15. Simonin (1867) p. 438, fig. 145.
16. Personal correspondence (JG/LM 2002).
17. Ibid.
18. Brooke (1967).
19. Schwartz (2000) p. 75.
20. Paige, R. T. *The Tamar at Work* (Dartington Trust 1982).
21. Troon WI (1952) p. 16.
22. Mills, Mary The Cornish Coif; *Old Cornwall* (1973) pp. 140-3.
23. Paynter, S. Winifred *Old St Ives; the Reminiscences of William Paynter* (Lanham 1927).
24. Personal correspondence (JG/LM 2002).
25. Tangye (1988) p. 54.
26. Troon WI (1952) p.16.
27. Sara (1970) p. 195.
28. Tremellin (1841).
29. Personal correspondence (JG/LM 2002).
30. Leifchild (1855) p. 164.
31. Pepper (1862) p. 27

Chapter 4

BAL MAIDENS AT THE COPPER MINES

Mention has yet to be found of women or girls at the copper mines in Cornwall before they became independent of the Mines Royal in 1689, and the first definitive records of females being employed come from the 1720s. However, copper mining was beginning to develop under private ventures before the end of the 17th century, when over 1,000 tons of Cornish ore were being shipped each year to smelters in Swansea and Lower Redbrook in the Forest of Dean. It is probable, therefore, even at this early stage, that female labour was being used in the ore-dressing process.

At the turn of the 18th century, the protracted wars with the French were creating new demands for copper armaments, as a result many new mines opened in West Devon and Cornwall to supply this market. The most successful of those early mines were at Tolgus Downs near Redruth, and Poldice near St Day. By the 1720s, the copper mines in West Devon and Cornwall (the most productive of which were Dolcoath, Cook's Kitchen, Relistian and Bullen Garden) were producing 6,000 tons of ore per year, which was half of the national output.

Over the subsequent 150 years, there were two major booms in copper trade in the South West. The first occurred in the 1740s, after the installation of better pumping machinery to enable mining at depth, and newly designed horse whims for bringing the ore 'to grass'. As greater quantities of ore were won per month than ever before, a much greater workforce was required for the dressing operations. Most of the copper ore mined in the South West was soft and easily lost by over-crushing, so mechanisation was not necessarily the solution to the accumulating quantities of ore-stuff at the surface. The manual crushing and separating operations did not require great strength, but rather dexterity, patience and a good eye. The most obvious and cheapest candidates for this work, therefore, were women and children. They were employed in the copper mines in ever-increasing numbers, and during this time many families migrated from the rural parishes of Cornwall into the mining areas to take up this type of work.

In the 1770s, however, there was a catastrophic slump in copper prices, partly because copper had also been found at Parys Mountain in Anglesey. As this copper could be obtained by the opencast method, it was much cheaper to extract than the copper from the deeper Cornish mines. As a result many copper mines in Cornwall had to be abandoned. Even Dolcoath, the largest copper mine in the South West, closed in 1787 with the subsequent dismissal of a large proportion of the workforce, including the women and children. This was a time of desperate poverty and deprivation in Cornwall, as it also coincided with some of the worst consequences of the *Land Enclosures Act*, when many rural families were left landless and with no means of economic support.

Eventually, with the exhaustion of the Parys deposit by the turn of the 18th century, coupled with an increase in world copper prices, some of the mines were able to re-open, or new ventures made. The largest employer by 1806 was Dolcoath again, with a total of 1,600 workers. How many were women or girls is not known exactly, but it was probably at least 400. Meanwhile, other copper mines were opening, and also employing considerable numbers of women and children. At the east end of Cornwall, when Rev. William Swete visited a copper mine *'on the Callington Road'* in 1792 (believed to be Old Gunnislake or Gunnislake Clitters) he stopped to watch girls cobbing and bucking ore.[1] Similarly, over the border in Devon, Wheal Friendship and the adjacent Wheal Jewell were in full operation when Charles Hatchett visited them in 1796. He too saw women and boys dressing ore at surface.[2]

Over the next four decades, until about 1855, there followed another time of boom (the second peak of production) for the copper mines of Cornwall and West Devon. The total number of mines operating, as well as their output, continued to increase during this period. By 1838, 151,000 tons of copper ore was being raised per year. Although there were continual improvements in the technology of the underground operations at this time (e.g. the introduction of safety fuses), there was very little change in the methods used on the dressing floors. These processes, using a combination of hard manual labour, a skilled and observant eye, and some fairly simple labour-intensive technology were still much the same in the mid 19th century as they had been a century before. This lack of technological development on the dressing floors can be seen by studying the illustration of Dolcoath Copper Mine (c. 1831) by Allom (Fig. 2). It shows the various stages in the dressing procedure, clearly recognisable as those described by Pryce in 1778, and yet not so different from later accounts of 1842, or of the carefully observed drawings of James Henderson of 1858 (Figs 20-24).

This was a time, then, when the cheap but dexterous manual labour of women and children was still required, and the demand (for the moment) was continuing to increase with the expansion of the industry.

THE DRESSING FLOOR

The copper-dressing processes were divided into two distinct phases. The first was the physical breaking down and separation of ore from waste rock as it came from underground, and the second was the use of water to separate out these components further, by using different sedimentation techniques. The physical layout of the dressing floor in the early years was usually determined by two main factors: the most efficient in terms of human carrying capacity, and the availability of water. To minimise human effort and wages, the first dressing processes, therefore, tended to take place nearest to where the ore was landed.

Originally, ore was brought to surface in kibbles. Subsequent processes would take place downhill from there, wherever possible, so that movement of ore was by a system of gravity and chutes, or by hand barrowing. From about 1830, ore was moved in wagons on tramways, when the layout of the dressing floors often needed to be redesigned to allow for appropriate angles and gradients. Water was needed for the initial washing of the ore-stuff, and then for the various sedimentation and separation techniques used later in the process. Water was a vital commodity, and the dressing floors had complex systems of launders and leats to provide the necessary quantities. The water was often brought many miles by launder in order to ensure constant supplies. For instance, at Devon Great Consols it was brought in a leat for two miles, from the Tamar at Latchley. It was such a precious commodity that it was re-used wherever possible, and carefully conserved. Even so, the supply often failed, especially in the summer months.

In the early days, the majority of the tasks were performed in the open air. From about the 1840s onwards, some of the activities were carried out under primitive shelters with no sides, but referred to as 'sheds' or 'hutches'. As late as 1864, the Kinnaird Report remarks on the inadequacy of provision at Fowey Consols:

'The greater number of females employed on the surface work are in the open air. There are some sheds, but as they are only provided with roofs, without any sides, there is such a strong draught of air through, that the girls prefer being out of them. In case of wet weather, inasmuch as the mine is not working very extensively, the females stop work, they being able to dress all the ore in fine weather. There is a good house in the eastern part of the mine which is used for dressing purposes in wet weather.' [3]

THE DRESSING PROCESS

The aim on the dressing floor was to remove as much waste as possible, with minimum of loss of ore, and minimum of expenditure. At each stage of dressing, the material was usually divided into three different grades of components; prills, deads, and gangue or drage (dredge). The pieces of pure ore (prills) would need no further dressing and would be moved away from the dressing floors ready for sampling and sale. The poorest materials (deads) would be rejected as waste, even though they may contain small amounts of ore. Gangue or drage, the medium-quality ore-stuff, was either sent on to a more refined dressing process, or recycled again through previous processes, depending on the richness and nature of ore remaining in it. The amount of ore discarded in the deads would depend on the current market price. When prices were low, it was not worth the cost of extracting very low concentrations of copper. At times of high prices, it would be economic to retrieve copper from material at quite low concentrations. The average amount of copper ore retrieved for sale, however, was not usually more than 8% of its original volume.

Because the nature of both the ore and the waste would vary from mine to mine, each would develop their own unique systems of dressing. Darlington eloquently makes the point in his paper on ore dressing that *'It is scarcely possible to observe the same system in any two distinct concerns.'* (Darlington 1878 p. 161)

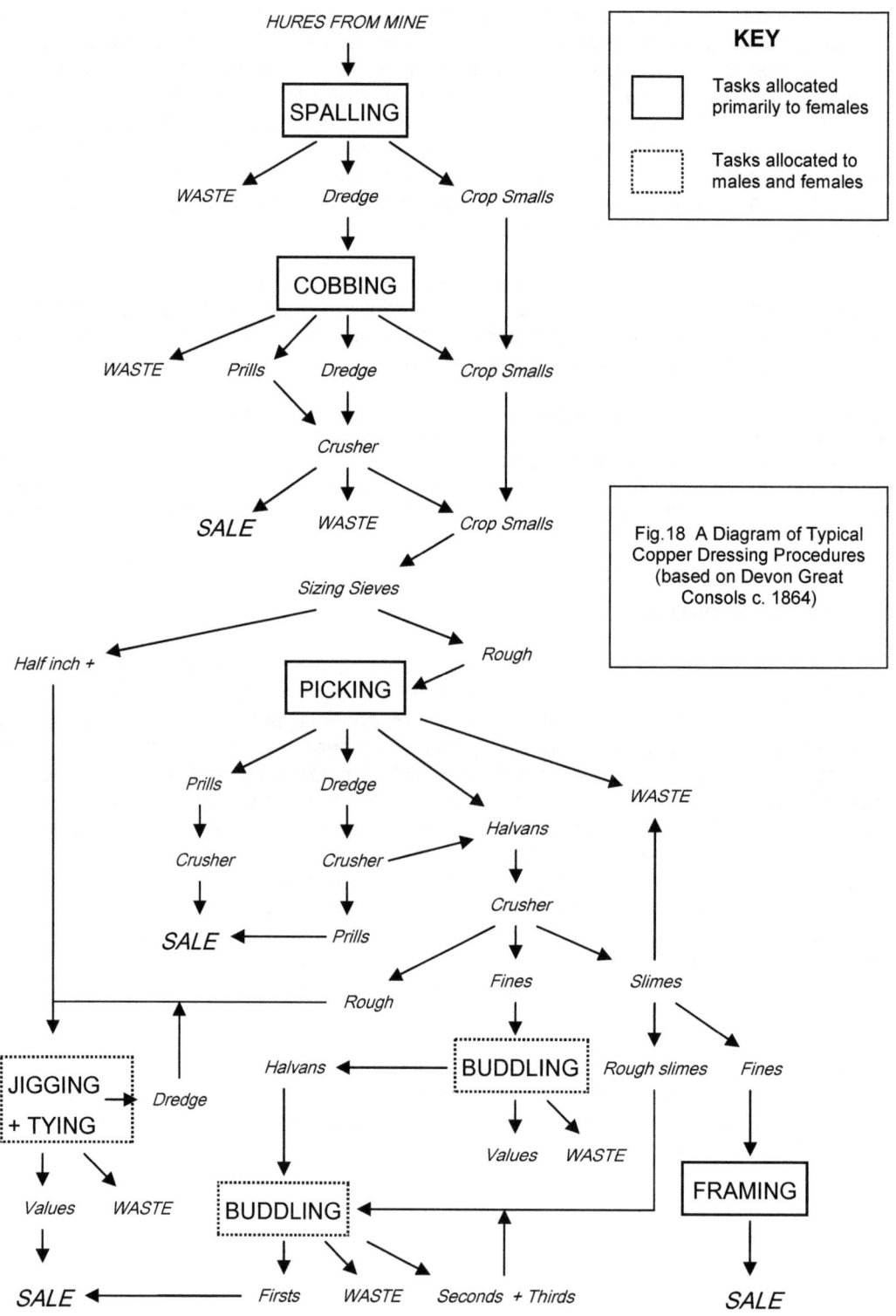

Fig.18 A Diagram of Typical Copper Dressing Procedures (based on Devon Great Consols c. 1864)

Despite variations in the detail of processes from mine to mine, two 19th century writers give us a very useful overview of what happened on the dressing floors at that time:

'The ores, or, as the miners term them, 'hures' are all dressed by women and boys, who cob them, pick them, jig them, buck them, buddle them and splay them as they may require. In order to prepare copper ores for market, the first process is to throw aside the deads, or rubbish; and this operation is very cleverly performed by little girls of seven or eight years of age, who receive threepence or fourpence per day. The largest fragments of ore are then cobbed, or broken into smaller pieces by women; and after being again picked they are given to what the Cornish miners term 'maidens' that is girls from sixteen to nineteen years of age. These maidens buck the ores; that is with a bucking iron, or flat hammer, they bruise them down to a size not exceeding the top of the finger; and the hures are then given to the boys, who jig them, or shake them in a sieve under water, by which means the ore or heavy part, keeps at the bottom, while the refuse is scraped from the top. The part which passes through the sieve is also stirred about in water, the lighter part is thrown to the surface, and the ores, thus dressed, being put into large heaps of about a hundred tons each, are ready for the market.' [4]

'The youngest girls are employed in picking out the best fragments, which they soon learn to do with much dexterity - the ore being spread out on a table, and receptacles being provided for the good and bad portions. The riddling is done by the elder girls and young women. Larger masses are ragged by men, those of somewhat smaller size are spalled or broken by the elder girls and with hammers that are not quite so heavy. The youngest boys wash or clean the stones in a trough, through which a stream of water flows. The fragments are next cobbed, being broken still smaller by girls of medium age who use a short handled hammer. The ore is then bucked or broken into pieces an ounce or two in weight, by girls who stand at a sort of bench, having several iron anvils fitted into it, this is done with a broad square hammer 2-3 lbs in weight, and is considered to be the hardest work at which the mine girls are engaged. The crushing mill is now coming extensively into use, as a substitute for the laborious bucking process. Machinery is now employed to keep the sieves jigging, and children are well able to supply and remove the material. When the ore is brought to a great degree of fineness it is collected into a heap sometimes weighing many hundred tons, and, when at intervals, varying from 2 weeks to two months in different mines, the ore is sampled for the smelter to inspect and buy it in lots, girls are employed to wheel barrowfuls of it into distinct heaps each to form one lot or parcel on the day of sale.' [5]

Due to the different levels of skill and strength needed for the various dressing processes, as noted above, there was a rough division of labour by age and gender. This is illustrated in this description of 1862:

'On the outskirts (of the mine) may perhaps be seen a great number of fine healthy children (boys and girls) of tender years, engaged at the buddle pits, or in jigging, screening, picking and dressing the ore; a little further on may be seen a number of stout girls and women, occupied in cobbing, breaking and assorting ores.' (WB 28th March 1862)

Generally speaking, the younger girls were involved in the lighter work of sorting and washing, while the older girls and women would carry out the heavier work of breaking down ore, and barrowing it around the site.

A smooth transition between dressing operations was crucial to prevent either bottle-necks, or idle times for the dressers. The inter-relationship between the processes and the different groups of workers is illustrated in this description of Devon Great Consols (probably from about 1860):

BAL MAIDENS

'The hot water was used by the older men and boys to wash the rock which the bal-maidens had reduced to the size of a coconut. These were packed into trays and passed into the women, who stood all day long at the two long, low tables in front of the windows. Each woman was armed with her own hammer, with which she cracked the small rocks to pieces in order to pick out the metals they contained. Each, had, of course, been taught to discriminate among the many minerals likely to be found.' [6]

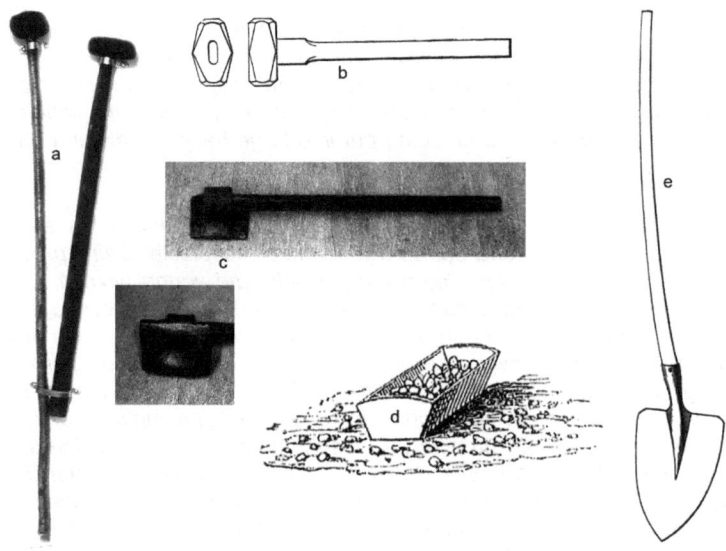

Fig. 19 Bal maidens' Tools of the Trade: a) Spalling Hammers *(courtesy of Helston Museum)*; b) Cobbing Hammer; c) Bucking Iron *(Courtesy of The Wayside Folk Museum, Zennor)*; d) Prill Box; e) Cornish Shovel

Spalling

Copper ore was originally brought to surface in iron kibbles (buckets), but, by about 1830, these had been replaced at some of the larger mines by wagons. Once landed, the largest lumps of material (spalling stuff) were broken into smaller pieces by male surface labourers, using ragging hammers which weighed from between eight to ten pounds.

The next stage in the physical separation of the ore-stuff, spalling, was nearly always done by women. The object of spalling was to break the gangue into an appropriate size for cobbing, or for sending on to the stone crushers, and to remove as much waste as possible at this early stage. This reduction in the volume of material going to the crushers, or onto other manual operations was crucial to the economy of the mine. Both ragging and spalling required a firm surface on which to break the ore, and areas of cobbles were usually set immediately around the landing area for these tasks.

In the 1831 engraving of Dolcoath Copper Mine (Fig. 2), a young woman can be seen spalling ore. Ore has been brought to her by one of the 'surface labourers', in a wheelbarrow, and tipped into a heap. She is working in the open air, near to where the ore is landed. She is using a long-handled hammer, with a blunt end, to break up the larger pieces of ore. The picture of spalling maidens drawn by James Henderson also shows the style of hammer used (Fig. 20). The hammer head was made of iron, or latterly, cast steel, and weighed about one pound. This was fixed on a light, slightly pliant handle, giving a total weight of three pounds or more.[7] These handles were made of ash or blackthorn, giving good flexibility and adding to their effectiveness (Fig. 19). Considerable skill lay in hitting the ore-stuff in its natural shattering plane, as dictated by its crystalline structure.

This very demanding task, which required wielding hammers for hours at a time, was normally thought to be only suitable for girls over about 16 years of age. In reality, younger girls were often involved. Only two out of the six spallers interviewed in 1841 were 16 years or over. Christina Pascoe and Martha Buckingham, who both worked at Consolidated Mines, had sometimes been called on to spall ore when they were only 13 or 14 years old. Similarly, Mary Buller (spalling at Fowey Consols) and Mary Johns (at Tresavean) were only 15 and 14 years old, respectively.[8]

Fig 20 Bal Maidens Spalling
Henderson c. 1858

Even in the late 19th century, it was crucial to minimise the amount of waste going to the crushers and Darlington, writing in 1878, still advocated hand spalling as one of the most economic ways to do this. He also believed that an experienced spaller could produce about a ton of ore-stuff per day '*but the quantity must necessarily depend on the hardness and nature of the stone*'.

It is not clear whether the spallers actually carried out any sorting of the ore they broke, or whether it was just left for the riddlers. It is probable that they may have carried out a very primitive level of sorting. It may be that, at some mines, they also carried out all the riddling and sorting of the spalled material themselves, before the gangue was barrowed away to the pickers and cobbers.

Riddling (or Griddling)

Riddling was usually the next process, when the smallest of the spalled ore was separated through a sieve, leaving the largest pieces needing to be re-spalled. The sieve used was made from an oak hoop, eighteen to twenty inches in diameter, with about a one inch iron or wire mesh. This sieving was also usually carried out near to the shaft and, in 1841, was still being done in the open air. The smaller material retained in the sieve (the picking rough) was sent on to the washers and pickers. That which passed through the sieve (the shaft small) was sent on to be bucked or crushed. Any waste was discarded.

It was mainly women and girls over 16 years of age who were employed at riddling. At Fowey Consols in 1841, there were twenty-seven girls employed in this way. Of those, only four were under 16 years old, and the rest were between 16 and 18 years old. Jane and Mary Ann Harvey, Hannah Davis, Elizabeth Howerd, Mary Barkle and Elizabeth Minhennett were all *'griddling'* copper at East Wheal Russell in 1857. In addition, riddling was also done at other stages during the dry dressing processes. Henderson's drawing of girls at a bucking table includes two girls sieving the newly bucked ore (Fig. 23). They would return the larger pieces that had escaped crushing to the bucking table for reprocessing. The material which passed through the sieve would be ready for jigging. By the late 1850s, though, this gruelling task had been partially mechanised, and the ore was separated on a hand cranked revolving griddle, with young girls or boys picking the best ore from a trommel.

Washing

If the larger ore needed washing, it was done in a strake (trough) with an iron plate in the base. One girl would load the strake with ore-stuff, and another girl would stir the material with a Cornish shovel or rake, so that the mud and fine ore sediment was washed through into collection tanks. Of the large material left in the strake, the best ore would be raised to the top due to its relative density. Another girl or surface labourer would empty the strake, separating the best ore from the mixed gangue, ready for further dressing. In 1858, James Henderson (Fig. 21) observed a slightly different arrangement for washing ore:

'When the ore to be 'picked' is brought to the picking table, it is thrown down on a perforated iron plate, called a 'washing-plate'. Water is then admitted, and the ore is stirred with a shovel. The finer portion is washed into the hutch beneath the washing-plate, whist the remainder is thrown up on the table to supply the 'pickers'.' (Henderson 1858 p. 210)

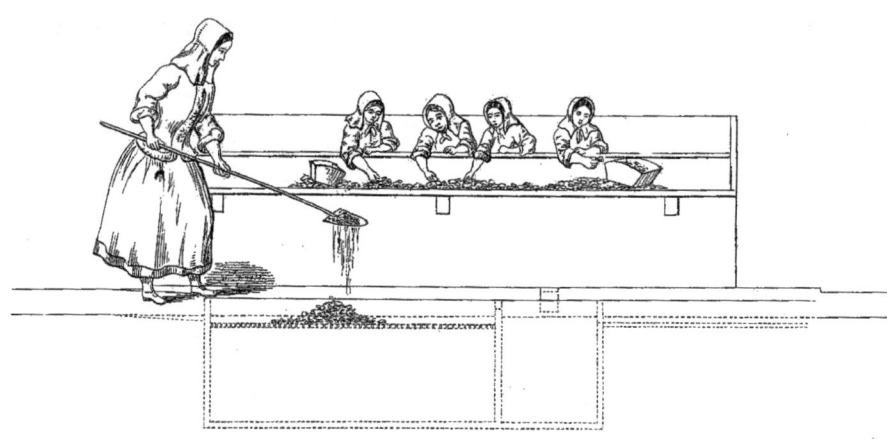

Fig.21 Bal Maidens Washing and Picking
Henderson c. 1858

Smaller material was sometimes washed in a short-legged trough with water running through, by the youngest girls or boys. They would throw out waste material on to the ground, or into barrows, to be carried away. Sometimes, the washing was done using hot water from the mine engine outlet. This was certainly the case at Devon Great Consols.

Picking

Picking the spalled, riddled and washed ore was one of the first tasks that the young boys and girls were given when they came to the copper mine to work. Girls as young as 7 or 8 years old may have been brought to this work, but generally they came to the tables from the age of about 9 or 10. Although boys would start at the picking table alongside the girls, they would very soon be moved to other jobs, usually at the buddles or underground, whereas the girls could remain for several years at this one task. The fine dexterity of the younger children meant that they were well suited to this type of work.

Most of the copper ore mined in Cornwall was in the form of chalcopyrite, and was fairly easy to identify due to its bright, golden colour. Some other copper ores were also quickly identifiable: the bright blue-green of malachite or the green, blue, gold and purple colours of peacock copper. However, not all copper came in readily identifiable forms. An added complication was that sometimes it was brought to the surface mixed with other types of ore, such as tin, lead or zinc. On occasions, then, the sorting task was quite difficult and complex. When Murchison visited Devon Great Consols in 1850, he had this to say about the identification skills of the young ore-pickers:

'*When the ore is mixed with a good deal of mundic, spar and other materials it is first picked by young women and boys, who show great proficiency in their knowledge of their business.*' (MJ 26th Oct 1850 p. 506)

De La Beche also remarked on the skill required by such young people:

'*When ores are mixed with much foreign matter they require to be picked with care, and to the stranger the little picturesque groups of children thus employed, and the practical judgment they have usually attained, are generally subjects of interest.*' [9]

Because the ore being brought to the picking tables had often just been washed, this work could be incredibly wet and cold. In the early days, the women and children would sit on the ground in the open air to sort the larger pieces of washed ore, which would just be tipped out in front of them. Later, the spalled and sieved pieces of washed rock and ore were tipped out onto picking tables, under very primitive shelters. As easy access was required for supplying material to the tables, and for the removal of the various sorted portions afterwards, these children often worked with only minimal protection from the weather. They were usually seated before a low bench, over which they leaned, to pick out the best ore (prills). Sometimes they stood up in order to reach, or just to ease stiff joints. The prills were thrown into special boxes placed on the top of the picking table. These picking boxes were made of deal, 16" long, 7" wide at the base and 10" wide at the top, and 7" deep (Figs. 19 + 21). Sometimes these boxes would also have a wooden handle. When the pickers had finished picking out the pure ore, they would then remove the 'deads' and throw them down into waste boxes underneath. This would leave only the mixed quality ore on the table, ready to be sieved and then barrowed on to the cobbers.

Of the five girls interviewed in 1841, who had spent time at the picking tables, Martha Buckingham and Mary Verran (both 14 years old, from Consolidated Mines) had spent about four years picking ore. 11 year-old Caroline Coom, at Fowey Consols, and 13 year-old Christina Pascoe, at Consolidated Mines, had both been picking ore for two years. At the United Mines (Gwennap) a total of fifty-three girls were employed picking ore, most of whom were under 13 years old. In comparison, of sixty girls at the picking tables at Fowey Consols there was a more mixed age range. Twenty-three were aged 10 to 12 years old, three were 13 to 15 years old, and twenty-four were 16 to 18 years of age.

It was not only very young girls who were put to this work. Minnie Andrews, described as *'the last bal maiden'*, was one of two people (herself and an elderly woman) who were employed to pick copper ore at Carn Camborne, in the 1880s:

'I helped an old lady called Anna Sincock pick over copper ore at Carn Camborne. They used to pull down the thing and the water would come down in the strip and wash the copper. We was picking out all the bad ones and letting the best ones there.' [10]

Cobbing

Writing in the 1770s, William Pryce described how cobbing was carried out at a stone anvil using a *'flat-polled hammer'*. This, presumably, was very like the process shown in the Dolcoath engraving (Fig 2). Five young women are shown kneeling, each at a stone block measuring about twelve inches in each dimension. On this, they are breaking down ore-stuff with a short-handled hammer.

Fig. 22 Bal Maidens Cobbing
Henderson c. 1858

Although the 1831 engraving of Dolcoath shows cobbing taking place in the open air, by 1841 it seems that it was mostly was done under in a 'hutch' or 'cobbing shed'. These were occasionally built much earlier; Wheal Towan had built theirs by 1809.[11] Here, instead of kneeling at a primitive anvil, the girls now usually sat in a slightly more comfortable position, on low benches. These benches had an iron anvil set in at the end, on which the girls broke the ore. They used a short-handled hammer with a tapering end. The heads of these cobbing hammers were four to eight inches long with a slight curve away from the handle, and weighed between 2 and 4 lbs. Later hammers seemed not to be curved (Fig.19). In some cases, the cobbers had their feet and legs protected by a screen, but, as in James Henderson's sketch of 1858 (Fig. 22), often the damp, cold debris was left to gather around their feet and legs.

Girls of about 16 or 17 years old were generally set to this task. They broke the mixed ore to hazelnut-sized pieces, separated out and rejected any waste rock, and placed the remainder into hand barrows ready for bucking. At Dolcoath, in the mid 1850s, the cobbing shed was known as the 'Roarer' on account of the terrific noise generated by the sixty girls working there.[12]

In 1841, five cobbers were interviewed, and all were 16 years old or over. Elizabeth Curnow and Christina Pascoe (at Consolidated Mines) were 24 and 17 years old. Grace Bowden (at Trethellan), Jane Sandow (at Wheal Gorland), and Jane Uren (at Tresavean) were 18, 17, and 16 years old, respectively. Although cobbing was considered very demanding, and only suitable for older girls, at Fowey Consols, three were between the ages of 13 and 15 years, and one girl was under the age of 13. Only four of their cobbers were aged 16 years or over.

In 1841, Jane Uren, at Tresavean, reported she usually cobbed over two hundredweight of ore-stuff per day. (This is probably the weight of dressed ore she produced). In 1878, Darlington, estimated that an expert cobber could '*prepare about 10 cwts of tolerably hard stuff per ten hours*'. In contrast, this is probably the amount of un-dressed material brought to be cobbed. George Henwood remarked on the speed with which women or boys could do this work:

'*...which they do with amazing rapidity; during this process they eject any extraneous substances that may have escaped the notice of the spaller.*' (Henwood 1855 p. 8)

Bucking

Bucking was considered the hardest task carried out by the women and girls on the dressing floors, and involved reducing the cobbed ore-stuff to small granule size. The bucking girls and women stood at a bench or a mound of stone packed with earth, into which was set an anvil. In the 18th century, a flat stone was used, set at slight angle to the bench or mound, but this was later replaced by a cast iron block about 16"square and 1.5" thick. The material to be bucked was delivered to the table from above, either from a hand barrow (Fig. 23) or down a chute.

Fig. 23 Bal Maidens Bucking, Barrowing & Riddling
Henderson c. 1858

Sometimes, the girls stood on a small platform at the bench in order to keep their feet clear of the debris. Some wore 'kitty bags', a kind of leg protector, to keep their legs dry.[13]

The girls would sweep the ore-stuff from the accumulated heap onto the anvil with one hand, and beat and pound it with a 'bucking iron' with the other. This hammer weighed three or four pounds. It had a wooden handle inserted into a stirrup of iron, attached to a flat end about 6" square and 1" thick made of cast iron (Fig. 19). Once the material had been crushed to powder, the bucking girls would then sweep it away with their left hand onto the floor. When about a barrow-full had accumulated the girls would shovel up the bucked ore and sieve it. They would then return the coarser material to the table to be bucked again. The finer grade would be barrowed away to the buddles. Darlington hinted that it was custom for the bucking girls to keep up a rhythm of working, hammering in time with each other.

As hand bucking was so difficult and demanding, it was one of the first processes to be mechanised. Crushing rolls were introduced, but in the first instance they were only suitable for the harder ore types. John Taylor installed such machines at Wheal Crowndale in 1804, and at Wheal Friendship in 1806. Reputedly, the former action was to break a strike by bal maidens, however, Taylor's own account was rather different:

'I had constructed the first [crushing mill] *for copper ore at Wheal Crowndale, near Tavistock, in the year 1804, at which time this mine produced large quantities of ore of low produce, and being situated in a district where women are not accustomed to work on the dressing floors, as they are in the more western districts of Cornwall, a difficulty had been felt in getting hands to dispatch the work.'* [14]

By 1830, De la Beche reported that the best ores were being broken by steam-driven crushing machines in most of the principal copper mines. This was confirmed by Henwood in 1832, and certainly one was in use at Trethellan Mine in 1841. Unfortunately, it was found that the crushers generated even more dust on the dressing floors than the conventional bucking.

From the 1831 Dolcoath picture, it seems that bucking took place out doors, but by 1841 it was generally being done inside, along with the cobbing. Bucking could only be carried out by the biggest and strongest girls and women. By the time of the *1842 Commission*, only three of the girls interviewed had been employed in this type of work. Two of them were Elizabeth Carkeek, aged 18 years, and Sally Fall, aged 19 years. Both were buckers at Tresavean Mine. The third was 17 year-old Jane Sandow of Truro, who had only been at the bucking tables a very short while before she was unable to continue, as it had been too hard for her. The total employment numbers at United Mines, in 1841, indicated that there were thirty girls working in the bucking sheds, of whom two were actually under 16 years old, and the remaining twenty-eight were between the age of 16 and 18 years old. Henderson reported that hand bucking had been discontinued in all but the smallest mines, by 1858.

Jigging

In the early days of copper mining, this very laborious task was done by boys or older women, and was also referred to as 'hutch work'. The work involved shaking brass wire sieves, holding gangue, in wooden boxes of water. The lightest material washed through, and the material left in the sieve would settle into layers. By the end of the 18th century and beginning of the 19th, hand jigging was done almost entirely by boys, and was found to be very injurious to their health. When Pryce wrote in the 1770s, he described how a girl would throw ore into the jigger, while a boy held it. After the shaking process, done by the boy, the different grades of sediment would be shovelled and separated by them both. The heavy purer ore was sent for sampling and sale, the medium mixed ore was sent for reprocessing and the poor ore was rejected.

Fig 24 Bal Maidens Jigging
Henderson c. 1858

From about 1830, semi-mechanised jigging boxes were introduced, which could be operated fairly easily, by either girls or boys. They consisted of large wooden boxes, in which the jigging sieves were set, but which were shaken by means of a very long-handled horizontal lever. (The type illustrated above was found to be awkward to operate. A much more successful design incorporated a 'Y' shaped lever.) Even though jigging with these machines was so much easier than jigging by hand, the operators still reported back pain. The only two named bal maidens that are known to have operated jigs at a copper mine were Mary Ann Dodd and Maria Rimmett (of Peter Tavy), in 1861. By the 1880s, jiggers had become fully mechanised and were belt-driven, using water or steam power, and only required to be manually filled and emptied. It was then usual for boys to be responsible for these machines.

Buddling

In the early part of the 18th century, it seems that both boys and girls worked at the buddles. It was here that the very fine waste from jiggers and settling pits was taken, to extract some more of the remaining ore. The early buddles were long, rectangular sloping pits or wooden troughs where waste was washed out from ore-stuff, leaving heavier copper ore to settle at the 'head' of the frame. To aid separation, the boys or girls agitated the mixture with a heather broom, or by standing up to their ankles in the buddle and using their feet. Pryce said these children were called 'lappiors' (dancers) in the earlier part of the 18th century. By the 19th century, the actual 'buddling' was done primarily by boys. However, girls were often responsible for 'serving the buddles'. This might involve controlling the flow of water and ore-stuff through the sluices, strips and launders to the buddle; as well as helping to barrow, load or unload the increasingly purified ore.

Barrowing and Tramming

The efficient transportation of the ore-stuff, waste and copper ore around the different areas on the dressing floor must have been one of the most difficult logistical challenges for the surface captain. In order to keep the flow, teams of men and girls were continually employed just to barrow material from one place to another. (Fig. 3) Even after the introduction of wagons onto the dressing floor, there were some areas where it was still necessary to hand-carry materials, and hand barrows were still being used in the late 19th century. Apart from the regular barrowing teams, girls were also called away from other tasks to help on an 'as needed' basis, when there was a bottleneck at one of the processes. Generally, it was the male surface workers who used wheeled barrows, and the women and girls who were given hand barrows.

In the early days, it seems that the hand barrows used at the copper mines held three hundredweight of ore. It was estimated that allowing for the weight of the barrow, the ore plus the water held in the ore, the weight to be carried could total as much as four hundredweight. In 1817, it was observed:

'This is an enormous burthern, which is borne by all descriptions of persons who are employed in dressing and weighing. Labour so disproportionate to the degree of strength possessed by ordinary individuals, has given rise to a most pernicious custom, generally adopted by persons, women as well as men, who are employed in mixing, dividing and weighing ore; that of drinking large quantities of spirituous liquors, from the false idea that they are thereby invigorated to perform the labour required of them.' (WB 25th Apr. 1817)

It seems that, historically, the hand barrow was designed to have the same capacity as the sacks used for transporting ore to the smelter, which was three hundredweight. One mule could carry two of these sacks, one on each side. By about 1780, it was decided to halve the sack sizes used on the tin dressing floors, due to the number of injuries incurred by the surface men and carriers in lifting them. As a result, the corresponding barrow size was also halved to contain one-and-a-half hundredweight as well. The same observer wrote:

'What has been done in the case of the load of tin ore will, I hope, be shortly accomplished in that of weighing copper ore.'

As all references, both in tin and copper mines, in the *1842 Commission* are to hand barrows with a 1.5 cwt. capacity, it seems that this change was made. These hand barrows were shallow wooden boxes made of deal. The total length, including the handles, was 5' 6" long, and the carrying box being 10" x 18" at the base, 18" x 24" at the top and 9" deep. The girls and women used a Cornish shovel to fill them. This had a curved and roughly triangular blade about 11" wide at the top and 13" from the shank to the point. It was initially made of hammered iron, and later pointed with steel. The hilt was normally of ash, and slightly curved. The whole shovel weighed about four pounds.

In his *Mining Journal* article on bal maidens in 1858, Henwood describes how two women were called to barrow ore when there was a shortage of male surface labourers, and that they were carrying a weight of three hundredweight between them. It is not clear whether he had mistaken the size, or whether, at this particular mine, the larger hand barrows were still in use:

'*There being a scarcity of hands (men) on the floor Mary and Nanny were called. On which two amazons rushed forward. Hand barrows filled with copper ore contain 3 cwt, 7 to the ton (21 cwt). These girls were employed to fill these barrows with the long handled Cornish shovel, and to carry them several yards to the scales. Then further to the heap, where they upset the ore, and returned to the pile to refill.*' (Henwood 1858 p. 36)

It seems that any strong adolescent girl or woman could be called on to barrow at a moment's notice, as with Mary and Nanny above. In the *1842 Commission*, we are told that Martha Buckingham and Mary Verran, both aged 14, were occasionally called on to barrow at the Consolidated Mines. As a full-time task, however, it was often allocated to girls in their mid to late-teens. In 1841, for instance, 17 year-old Fanny Francis was a full-time barrow girl at the United Mines.

Hand wagons were used throughout the industry, from at least the second quarter of the 19th century, but there are few records of women being employed to tram them at surface. However, an elderly woman and her younger colleagues at Carn Brea were responsible for pushing their ore wagons to the copper crushers, when Rideing visited the mine in 1880 (Fig. 58).[15]

SAMPLING AND ASSAYING

Once every two months or so, activities on the dressing floor changed dramatically in order to prepare the ore that had already been dressed for sampling and sale. This sometimes took up to two weeks to complete, so, at some mines, extra women and girls were drafted in. For instance, Sarah Michell was employed at 'weighing up' at Dolcoath in August 1789, and was paid 1s 2d. At East Wheal Crofty in the 1840s, a designated team of women and girls were 'shared' with an adjacent mine, and were employed just for sampling for a month at each mine, alternately. In most other mines, some of the normal dressing activities were stopped, and those workers sent to help with the sampling.

Sampling proceeded in different ways, depending on the dressing arrangements at each individual mine. Where ore was raised and dressed by separate tribute teams, each tribute team would prepare their own ore for sampling. Where ore from the different teams was dressed by surface dressers employed by the mine, then each teams ore would continue to be prepared separately.

Either way, the principles involved were the same. Each heap of dressed ore would be thoroughly and carefully mixed to try and ensure complete uniformity of content. Because some of these heaps would be very large indeed, sometimes consisting of many hundreds of tons, the mixing could take a long time. The thoroughly-mixed ore would then be shared out as fairly as possible into 'parcels' or shares, according to how many people had an interest in the ore (which would include the tributers, shareholders, mineral lord etc).

Within each parcel, the ore would be barrowed and laid out into neat 'doles', flat-topped circular piles about two or three feet thick, ready for the assayers to sample.

This complicated procedure of sharing out into doles at sampling was sometimes directed by one senior woman or girl, appointed by the surface captain. The rest of the women and girls were organised into groups of four, one pair shovelling and the other barrowing. At allotted times, the two pairs would change over tasks.

A document from 1813, describes how girls were also employed in the final stages of selecting a representative sample of ore for assay. After mixing portions from selected doles, a 20 lb sample was finely ground and sieved. A girl would thoroughly mix a 5 lb portion of this, stirring it and passing it *'from hand to hand five times'*. After a final sieving, a 2 lb sample was then taken from this final mixture for assaying.[16]

OTHER TASKS AT THE COPPER MINE

Women were sometimes employed to provide transport for goods to and from the copper mines. Before 1820, this was done by mule train or pack horses. Keturah Blewett was regularly hired at Cook's Kitchen, between 1781 and 1785, to carry copper ore from the mine to the port (probably Portreath). She was paid 7d for each journey. From time to time, she was also paid 8d for taking *'8 horses to collect clay from St Agnes'* (presumably the clay which the miners used to attach candles to their hats, which was quarried from the north side of St Agnes Beacon).

In the early days, ore was hoisted to the surface in kibbles (buckets) using horse whims. In the more effective and safe form, the horses were usually harnessed, in pairs, to one end of a long beam attached to the whim. This beam was counterbalanced by a heavy weight at the opposite side of the pivot. The driver would sit on the beam, between the horses and the centre, and direct them to trot around the circumference. The overhead drum would then simultaneously wind one kibble up, while lowering the other. The driver would know how just many turns of the whim were required for the kibbles to be raised or lowered to each level, and would slow the horses accordingly. In the Whitehaven Coal Pits, in 1802, the whim horses were changed every 8 hours, while the drivers worked for 12 hours. It is not clear what the practice was in Cornwall; however, both women (probably the horse owners) and children were sometimes employed for this very responsible work.

Women were employed at Poldice Mine in the early 19th century. In 1806, Jane Annear, Alice Jeffery, Ann Martin and Ann Richards were paid different rates per 100 kibbles of ore-stuff that they landed, indicating that they were probably raising it from different levels. For instance, in June 1806 Jane Annear raised 400 kibbles at 16s, and 827 kibbles at 10s 6d per hundred. This averaged about five kibbles per hour. There had obviously been a serious accident in the June of that year because Jane was paid *'10s for horse kild* [sic]'.

Towards the end of the 18th century, Grace Briney was apprenticed to the surface captain, at a very young age, to work at the horse whim at the Treskerby Mines. Eventually, she went on to be the only known woman 'kibble lander' at the horse whim, and in later life, a mine wagoner. (Her story is told more fully in Chapter 12).

Women and girls could also be found at an assortment of other tasks, especially in the early days of a mine. At Poldice Mine in February 1798, two women were paid 4s each for *'cleaning bricks'*, and several others were paid 1s for *'being about bricks'*. In June 1806, Elizabeth Phillips was also paid 5s for brick cleaning. At the same mine, Grace Morcom was paid 9s 0d for *'holing 2 copper bottoms'* in March 1789. This was probably punching out the very fine holes in the copper base of the jigging sieves.

WASTE PICKING

During the tin mining operations of the early 18th Century, the value of copper was not necessarily recognised, and copper ore was sometimes discarded as worthless along with the other waste. In the late 18th or early 19th century, copper ore was subsequently retrieved from these waste heaps, sometimes at great profit. When copper prices were high, it also became economically viable to re-dress the waste heaps from previous copper mining ventures for the copper that had been left when prices had been low. Mine adventurers would either employ their own dressers for this task, or sometimes lease out the work.

THE FINAL COPPER YEARS

New technologies were already heralding the reduction of the use of manual labour on the dressing floors when, in 1855, there was an enormous slump in copper prices. Many copper mines in Cornwall, previously in their heyday, closed, resulting in huge job losses. Some copper mines found tin at depth and were able to convert to mining tin. This happened at Dolcoath, Tincroft, and Cook's Kitchen, for instance. However, the transition process was slow and, as tin dressing was usually less labour intensive than copper, job losses for the women on the dressing floor, even in the surviving mines, was inevitable. As a result, women and children were never again to be employed at the Cornish copper mines in such numbers as in the 1850s.

In 1866, there was another depression in the copper market, which heralded the final decline of the Cornish copper industry. Copper production in Cornwall had halved between 1860 and 1870, and halved again between 1870 and 1880. Also, many of the most successful copper mines, which had been in continual production for sixty years or more, were becoming exhausted. As a result, by 1885, only thirty-five mines were producing any copper at all, and, by the turn of the century, the only copper being produced in Cornwall was as a by-product of the tin mines. Over the border in Devon, Great Devon Consols continued to extract some copper, although its main product by now was arsenic, and even this major mine closed in 1901. So, from 1866 onwards, there were huge job losses on the dressing floors of the copper mines, with many women and children thrown out of work. The mining parishes that depended almost entirely on copper mining were the worst affected, and there was desperate poverty and hardship.

However, the contribution of these copper mines to the world economy should not be under-estimated. During the 18th and 19th centuries, Devon and Cornwall gained four times as much revenue from copper as it did from tin, and, at the peak of production, it provided 50% of the national output. The impact on the course of world economics, history and trade is impossible to quantify. This copper provided the nation with high quality domestic ware and copper coinage in the 18th century. It also had it's darker side; providing much of the copper necessary for commodities for the transatlantic slave trade and armaments for the long term war effort against Napoleonic France. It also formed an important component of Britain's 19th century colonial trade. During all these years of production, the dressing of copper ore was hardly mechanised at all and relied almost entirely on armies of women and children and their corporate manual effort. They were one of many crucial links in the booming economy of mid 18th and 19th century Britain, which, for better or worse, had such far-reaching consequences around the world.

FOOTNOTES

1. Swete, Rev. John *Travels in Georgian Devon* (Devon Books 1997) Vol. 1 p. 133.
2. Hatchett, (1796) p. 23.
3. Kinnaird (1864).
4. Watson (1843) p. 16.
5. The Mines and Miners of Cornwall *Chamber's Repository* (March 1853) or Honor (1869) p 37.
6. Paige, R. T. *The Tamar Valley at Work* (DART 1982) p. 58.
7. Many of the descriptions of dressing apparatus and tools are taken from Darlington (1878) especially pp. 18, 78, 80, 84, 120 and 156.
8. Information throughout this chapter is drawn from material gathered in 1841 for the *1842 Royal Commission on the Employment of Women and Young People* [CEC] especially pp. 53, 55, 57; Tables 17, 18; Evidence Nos. 6, 19, 20, 21, 33, 47, 86, 89, 112, and 114.
9. De La Beche (1839) p. 594.
10. Brooke (1967).
11. Hamilton Jenkin (1978) *St Agnes – Perranporth* p. 9.
12. MJ 15th February 1879.
13. Henwood, G. (1855) p. 8.
14. Collins, J. H. *Observations on the West of England Mining Region* (1912) p. 268; Taylor (1831) pp. 82-7.
15. Rideing (1881) p. 808.
16. A General Survey of Cornwall 1817 *Cornwall Gazette* Section 15.

Chapter 5

BAL MAIDENS AT THE TIN MINES AND SMELTERS

Cassiterite (tin ore), like copper, is found in lodes and deposits where the sedimentary rocks meet the granites of the South West. Unlike the copper ores found in Cornwall and Devon, however, it is relatively hard and can survive in very small dense particles, even after the minerals in which it was deposited have been physically or chemically eroded away. This means that viable amounts of tin ore have been found in stream beds and even on the sea shore, often far away from their point of origin, when the parent rock has long since been washed away. The tin in this form has been weathered over many years and is very pure, making it relatively easy to access and requiring very little dressing. This kind of tin has been collected over the centuries, sometimes by comparatively simple methods, without the need for complicated equipment or the investment of large sums of money. These types of tin recovery are known as tin working or streaming, sea tinning, and blown tinning. When these sources of relatively pure tin from rivers and streams were exhausted, deposits began to be exploited underground, by shode, drift, or deep mining. However, tin from these sources is less pure, still being incorporated in the parent rock, and requires far more preparation and dressing before it is ready for smelting.

TIN STREAM WORKS, AND EARLY SHALLOW MINING

Evidence of tin stream workings has been found out on the Cornish moors from very early times. It is believed that tin has been extracted in this way and smelted for at least two thousand years in Cornwall, more or less continuously through the Roman and medieval period, right up to the first half of the 20th century, often with little change in technology. The first records for tin working in Devon (on Dartmoor) date from the 12th century.

The simplest early process of obtaining tin was similar to that of panning for gold. Tinners would collect a small quantity of sandy river deposit in a wooden bowl of water, and swirl the mixture, allowing the 'values' to settle to the bottom. Repeated discarding of the lighter waste would eventually concentrate the small quantity of ore in the bottom of the bowl. This method could be used by men, women, and children, alike.

When the tin in the recent deposits of a stream was exhausted, the prospecting for tin deeper in the river bed would begin. Owing to the heavy nature of the ore, it would collect, over many years, in pockets on the granite bedrock under the stream or river, having been washed there as the parent rock had been eroded and carried away in the water. Sometimes these pockets were a considerable distance from the source of the mineral, collecting where water movement was significantly reduced.

Stream works, to exploit the deeper deposits, were built at the downstream side of the location where tin was suspected to lie. A shallow pit would be sunk to the stanniferous gravel layer, and then drained by buckets, or simple water-powered pumps. Work would progress back up the watercourse. Ore was collected by building a series of wooden leats and strakes, whereby river deposits were washed in a current of water. In the very early days, the tin ore was raked up onto a piece of turf at the top of the strake, which acted as a sieve. The turf was then carefully rolled, and carried to a large wooden bowl, usually about two feet in diameter, where the ore was washed out and collected. Latterly, the tin-stuff was worked against the current with a rake or brush, by a person standing in the strake. The heavy ore then separated out at the top, while the lighter waste and ore was washed away into collection pits for further separating. From this simple strake, the first buddles evolved, being larger rectangular troughs sometimes built out on trestles, and sometimes sunk into the ground. The ore that was extracted from the stream beds tended to be very pure, and therefore needed little dressing. Small pebbles and coarser gravels would be dug out separately, and left in piles for picking over. They would then be ground and washed out in a strake. When the ore from one area had been removed, the waste would be back-filled into the hole.

As work proceeded, material from the streambeds would become exhausted, but, with diligence, miners were often able to locate and expose the tin lodes which had been the source of the stream tin. They did this by looking for the 'shode' stones (stones found in the river bed, containing tin, but with little sign of being rounded into pebbles by water erosion) indicating that the parent lode was not far away.

On discovering the tin lode, which was the source of the stream tin, a drift mine would then be driven into the valley sides. Alternatively, shallow pits or trenches could also be worked along the 'lode back' from the surface. Evidence of this latter type of tin working has usually been destroyed by later deep mining at the same sites, but evidence of openwork can still be seen, for instance, at Wheal Prosper in Lydford, Devon. The material mined in this simple way had not been exposed to the elements and broken down in the same way as the stream tin, so needed more dressing to remove it from the substrate in which it was found. Originally, all the picking, sorting and crushing that was required was done by hand. The crushing was done by placing the tin-stuff in hollows in granite blocks, or in specially made mortars, and beating with hand-held rocks, until it was the consistency of fine sand; this was called crazing. Later, it was done using a hand-operated 'crazing mill', not unlike a flour mill, where the material was ground between two flat rotating stones.

During the middle ages, hand-operated crazing mills were replaced with larger versions powered by horses or water. Eventually, by the 16th century, most of the crushing of tin-stuff was done by water-powered log 'stamps', which acted as huge battering devices. Even then, the 'leavings' were often recycled through the water-powered crazing mill as well, in order to extract more tin.

The first detailed documentation of the tinning industry in Cornwall and Devon survives in court records from the middle of the 12th century, with the signing of the Charter of the Stannaries in 1201, which sought to regulate tinning in the South West. Mining was then under control of the Crown, and was organised in four Stannaries in Cornwall, and four in Devon. From very early on, large areas of moorland were allocated to named tinners, and each site or 'bound' was described and named. In these early days, it seems that the dressing was not necessarily carried out as soon as the tin-stuff was extracted. Instead, it would probably be left until the weeks immediately before the quarterly coinage (presumably, to reduce the risk of theft of the black tin). From this, we would deduce that any women and children employed specifically for this final dressing would not be working full-time.

The tin stream works and shallow mining continued in this way for centuries, with varying degrees of success. Tin mining in Cornwall and Devon went through the doldrums in the 15th and 16th centuries, but began to pick up again when the Crown released its monopoly on the Mines Royal, and allowed the landowners to apply for mining rights. Private arrangements were then made between the landowners (mineral lords) and individual venturers who applied to search for tin.

Even though tin stream working was to be largely overshadowed by deep mining from the 18th century, new stream deposits continued to be discovered. In the first half of the 19th century, the Wendron tin streams were second only in extent to those in the St Austell area, with twenty companies operating on Porkellis Moor alone.[1] The Carnon tin streams were also extensive, and covered an area of 9 or 10 miles, stretching over five parishes from Carn Brea to Perranworthal, Feock and Mylor. It seems that in some cases these extensive stream works continued to operate well into the industrial era, often evolving into 'second streaming' operations; i.e. collecting the tin carried away in the waste water from the dressing floors of deep mines, further upstream.

The degree of involvement of women and girls in the tin stream works and drift mining ventures over the centuries is unclear. Certainly, many of the simple dressing operations, such as picking, buddling or straking, crazing, and framing are activities which could have been done by women or girls, and all of these tasks, or their equivalents, were definitely performed by them from the early or mid-18th century onwards. Whenever these tin stream works or drift mines were being run by family units, or community groups, it would be fairly safe to assume that women and children would probably have had their allotted tasks.

The earliest definite reference, however, to females as part of the tin mining workforce is in 1357, where Abraham the Tinner was employing three hundred men, women and children at mines and stream works at Crukbargis (on Bodmin Moor). Another early record is of female tin workers brought before the Stannary Court in May 1364. They were Meliora Phelny, who was summoned to Redruth, and Christian Wrehans who was summoned (with her husband) to Marazion. All had been employed by a John Polper, and had been absent from their work.[2]

Even though evidence of female employment is scarce during this time, there are indications of their involvement across the tin industry. In the mid 16th century, Alice Nosworthy and Margery Bradeley seem to have been working tin illegally at Hethefield,

Ilsington. Also in Devon, Joan Winsland was leasing a tin mill at Walkhampton in 1569, and Juliana Rede a knocking and blowing mill at Keigella Borowe in 1577. Women sometimes appeared as joint lessees to tin works in the 17th century. For instance, Agnes and John Jutsham, of Shaw, were leasing Cuccold Tin Works, Plympton St Mary from William Strode in August 1647. Similarly, Margaret and Benjamin Surfe were joint lessees of tin works at Bottle Hill in December 1655.

In addition to being involved in tin works themselves, women sometimes took over a tin trading role on the death of their husbands. In 1303, 'Isobell of Northworthi' and 'Sarra of Holne' took tin to Ashburton, and Clarice Lyne took tin to Chagford, for coinage. In 1477, tin trader Agnes Stannon took Henry Wynneslond to the Stannary Court at Tavistock for selling her corrupt tin in Buchland Monachorum, two years previously. Later, in 1531, a few women traders were still recorded: with Rachel Bownde and Matilda Browne taking tin to Plymton; Elizabeth and Isabella Bradeley, Alice Nosworthy, Joanna Wyncheat, Elizabeth Dolberre and Catherine Hamlyn to Ashburton; and Alice Hanworthy (Hanfforde) to Tavistock.[3]

It is about two centuries between these fascinating entries and any subsequent references to women or girls employed in the tin works. In 1778, Pryce described how both boys and girls would work barefooted in the buddles, and had previously been called by an ancient name 'lappiors'. Women and girls continued to work at the tin stream works through the 19th century. For instance, in the mid-1830s, 2 women and 36 children were working at Carnon Streams, Redruth, and 5 children (gender not specified) were working at the Pentuan Stream Works at Mevagissey.[4]

SEA TINNING

As considerable amounts of tin ore are continually washed down onto the beaches from streams and from the adits of tin workings, sea tinning was one of the easiest ways of all to collect tin ore. It required little more than some wooden frames, sieves and a shovel, plus a means of transporting the ore to the stamps. Collection of sea tin, however, was not usually a continuous occupation, and could only be done after allowing a sufficient amount of deposit to accumulate, probably over a period of several years.

Due to its greater density, after the tin was washed onto the beaches, it would slowly sink through the sands or shingles with successive tides and collect in pockets on the bedrock, in much the same way that it collected under the riverbed gravels. Once one of these pockets had been located, the miners would simply dig down to it, extract it and separate it from the sand and shingle in which it had collected. This was done using a series of sieves and simply built washing strakes. It would then be transported by mule or cart to the nearest tin stamps for crushing and dressing.

There is very little documentation about sea tinning in Cornwall, but it is known to have taken place at Priest Hole at Cape Cornwall during the 19th century. It was also recorded at Pendeen, Lelant, Loe Pool, Chapel Porth, Trevaunance, Trevellas and Perranporth at the end of the 19th or into the 20th century. When Mr. David Stephens was extracting tin from the beach at Gwithian, he used just twelve frames and three buddles. In this way, he was able to obtain 9 lb tin from every 1 ton of sand. No record of females helping at these enterprises has yet been found.[5]

A similar venture that took place on the shoreline was the collecting of 'blown tin'. This was opportunistic mining at its best. Under certain weather conditions, as ore washed down on to the beaches, it could be blown into concentrated deposits. For instance, the accumulation of blown tin at Porthrepta, near St Ives, was usually seasonal, and depended on a north wind to give a good 'coat' of tin on the sand. Under any other weather conditions, the sea remixed the tin with sand, making it uneconomic to collect. During the last half of the 19th century, 'beachwork' there was taken to the six-headed stamps and dressing plant on the shoreline, for processing. In 1887, five workers were employed but their gender is unknown.[6]

DEEP MINING FOR TIN

By medieval times, some tin was being mined from deep pits, or by driving drift mines into the valley sides. The depth of a tin mine at this time, as with the copper, was limited by the height of the water table, and also by the efficiency of any primitive pumps, used to keep the mine dry. Medieval accounts of mining for tin in Cornwall, describe an all-male workforce, most of whom were employed in keeping the mines clear of water.

When tin and copper mines became free of Crown control by the end of the 17th century, landowners were allowed to lease out their mineral rights to private adventurers. This change was followed almost immediately by the development of improved pumping and lifting technology, so that, from the beginning of the 18th century, deposits could be exploited at greater depths than before. Improved tin stamps also meant a more efficient dressing of the ore. Although the initial emphasis was on opening up the copper mines for the escalating copper market, a few deep tin mines were developed, and operated on a far greater scale. Some of the earliest successful tin mines opened were Rosewall Hill Mine, Polberro, Polgooth, Great Work and Wheal Vor. By the end of the 18th century, deep mining was also underway on Dartmoor, with the development of such mines as White Works, Hexworthy and Vitifer. It was at this stage that the workforce at the tin mines began to expand rapidly, with the need for large numbers to work on the dressing floors. From about 1720, women and girls are believed to have been employed in increasing numbers at these deeper mines.

By 1770, when employment of women and girls was well under way at the copper mines, copper prices were falling, resulting in mine closures. The copper mine workers put out of work often offered their services at the tin mines, which enabled an initial increase in output. It was just at this time, though, that pewter for domestic tableware and kitchen utensils fell from fashion in favour of earthenware, so the price of tin then dropped, causing more mine closures. How many bal maidens were effected by these economic down-turns is unknown.

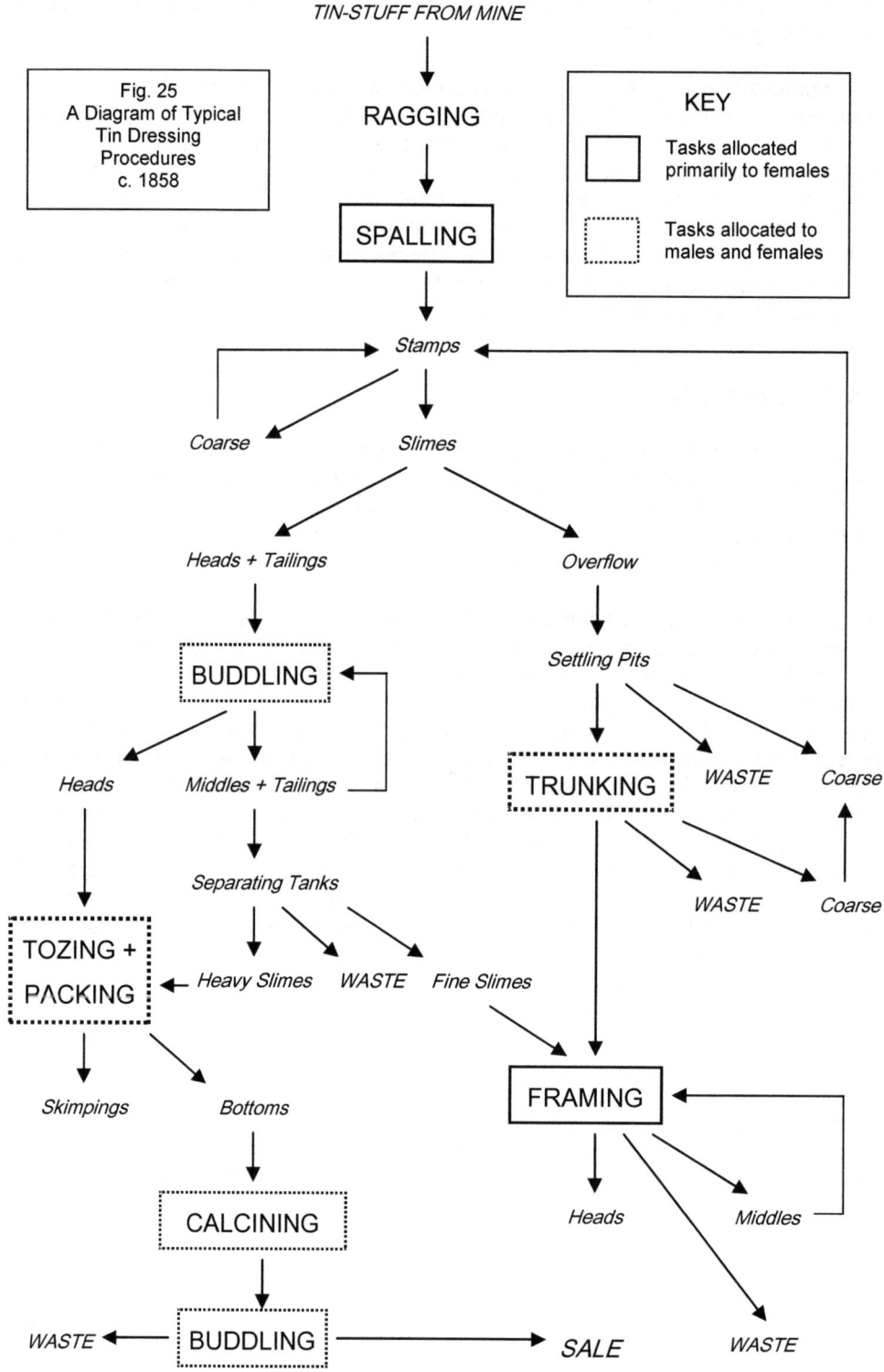

Little documentary evidence seems to survive confirming female involvement at the tin mines before about 1770, but Pryce indicated that by 1778 it was quite the norm for women and girls to be filling buddles, sieving or trunking. Eventually, by about 1800, both copper and tin prices began to pick up again, and mines in Devon and Cornwall came back into production. During the first half of the 19th century, however, tin was never as important as copper, and it was to suffer the same vagaries of trade depressions, especially in 1837 and 1838, when many of those working at the tin mines, including women and children, were laid off again. The total number of women and children at the tin mines was always much less than the number at the copper mines during the 18th and first half of the 19th century.

Tin eventually came into its own from the mid-1850s, and, after an alarming slump in tin prices between 1865 and 1867, peaked in production around 1873. During this time, many women and girls were employed to work at surface, eventually outstripping the number employed at the copper mines as they closed, from about 1856 onwards. Probably the highest number of females employed at the tin mines was between 1855 and 1860. A description from this time gives some idea of their working environment:

'Soon the scene presented another abrupt and extraordinary change. We had hitherto been walking amid almost silence and solitude; but now with each succeeding minute strange, mingled, unintermitting noises began to grow louder and louder around us. We followed a sharp curve in the tramway, and immediately found ourselves saluted by an entirely new prospect, and surrounded by an utterly bewildering noise. All about us monstrous wheels were turning slowly, machinery was clanking and groaning in the hoarsest discords; invisible waters were pouring onwards with a rushing sound; high above our heads, on skeleton platforms, iron chains clattered fast and fiercely over iron pulleys, and huge steam pumps puffed and gasped, and slowly raised and depressed their heavy black beams of wood. Far beneath the embankment on which we stood, men women and children were breaking and washing ore in a perfect marsh of copper coloured mud and copper coloured water. We had penetrated to the very centre of the noise, the bustle, and the population on the surface of a great mine.' [7]

The Dressing Floor

As with the copper dressing floors, the layout at the tin mines was designed to minimise effort in transporting ore, but was also dependent on good supplies of water. In mines where there was no regular supply of water ore was carried to nearby stamps, which had been built where the water supply was more reliable, for dressing. This was done by mule or pack horse in the early days, or by wagon later on, Even so, stamps could sometimes lie idle from May to October, for lack of water. These separate stamps were sometimes managed by the mine, but were frequently privately-owned. In the parish of St Agnes, in 1790, so much tin was being raised that twenty-five different stamps were at work in the parish, employing a total of one hundred and fifty people. At about the same time, six different privately-owned tin stamps were operating in the Redruth area, all of which received tin-stuff for crushing from Wheal Sparnon. In the late 19th century, ore-stone was sent down from by tram East Pool Mine to be crushed at the stamps at Tolvaddon. The women and girls who worked at the stamps were sometimes referred to in the census records as *'tin stamps workers (or girls)'* or *'stamps maids'*.

The Dressing Process

In contrast to the tin extracted from the river beds or the sea, tin mined from depth had not been weathered, and therefore needed much more dressing and preparation. Also, unlike copper, which can be smelted as small pieces, tin needed to be reduced to fine grains first. As a result, the mines had to set up extensive dressing floors to prepare the ore for smelting.

Some of the processes required for dressing tin ore were quite different from those used for dressing copper, due to the very different nature of the two ores. Even the words for the material brought to grass were different. At the copper mines, it was referred to as ore-stuff, or 'hures'. At the tin mines it was called 'tin-stuff'. Although there were some processes in common, such as washing and picking, spalling, buddling and jigging, other processes were developed which took into account the much heavier and more robust nature of tin.

On landing, the tin-stuff was picked, and washed, with larger pieces being spalled, in much the same way as copper. Unlike copper, however, all the tin-stuff was then taken to stamps for crushing, instead of being manually cobbed and bucked. In 1839, Ure sums up the process of dressing of tin at Polgooth Mine in this way:

'The ore on issuing [from the stamps], *deposits its rough in the first basin, and slimes in the following basins. The rough is washed in buddles and tossing-tubs, and the slimes in trunks and upon a kind of twin tables, called racks.'* [8]

Here, we are given a very simple over-view of the fate of the two main portions of tin-stuff which were separated after passing through the grate at the stamps; the coarser sandier part, and the finer 'slimes'. While each part of the process would entail many stages of washing and various modifications in different mines, the general principles followed here in the early 19th century were not to change significantly until the 1890s (Fig. 25). Each mine tended to develop its own procedures, according to tradition, the economic climate and the properties of the minerals involved.

As with copper, each process usually involved the dressers in recognising and separating three grades of material: the ore that required no further dressing and was pure enough to be sent for sampling and sale, mixed materials with enough value to warrant further separation, and waste.

The main technological improvements made in the tin mines during the 18th and the first half of the 19th centuries were made in below-ground extraction techniques. The introduction of mechanisation on the dressing floor was much slower, the most significant development being the improved effectiveness of the stamps. Other innovations, such as self-acting frames, were not introduced until about 1860. These were followed fairly rapidly by other mechanisations in the 1880s and 1890s so that most of the female labour on the dressing floor had been replaced by the early 1900s.

Picking and Washing

In the early days, the tin-stuff, on being landed, was loaded into hand barrows and tipped into heaps to be sorted and washed. This mixture of ore and waste was called 'spaller' [10] and was generally hand-picked by young girls. Sometimes the picking was done after spalling, rather than before. Either way, the task was the same in principle. Bal maidens discarded the waste, and selected the good quality tin-stuff of a suitable size for crushing. The pieces that were too large, or had medium ore content were then spalled. This sorting was not an easy task, as the 'values' were often difficult to distinguish from waste. Due to the more difficult nature of this task it may have been that older girls were used than at the copper mines. At Charlestown Mines in 1841, the three girls who were employed picking were all between the ages of 16 and 18, whereas at the copper mines girls of 9 or 10 were commonly employed. Other girls or women would also wash the ore, if required (Fig. 21).

Spalling

Tin-stuff (after being ragged by the men) was broken (spalled) with a long-handled hammer weighing between three and seven pounds, into fist-sized pieces. As with copper, this would be done on special cobbled dressing floors near to where the tin-stuff was landed. (For instance, the remains of one of these floors can still be clearly seen at King Edward Mine.) At some mines where dressing space was limited (such as on steep hillsides or on cliff ledges), it is thought that 'spalling braces' may have been installed instead. These consisted of platforms built on the shaft tackle, by attaching beams to the shaft legs. Such an apparatus is believed to have been used at Cape Cornwall.[9]

The spalled pieces would then be re-picked to remove more waste, and the remainder sent to the stamps. Spalling was often carried out in the open air, and sometimes under appalling weather conditions:

'On the hill at Dolcoath the girls had to face wind and rain, and soon had to 'touch pipe' as they were drenched and cold, and when standing before the fierce fire in the little shed the steam rose in clouds from their garments; yet they soon resumed their labours.' (Cornishman 5th Jan. 1893)

The quantity of material that bal maidens were able to spall varied with the quality and type of tin-stuff. At Dolcoath in 1893, it was estimated that one woman or girl could spall between three and five tons of rocks per day. As spalling was a very demanding task, it was generally carried out by the older girls and the younger women. Herbert Thomas had this to say about the skills and strength required:

'Even for strong girls who have the knack of striking rocks at the right spot and breaking four or five tons a day to a size suitable for the stamps, the wages are decidedly well earned.'

However, it was not just older girls who were put to this task. When 17 year-old Elizabeth Hocking was interviewed by the *1842 Royal Commission*, she had been spalling tin at the Charlestown Mines for three years.[10] Annie Roberts broke stone from East Pool Mine, ready for the tin crushers at Tolvaden Stamps, during her teenage years in the 1890s. Annie Martin, a spaller at Dolcoath Mine, was slightly older (23 years old) when she was involved in quite a serious accident in 1892.

Figs. 26 & 27 Tincroft Spallers
(above, *courtesy of Paddy Bradley*, below *courtesy of Cornwall Centre Collection*)

Stamping

After spalling, the tin-stuff was taken to the stamps or the crushers. In the earliest days, the moving of stuff to the stamps, if on site at the mine, was done by hand barrowing with an army of girls and women. If the stamps were some distance away, material was carried on mules, or in carts. Latterly, it was trammed in wagons. Ore was usually gravity-fed under the stamp heads. There the tin-stuff was forced through a fine copper mesh into a series of collection pits. When settled, the fine particles of tin and quartz-rock sediment were dug out of these pits and sent for further processing.

Serving the Buddles

By the mid 19th century, the collection pits were replaced by longer sedimentation areas called strips. Using a Cornish shovel, bal maidens would stir the tin-stuff in the flowing stream of water to allow the lighter waste to wash away. After settlement, they would dig out the different grades from the strips, ready to be taken on to the next processes (the best going to the buddles). In 1858, Henderson described how there would normally be two such strips supplying each buddle.[11]

The coarser sediments were separated by buddling, in much the same way as copper. Initially, in the late 18th century, square buddles were used, which were wooden boxes approximately 7 ft x 3 ft x 2 ft, with a 2 ft incline. A dresser stood or sat on a board across the buddle, and worked the ore with a broom or bare feet to help separate the different grades of particles. By 1850, square buddles were still in use, but were gradually being replaced by the Cornish round buddles with mechanised sweeping arms.

It took about ten hours for each of these large buddles to be filled. As at the copper mines, boys usually looked after the buddles, but girls were sometimes involved in assisting them. One of these was Minnie Andrews who worked at Tincroft, in the late 1880s:

'Then I used to buddly in the strip and used either to work with a shovel in the strip, keeping them going, water coming down, washing it all down and filling up the buddle. A buddle would go round with sweeps to it, and then the young men would clean un up and then I should fill un again. I filled twice a day.' [12]

This work was also remembered by a Troon bal maiden, in later life:

'The buddles used to fill up and had to be cleaned out three times a day. They had to be cleaned out about half past nine, then again before dinner and again in the afternoon. Four men cleaned out the buddles. They wheeled the head to me in a wheelbarrow and I had to return it to the buddle again for another washing. That was done three times, then it had to be taken to the packing house. I liked a sharp shovel, the sharper the better. I used to take mine to the men to be sharpened.' [13]

In 1841, three girls between the ages of 13 and 18 were employed in *'serving the buddles'* at Wheal Vor. By the 1880s, it was older girls and women who assisted in this way, as can be seen in the photograph of Wheal Basset.

Fig. 28 Serving Buddles, Wheal Basset c. 1900. *Courtesy of Paddy Bradley*

Tozing, Chimming and Packing

The medium-coarse sediment from the stamps, or lower-grade ores from second buddling, was sometimes shovelled into large kieves (barrels), about three feet in diameter, which had already been half-filled with water. Two boys or girls would carry out this task, carefully tipping the sediment down the side of the kieve with a shovel, whilst a third child constantly stirred the mixture with a shovel. This stirring was carefully done in one direction only, in order to assist separation of the ore from the lighter waste. Sediment would continue to be added until the water level had risen to within two inches of the top of the kieve. When this was done, one of the boys or girls would then strike the kieve with an iron bar, which was usually fixed into the ground at one end, to settle out the sediment. This could take between fifteen and sixty minutes, and needing about one hundred blows per minute. Burritt describes a bal maiden carrying out this task with a slightly different hammer arrangement:

'One process was quite primitive and amusing. At a certain stage of purification the solution was put into large tubs and a great wooden hammer, like a beetle, was hung by a cord suspended from a beam over-head. This was swung by a girl against the tub, to assist the settling of the metal at the bottom.' (Burritt 1855 p. 319)

TIN MINES & SMELTERS

Fig. 29 Tozing and Packing Tin
Henderson c.1858

When the packing was finished, the surplus water was baled into a second kieve alongside, ready for the next tozing. Then, the thin top layer of waste or mixed ore (not more than half an inch) was removed using a 'limp' (semi-circular piece of wood) and put aside to be rebuddled. The settled white sediment in the bottom of the kieve was ready for roasting, to remove any arsenic impurities. This sediment was called 'whits'. After roasting, the whits were usually returned for re-buddling, or kieving. From 1860, mines began to install water-powered wooden hammers for this laborious task of packing. In 1858, Henderson recorded: *'This saves the time of the child who might be more usefully and certainly more comfortably employed. The occupation of packing being anything but a pleasant one during the winter season.'* Chimming was a variation on tozing, where the kieve was tipped at an angle of 45 degrees.

Dilluing

This was an ancient process, and was mentioned by Pryce in 1778, as well as Henderson in 1858. The tails (waste) from the buddles were sometimes placed in a hair-bottomed sieve and shaken in a kieve of water. With dexterous working, the light particles could be washed off, similar to gold-panning, and the remainder returned to the stamps. The fine particles in the bottom of the kieve (dilluing smalls) would then be re-buddled. This task was performed by women or boys.

Jigging

In the 18th and early 19th century, the finest sediment from the stamps was taken for jigging, as at the copper mines. It was passed through a very fine copper-based sieve, shaken in a hutch (barrel) of water, and the pure tin ore left in the bottom of the sieve was sent for sampling. The even finer sediment in the bottom of the hutch was sent on to be framed. Jigging was generally done by young boys, but occasionally by young women. This was very difficult, wet and heavy work. The process was semi-mechanised by the 1830s, and fully mechanised, except for filling and emptying, by about 1860 (Fig. 24). Bal maidens Elizabeth, Mary Ann and Margaret James of Carnyorth Moor had all *'worked the jigs'* during the 1860s.

Trunking

The finest of the slimes collected after stamping were dried and the taken to the trunks. These consisted of a circular strake, sluice and settling area. The slimes were agitated with water in the strakes, and then allowed to flow out through the sluice into a rectangular settling box. The purest tin settling out at the head was then barrowed to the frames, ready for framing, and the rest was either disposed of as waste or re-trunked. Trunking was usually done by girls. At Wheal Vor, in 1841, there was one girl responsible for *'trunking slimes'* in this way, and she was under 13 years of age.

Framing

This was also known as racking (or recking), and was the process of separating out tiny tin particles from the very finest grade of waste. It was the most delicate process in the dressing of tin ore, and interestingly, in 1778, Pryce describes this task being carried out by boys and elderly men. However, it seems that certainly by the 1840s (if not considerably earlier) it was done by women and girls. The skill required (before automation), as with buddling, was considerable. This separation took place in wooden frames, usually built in ranks. Each frame was made up of two main portions, the head and the body, all inclined at a slope of about one in seven. The fine tin-stuff was laid in ridges on the 'jagging board' at the head of the frame. Furrows parallel to the flow of water were made by the bal maiden 'jagging' with the edge of a rake. By careful management of the water flow, the tin particles collected at the top of the frame, while the lighter waste sediment would run off at the bottom. The girl in charge of the frame would stand to one side and encourage this separation with a light brush or feather, or, later, by a toothless rake. When the separation was complete, she would then tip the frame over, using a fork or rake, and wash the tin concentrate into the two collecting hutches, or chests, underneath. The top hutch would collect the purest ore; the lower one the mixed grade (which would be taken for re-treatment).

The first technological development of the frames came with a self-supplying design. Prior to this, one girl operated two frames, one on either side of where she was standing (Fig 30). These new ones seem to have been installed in two lines of eight, with one girl responsible for four at a time - four girls to each section.[14] However, by the end of the 1850s, some self-acting frames were beginning to be used, which would tip up and empty automatically. This meant that one boy or girl could oversee twenty or thirty frames at once. Among the first installed were at St Day United Mines. Apparently, the mechanically tilting frames did not prove a success and were not used universally. A photo from Dolcoath, in the 1890s, appears to show double frames, ranked over each other, with one woman responsible for about fifty (Fig 10).

TIN MINES & SMELTERS

Fig. 30 Bal Maidens at Racking Frames
Henderson c. 1858

Framing was usually carried out by young girls in their mid or late teens. Only two of the girls interviewed by the *1842 Royal Commission* worked at the racking frames. They were Elizabeth Hocking and Elizabeth Davey, both employed at Charlestown Mines, who started framing at the ages of 13 and 17 years, respectively. Of a total of thirty-seven girls employed at the frames at Charlestown, all were between the ages of 16 and 18. In the census, it was unusual for particular dressing tasks to be recorded, however, in 1861, Elizabeth Foy, aged 13 years, from Porkellis, and Peggy Phill, aged 61 years, and Margaret White, aged 18 years, of Amalebra were described as a '*stamps framers*'.

In the early days, when one girl was responsible for just two frames, it seems that this work was done under cover, in open-fronted sheds, built in ranks. The later self-supplying and self-acting frames, constructed in large blocks, were generally built in the open air. Minnie Andrews gave a graphic description her outdoor work at the frames, in about 1882:

'*I first went to work when I was nine year old. I was turt* [taught] *to the frames and cleaning the holes and getting the water to run, and taking out gravels out from the holes; it did choke up the holes, you know, they things. Oh, I worked awful hours, mister, because I been dying with the cold, my hands, no wonder they go dead, I didn't, they don't go dead, my lor.*' [15]

In addition to looking after the frames, the bal maidens sometimes also 'stanked widths'. This involved treading (puddling) the tin-stuff that had been separated at the frames into the collecting tanks underneath, so that the water rose up out of it and was drained away. The tin ore was then relatively dry for carrying to the calciner (if containing arsenic) or for sampling.[16]

Fig. 31 Bal Maidens at Racking Frames, South Wheal Frances, c. 1890
Courtesy of Paddy Bradley

Barrowing and Carrying

As in the copper mines, a continual flow of tin-stuff, ore, and waste, through the dressing operation was vital, and so the effective barrowing between different processes was very important. Most of the barrowing was done by girls and women, using hand barrows of the same design as at the copper mines, with a carrying capacity of one and a half hundredweight (Fig. 3). Some of the hand barrowing was replaced by wagons, tramways or overhead 'telepherage' by about 1860. However, some mines, for example Old Wheal Vor, continued to hand barrow beyond this date, especially over rough ground.

The bal maidens were also sometimes moved from their normal jobs to other carrying or lifting tasks on the dressing floors. For instance, Mrs. Collins, of Troon, remembered how she was sometimes called away from the strips to help with moving kieves of water when she worked at Wheal Grenville:

'*Sometimes we had to help the men. We filled the kieves with water from the launder and then carried a kieve of water across to the men, as much as two of us could lift.*'

TIN MINES & SMELTERS

Fig. 32 Bal Maidens Barrowing, West Wheal Seaton c. 1890
Courtesy of the Cornwall Centre Collection

SAMPLING

The complete process of dressing tin ore took from eight to ten days, during which time the concentration of tin was raised from less than 2% in the tin-stuff brought from the mine, to between 60 and 90% in the samples that were ready for sale and smelting.[17]

As at the copper mines, normal work on the dressing floors was suspended on a regular basis, in order to prepare the dressed ore for sampling and sale. At these times, the women and girls were often diverted from their normal tasks, in order to mix the dressed ores, and then barrow them into the separate parcels. This is illustrated by the night captain's entry for Dolcoath for 1823:

'They have been mixing the tin very late tonight and there has been little drawing.' [18]

This process was carried out as for copper. Some of the women in the West Wheal Frances (Fig. 30) appear to be involved in sampling, with one of the doles of ore being laid out in the background on the right hand side of the picture.

Women were sometimes employed in the sampling office, as assistants to the assayer. 21 year-old Emily Richards of Camborne, and 23 year-old Margaret Bennett were both described as a *'sample refiner'* in 1891. Around the same time, a Miss Bickerleg was employed at Dolcoath. Her story is told more fully in chapter 12.

OTHER TASKS AT THE TIN MINE

As at the copper mines, women or girls were also employed at the horse whim to draw kibbles (buckets) of ore up from the mine to surface. In 1857 and 1858, Charity Jewell was working at the East Whim at Wheal Widden (Trumpet Consols) raising ore, as well as occasionally drawing water. In February 1857, she raised 707 kibbles and was paid 4s per 100. She was sometimes recorded as working with a partner, and her wages were paid over to Henry Jewell (described as a *'mine horseman'*), possibly either her father or husband. At the same mine, Jane Carter (presumably a small child) was paid 1s 10d and 1s in June 1861 and 1862, respectively, for 'weeding' at the mine.

SECOND STREAMING (TIN STREAMS)

From the early 18th century, individual families or venturers often applied for leases to search riverbeds and streams for waste tin washed down from the waste outlets of the deep mines. This involved collecting the very fine tin which had escaped the final dressing processes. This was formally referred to as 'second tinning' (or tin salvage or recovery) but confusingly referred to, in common parlance, as 'tin streaming'. (Not to be confused with the original tin streaming, which exploited naturally-weathered tin, deposited in the river beds over many years).

One of the first references to females being involved in this type of streaming comes from the pen of William Pryce. He describes how many poor people of Perranworthal parish scraped a meagre living from the tin washed down from the tin mines on the Perran, Carnon and Kennal rivers, some seventy years previously:

'The low sands under Perranworthal, which are covered almost every tide by the sea, have, on its going off, employed some hundreds of poor men, women and children incapable of earning their bread by any other means occasioned by the refuse and leavings from the stamping mills which are carried by the rivers down to the lower grounds, and after some years of lying and collecting there, yielded some money to the laborious dressers.' [19]

A. K. Hamilton Jenkin's forebear, William, was steward for the Devoran Estate in the 1720s. He described how these tin streamers did not have to pay dues to the mineral Lord, but only the rent for the water to wash the tin-stuff.[20] In 1775, Cunnack gave even more detail:

'At low spring tides when the creek is low, wash works can be seen. Some time ago the country people began to wash the mud, and poor people can often make 30 to 40s and up to £3 per month.'
(Cunnack 1775 p. 22)

In the 1850s, it was calculated that between 17% and 33% of tin from the deeper mines was never recovered. It was this 'lost tin' which was the lifeblood of the second streamers. It became even more profitable to reclaim this tin during the early part of the 1870s. This was because the deep-mined tin tended to be very fine-grained, and the newly designed Californian stamps liberated more of this fine tin from the tin-stuff than the Cornish stamps previously. As a result, higher levels of fine tin accumulated in the 'slimes' after stamping. However, not much of this newly available fine cassiterite was recovered during the subsequent dressing operations. This meant that huge quantities of tin found their way into the rivers and streams serving as outflows from the mines, and some estimated that as much as 40% to 50% of the tin was being lost at this time.[21] Barton described it in this way:

'The only aspect of production which failed to keep pace with this technical revolution was tin dressing and a great deal of cassiterite stamped out of the ore was certainly being lost.'

Because most of the tin to be extracted from these water courses had already been through long processes of dressing, its recovery required little investment. Most tin streams operated with water-powered stamps, buddles and frames. These tin stream works were often set up in sequence down a stream or river bed, over many miles. In 1877, it was estimated that machinery worth £40,000 had been installed just on the one and a half miles of the Red River below Tucking Mill. By 1879, one eighth of all Cornish tin came from stream works and on the Red River alone, at least twenty tin stream works were in operation.

Despite these comparatively simple operations (requiring less capital investment), the tin streams were as sensitive to tin prices as the deep mines, and many operations closed in the depressions of 1879 and the 1890s, probably contributing considerable numbers to the total who became unemployed in those years, and causing a crisis situation for Cornwall on both occasions. The tin streams, unlike the mines though, were able to respond more quickly when tin prices picked up again. For instance, by 1884, there was once again a thriving tin stream industry with twenty-eight operating in the Red River Valley (employing over 850), nineteen on the Portreath River (employing 139) and a further ten (employing 120) elsewhere in the county. The most notable of these were on Crinnis Moor (St Austell), and at Darley Ford (Linkinhorne) and Wheal Vor Flow (Breage). A good proportion of these employees would have been women and girls.[22]

Although the tin streams required little investment, they were very labour-intensive. Some stream works employed very large numbers, mostly children, and sometimes tin dressing continued around the clock, with the women and children working shifts.[23] Reskadinnick was one of the largest, with 210 people employed in the 1870s. It had three quarters of an acre of settling pits, buddles and frames. In 1877, a total of over 2000 frames and about 100 buddles were in operation at nine tin streams in one and a half miles of the Red River. When Relubbus Streams, in the Cobor Valley, was put up for sale in 1881, there were eight water wheels, three scoop wheels, eight heads of stamps, one hundred framing frames, and fifty-seven dead frames for auction, giving an indication of the number of boys and girls who may have been employed there.

Muriel Sara remembered visiting a 'courtesy aunt' who worked at a tin stream (either at Gwithian or Portreath) in the 1890s. This is how she described the working conditions:

'These tin streams were rather like a field of red water and sand, with wooden bridges or planks that led you over it, and at certain places there were big brush machines that the bal maidens worked. Aunt Harris would show us how things were used and let us try at times to work the great brush, not so easy as it looked.' [24]

In 1895, the tin streams on the Portreath River returned over 25% of the total tin sold in the area, and some proved to be more profitable than the deep mines which had lost the same tin in the first place. Mr. B. Bennetts, whose family owned one of the tin streams near Dolcoath for many years, estimated that, at the turn of the 19th century, at least 500 women and girls were employed on the Red River group of tin streams alone.[25] Some bal maidens were still working at W. G. Hocking's Tin Streams at Reskaddinick in 1915, and they were described in this way:

'There were about a dozen bal maidens working there then. They were all good maidens. Some of them was [sic] strong, like men....They worked hard, wheeling barrows to the buddles and keeping them tidy. They also looked after the round frames, there was one maiden to each. One of their jobs was 'stankin widths', that is treading heavily on a width of tin stuff that had been through the frames. All the water would then come up from it so that it was pretty dry before it went to the burning house.' [26]

The tin streams on the Red River were the most tenacious of all; Reskadinnick being the very last one operating. It eventually closed in 1920. (It subsequently re-opened but only for a short time).

RE-PICKING OF TIN WASTE

As with copper, there were occasions when it became economically viable to re-pick old tin waste. For example, Emma Jane Jenkin, 18 years old, was recorded as working at the tin 'burrows' in the Marazion area in 1861, and Mary Oats of Ludgvan Leane was working at 'tin burrows' in 1871. The waste burrows at Balleswidden and Ding Dong Mines were re-sorted and stamped at about the time of the First World War. New Cornish stamps were installed at Ding Dong and nearly 14,000 tons of ore, yielding 51 tons of black tin, were extracted between 1912 and 1915. Similarly, during the Second World War, re-dressing of waste heaps was carried out at a number of mines, such as Wheel Reeth, Dolcoath and Drakeswall. These tasks may have been carried out by women or girls, but no records have yet been found.

Apart from formal employment at these waste heaps, re-dressing had probably been the source of money through the informal economy for as long as mining had occurred in Cornwall and Devon. Unemployed miners and their families would eke out a living from re-picking tin and selling it to local tin stamps. This was particularly true in times of high unemployment such as during the 1880s and early 1890s. Small groups of tributers were working in this way at Poldice and Gwennap, where they sold over 5,100 tons of tin stone to stamps at Bissoe or on the Red River in 1890. Similarly, an amazing 120,000 tons of tin stone is believed to have been collected and sold from old burrows at Clifford Amalgamated Mines, after its closure in 1870.[27]

TIN SMELTING

Until the turn of the 18th century, tin was smelted in blowing houses or 'ore hearths', usually built near the tin works. They required charcoal or 'moor coal' (peat) for fuel. They were usually built in exposed places that could provide good ventilation to the furnace, in order to achieve the very high temperature required to melt the tin ore. It is not known whether women were involved in these early smelting processes.

By about 1700, finding wood for charcoal, or suitable moor coal, was becoming increasingly difficult, with much being brought by mule from distant places, such as Dartmoor. As a result, in 1703, the first iron furnaces were built in Cornwall. They used fossil coal from Wales, and could also process larger quantities of tin quickly. The first furnaces were in operation in Newham by 1703, which were superseded by Calenick by 1711 (both near Truro on the Fal) and at Angarrack, near Hayle, by 1704. These smelters, in contrast to the hill and moorland positions of the blowing houses and ore hearths, required easy access to the shore or a harbour to enable delivery of coal and other commodities. A third such reverbatory tin smelter was also opened on th Fal by a different operator about a mile away from Newham, at Treyew.

From cost and receipt books for Newham Smelter from 1704 to 1707, there are regular entries for women carrying this coal from the shore to the yard, for which they appear to have been paid between 2d and 2.5d per ton:

'*Twenty second day of November 1704 received by the barrow women for carriage of thirty two tons weight £3 5s 6d, signed* [mark of] *Martha Crips, Elizabeth Traffon.*'

On 31st May 1706, Ann Stevens was paid three shillings for carrying 1,500 bricks ashore. If these women were using the standard 1.5 cwt hand barrow for carriage, this means that they were being paid 2d for about seven journeys, which presumably would involve the filling and emptying of the barrows at either end. If their round trip from the smelter to the shore took as little as fifteen minutes, they may be able to earn about 6d to 8d per day.

Specific entries indicate when women were paid for barrowing coal from the ships to the smelting yard, when they were paid by the ton. Other entries show that women were also barrowing ore, coal, lime etc. at the smelter itself, but for this they seem to have been paid a daily rate. This barrowing was combined with sifting slag, culm and cinders, and the going rate was 6d per day. Presumably, these tasks involved sieving the coal on arrival, to remove fine dust and particles before it was used to fuel the furnace. Sieving of the slag and cinders could only be done when they were cold, and this would be to recover ore for re-smelting, or re-usable coal.

It is possible that women and girls were also employed at Treyew Smelter, whose manager was charged, in 1713, with luring away '*covenanted servants*' (presumably apprentices sworn to secrecy over these new processes). In the court case, it was stated that at Treyew '*day labourers were employed at the usual wages*', some of whom may have been female.[28]

There is very little subsequent information about females employed at tin smelters. However, Mary Curnow of Lelant was described as a tin smelter in 1841, and Eliza Bryant and Susan Thomas are both described as working at a smelting works in Redruth in 1871. In 1891, 40 year-old Amelia Rowe, and her 17 year-old daughter Kate (from Chenhalls, St Erth) were working at a tin smelter, probably at Chyandour, on the outskirts of Penzance.

THE FINAL YEARS OF TIN

From the 1850s onwards, innovations on the tin dressing floors meant fewer people were employed. With public feeling growing against the employment of women and children at mines in general, it was hardly surprising that it was the girls and women who were often the first to lose their jobs. For example, when a new water wheel was installed at Great Wheal Busy in 1857, to work a set of thirty self-acting frames, one small boy was employed to do the work of six or seven girls! [29]

As copper prices fell, some copper mines struggled on and eventually found tin at depth, such as Dolcoath, West Wheal Basset, West Wheal Frances and South Condurrow. They installed tin dressing equipment to replace the existing machinery, including new stamps, and continued to employ some girls and women at spalling, picking and to operate the framing frames. At Providence Mine, the improvements included roofing the entire dressing floor, giving shelter to all 150 working there (although providing shelter was not a universal feature at this time). Another mine that offered covered working areas for dressing in the 1870s was St Ives Consols. The advertisement listing items for sale, when the mine closed in 1875, gives an indication of the equipment used at this time:

'Tin floors, together with the excellent and lofty woodshed covering the same, 21 large centre headed buddles, 6 square ditto, 124 self-acting and other tin frames, Brunton's Calciner and waterwheel, 4 water wheels for dressing machinery, tin kieves and all the necessary dressing tools for a large mine.' (MJ 16th Oct. 1875)

Tin production stayed at reasonable levels from 1870 until 1890, although tin prices started to drop again from about 1873, resulting in more closures. In 1873, there had been over 230 mines producing tin in Cornwall but only 98 remained open in 1877, with massive loss in the jobs of both underground and surface workers. Those tin mines that stayed open found it economically expedient to remodel their dressing floors yet again and install improved or semi-automated equipment, so that, although the total amount of tin produced did not radically alter, it was raised and dressed by half the number of people. This reduction was mostly in the number of children, especially in the younger age group, because they could no longer be employed after the passing of the *Factory and Workshop Act of 1878*. As many as 60 young people were dismissed from Dolcoath at this time. However, Dolcoath was to continue to employ bal maidens in fairly large numbers, with 745 surface workers employed at the peak of its tin production in 1893.

In 1893, there was another drop in the price of tin, so, by 1897, only nine tin mines remained open in Cornwall. In 1895, for instance, the 70 surface workers were laid off at South Condurrow. Between 1891 and 1898, the number of surface workers employed at the tin mines in Cornwall had fallen from nearly 6,000 to 2,500, most of these losses being women. At Dolcoath in 1908, the tasks left for women were spalling, (still considered by some to be the most economic way of reducing waste at the point the tin-stuff arrived from underground), sorting and framing. In 1910, Tincroft was still employing a few women, but just 67 out of the total workforce of nearly 1,000.

Eventually even these tasks were mechanised. Hand sorting was replaced by automated shaking and separating tables, Californian Stamps and Husband's Stamps replaced the spallers, and Frue Vanners were used to separate the finer wastes, replacing the women and girls who attended the frames. These processes only required one or two employees to oversee them where, previously, dozens had been needed. Training to operate these machines was always given to male employees. The last women at the tin streams seem to have finished by the end of the First World War and the last spalling maidens at the deep mines were dismissed from Dolcoath in 1921.[30]

Fig. 33 Women at Geevor Picking Belt, Second World War
Courtesy of Geevor Tin Mine

There was a final brief recall during the Second World War, when women and girls were needed to replace some of the surface men who had volunteered for war service, at Geevor Tin Mine. At 16 years old, Richard Lawry was one of eight boys who normally worked on the picking belts. He described the day when this was to change dramatically, when they were all moved into new jobs:

'One day, at the age of 16, I was asked to show the girls how to tell the difference between a granite stone from the others, and what to do with those stones.'

He taught the six new recruits to distinguish the white and black flecked granite, which they then needed to lift out and throw down a chute onto a conveyor, to be carried to the waste heaps. They would leave the remaining material (which contained tin, copper, spar and mundic) on the belt, to be taken on to the crushers. From that day, Richard no longer worked at the picking belt himself. Instead, he had sole charge of operating the picking belt machinery, and of overseeing the women and girls at their work. Many years later he could still remember the names of those recruits: *'Cora Collins, Bella Prowse, Jean Polglase, Josephine Mathews, Sylvia Angove, and Phyllis Mathews down Lower Boscaswell.'* [31] These women were employed until the end of the war. This, finally, was the end of a very long association between women, girls and tin mining.

FOOTNOTES

1. Brooke (1994).
2. NTA: PRP SC.2,161/81 p. 64.
3. Greeves (2006) p. 8; Tin Works Leases (PDRO: 72/990/ Part 4 + 6).
4. Lemon (1838) p. 74.
5. Personal correspondence (PT/LM 2001); RCG 12th Oct 1877.
6. This chapter draws heavily on information from Barton (1989) especially pp. 84,138, 169, 175, 182-3, 211, 230 and 242.
7. Collins, Wilkie *Rambles Beyond Railways* (1861) in Messenger (2001) p. 32.
8. Ure's (1839) p. 1250.
9. Von Arx, R. 'A Glimpse at Cape Cornwall Mine' *British Mining* Vol. 43 Memoirs (1991) p. 43.
10. Throughout this chapter information is drawn from the *1842 Royal Commission on the Employment of Women and Young People* [CEC] especially p. 55, Table 17, and Evidence Nos. 103 + 104.
11. Throughout this chapter information is drawn from Henderson (1858) especially pp. 195-208.
12. Brooke (1967).
13. Troon WI (1852) p. 17.
14. Salmon (1860) p. 23-24.
15. Brooke (1967).
16. Tangye (1988) p. 53.
17. Fergusson (1873) p. 129.
18. Buckley (2007) p. 45.
19. Pryce (1778) p. 136.
20. Hamilton Jenkin, (1967) p. 42.
21. Salmon (1860) p. 215.
22. HMSO. *Mining and Mineral Statistics of the United Kingdom* 1884 p. 252.
23. Barton (1968) p. 56.
24. Sara (1970) p. 43.
25. Troon WI (1952) p. 4.
26. Tangye (1988) p. 53.
27. Minutes of the Cornish Tin Mining Advisory Committee (CRO: X 161).
28. Barton (1970) p. 97.
29. Henwood, G. (1857) p. 157.
30. Troon WI (1952) p. 12.
31. Lawry, Richard Nicholas *Scrapbook of Memories of a Pendeen Man; My Early Life* p. 23.

Chapter 6

THE 'CLAY' MAIDENS

Although the majority of women and girls employed in the mining-related industries in Cornwall and Devon were employed in the tin and copper mines, a considerable number also worked at the various clay pits. A few also worked at the soapstone quarries and glass (potash felspar) mines.

The granites of South West Britain have, in places, been extensively altered. China clay and china stone has been extracted where felspar, one of the chief minerals in the granite, has been broken down by fluids and vapours and converted into kaolinite. Commercial china clay is made up almost entirely of kaolinite, hence its alternative name, kaolin. This kaolinised granite is often found in association with veins of tin, but was little used before the second half of the 18th century. For instance, Carclaze, which was to produce significant amounts of china clay, was initially mined for tin for well over a century, with the china clay being discarded as waste.

When well-kaolinised ground was soft enough, it was washed out as a thick slurry of mineral particles, the finest of which was kaolin. The coarser waste particles of mica and sand dropped out of the suspension in successive settling pits, and the remaining fine clay was settled in pans and slowly dried before cutting into blocks, ready for sale as china clay. In harder ground, where the granite was only partially kaolinised, the mineral was quarried and sold in lump form as china stone, or ground and sold as china stone powder.

It was not until the 1760s that the full potential of these products in the manufacture of fine porcelain was realised. The Bristol, Worcester, and Staffordshire potteries took both china clay and china stone in equal quantities. However, during the 19th century, many other uses were found for the china clay, especially as a filler in fabrics and paper. During this time, production expanded enormously.

CHINA CLAY HISTORY

Whilst china clay working is mostly associated with the St Austell area, the first commercial exploitation in Cornwall, in 1746, was at Tregonning Hill, between Helston and Marazion. Good quality clay was then also discovered at Carloggas, near St Stephen-in-Brannel. Prior to this, only very small amounts had been dug out by the farmers or landowners, and sold to local potters for earthenware production, or used for making bricks, fireboxes for mine steam engines, or casting moulds.

China clay was quarried in a small way in the 18th century, but during the 19th century it became a large-scale industry. By 1809, 3,000 tons of china clay and stone was being exported through the Charlestown Docks. The earliest mention of women and girls working at the clay pits was in 1812, and refers to Trethosa Clay Work, along with others:

'It is probable also that from time to time, and in other small works then active, women and children were also employed on the simpler and lighter tasks.' [1]

Although the word 'bal' was not applied to the clay works, it is interesting that the term 'bal maiden' was thought to have also applied to the women and girls who worked at the clay pits, as well as at the mines.[2] They were involved in drying, cleaning and packing of clay. In census returns, more functional descriptions were used such as *'clay worker'*, *'china clay labourer'*, *'clay scraper'*, *'clay cleaner'* or occasionally *'china clay girl'* or *'clay refiner.'*

By 1845, at least forty-five pits were open, and by 1851 the volume of clay produced had increased to 98,000 tons. By 1852, it was estimated that the total number of employees at the West of England Clay Works, operating in the Hensbarrow area north of St Austell, was about 7,200, of whom a proportion would have been women and girls. In 1864, the five 'china clay' parishes of the St Austell area (St. Austell, St Stephen, St Dennis, St Mewan and Roche) employed a total of 1,700 clay labourers out of a total population of 30,000, but no separate figure was given for the 'maidens'. When Esquiros travelled through Cornwall in 1865, he noted that:

'The china clay works in the St Austell area employ a large number of men, women and children.' (Esquiros 1865 p. 43)

While the largest clay works were opened around St Austell, from the late 1830s china clay deposits also began to be exploited on the southern edge of Dartmoor at Lee Moor and Wotter. Women and girls were employed there too, but with the earliest written records coming from the *1861 Census*.

From about 1865, the clay pits often offered employment when other mines in Cornwall were laying people off, but, even so, there were times when there was also desperate poverty in the clay-mining areas. During 1868, corn prices were so high, and the wages at the mines and clay pits so low, that soup kitchens were set up at Blowing House Hill, Wrestling Green, for the china clay workers. This 'Parish Relief' was available three days per week, at 1d per quart.[3]

During the 1870s, the china clay industry was actually expanding, at a time when the copper mines were in very deep trouble, and employment levels at the lead, iron and tin mines were also dropping, either due to closure or increased technology. As the market developed for the china clay, new clay pits opened. According to Hunt's annual *Mineral Statistics*, 1874 was the peak year for the number of active clay works, when one hundred and nineteen enterprises were reported for Cornwall, and ten for Devon. Most of these were in the St Austell and Par area, but some also opened in other parts of Cornwall, such as Breage, Germoe, Towednack, and Ludgvan. There is evidence of movement of personnel between these different china clay producing areas. For instance, Ellen and

Amelia Hooper, who were working at the clay works in Tresowes, Germoe in 1871, had been born in St Austell.

China clay extraction has continued to the present day, but with inevitable closures, amalgamations, and mechanisation. From 1845, coal-fired dries (or pan kilns) began to be used at the clay pits, instead of the sun pans. This meant that it was possible to dry the clay more quickly and that clay could be ready for market all the year round. As a result, where these changes were made, the women and girls were no longer required to scrape clay blocks. They were now dried in a clean state and were loaded straight from the dries into wagons by men.

Some clay works, however, continued to use the sun pan process for drying into the 20th century, as at South Carloggas, but eventually it was replaced by pan kiln drying in all the clay works, so that the women were no longer needed. Nearly all the females involved in the drying and scraping processes were laid off by the beginning of the First World War.

This was not the last time that women were employed at the clay pits, though, as some were recruited to take over the process of extracting clay when there was a shortage of employable men during the First World War. Some women were also employed to mill and pack the waste china clay sand for sandbags during the Second World War.

THE CHINA CLAY PROCESSES

Initially, the china clay 'matrix' was dug up and dumped into pits using manual labour. In these pits, it was thoroughly agitated with water, so that the clay could be decanted in suspension. By the end of the 18th century, most producers were using the less laborious technique of breaking up the clay in situ, and diverting streams of water over it. The finer particles were washed out, leaving the coarse material behind. This was then drawn up onto the waste heaps (sand-burrows). The stream of 'fines' was pumped out of the pits and then channelled in such a way that the coarser particles would sediment out sequentially into the sand and mica 'drags' (pits). These preliminary separating tasks were normally carried out by male employees; however, in the *1841 Census*, 70-year old Jenepher Jacob of Barbellingey was described as a *'sand settler'*.[4]

Eventually, only the lightest clay portion remained in suspension. This fine clay slurry was run into shallow tanks, usually about 40 ft x 12 ft and 14-18 inches deep, called sun pans. Each pan was lined with granite blocks and, before the clay slurry was poured in, it was made waterproof by lining the cracks with moss. A young child was paid to go out on to the moors to collect the moss and to fill these cracks. The bottom of the pan was then covered with sand, prior to being filled. [5]

The time it took for the settling and drying of the clay depended on the weather, but generally the clay collected in the summer and left to dry over winter (called the 'winter saving') took about eight months, and was ready for lifting sometime between March and May. The clay collected in the spring months (the 'summer saving') took about four months to dry and could be lifted in the late summer or autumn.

When the clay was dry enough to be moved (between 15% and 20% water content), it was cut up by two men using a large knife with a blade at right angles to a long handle. In the early years, various sizes and shapes were cut, including prisms and nine-inch blocks. Latterly, they were standardised to twelve inches. The men would lift these blocks out onto wooden boards placed at the side of the pans. In good weather, these blocks would be carried out onto the hillsides to dry. This is how the scene was described in 1852 and 1861 respectively:

'The scene was animated by the constant passage of women with white bonnets, aprons and sleeves carrying cubes of clay for placing beneath reeders, in sheds or in their hundreds on drying grounds on the surrounding hills, by the comings and goings of heavy sand wagons, the creak of pump and horse whim and the sound and motion of countless water-engines about their endless tasks.' [6]

'The diggers fling the lumps on a board, and boys and women carry these to the drying ground... watching the women and boys as they spread their burdens on the drying ground, all as white as only clay workers can be.' [7]

Fig. 34 Cleaning Clay Blocks Under Reeders
Courtesy of China Clay Country Park Mining & Heritage Centre

If the weather was not good enough for drying on the hillsides, the clay was carried straight to the 'reeders'. The women and girls would build the blocks into an airy tower, separating the blocks with layers of sand or straw to prevent them from adhering to each other. These towers were usually protected by a thatched roof or thatch-covered hurdle over the top, and often around the exposed sides as well, hence the name 'reeders' (Fig. 34).

When dry, it was the job of the 'maidens' to scrape the sand, straw and algae off the blocks, clean them generally, and load them into casks. Charles Thurlow suggests that it was only the better grade of china clay that was scraped in this way.[8] The cleaning was usually done in the open air, or under a simple movable shelter made from three thatched hurdles. The girls or women stood at slatted trestle tables, working on individual blocks. They used a triangular iron scraper to remove the dirt and sand (Fig. 37). Walter White, during his travels of 1854, describes the blocks being scraped with an instrument like a Dutch hoe. Alternatively, the women placed the blocks on a board held against their chests, and cleaned them by dragging a specially designed knife towards themselves, over the surface of the clay. The scrapings and other waste were collected and rewashed.

Women and girls were not just employed at the clay works for cleaning, carrying, stacking and packing the china clay. From the 1830s, rather simple bucket lift pumps were commonly used in the clay pits, when they began to operate at moderate depth. Both men and women were employed at the physically demanding task of operating them. They would work in relays, throughout the day. Such a hand pump was still operating at

Screeda as late as the 1850s (Fig. 35). In the 1920s, people could still remember women at this work, which probably ceased between 1865 and 1870.[9]

Female wagoners were contracted to cart china stone from Wheal Prosper Quarry, probably to the railway at Burngullow. A few were working in 'husband and wife' teams such as Mary Ann Williams, working with her husband William, and Catherine Boundyn, working with her husband James, in 1858 and 1862 respectively. Some, however, seem to have been working in their own right, such as Nancy Phillips and Ann Key who were transporting loads of 7.5 or 15.5 tons of china clay in 1864. They were being paid between 2.5d and 3d per ton.[10] In the *1891 Census*, Amelia Pearce and her daughter Ellen, of Boscell Farm were also recorded as a clay wagoners.

Women and girls also stepped in to do mechanical tasks when there were emergencies. During the First World War, Hettie Julian often went down into Bluebarrow Clay Works in the middle of the night to clear blocked pumps. Similarly, Helen Baker remembers how her sister would sometimes be responsible for opening or closing the mica drags 'out of hours' at the Castle an Dinas Works in Nancledra.[11]

Fig. 35 Sketch of Women Operating Hand Pumps at Clay Works
Courtesy of British Geological Survey

Women were sometimes called in to replace male clay washers who had joined the armed forces during forces during the First World War. This certainly happened at Rocks and Bluebarrow Clay Works. Two photographs in a Pochin's manual from about 1920 also show pairs of women working at the monitors at Gother's clay pit, indicating that the practice was possibly more widespread. Their work required them to handle the heavy water jets under very wet and slippery conditions, on the clay pit sides or at the bottoms. The hoses could discharge up to 750 gallons per minute, at a pressure of 100 lbs per square inch.[12]

Women were also employed at Little Treviscoe during the First World War, in the old cooperage, where they bagged powdered china clay from hoppers. This was sold as scouring powder called 'TREPOLPEN'. During the Second World War, at least four women were employed at Great Treverbyn Mill, at Par Moor, where they also worked at the mill hopper, bagging china clay (Fig. 36).[13]

Fig. 36 Great Treverbyn Mill Women Workers (Second World War)
from L-R: Audrey Brewer, Barbara Beard, Olive Hughes, and Phyllis?
Courtesy of China Clay Country Park Mining & Heritage Centre

Fig. 37 Women Clay Dressers with Scraping Tools
Courtesy of China Clay Country Park Mining & Heritage Centre

WORKING CONDITIONS

Most of the Clay Works were run on the Cost Book System, like the other Cornish mines, and used the same employment practices. So, the 'maidens' were paid monthly, either one or two months in arrears. The women and girls seem to have been paid in different ways according to the task and varying from works to works; whether laying out clay on the hillside, stacking clay in the reeders, or scraping or packing the clay blocks, once they were dried. The child who collected moss to seal the granite blocks in the sunpans at Lower Ninestones in 1828 was paid 7d per day. At Goonvean, the women and girls who carried the clay blocks out on to the moors to dry worked in teams of about eight. They appear to have been hired by a subcontractor, who was paid by the number of yards of blocks that the women had laid out, normally 1d per yard. In some cases, it seems, there was a woman in charge of the group, for example Kitty Grigg and Ann Brook, who received payment for them all.

Some women were paid for their work by the ton; 4d or 5d per ton at Goonvean, for instance, in March 1835. This seems to be the rate for stacking clay blocks in the reeders, or packing them in the casks. Other women were paid by the day, and these were probably the women who cleaned the blocks; for instance, the women *'scraping clay'* at Goonvean were being paid 4d per day between 1833 and 1836.

A decade later, in the 1840s, the boys and 'maidens' at the clay works were still earning much the same; 4d to 6d per day. After pressure from clay workers on the management to increase their wages in 1853, when china clay was fetching good prices, the maidens' average wages were increased from 8d to 9d per day, but only at the expense of a longer working day.

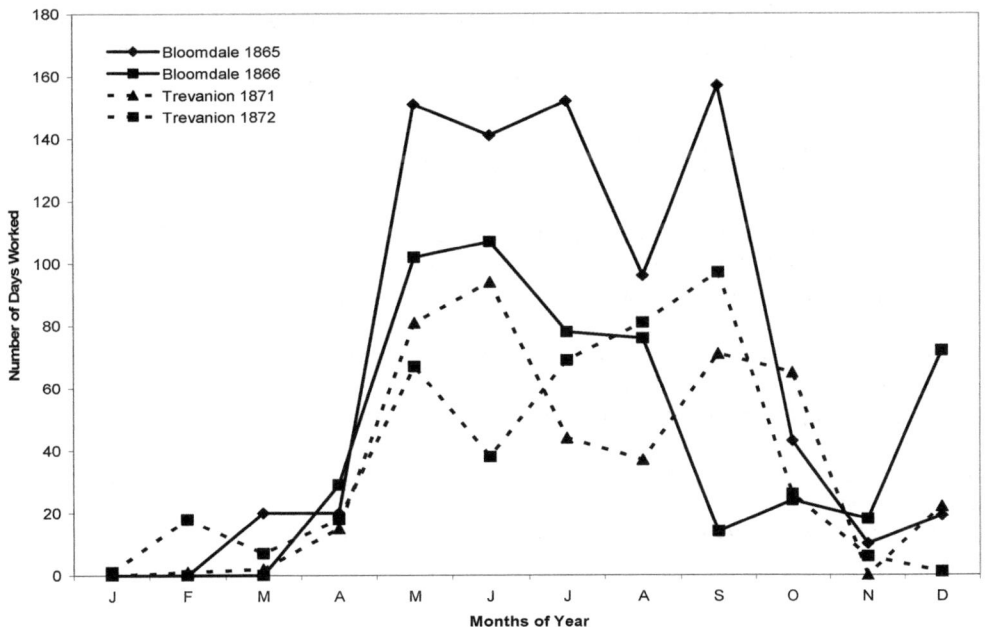

Fig. 38 Seasonality of Female Employment at Bloomdale and at Trevanion Clay Works

At Trevanion Clay Works, the women and girls were being paid between 9d and 12d per day in 1870. At Bloomdale Clay Works in St Stephens, all the females were being paid 12d per day in the same year. In the 1880s, the rate was still about one shilling. This continued to be comparable with pay at the tin and copper mines. Mary Ann Bray and Elizabeth Fisher were paid this amount for scraping clay at Wheal Henry Clay Works between 1882 and 1886.[14] There was no increase in this level of pay over many years, and the clay maidens were still earning this amount in the early 20th century.

There seems to have been a degree of seasonality to the work done by the females. Surviving cost books show that there was usually higher employment from March through to August or September, with virtually no women employed in December or January. At Ninestones, two women worked from May until September only in 1828, and five or six women were employed for March and April during 1831. An unspecified number of women worked at Goonvean for the equivalent of between 160 and 190 days per month from March to August, and for 30 to 80 days from September to December 1834. The numbers employed in the spring and summer months also fluctuated, and presumably were dependent on weather conditions. A graph (Fig. 38), shows the number of days worked by women at Bloomdale and Trevanion Clay Works, illustrating this 'two season' working year (peaking in different months depending on the weather patterns). In May, June or July, it was not uncommon for women and girls to work between 35 and 40 'days' per month, which must amount to at least time and a half, and a six day week. It seems that work was offered on a much more casual basis than at the mines, with workers being called in at short notice, and presumably laid off at short notice as well.

As these women were only employed full-time for a very short time each year, they were sometimes employed as 'flying teams' to be moved from one clay works to another. For instance, it seems there was an interchange of personnel between South Caudledown, Greensplat and Gunheath in the 1830s. Similarly, *'Gunheath'* girls were employed alongside regulars at South Caudledown during the summers of 1849 and 1859, and *'borrowed girls'* (from South Caudledown?) were employed at Gunheath in July 1851.

All of the work carried out by the women and girls could only be done in dry weather, in order to keep the clay dry, and every opportunity had to be taken to complete the tasks before the weather broke. Sometimes, work continued long after dusk, both in winter and summer, and this would be done by the light of lanterns or candles. There was some recompense for having to work late, it seems, as this entry in the cost book for Lower Ninestones for November 1832 shows: *'12 quarts of beer on scraping by night 10s 10½d.'*

Although the tasks performed by the women and girls at the clay works were very different from those undertaken by the bal maidens at the mineral mines, the clothes they wore for work were recognisably the same. Esquiros describes them in this way:

'The scene was animated by the constant passage of women with white bonnets, aprons and sleeves, carrying cubes of clay for placing beneath the reeders or in their hundreds on drying grounds on the surrounding hills...and it is curious to see them carrying to the surrounding hills a clay whiter still.' (Esquiros 1865 p. 43)

When Stocker described these groups of women in 1862, he was obviously somewhat intimidated by them: '*As they surround their scraping tables,* [they] *present a formidable appearance.*' [15]

In the 1880s, women were employed at the Castle Dinas Clay Works near Nancledra, between Hayle and St Just. The daughter of the clay works manager described her early memories of them:

'*The blocks were scraped clean by several ladies, clad in longish full skirts, three cornered shawls, hats or bonnets tied under the chin, and, of course, the inevitable 'towser'. They worked not far from the water-wheel which pumped the liquid clay from the pits into the tanks*'.[16]

The photograph in Fig. 34 appears to have been taken in the summer months, as the women are wearing a cotton 'gooks' and dresses. They are also wearing hessian aprons, with one bal maiden wearing removable protective sleeves. In contrast the photograph in Fig. 37 looks to be winter time, with the women wearing thick woollen skirts, thick stockings and warm shawls. Surprisingly, they appear to be working bare-handed (even though their hands must have become very cold, coarsened and sore). They seem to be wearing lighter shoes than some of the bal maidens who worked at the copper and tin mines, presumably because they were generally working in a drier environment.

THE NUMBERS OF CLAY MAIDENS

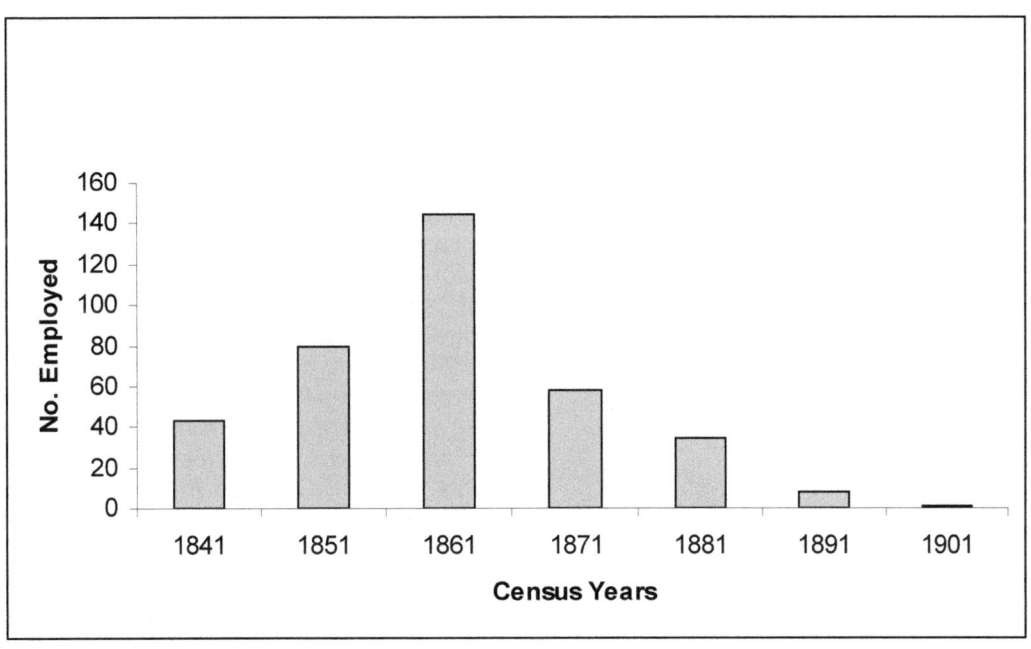

Fig. 39 Number of Females Employed at Clay Works
from Census Records

The proportion of women and girls employed at the clay works was never as great as at the copper, tin or lead mines. Generally, the highest numbers employed seemed to be at the time that the clay was being laid out to dry, and for scraping. Some surviving cost books record women and girls employed in small numbers from the late 1820s onwards. Subsequently, most clay pits employed only a handful of women, with the maximum probably being between twenty and thirty. By 1841, the census recorded a total of 41 females at the clay works in Cornwall. This had risen to 144 by 1861, then dropped to 58 in 1871, 8 in 1891 and 1 in 1901 (Fig. 39).

With quite low numbers, it might be expected that the age range of females recruited to the clay works might differ from that at the mines. However, most were also between the ages of 15 and 20 years old. Unlike the mines, very young girls have not yet been found; the youngest girl being 12 year-old Georgiana Poad of Washaway (in 1861). One of the oldest women was 70 year-old Jenepher Jacob of Barbellingey, who was described as a 'sand settler' in the *1841 Census*. It is thought that she worked at Ruddle Pit.[17]

WOMEN CHINA CLAY MANAGERS

An unusual feature of the china clay and china stone business was the number of women who appear to have become involved in management, and who sometimes took significant steps in the development and progression of the industry. For instance, Sarah Michell managed Carbeen, Bluebarrow (Bunny), and Yondertown Clay works from 1848 until about 1868, after the death of her husband. In 1851, she sent samples of her clay to the Great Exhibition at Crystal Palace, which appear in the catalogue described as:

'Michell, Sarah, St Austell - Producer White china-clay, for manufacturing china and earthenware, also for bleaching paper, calico etc.'[18]

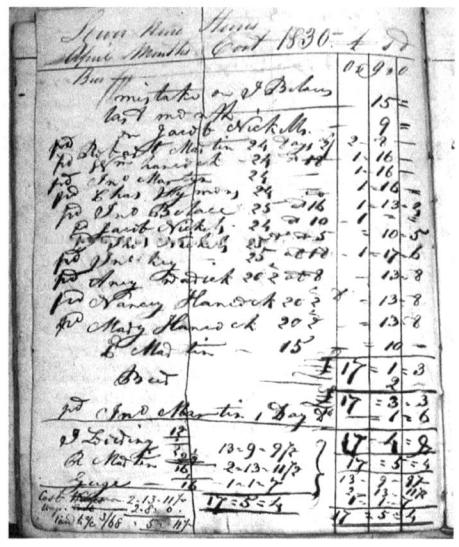

Fig. 40 Lower Ninestones Clay Works Cost Book April 1830

Phillipa Lovering also took over management of her husband's business interests at Lower Ninestones, when he died in 1834. Phillipa was in her late forties, and continued to manage these works until her son, John Lovering Jnr., was of age (by about 1845). The Lower Ninestone Cost Books 1828-1836, which survive in the Wheal Martyn archives, were written by Phillipa, so it seems that she was working as her husband's bookkeeper before his death (Fig. 40). Phillipa and her son subsequently took leases on Stents in 1850, Carclaze in 1858, Luxulyan China Clay Co. in 1860 [19], West Goonbarrow in 1868, and Carbeen and Bluebarrow in 1870. It seems that Phillipa was a very able women, described as *'a lady of great strength of character and activity'* and *'a capable business woman.'*

Mrs. Thriscot managed Caudledown after the death of her husband Thomas, from about 1858.

By 1878, an Emily Sophia Truscott was in partnership (one third part) with Henry Adolphus Bell at Caudledown, and together they renewed the lease one month later. Emily had given her address as Newington, Middlesex suggesting that, if she was the original Mrs. Thriscot, she was no longer an active partner.[20]

Another woman who appears in the census returns as a clay works manager was Mary Ann Phillips, of the Lee Moor Porcelain Clay Company. In May 1861, she was described as employing eighty-nine men at the clay and brick works. This was shortly after her husband's death, and, within a few months, the works were taken over by the other shareholders. They subsequently leased the works to Rebecca Martin in November 1862. It seems that Mary Ann's time as manager had been a very brief 'caretaking' affair.

A Mrs. Margaret Spargo was also described as a China Clay Merchant in Gunnislake in 1893, but we know little of her.[21] However, the most notable female 'clay baron' was Rebecca Martin who managed several large clay works and was largely responsible for initiating co-operative practices in the clay industry, in the mid 19th century. Her story is covered more fully in Chapter 12.

By the third quarter of the 19th century, it seems that this window of opportunity for females to take over management roles in the clay industry was closed, and the likes of these strong and capable women were not seen again in these powerful positions.

SOAPSTONE

In Cornwall, soapstone, or soap rock clay, was found uniquely in veins of serpentine on the Lizard peninsular, and was exploited briefly from the mid 18th century until about 1818. It was an important constituent of soft porcelain, but was quickly superseded by china clay, which enabled the major potteries to produce the more desirable and better quality hard porcelain.

One of the earliest references to the mining of this product is from Dr. Richard Pococke in 1750, who described soapstone being shipped from the Lizard to potteries in Bristol.[22] Majendie lists soapstone being extracted at Trethvas, Predannack Downs, Mullion Churchtown, on the North West Coast of the Lizard, as well as Gew Graze, in 1792.[23] In 1801, Britton and Brayley described the soapstone in this way:

'The serpentine is occasionally intersected with veins of steatites, most contained in the celebrated soap-rock situated between the Lizard and Mullion. Its colour is whitish or straw yellow, with streaks or veins of green, red and purple. It is found in three degrees of purity. The first is called best-best, and is most beautifully white. It possesses an absorbent quality, and will imbibe spots of grease or oil from silk without injuring its colours.' (Britton and Brayley 1801 p. 331)

Gew Graze Mine, situated in a deep valley three miles south of Mullion, had been worked by the Worcester Potteries from about 1757 until 1775. In 1780, the lease was taken over by the proprietors of the Caughley Manufactory. Although Paris describes Josiah Wedgwood as one of the lessees, there are no supporting documents for this, but it is from this mine that the only reference to women being employed has been found.[24] It comes from the writings of Rev. Richard Warner as he travelled through Cornwall in

1808.[25] He describes the operations at Gew Graze, the mine then being leased by Messrs. Flight and Barr, who owned potteries in Worcester.

At this time, five men, who dug out about five hundred pounds of soapstone per week, were employed at Gew Graze. This was graded into fine and coarse steatite at surface. It seems that the steatite at Gew Graze came in mixed colours, with the white being in great demand, and needing to be separated from the red and other colours before sale. It was graded, and then packed into casks, by 3 or 4 women working in a nearby building. The casks were then shipped from Mullion Cove to Worcester. Gew Graze Mine was still being worked in 1818, but only producing about twelve tons per annum, and by 1819 it seems to have ceased production altogether.[26] It is not clear whether women were also employed at the other soapstone mines on the Lizard.

DEVON BALL CLAY

Considerable deposits of ball clay have been found in the Teign Valley in what is called the 'Bovey Basin' (around Bovey Tracey). It contains ultra fine particles of clay and also contains high levels of kaolin, making it easy both to mould and to fire successfully at high temperatures, when used in conjunction with china clay. It had been used for clay pipes from the latter half of the 17th century, and then more generally for local pottery. Its unique qualities were soon recognised, and it has been exported to major potteries all over the world.

These ball clays were traditionally cut into cubes, by hand, from open pits and then left to be weathered for several months. There is no evidence, so far, that women or girls were involved in this process, although they were employed in large numbers in the actual potteries in the Bovey Tracey area during the mid to late 19th century. Here, they carried out at a range of tasks, from powering the lathes to applying transfers and delicate hand painting.

POTASH FELSPAR

In Cornwall there were at least two orthoclase mines operating during the 19th century in the St Austell area. One was Tresayse Mine, locally called Polpuff Glass Mine. It was open for ten years from about 1870 but closed when the best material was thought to have been mined out, leaving the quarry unable to compete with good quality ore imported from Norway and Sweden. Very little is known of the workings of this mine in 19th century, and it is not known whether women and girls were employed at that stage.[27]

Despite it being thought that only lower grade ore was left, it became necessary to re-open the mine during the First World War, in order to obtain the felspar for specialist glass production, as supplies from Norway could no longer be guaranteed. Glass was needed for such vital items as clinical thermometers and, the workers believed, for periscope glass. On re-opening it was found that Polpuff still had considerable quantities of very high-grade material. Although Russell (1998) reported that the mine reopened in 1917, John Tonkin believes it may have been functioning as early as 1914, and continued in production until about 1921, with at least fifty women or girls working there at its peak.

Most of the information about the working of this mine in the First World War has been preserved by the foresight of John Tonkin, who started archiving material and interviewing individuals in the 1970s. Without this, we would know almost nothing about Polpuff, its employees, or the processes involved.

Fig. 41 Polpuff Dressing Tables
Courtesy of China Clay Review

The rock being worked at Polpuff contained quartz, tourmaline and mica, as well as the potash felspar. After being quarried, the potash felspar needed to be separated from as much of the waste as possible, and this was done by women and girls. The material was brought from the quarry to the picking table in wagons, along a bank about twelve feet above the pickers. The teenaged male trammers would tip the material from the wagons down onto the bank. The women and girls would pull the ore-stuff, as required, down the chutes onto their picking table. Each bal maiden had a small cobbing hammer for separating the waste from the felspar.

A photograph was taken of the women at work, dated about 1918 (Fig. 41). It was taken from the wagon-way along which the felspar was delivered, and shows the slope of ore from which the women and girls worked. Approximately thirty women and girls are shown standing at the picking table (which looks about forty feet long and three feet wide) under a crude iron roof (about six feet wide) with no additional shelter on any side. The women in the photograph are all working bare-headed, in long skirts and blouses, or dresses. Some seem to be wearing long aprons, and protective sleeves.[28]

There are two other known surviving photographs of these women. In a photograph of forty-eight women, believed to have been taken in the autumn of 1918, the women and girls are all wearing a variety of overalls or aprons, over long-sleeved dresses or blouses (Fig. 42). They are mostly bare-headed. In a photograph of a smaller group of six, several of the same women can be identified, and they are wearing much the same as before, and are all holding their cobbing hammers. They are photographed with two men, presumably the two surface captains. Both photographs must have been taken before they started work, as they are all in beautifully clean clothes, and in summer time, as they are wearing light summer cottons. Most of the young women look as if they are in their late teens or early twenties, but with a small number looking as if they are of school leaving age, about 14 or 15 years old. Many of these women were interviewed by John Tonkin in the 1970s, and of six for whom a date of birth is available, the youngest would have been 15 years old, four of them 16 years old, and the eldest 20 years old in 1914.

Fig. 42 Women Orthoclase Dressers at Polpuff Mine, First World War
Courtesy of John Tonkin

The women were paid piece-work for a given number of boxes filled with sorted and dressed ore each day. Each woman had a box number, and, on completion of the box, would have the box tallied against her name. The ore stuff would be sorted, with clean potash felspar being placed straight into the box, and the quartz and other waste being thrown as 'deads' into a pile behind. The dressed boxes would then be taken by a male surface labourer who emptied the box into the leat which ran behind the women. After washing the ore in the leat, it would then be raked out onto the concrete wharf to drain and dry, ready for shipment. It is thought that this team of forty to fifty women could probably dress about one ton of ore per day.

Periodically, the pile of 'deads' was graded through a sieve by a young boy, and the larger waste returned for cobbing and re-sorting. As this task gave much lower returns, and very often the material was very wet and cold, the job was the least popular; so the women took it in turns.

During the summer months, two or three of the most skilled of the women were selected to work out on the wharf, where they broke some of the dressed ore into two inch cubes. This was a slow job, and they would only finish a few boxes per day, and were on a different rate of pay. This dressed ore was shipped to South Wales to be used in the coal washing process.

The women were generally superintended by the two 'treatment captains' who literally 'oversaw' from the top and bottom levels of the dressing floor! Mary Higman from Luxulyan was the 'shift manager', and 18 year-old Gussie Retallack, who was the daughter of the surface captain, was the tally checker for the women's boxes. Trammers sometimes favoured particular workers, and would deliver better quality ore to them. As a result, some women finished their allotted task much more quickly than others, with the older or 'unpopular' women often finishing last.

The working day began at 7 a.m. The women travelled from such places as Enniscaven, Whitemoor, and Luxulyan, involving a walk of two to five miles, across very exposed countryside, in all weathers. Hazel Varcoe worked at Polpuff, and lived in Enniscaven. Her father was responsible for the 'dry' at Polpuff. When she was interviewed at the age of 78, she was able to boast that she had never been late to work despite the three-mile walk in all weathers. Annie Andrew who lived in Currian Road, Nampean, used to leave home at 6 a.m., with five of the other women, to reach work in time. She described how sometimes, if she worked hard, she could finish her allotted task for the day by 2 p.m. and then would be allowed to go home early.

Some women were conscripted against their will to work at Polpuff during this time. One described how she had trained as a music teacher when she was called to work at the mine. When she arrived she was issued with clogs to wear, but because the dressing floor was so uneven, she found it more comfortable to wear her own shoes. She remembered how quickly clothes wore out at the picking table. Several of the women remarked on the difficulties of dressing the ore under winter conditions. The winter of 1920-21 was particularly severe, when the ore-stuff froze to the galvanised chutes, and to itself. Polpuff Mine eventually closed in 1921. Varcoes, who owned the mine, also owned a knitting factory in Newquay, and it seems that some of the women were offered alternative employment there.

FOOTNOTES

1. Throughout this chapter information is drawn from Barton, R. (1966), especially pp. 42, 48, 88, 95, 98, 101, + 103.
2. This chapter also draws on the research of John Tonkin, into both clay works and Polpuff Glass Mine. (Personal correspondence JT/LM 2002).
3. WB 23rd January 1868.
4. Personal correspondence (AJ/LM 2003).
5. Ninestones CB (WM: 1988.367).
6. Stocker (1852) p. 78.
7. White (1861) p. 187.
8. Thurlow (1996) p. 24.
9. Coon, Joseph M. The China Clay Industry, *Roy. Cornwall Polytech. Soc.* Vol. 6 (1927) p. 56.
10. Personal correspondence (JT/LM 2002).
11. Baker, Helen (1951) p. 33.
12. Pochin, H. D. & Co. Ltd. *Pochin's China Clay* p. 8 (WM: 5c 2002.45).
13. WM Archives.
14. Personal correspondence (JT/LM 2002).
15. Esquiros (1865) p. 79.
16. Baker, Helen (1951) p. 33.
17. Personal correspondence (AJ/LM 2003).
18. *Great Exhibition (1851) Cat.* Vol. 1 p. 133.
19. Luxulyan China Clay Lease (CRO: CF/1/3921).
20. S. Caudledown Lease (CRO: BRA898/51).
21. *Kelly's Directory 1893*.
22. Chope (1967) p. 97.
23. Majendie, A. (1818) 'A Sketch of the Geology of the Lizard' *Trans. Roy. Geol. Soc. Cornwall* 1. pp. 32-37; Britton & Brayley *The Beauties of England and Wales* Vol. II Cornwall (1801).
24. Paris, J. A. (1818) 'Observations on the Geological Structure of Cornwall', *Trans. Roy. Geol. Soc. Cornwall* 1. pp. 168-200.
25. Warner, Rev. Richard *A Tour Through Cornwall in the Autumn of 1801* (Bath 1808) p. 224.
26. Paris (1818) p. 200.
27. Collins (1878) p. 26.
28. *China Clay Trade Rev.* Vol. 1. (June 1919) p. 11.

Chapter 7

BAL MAIDENS AND OTHER MINERALS

Despite tin and copper mines being the major producers of minerals in Cornwall and South and West Devon during the 18th and 19th centuries, other mines were in operation which employed a considerable workforce of women and girls and which were making a significant contribution to the economy of the nation. These mines, or quarries, were producing lead, zinc, manganese, wolfram, and slate. Some other mines also seem to have employed small numbers of women or girls, such as the iron, antimony and uranium mines.

MINES PRODUCING MIXED ORES

A good number of mines were producing more than one mineral, which required careful separation, often dependant on the careful judgment, not just of the surface captain or agent and underground miners, but also of the ore dressers themselves. For instance, other secondary minerals, mined in conjunction with copper or tin, included arsenic, silver, gold, and cobalt. Silver was invariably mined with lead, as was zinc. Sometimes these ores were raised separately from different shafts, in which case they were dressed totally separately, but in many instances, they would come to the surface mixed. For example, in 1854, Great Wheal Baddern Lead Mine was producing *'mundic* [arsenic], *jack* [zinc] *and lead'* from one three-foot wide lode, while silver and copper were being extracted from other parts of the mine.[1]

The stage at which mixed ores were separated from each other depended on the relative quantities and type of ore. Some could be separated by feel or by eye, depending on texture, colour, or density. In such cases, they could come to the surface already roughly separated by underground workers designated to this task. They could be further separated at the picking table, and subsequently by the spallers, cobbers and buckers. Some minerals were much more difficult to distinguish from each other or from the parent rock, but the ore dressers soon became skilled at discerning one from the other. Wolfram, for instance, was very difficult to distinguish from tin, and in the early days was rejected as waste. It was only in later years that it was exploited for tungsten. Henwood described wolfram as:

'So nearly in appearance when in the stone, that none but the experienced tinners can tell the difference.' (Henwood 1855 p. 10)

No doubt an experienced bal maiden would be expected to be able to distinguish wolfram from tin. Others minerals were not easily distinguished by eye, but could be separated out by gravity at the buddling stage:

'The purpose of the revolving arms with their drags was to distribute evenly the slime, so that the minerals could arrange themselves according to their specific gravities. Cassiterite (tin oxide), being the heaviest, would settle in the head of the buddle. Then following outwards would be the copper, zinc, iron and arsenic sulphide, and the lightest quartz as the tailings. The sulphides and tin oxides were calcined. The other oxides were buddled again, then the copper oxide treated with sulphuric oxide and precipitate out of solution using scrap iron. Zinc oxide was removed by buddling.' [2]

The problems involved with separating mixed ores were mentioned in a report to the Boiling Well Mine in 1858. It is not clear whether the *'expensive and tedious'* separating methods in place were at the picking or buddling stages, but the recommended remedy was to install specialist machinery:

'Your mode of separating lead from the blende and copper is very expensive and tedious. It may be much facilitated in time and with less expense by a Vian's separator.' (MJ 28th Aug 1858 p. 118)

Others were either so intermixed, or had such a similar density, that they could not be separated either by appearance or by gravity, and could only be separated at differential temperatures during smelting. This included such mixtures as silver and lead.

Because of the complexities of dealing with mixed ore, each mine would have to develop its own sequence of processes to exploit their ores to the best. The complicated process of separating ores is summed up in this description of 1819:

'Iron ores are rejected as far as possible, and tin and copper completely separated from each other. But sometimes they are so intimately intermixed that much judgment is required to decide whether they can be dressed with greater advantage as tin or as copper.' (Boase 1819 p. 383)

The major decisions regarding these processes would be made by the surface captains or mine agents. However, the efficiency of separation also depended on the skill, eye and dexterity of the picker, cobber, bucker and buddler. Depending on the ore raised, they would sometimes need to discern several different types of ore. Not only would they be selecting for the main Cornish ores such as tin, copper, lead, silver and zinc, but might also need to identify such minority minerals as cobalt, manganese, wolfram, or molybdenum.

ARSENIC

In Cornwall and Devon, the element occurring most frequently in combination with other minerals and in significant quantities, was arsenic. Most of the tin and copper ores in the South West contained arsenic as a naturally occurring impurity. In the early years, its commercial value was not recognised and it was treated as unwanted waste, as it interfered with the smelting process. This removal of arsenic was usually an integral part of the dressing process.

In this early era when arsenic was just deemed a nuisance to be burned off, women and older girls were often paid to tend the 'burning house'. The earliest references found are of Catherine Sims who was paid about 12d per day at Wheal Unity Wood in 1774, and Mary and Sarah Davies who watched the burning house by night at Wheal Union and Owlacombe Bean Mine in 1809 and 1810.[3]

Where the arsenic occurred with copper, the best copper ore was picked out, and the copper and mispickel ore that had high arsenic content was sent to be roasted, originally in open hearths, and later in special calciners. Where the arsenic content was lower, the ore-stuff was sent to the crushers and jiggers for further separating first. In the same way, if the arsenic was found with tin in high concentrations, it was roasted in road-stone sized pieces, and then stamped for tin and roasted again. If the arsenic content was low it went straight to the stamps and then on to the calciner. In some mines, it was possible to remove the recognisable arseno-pyrite ore at the picking stage.

By 1830, it was realised that there was a commercial market for arsenic in the manufacture of pesticides and medicines, for instance, and methods were required where this by-product could be collected. Brunton's calciners were designed and developed, whereby the 'whits' (ore concentrate) could be fed from an upper floor through a hopper onto a revolving hearth below, in the top of the furnace. The arsenic fumes were then carried away through lengthy flues, sometimes for several miles, where the arsenic eventually deposited out in a white powder form on the flue sides. These residues were then carefully collected and sold. The purified roasted copper or tin ore which remained in the calciner was then cooled and dressed in the usual way.

Fig. 43 Bal Maiden Feeding Brunton's Calciner Hopper
Henderson c. 1858

James Henderson's 1850s drawing of a Brunton's calciner suggests that older girls or women were sometimes responsible for feeding the ore into the hopper. Similarly, when Esquiros describes the mining operations at Botallack in 1865, he describes women and children as being involved in *'burning'*. Elizabeth Whitta (of Peterville, St Agnes) was described as a *'tin burner'* in 1871, and in 1881 Philippa Reynolds was a *'burner at stamps'* in the Coombe area of Gwennap. In 1882, Ann Gribben was paid for *'burning tin'* on Sundays at Wheal Coates. Cecilia Davey of Baldhu was also described as a *'tin burning house labourer'* in 1891.

It seems from Robert Hunt's description of the calcining process in 1878, that the hopper was actually charged with a mixture of 6% salt and ore, presumably prepared by the bal maiden responsible for filling the hopper:

'The furnace is charged with ore and salt by means of iron hoppers placed immediately over the centre of each of the hearths. For the supply of each hopper, a heap of about 14 quintals of ore (one quintal = one cwt), with 5 or 6 per cent of salt, is prepared from time to time upon a small platform on top of the furnaces...'

About one quintal of ore and salt needed to be fed into the hopper per one revolution of the hearth, and it took fifteen to twenty minutes per revolution. This would need the bal maiden responsible to shovel about five to eight pounds of ore per minute. This would not be a very arduous task, somewhat boring perhaps, but needed the greatest of care. Where several calciners were installed together, she presumably would be responsible for charging the hoppers for each one.[4] In 1879, there is a note in a Penhalls and Blue Hills minute book which indicates that the man working at the calciner was to be replaced by a woman or child, in order to reduce labour costs.[5]

As the tin and copper mines began to fail from the 1870s onwards, some mining was carried out specifically for arsenical ore instead, as at Devon Great Consols, Gawton, Okel Tor and Lady Bertha in the Tamar valley, either by redressing the waste heaps, or by revisiting the galleries below ground to retrieve what had previously been left as worthless. At Devon Great Consols, for instance, it was found that, where four or five feet of material had been removed from a copper lode, there was another similar depth of mispickel to be exploited on either side. Total production of arsenic peaked in Cornwall between 1880 and 1890, at about 1,400 tons per year. In Devon, nearly thirty mines produced arsenic during this period and into the first decade of the 20th century, where women and girls continued to be employed in the dressing of these ores. By 1903, however, only a few mines were still open. There was a temporary recovery in 1907, but shortly after the industry closed completely.

There are very few references to females working specifically with arsenic in the census records. Grace Gilbert (of Mount Hawke) and Ellen Morcom (of Bolster) were described as *'dressing mundic'* in 1871, and Eliza Nettle (of Gwennap) was a *'mundic miner'* in 1881. Over the border in Devon, Elizabeth Boundy, Mary Ann Easterbrook, Elizabeth Jane Floyd, Mary Elizabeth Jones, Emma and Irena Maunder, and Jane Penrose were all *'mundic cleaners'* at Mary Tavy. In 1891, 82 year-old Eliza Kellow, an inmate of the Truro Workhouse, was recorded as previously having been a *'labourer at the mundic mine'*. The latest recorded arsenic dressers from the census were Rita and Lillie Waters (of Calstock) who were *'picking mundic'* in 1901.

At what stage the dangers of working with arsenic were appreciated is hard to judge. Pryce, writing in the 1770s, describes the utter devastation of the surrounding countryside when arsenic was burnt in the early calciners, and the agents at Wheal Vor reported how employees became ill when the fumes from the arsenic furnace were discharged into the centre of the mine. However, photos from the end of the 19th century of men collecting arsenic show the only precaution taken is the placing of cotton wool plugs in their noses and ears. Similarly, according to Henderson's diagram of about 1852, the woman filling the calciner hoppers is not wearing any protective clothing of any kind. However, in Robert Hunt's description of arsenic calcining in 1878, the care required to avoid the hopper filler being overwhelmed with arsenic vapours, was mentioned:

'...*a few shovels-ful* [are] *thrown in occasionally as required, taking care, however, always to have enough ore in the hopper to prevent the ascension of acid vapours, etc. from the furnace.*'[6]

Even though employing females to dress arsenic had probably ceased by 1910, six women were recruited from Tavistock during the First World War to dig over the 'burras' (waste heaps) at Wheal Friendship. These included Mrs. Jackman, Dorothy Luxton, Mrs. Remington and Mrs. Terrell.[7]

From about 1840, chemical works opened which processed the impure arsenic coming from the mines. Initially, they produced 'mineral green' for colouring paper, but, by the 1850s, they were producing sulphur products and sulphuric acid. It seems that female workers were also employed here, in small numbers. For instance, 25 year-old Eliza Datson (of Wheal Widden) and 22 year-old Mary Ann Pascoe (of Fernsplatt) were employed at one of several arsenic works in the Carnon Valley in 1881. The latter was described as a 'framer', so was presumably involved in further dressing of the ore.

LEAD, SILVER AND ZINC

Interestingly, the very first accounts so far found of female involvement in the mining industries of Cornwall and West Devon relate to women at the lead-silver smelters in Calstock in the early 14th century. At this time, a considerable deposit of silver and lead was found in the Bere Alston and Bere Ferris area on the Devon side of the river Tamar, and the Mines Royal developed mines there from 1295, eventually employing about 700 people. By 1302, the ore was being transported over the Tamar to Calstock for smelting because there was an ample supply of wood and charcoal to fuel the furnaces. The white and black ores, containing lead carbonate and galena respectively, were initially smelted in a traditional 'bole', but often the white ores did not fully separate, forming a black slag instead. This slag was retrieved and subsequently re-crushed and washed. It was then smelted again at a higher temperature, in a separate ore furnace, which burnt charcoal and brushwood. Unfortunately, detailed surviving accounts relate only to the smelting operations at Calstock. They do not give the names of women dressing or washing ore at the Bere Alston end of the operations, although almost certainly they would have been employed in considerable numbers there. Bucking hammers, washing sieves, and tubs all appear in the accounts for Bere Ferris indicating typical ore dressing techniques of the time. Unfortunately, no dressing floor archaeology survives.[8]

However, detailed accounts do record the names of women working at the Calstock smelters. It seems that some sort of horse-powered mill was usually used to crush the 'black work'. Some breaking of slag was also done by hand, with Mattillid de Suthecon being paid '*3d for breaking black ore*' on two and a half days in July 1304. The most common task carried out by the women, though, was the washing of the slag (confusingly also described as black ore). This washing was done in the watercourse next to the boles and furnaces at '*Davypulle*'. No details are given of the method of washing, but each washer had an '*assistant*' or '*servant*', which sounds like the equivalent of the 'server' at the dressing floors of the lead mines in the Pennines. Presumably, they used some sort of sieving or grading pans, which the women would wash and shake under a stream of water. Their assistants would help load the crushed slag, and then remove the cleaned residue ready for drying and re-smelting. The women were also sometimes employed washing and sieving tan bark ash which was used in separating silver from lead in the smelting process.

These women appear to have been working up to six days a week and were paid weekly. Agnes Oppenhulle seems to have been the first woman employed at the smelter in May 1302. During the summer months of 1306, about four or five pairs were normally at work. Mattillid de Suchetone began work initially as an 'assistant' but eventually was employed in her own right. Others working there during 1306 were Isabelle Cutard, Gunhilde de Bonn, Dyonis and Desiderata de Milleton, Emma de Falling, Matilda Bate (whose father was the furnace man), Joanna Cole and Agnes Sludde. Emma de Falling appears to be the longest serving female, and was employed intermittently between 1306 and 1313. In the last year, she was paid 1s 6d per day for herself and her servant, for a total of 226 days.

It seems all the surface workers were employed by the Mines Royal, and were supervised by an 'overseer'. Employment ceased in these early mining ventures with the advent of the Black Death. If mine workers survived the plague themselves, they were drawn away to work on the land, where there was a huge shortage of labourer. Agricultural wages had doubled, making it much more lucrative than mining.

When Pryce was writing about mining in Cornwall in the 1770s, he referred to the oldest known lead mines in Cornwall being at Perranporth, and that they reached out under the sea. He does not indicate a date for these. However, of the two major lead deposits in Cornwall, by far the more substantial was between Perranporth and Newlyn East, and several mines of note developed in this area during the mid 19th century.

Although some lead was being mined in Devon and Cornwall in the 18th century, the mines were small, and ore dressing presumably very simple. The major period of lead production was from 1830 to 1880, peaking between 1850 and 1860, with East Wheal Rose being the largest and most famous of these mines. Other lead mines producing significant amounts during the 1850s were several in the Callington and Bere Ferris areas around the Tamar, and Wheal Trelawney and Wheal Mary Ann in Menheniot. Lead mines also opened in the Teign valley, the most notable of which were Frank Mills and Wheal Exmouth. All were in decline by the mid 1860s. The major producers after that date were West Chiverton and Cargol (in Perranzabuloe and Newlyn East), and Lanescot (in Tywardreath). From 1845 until 1913, there had been about 170 mines producing lead in Cornwall, but mostly in conjunction with tin or copper.

Lead, being the most dense and the softest of all the ores mined in Devon and Cornwall, required its own combination of dressing processes; its most useful quality being that it was easily separated by weight. The relative densities of galena to the rock in which it was found was at most about 7:4, enabling good separation by gravity, when washed in water. The softness of the ore, however, meant that it was easily lost in the stamping process, so, in many respects, the dressing procedure was similar to copper (which is also very soft), and involved manual or very careful mechanical breaking down of the ore, prior to sedimentation. However, because lead ore very often needed to be crushed or bruised to a smaller grade for smelting than copper, it generally took longer to dress.[10] For instance, in 1841 lead dressers at Old Cornubian Mine were dressing only three barrows of ore per day, about half of the amount processed at most copper mines in the same amount of time.

The earliest dressers in the very small mines operating in the late 18th or early 19th century hand sorted and hand crushed the ore-bearing material. This was then separated from the waste by sieving in water, the larger ore being picked out. The lighter waste, and ore that passed through the sieve, was then separated out in a stone lined buddle. Many of these processes were carried out by women and children. Initially, as with tin and copper dressers, the lead dressers were employed by their own tribute team to dress the ore that they raised.

From the early 1800s, the dressers began to be employed by the mine, each tribute team being charged for the dressing of their ore. By the 1850s, dressing was still the province of female and child labour, with some male labourers carrying out the heaviest of the work, and all supervised by the surface captain. The ore-stuff was raised in kibbles or rolled out of the levels in wagons and would be deposited in piles or hoppers and then taken for dressing as needed. It would first be spalled or put through stone-crushers to break it down into manageable pieces (Fig. 20). In lead mines in Scotland, a young boy was responsible for supplying the crushers with ore, so it may well have been the task of a child at the lead mines of the South West.[11] After crushing, the ore-stuff would then be barrowed (in the earlier days) or trammed to a hopper and sent down a chute onto a picking table, where it was washed and picked, in the same way as copper and tin ore (Fig. 21).

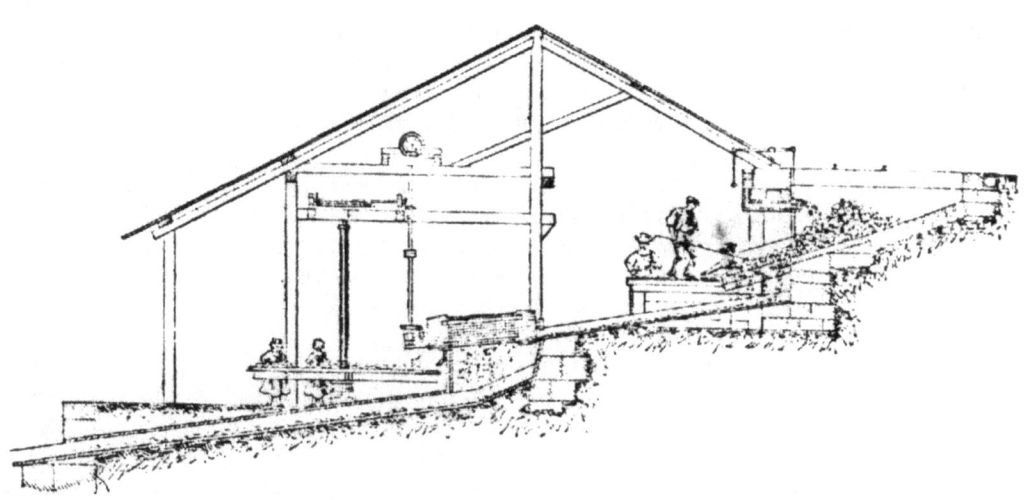

Fig. 44 Bal Maidens Picking Lead from a Rotating Trommel (1884)

By about 1860, the picking was fairly mechanised, with ore (after washing) being sized in a rotating trommel or sieve, and with a final hand picking out of the larger waste, by boys or girls, from a rotating table. Pure ore was taken away to be stored, ready for sampling and sale. The ore-stuff that passed through grate was fed down a slope onto another sizing trommel, which separated 'rough' from 'fine' smalls. These rough smalls were also picked over by young children (Fig. 44). The fine smalls were crushed and jigged. The labour requirement of the wash kiln and trommel was one man to rake material onto the grate, two girls on each of two picking tables at the grate, four children on the rotating picking table, and several men or strong boys to remove waste to tips. In this way, twenty tons could be dressed in ten hours at a cost of 4d per ton.[12]

The medium quality ore would then be cobbed into pieces about half to one inch across, and the waste discarded (Fig. 22). The cobbed pieces which still contained waste would then need further separating by hand bucking or at the crushing mill (Fig. 23). Some ore was too hard to be bucked easily, and, as early as the 1790s, stamping mills were possibly used for this purpose.[13] As with copper, if stamps were used at all, it was usually used for the 'halvans' (or poorer grades), as at Wheal Mary Ann and Wheal Exmouth.

Specially designed crushing machines gradually replaced hand bucking. However, even as late as 1878, bucking was still being done by hand at the smaller mines. As with copper, the ore was bucked at a bench, sometimes brick-built, with a slab of iron used as an anvil. The women and girls would stand on a rock or box to keep their legs free of the dressed ore-stuff. In 1841, the dressing captain at Cornubian Lead Mine reported that the females on his dressing floors were able to buck 4.5 cwt of material per day. Nine girls were involved either in bucking or cobbing at this time, of which one was under 13 years old (the others being between 13 and 18 years old).

The fine gravel-textured material from the bucking mill or the crushers would be separated by jigging. In early days, this was carried out by boys. After the development of semi-mechanised jiggers, filling, operating the lever to shake the boxes, and emptying were still done manually. Sometimes, girls were employed at these tasks. Wheal Betsey was one of the first mines to install these improved jigs, in about 1830.[14]

The sediments from these processes were continually rewashed and cleaned, and then on to the buddle. Buddling was overseen by boys, and, after 1876, when full-time child labour was illegal, by men. However, older girls and women assisted them at the 'strips' where they rewashed the best quality ore-stuff from the buddle and returned it for reprocessing.

Because lead ore was invariably impure and contained traces of other valuable ores with it, various techniques were used to separate the minerals. Zinc, for instance was separated at the buddling stage, when it could be found in the lower sedimentation zones in the buddle, whereas the lead would accumulate around the cone. For mines that raised lead with zinc, a further separation process may have been used which was the equivalent of the tozing and packing stage in tin. In the north, this was called 'dollying'. The tub was one metre high, with a vertical axle (dolly) with two or four paddles rotated by a handle. The dolly was turned while slime ore was poured into the water-filled tub. As the ore was settling, the tub was hit on the side to keep lighter clays and waste afloat, while metals precipitated to the bottom.[15] This task, as with tozing and packing, was almost certainly done by adolescent boys or girls.

Some lead slimes were trunked and treated at the racking frames, in the same way that tin was separated. Girls and women were responsible for this part of the process, and at the frames one girl could wash thirty hundredweight of lead slimes per day, but using as much as 600 gallons of water.

Statistics of the numbers of women and girls working in the lead mines are difficult to find. In the returns sent to the *1842 Royal Commission*, 57 females were working at three lead/silver mines in Cornwall, and 33 in two lead mines in Devon. Although the ten yearly census records probably under-reported the numbers of bal maidens employed, we can perhaps glimpse a trend in the figures. In 1841, only 27 female lead dressers were recorded (all resident the Perranzabuloe and Newlyn East areas). This increased dramatically to about 300 in 1851 and to 325 in 1861, and now included the Liskeard, Bere Ferris and Teign Valley areas. By 1871, the number had dropped again, to about 150, and then to just 11 in 1881 and 3 in 1891.

Fig. 45 Bal Maidens at Silverbrook Lead Mine, Ilsington, c. 1858
Courtesy of Torquay Museum

Although the lead mines were fewer in number and generally smaller than the copper and tin mines, there were some which employed a reasonable number of women and girls. One of the earlier lead mines, Trewavas (in Breage), was employing 42 females and 17 children in 1836.[16] In the later years, the lead mines in the parish of Menheniot were one of the main employers with 140 women and 152 children recorded in 1851, 260 women and children in 1856, and 132 surface workers in 1868.[17] No separate figures were given for the female surface workers at Frank Mills and South Exmouth Mine, in the Teign Valley. However, in 1864 there was a total of 90 surface workers, when it was reported that all of the bal maidens were dressing lead under cover.[18]

At South Tamar Consols in the summer of 1856, the 130 surface workers (men, women and children) were dressing an average of 100 tons of lead ore per month. Sadly, that autumn the mine was flooded, when the waters of the Tamar broke through into the levels, and all hands were laid off. The mine never re-opened.[19] In contrast, just eight bal maidens were employed at Carn Vivian in 1856 (four bucking and four *'dressing'*). Another lead mine employing females in small numbers was North Porthilly, with only four in 1862.

In 1841, East Wheal Rose seemed to be employing very young girls. There were a total of nineteen girls under 13 years old (of whom six were under 10), with twenty-seven between 13 and 18 years old. The youngest worked at *'trunking slimes'* or at the picking tables; the older girls were cobbing or bucking, with one child under 13 years old also at the cobbing bench. A Cost Book for Lady Bertha Lead Mine shows that up to eighteen females were employed at a time, between 1855 and 1857. Among them was Mary Sleep of Bere Ferris, who had was already a bal maiden by 1841, when she was just 10 years old. She was by no means the youngest lead dresser; Caroline Tregoning was 7 years old and Mary Ann Kempthorne was only 6 years old, when they were employed at mines in Newlyn East in 1851 and 1871 respectively. Ann Polmear who worked intermittently at Carn Vivian from 1860 to 1862 was also probably very young, as she was only paid 3d per day.

As at the other mines, women and girls were also employed for tasks other than ore dressing. In 1866 and 1867, Mary Peak was employed at New Trelawney for *'making sacks for underground work'* at 1s per sack. Also, a Mrs. Elizabeth Hill was paid for carriage. Her donkey and cart collected 'oils from Callington to the mine' for 1s, and on one occasion made *'four journeys to Liskeard and two to Callington'* for 4s 8d. Similarly, at North Porthilly Lead Mine in 1861 and 1862, Christiana Richards was paid for regular journeys with a horse and cart (or gig). She was paid 3 or 4s for trips to Bodmin, Tregardock, Washaway or Wadebridge. On occasions, she drove to Great Onslow Consols to collect various mining equipment (including a pump). For these journeys she was paid 5s.

Other than the 14th century Calstock records, few reports have been found of women or girls working at lead smelters in Cornwall or Devon. However in 1851, sisters 12 year-old Ruth and 16 year-old Eliza Williams, plus 24 year-old Jane Eselby, were working at Weir Quay Smelter in Bere Ferris. In 1861, 34 year-old Grace Richard (of Come to Good) and 56 year-old Mary Ann Martin (of Quenchwell), both in Feock, were also described as working at a lead smelter (presumably at Point, at the mouth of Restronguet Creek).

Invariably in North Cornwall, lead was found in conjunction with silver. The mines around Newlyn East were particularly rich in this valuable ore, sometimes yielding up to 35%

silver. One of the most famous silver mines was at Huel Mexico in St Agnes, but no employment records survive.

All Cornish silver was extracted along with lead ore. From 1870 to 1880, there were eleven mines producing silver in any quantity, the main mines being Newton and Prince of Wales (St. Mellion) and Great Crinnis (Charlestown). As the silver was separated from lead at smelting, the dressing process was as for lead. In mines where valuable quantities of silver were retrieved, security must have been an issue. A 16th century picture of a German silver mine appears to show workers being body searched, but no information has been found about the security measures taken in the Cornish lead and silver mines.

About fifty Cornish mines extracted zinc, occasionally on its own, but usually in conjunction with copper, tin or iron. The main producers in these combinations were Great Retallack and Budnick Consols in Newlyn and Perranzabuloe, and Penrose Consols (British Silver and Lead Co.) in Sithney; the output being greatest between 1850 and 1860. There were about forty mines which extracted zinc with lead, and, of these, the chief producers were West Chiverton and Cargol. Creegbrawse (in Kenwyn) was another mine which produced good quantities of zinc in the first half of the 19th century, along with copper and tin.

Zinc was separated out from the other minerals during the buddling or jigging stages and was dressed in much the same way as copper.[20] Very little information is available about employment of females at the mines producing any quantity of zinc. However, Creegbrawse was employing five women and ten children in its dressing operations in 1838.[21] At the same time, Pembroke Mine (in Par) was producing zinc with tin and employing a total of twelve women and fifty two children. Zinc dressers were very rarely recorded as such in the census returns; however, nineteen women and girls are described as *'blende dressers'* in the parish of Perranzabuloe for 1861. They were living in the Goonhavern and Carnkief areas. The youngest among them was 9 year-old Georgianna Menadue of Polvenna, but most were aged between 12 and 18 years old. Later, in 1865, twenty females were employed in the dressing of zinc and silver at Rosewarne United (in Gwinnear).[22]

MANGANESE

Very little is known about the mining of manganese in Devon and Cornwall, but it is believed that it was first mined in the Newton St Cyres and Upton Pine areas (in the Exe Valley) at the end of the 18th century. An early cost book for the manganese works at Pound Living, Newton St Cyres indicates that women were employed, and were paid 2s *'for Christmas'* in 1790.[23] It is also believed that women were involved in washing manganese in a dammed stream at nearby Hayne Farm, Woodley, as well as picking the ore at *'The Landings'*.[24]

Manganese was also exploited in the Tamar region from about 1805, when small mines were worked in the Launceston and Tavistock area, especially in the five parishes of Milton Abbott, Marystow, Coryton, Lifton and Brentor. Between 1805 and 1820, the manganese from the Tamar area was the main source of this mineral for use in glassmaking in the UK. Later, it was also used in steel manufacture and chlorine production. Such was the local impact of these mines that the population at Lifton, Coryton, Stowford and Lewtrenchard doubled between 1801 and 1851.[25]

In addition, there was some manganese mining in the Teign Valley during the mid 19th century. However, most of the manganese in Devon had been mined out by about 1860 and the industry went into decline. The exception was Newton St Cyres Mine, which was reopened from 1872 to 1879, but few records survive.

This Devonshire manganese was mostly found in irregular nodular masses, and usually at very shallow depths. As a result, the earliest operations were often very simple excavations made by farmers, as they discovered these deposits in their fields. As these surface deposits were exhausted, the manganese was then worked by very simple methods, either by open cast mining or sinking shallow pits.

By about 1845, as the surface deposits and open cast workings were also worked out, some of the mines developed into more extensive underground mines. The largest working was at Hogstor, near Chillaton, where over 50,000 tons of ore was produced. Other mines operating on a fairly large scale were at Monkstone (Brentor), Coryton, Dippertown (Marystow), and Ramsdown (Milton Abbott).[26] Manganese was also mined in a small way in parts of Cornwall. One such mine was Falmouth and Sperries in Kenwyn, where manganese was mined with copper, tin and lead. It was also mined with iron and tin at Ruthers in St Columb.[27]

It seems that, because manganese dressing was relatively simple, a much smaller proportion of the mine workforce were involved in dressing than at the tin, copper or lead mines. When brought to the surface, the ore readily lent itself to hand picking, the black manganese ore being easy to distinguish from the slate and chert usually brought up with it. The 'fines' and 'dredge' ore were then treated by jigging and the finest portions buddled, in the same way as copper ore. After these three operations, the ore was generally taken for milling.

Women and girls were employed in the picking and dressing process at these mines. Manganese mines in Milton Abbot (probably Chillaton and Hogstor) and Lewtrenchard were mentioned in the *1842 Royal Commission*. In 1841, they were employing ten girls under the age of 13, and thirty-three girls between the ages of 13 and 18. No figures were given for women working above that age. The *1841 Census* tended to give little information on women's occupations, but still recorded eight females working at the manganese mines who were resident in Christow, Lamerton, Milton Abbot or Marystow. A larger number were recorded in the *1851 Census*; twelve in Coryton and twenty-one in Lifton. In July 1856, five females are known to have worked for between thirteen and seventeen days at Coryton Manganese Mine, and were paid 4 or 5d per day.[28] In the *1861 Census*, there were just five manganese dressers recorded; in Stowford and Lifton.

After the ore was dressed by these women and children, it was transported by mule, or later by horse and wagon, down to water-powered mills in the river valleys. There were manganese crushing mills at Hamlyn's Marsh (Exwick), Shillamill (Tavistock) and Slimeford (Calstock), but the largest mill was at Morwellham.[29] Here, the mill and manganese quay were constructed away from the copper quays, in order to prevent contamination (Fig. 46).

OTHER MINERALS

Fig. 46 Morwellham Quay c. 1868, showing Manganese Mill (arrowed)
Courtesy of Morwellham & Tamar Valley Trust

Manganese was exported from Morwellham from at least 1820.[30] Hearder, in his *Guide to the Tamar* of 1841, notes that women were probably employed at the manganese mill.

'At Morwellham, which developed as the chief port of Tavistock and the mines of that area, there were also mills for crushing manganese ore, certainly in the 1840s. After crushing, the ore was carefully packed in large casks which are then stored on the quayside. It is almost certain that the women in Morwellham were involved in this dressing and packing of manganese.' (p. 55)

At these mills, the women or girls would feed the roughly dressed manganese into the mill where it was crushed to a fine powder. They then packed the powder into 4 cwt casks ready for export. Unusually, in 1845, a three-shift system was operating at the mill, so that there was a continuous supply of dressed ore for shipping.[31]

WOLFRAM

Wolfram was almost indistinguishable from tin, and, up until about 1900, was discarded as waste, despite being recognised as a potential hardener for steel as early as 1785.

With a developing market for steel, from 1900 some of the waste heaps of the Cornish mines were reworked for wolfram, as at Gunnislake Clitters mine. Wolfram was probably also extracted from Wheal Mary Ann (Menheniot) when reworking for lead between 1900 and 1908.[32] Whether females were employed at this time is unclear.

Wolfram was certainly recovered from the spoil heaps at Wheal Mary Ann during the First World War, when it was desperately needed for steel making for the war effort. A surviving photograph shows twelve women were working there at this time, under the direction of two foremen. The women in the photograph are named, and all appear to be in their late teens or early twenties. At least four of them were married, and sisters Nancy Bawden and Pol Pomeroy were both working there while their husbands were serving in the forces. They would have been 25 and 31 years old respectively in 1914.[33]

The very nature of their work meant they were working in the open air at the spoil heaps, so these women and girls were dressed accordingly, with long overcoats, long boots, and warm hats. Interestingly, however, as with their contemporaries at the clay pits, they appear to be working bare-handed. A photograph shows them with cobbing hammers and a short narrow type of rake, presumably used for dragging down material from the heap. One of the foremen is leaning on a long-handled rake for the same purpose. They do not appear to work at tables, as at the glass mine, but seem to be equipped with buckets for collecting the material they have dressed.[34]

Fig. 47 Women & Girls Dressing Wolfram at Spoil Heaps
Wheal Mary Ann, Menheniot, First World War
Courtesy of Brian Bawden

Several other mines were reworked for wolfram during the First World War. Among them were Gazeland, Cannaframe and Treburland on Bodmin Moor, and this second dressing continued at Gunnislake. It is not clear whether females were recruited at these mines or not. However, they were brought in to work at Hemerdon Mine in the parish of Plympton, but it seems that their efforts were not received very favourably:

'General labourers were therefore requisitioned for service in the engine room and stamps mills. Girls proved the only class of labour available for the concentration plant. The results obtained under these circumstances were far from satisfactory.' [35]

IRON

Major iron workings developed over the 'Great Perran Iron Lode' in the Newlyn East area and around Restormel (Liskeard) during the second half of the 19th century. There are just a few records of women being employed there. In 1861, Charlotte and Eliza Jarvis, 12 and 10 years old respectively, were described as *'iron ore workers'* and Elizabeth Ann Lampion, 17 years old, as *'iron ore dresser'*. All were living in the Rejarrah area of the parish of St Colomb Major. Around this time, micaceous haematite (shiny ore) was also mined in the Teign Valley. This was sold as 'Devonshire Sand' for drying ink on letters (in the days before blotting paper). In 1861, 25 year-old Harriett Yendall was the only woman recorded as working at the *'shining ore mine'* in Christow.

Fig. 48 Women Employees Outside the Washing Plant
Great Rock Iron Mine, August 1945
Courtesy of British Geological Survey

Fig. 49 Woman Working in the Mill
Great Rock Iron Mine, August 1945
Courtesy of British Geological Survey

The last working metal mine in Devon was Great Rock Iron Mine in Hennock. Women were employed there during the Second World War, to help with the dressing of the shiny ore, and were kept on until about 1952. When the ore from underground was tipped from wagons into a bin at the top of the dressing plant, one of the women would rake it across a screen and then hand pick the ore. Ore-bearing rock was dropped into a chute going to the crusher, the waste passing into a chute to go to the waste dumps. After crushing, washing and further screening in the mill, the fine mix was washed down into a series of sand collectors and baffles. This separation process worked in a similar way to that of china clay. It was here that a second woman oversaw these operations, as the micaceous haematite was separated from the heavier sand. She would ensure continual flow through the processes, and dig out and rewash the deposited sand as required (Fig. 49). The separated shiny ore was then channelled to the drying shed.

In 1943, two women were paid about £4 6s each for a 36-hour week, and a girl was paid £2 15s. for 44 hours. One woman was also employed as the equivalent of a post-war 'counthouse woman', and she continued to work at Great Rock until about 1965.[36] At least one woman also worked at Treamble Iron Mine during the Second World War. She was responsible for packing Fuller's Earth into bags ready for sale.

OTHER METALLIFEROUS ORES

Antimony, although very much a minority mineral in Cornwall, has a long history of exploitation, mostly being mined from the Endellion and Porth Quinn area. It was dressed in much the same way as lead. The ore dressers and washers at Newham Smelter were paid for washing antimony ore as early as 1704 and 1705. The only other reference found for bal maidens dressing antimony was much later, in 1891, when 17 year-old Jane Stephen of Tideford was described as an *'antimony miner'*.

In 1891, 27 year-old Janie Minors was recorded as a *'uranium mine girl'*, and seems to part of a small group of people employed at South Terras Mine in Coombe, in St Stephen-in-Brannel. Most of the uranium obtained from Cornwall in the late 19th century was recovered from spoil heaps, as its use had not previously been recognised at the time of the first working. Janie's work, therefore, was probably very similar to that carried out be the women at the wolfram mines.

SLATE

Although there were many slate quarries in operation in Devon and Cornwall during the 18th and 19th century, with 130 granite and slate quarries recorded in Cornwall in 1829, there are very few records surviving. The largest complex of quarries was at Delabole, on the north coast, and slate is still extracted from there today.

In one of the earliest references, tribute teams seem to have worked at Delabole under much the same system as at the copper and tin mines.[37] Although the presence of women in the workforce is not mentioned, we may assume that wives and daughters were probably part of the tribute team, dressing the slate brought out of the quarry by the men and boys. Certainly, women and girls were being employed as slate dressers at the quarries during the first half of the 19th century. The tribute system seems to have still been in place in 1864, long after the women and girls had ceased to work there.

Clifton's description of 1850, gives us an inkling of the environment in which these women and girls lived and worked:

'Two villages owe their origin to the Delabole quarries, Pengelly and Medrose. These quarries present one of the most astonishing and animated scenes imaginable. The traveller suddenly beholds 3 enormous pits, excavated by the uninterrupted labour of centuries, slowly encroaching on the domain of the farmer. Upon the edge of each quarry is the Papote Head or platform from which guide chains are stretched like the shrouds of a ship to pit bottom. The slate, after blasting, is placed on a truck, which being attached to a wheel traversing a guide chain, is drawn up to the Papote head by steam engine. Moveable hatches are run out 14 ft over the face on to which the truck lands and is then drawn away by horses to the workshops.' [38]

It seems that, in the early years, women and older girls may have been responsible for the most skilled aspect of slate dressing, that of the final splitting. They seem to have worked alongside the men in this task:

'For many years women and girls were employed in the splitting of slate and some were expert at their work. Sometime in the fifties it was necessary to reduce hands and in order to retain males the females were discharged, and since then none have been employed.' [39]

Turner also mentions *'cullers'*, or *'hullah bobbers'* searching the waste heaps for good slate. These were usually young boys, who were able to make a living from dressing the scraps. Although there is no evidence of women or girls working at the quarry at Delabole beyond about 1855, these tasks, ascribed latterly to boys, may also have been done by women and older girls.[40]

It would be at the 'workshops' that the female dressers worked. In early days, they would probably be working out in the open air, or in crudely erected sheds, the sides of which would be made from rejected slate, and roofed over with wood or iron. These sheds were only open at the front, giving more protection from the weather than their counterparts in the copper, lead and tin mines. In 1864, the dressing houses were described as having two sides at an acute angle with a roof over the top.

It seems that, in 1839, each tribute team had its own particular storage and dressing area. By 1864, the finished slates were stacked in a communal 'show yard', where they were marked with the tribute team's symbol, and recorded by the tally clerk. The slates were taken to the yard by 'pitchers' who carried them in V-shaped receptacles on their backs. Slates were usually stacked in rows of *'one hundred dozen'* (actually fifteen hundred, to allow for breakages) with each five dozen marked by a slate turned on its edge.[41] The younger girls employed at the slate quarries were perhaps involved in carrying, or stacking and counting the slates. Local custom has it that women and girls were also involved in slate stacking at Carnglaze Slate Quarries, although no written record has been found.[42]

As well as dressing, women were also involved in the transporting of slate. About 1836, one of the Delabole quarry companies bought six donkeys to carry the slates from the quarry to the 'slate depot' in Pengelly. They then employed a woman to drive the donkeys. Apparently, this method of transport was quite successful, and soon most of the carriage was done in this way. By 1850, bullocks and horses were being used instead, but these were probably driven by men. Women also packed slates from Delabole into the ships at

Port Gaverne. These women were employed by the ships' captains, not by the quarry managers and so fall outside the brief of this book.

Although the *1841 Census* for the Delabole area does not identify any women as working at the quarry, other than possibly two widows who are recorded as *'labour women'*, Delabole Slate Quarries were clearly employing females at that time. According to the *1842 Royal Commission*, there were nine girls under the age of 13 years, and seventeen between the ages of 13 and 18 in 1841, a total of twenty-six; but no figures were given for adult females. In 1842, 10% of the workforce of 700 were reported to be women. These women and girls were usually hired as daily labourers, with their wages ranging from 2s to 5s per week, depending on age. As at the copper and tin mines, a deduction was made from their earnings for their tools.

The *1851 Census* for St Teath gives much more detail than the census of 1841, mentioning twenty-six *'quarry women'* or *'quarry girls'*. In ten years, the average age of girls employed at the quarry had obviously changed. The youngest, Mary Tremaine and Elizabeth Lane, were just 13 years old, but most were between the ages of 14 and 17 years. The oldest was 48 year-old Catherine Killow, who was a widow. Twenty-five of them lived in either Pengelly or Medrose, almost adjacent to the quarry.

The *1851 Census* also records a 60 year-old widow working at a slate quarry in St Clether, and a 39 year-old widow, Mary Rush, in Tintagel. The latter entry is particularly interesting as her two young sons are also described as 'sorting slate'. They may all have been 'cullers' or 'hullah bobbers' as mentioned earlier. Lorigan [43] has traced the fate of some of the 1851 Delabole slate dressers. By 1861, one had died, four had moved from the parish, eight (one of whom was a domestic servant) had married quarrymen, and one was single and unemployed. It seems that no women were employed at Delabole after the mid 1850s, other than for office work.

FOOTNOTES

1. Murchison (1854) p. 118.
2. Corin (1997) p. 10.
3. Greeves (2006) p. 9.
4. Hunt, *Ure's Dictionary* (1878) p. 1004.
5. Penhalls and Blue Hills Minutes Book (CRO: STA/191).
6. Hunt, *Ure's Dictionary* (1878) p. 1004.
7. Greeves (2006) p. 9.
8. Personal correspondence (PC/LM 2002).
9. Throughout this chapter information is drawn from the *1842 Royal Commission* [CEC], especially Tables 13, 14,15, 17, 28 and Evidence Nos. 84 and 124.
10. Gill, Michael (1994).
11. Report by Joseph Fletcher for the Lead Mines of Lanark and Dumfries, CEC (1842) pp.4, 8.
12. Burt (1982) p. 15.
13. Hunt (1970) p. 92.
14. Hunt (1884).
15. Gill (1994).
16. Lemon (1838) pp. 70-76.
17. Bartlett (1994) p. 121.
18: Schmitz, Christopher 'The Teign Valley Silver-Lead Mines 1806-1880', *British Mining* No. 15 (1980) p. 73.
19. Hamilton Jenkin (2005) p. 27.
20. Henwood, G. (1855) Part 2 p. 10.
21. Henwood (1838) p. 59.
22. Spargo (1865) 2. p.19.
23. Russell, P. M. G 'Manganese Mining in Devon' *Devon & Cornwall Notes & Queries* (Summer 1970) pp. 205-13.
24. Hamilton Jenkin (2005) p. 142.
25. Toll (1958) p. 17; Booker (1974).
26. Richardson (1992).
27. Burt (1984) pp. 18-40.
28. Newman (1940) p. 111.
29. Massey, Roger 'Slimeford' *Tamar History* No. 12 (2002) p. 10-11; Toll (1958) p. 17.
30. Patrick (1990) p. 40.
31. Toll (1958) p. 17.
32. Personal correspondence (VFJ/LM 2002).
33. Messenger (1994) p. 116.
34. Flint-Johnson, V. *CFHS Jour.* 106 (2002) p.14.
35. Terrell, Ernest (1920) p. 86.
36. Brooks (2004) p. 60.
37. Borlase (1758) p. 94.
38. Clifton, Thomas *Handbook for Travellers in Devon and Cornwall* (1850).
39. The Cornish & Devon Post (1917).
40. Turner (1864) pp. 11, 14.
41. De la Beche (1839) p. 502.
42. Personal correspondence (CR/LM 2003).
43. Lorigan, Catherine *Delabole: The History of the Slate Quarry and the Making of its Village Community* (Pengelly Press 2007) pp. 42-44.

Chapter 8

THE COUNTHOUSE WOMEN

Apart from the large number of women and girls working on the dressing floors and at the stamps, there were usually other females at work at the mine counthouse. These 'counthouse women' were not often mentioned, but were an important part of the total workforce and had significant parts to play in the smooth running of the office management. Not only were they rarely included in descriptions of the mine, but they were not necessarily recorded in the cost books, sometimes just being included under 'general office costs'. Neither were they always named in the census material, probably alternatively recorded just as 'housekeeper', 'domestic servant' or 'employed at mine'. They were variably described as mine or counthouse servants or counthouse women. Occasionally, their work was described in more detail, such as 'cook' or 'washing and cleaning at account house'. Due to the scarcity of information, it is very difficult to find out much about individual counthouse women, and most of our information about their work comes from general reports of events at the counthouse. It seems that there were not the same arrangements made for a central office on site at the clay pits, so counthouse women were not employed there.

The mine counthouse had developed from very humble origins to become, by the turn of the 18th century, the organisational centre of a mining venture. In early days, or in very small mines, its equivalent was probably no more than a hut, where stores were kept and paperwork done. At remote mines or workings, it would sometimes be necessary for mine officers to remain overnight, so a multipurpose counthouse would then have been built. In Bottrell's *Hearthside Stories of Cornwall*, there is the following description of one such house on Trewey Downs:

'*The streamers built a much larger moor-house than was usual for such sized tin-works, because many men lived down in Ludgvan or Towednack: besides, as some always remained on the place be night, when there was much liquor to be disposed of. They soon got up a house more than 30 feet long and 12 feet wide, with a broad deep chimney in one end, and a wood corner that would contain a cartload of turves, and enough furze to do the cooking for the week. Between the fireplace and the end wall of the house, there was a place contrived to be entered from the wood corner, large enough for storing away a score of ankers or more, besides other goods which required to be kept dry. When the wood corner was full of fuel no person could see that the chimney end wall was double. Planks on stakes stored heath, rushes, ferns or straw for bedding along one side of the house.*'[1]

This particular counthouse was obviously used for more than just mining activities. Although it seems that the men were fairly self-sufficient at such a place, catching rabbit, game or fish for their food, it is not clear whether women were involved in the upkeep, or the smuggling activities, of these remote counthouses.

At the larger mines, from about 1750, permanent residential buildings, which served as an office as well, were often built on site by the managers. These buildings would be placed in some prominent position where the agents could keep an eye on the workforce, but far enough away from the worst of the noise and dust of the mining operation so as to make life bearable. As mines expanded around the house, or managers became wealthier, they generally moved away and built more extensive properties some distance from the mine. The old residence was then often used entirely for business purposes and termed the counthouse (account house):

'In the centre of this hive of activity [the mine] *is seen the counthouse, replete with comfort and convenience for the mine agents, clerks, and other officials, and where a most hospitable welcome is ever awaiting the curious visitor.'* (WB 28th Mar 1862)

The counthouse would have an office, or offices, for the manager and purser, where all book-keeping was done and business visitors received. In addition, there would be a large dining room, probably upstairs, where visitors and shareholders were entertained, and some had a separate 'map room'. There would also be the kitchen and various store rooms. Sometimes there was sleeping accommodation for captains on duty at night, or for emergencies.

Fig. 50 Botallack Counthouse 2003

In the early days, when the mine office and reception area were just part of the mine manager's residence, the domestic work was probably done by the manager's own household staff. Where the counthouse was independent of the main house, the management of the domestic arrangements in the counthouse was the responsibility of the counthouse woman. This was usually a woman of mature age, as shown in an advertisement in the *West Briton*, in 1889, where the minimum stipulated age was 40 years old.[2] The qualities required were *'a good character'* and *'experience of household work and plain cooking'*. Depending on the number of staff and visitors, the counthouse woman may have had one or two women or girls to assist her. In these situations, the senior counthouse woman usually fulfilled the duties of cook and housekeeper, with the others responsible for the general cleaning, laundering and kitchen duties. Dolcoath, the largest Cornish mine, had four counthouse staff in the 1890s; a cook, 'kitchen girl' and two maids. Unlike most other domestic servants and housekeepers, the counthouse women were not normally resident, but were usually drawn from the local mining community. For instance, Elizabeth Kitto, at Godolphin Hill, appears to have lived next door to the counthouse. A few who were resident were Jane Lean and Elizabeth

Roskilly (Fowey Consols) and Elizabeth Middleton (Gwallon) in 1841, Elizabeth Wittington (Fowey Consols) in 1851, and Sarah Ford (Wheal Maria) in 1881.

DAILY ROUTINE

The main duties of the day were to prepare a dinner at mid-day for the agents, purser and captains at the mine, and to keep the counthouse room clean and tidy, despite the amount of dirt and dust that must have been brought in throughout the day. Other duties revolved around the mine officers tours of the mine. In one of Seymour's cartoons of 1877, three men are depicted, almost certainly mine officers, in the washing sheds. They are soaking their feet in hot water and being provided with a hot drink, while their discarded underground clothes are being picked up by a maid and carried off to be washed. We are left to read into this cartoon picture what we will, but this picture fits well with a description of events in the wash-house that come from Moonta in South Australia:

'At nine-thirty every morning the captains began the ritual associated with their daily visits to the underground workings. This would begin when they entered their special changing-room, where white duck coats and trousers, flannel shirts and drawers, thick woollen socks, leather boots, and safety helmets had been laid out by the attendant. By the time they returned at two p.m. the boots they had removed before they went underground would have been polished by the attendant, who would also have sharpened matches ready for them to clean their nails, and would be ready to start laundering their towels and their underground clothes in readiness for their next visit. When they reached the changing room on their return they would strip to the waist, wash the upper part of their bodies, then put on their shirts before they washed their feet and legs in a bowl.' [3]

Fig. 51 Counthouse Woman (Seymour c. 1870)
Courtesy of Mining Communications Ltd

In Moonta, apparently the 'attendant' as mentioned was a male, but the Seymour cartoons show a female doing these duties. In Cornwall, it seems that the counthouse women were responsible for having ample supplies of hot water ready for the agents and captains on their return from their underground tours, or when they had been involved in dirty tasks at surface. Hot water for baths was probably obtained from the engine house outflow, or possibly heated in cauldrons over the fire in the kitchen. It would then have to be carried to the 'dry' or washing sheds, or to a designated part of the counthouse.

The women probably also kept the mine officers supplied with a fresh supply of clean protective clothes. This would involve continual laundering of duck jackets and over trousers. This may have been done at the engine outlet, where other women from the locality

Fig. 52 Cameo Sketch of Counthouse Woman
(Seymour c. 1870)
Courtesy of Mining Communications Ltd

often gathered to do their washing. The clothes were probably dried in the 'dry' or the counthouse kitchen. One of the earliest mine laundresses recorded appears to be Jenny Jenkins at Ailsborough Mine (Sheepstor) who was paid 10s a month, in 1815, for washing underground clothes. Between 1845 and 1848, Mary Ralph was paid 2s 6d per month for washing '*captains underground clothes*' at Wheal Maiden (Gwennap). Also, in the accounts for Coryton Manganese Mine in September 1856, a woman is paid 1s for the same task.[4]

The women would also have the men's boots and helmets to clean after each visit underground. It seems that they were also responsible for the general upkeep and repair of the 'underground' clothes. One person was paid a total of 6s at Wheal Comfort (St. Ives) in 1834 for '*washeing* [sic] *and mending agents' clothes*' over a period of eleven months.[5] Some women were also paid to make the underground clothes. At Cook's Kitchen, in 1781, Elizabeth Gribell made underground suits for John Cockin and James Williams; at 2s 6d each. Ann Thomas was paid 1s for making underground clothes at St Just Mine, in 1862; and, in 1886 and 1887, Ada and Anny Lawry were paid 1s per day for the same task.

Not only were the counthouse women responsible for the laundering and repair of the mine officers' underground clothing, but they were also expected to make sure that it was readily available in the right place and at the right time. Many mine officers were employed at more than one mine, or could be called out to conduct inspection or survey work elsewhere. For instance, Betsey West (the counthouse woman at Wheal Agar in 1823) was '*asked to send underground clothes up* [from Wheal Agar] *to Camborne Vean according to custom*'.[6]

An idea of the type of activities that went on at the counthouse can be glimpsed by the regular orders that appeared in the Wheal Prussia 'Receiving' Book between 1879 and 1882. Food items purchased included bread, butter, cheese, jam, sugar, tea, salt, rice, flour, mustard, pepper and potatoes (in 5 gallon quantities). Laundry and cleaning items included soap, starch, blue, soda and brushes. In addition, 'duck' was ordered at 1s 6d per yard, flannel at 1s 1d, and serge at 1s 11d.

The counthouses were most famous for their provision of very liberal hospitality, especially in the early part of the 19th century. According to George Henwood, people took advantage of this: '*Counthouses were more like regular hotels, with a bottle on the table, dinner open to anyone, with wine and punch.*' However, he noticed that, by 1857, most counthouses were more restrained in their expenditure:

'Counthouses are now what they were originally intended and ought to be - the proper offices for the keeping of mine accounts, for the meeting of the adventurers, for the receipt of persons of business, for the temporary residence and sleeping apartments of the captain when night captains were employed, or in cases of emergency.'

Nonetheless, even in the days of a more closely controlled budget, the counthouse women still had to be ready to receive unexpected visitors at a moment's notice. At the very least, 'visitors' meant the preparation of extra food for the mid-day meal. For those wanting to go underground, it would also involve finding suitable protective clothing and the provision of adequate washing facilities afterwards, as indicated in this conversation, reported by George Henwood, between a mine captain and the counthouse woman:

'Well, then Mary,…get out and air three suits in three minutes…send off the maid at once for a few pounds of beef steak, and a bit of fish, if she can get it; and some new bread, and tell her to go to my house for two bottles of wine and a bottle of brandy. These strangers ought to have something when they come up; and be sure and have plenty of hot water to wash. We shan't go down until twelve, and we come up at three; have'n all ready by four, tha'al do; have't all nice, now.' [7]

Leifchild was appreciative of the attentions and preparations of the counthouse staff in this way, after a visit to Botallack Mine:

'At the counting house, gallons of water are awaiting us, and tallow, mud, ooze, and iron-rust, all give way to the application of soap. Off go our miners' caps, and woollen jackets, and wide inexpressibles.' [8]

SETTING DAY, SAMPLING DAY AND MINE ACCOUNT MEETING

Apart from the daily routine and visitors to the counthouse, there were other special days for which the counthouse women had to prepare. Among then were Setting Day, Sampling Day and the Mine Account Meeting.

Setting Day usually occurred every two months and coincided with the payday for that month. This was the occasion when miners bid for new pitches at the mine. The auction would be conducted by the mine captain, outside the counthouse. If there were gentry visiting the area, Setting Day was often considered a good time to have a tour of a mine, as it was one of the few occasions when working miners were to be seen above ground. It was also of great interest to the visitors to see how the bidding was done. Once the setting was complete and all the employees had been paid, guests would then be taken on a tour of the mine, including an underground visit if required. When all was done, the mine officers invited their guests to dine. Henwood described such a scene at Great Hewas Mine:

'A neat, tidy, elderly woman appears to lay the cloth, which is soon done in the plainest possible manner. Savoury smells assault the nose, provoking an already keen appetite, seeing it is three o'clock; and the neat little woman re-appears with a goodly, plain sort of roast beef, accompanied by potatoes and cabbage. A jar of ale is brought from the public house two miles off, and a little bread and cheese completes the welcome repast.'

Sampling Day, like Setting Day, occurred about every two months, and was the day when the assayers and managers of the smelters would come to sample the ores for sale. These visitors might have several mines to visit in one day, so it was customary for the mine to provide dinner for them in their travels. There could be as many as thirty people attending. Henwood, again, described a typical meal:

'Roast beef, and a leg of mutton with wine. Followed by rice pudding, bread and cheese and then brandy.' [9]

However, the major event at the counthouse appears to have been the quarterly Mine Account Day. Under the cost book system, used throughout Cornwall and West Devon until almost the end of the 19th century, adventurers (shareholders) met every three months at the counthouse to receive reports, approve the accounts, and make decisions about the running of the mine over the next quarter. Each mine had its traditional day of the quarter for this meeting, for instance at Bosorn and Bollowell it was the third Friday, and at United Mines it was the Saturday before the second Monday of the month.[10] The meetings usually started at mid-day, and dinner was not served until the business had ended. After the two-course meal, the meeting continued with drinking into late afternoon or early evening.

In the early years, these meals were famous! In fact, some people invested just the minimum amount in the mines in order to attend the counthouse dinners. These people were known as *'knife and fork'* shareholders.[11] This probably romanticised and exaggerated view of the 'old times' was recorded in 1872:

'The old school of mine managers' creed was that a lode could not be found without proper dowzing of the ground, and dowsing of themselves with the strong contraband from the other side of the channel, that the cost-book could not circulate for signatures, unless the bottle, with a good drop of 'something short' in it accompanied it round the table - and the next six months' work would never be fortunate unless every equestrian, as he climbed on his nag, hours after dinner, fell over the saddle half a dozen times..., and every pedestrian had three or four snoozes...on his way home from the counting house.' (RCG 27th Jan 1872)

A typical scene at the Counthouse Meeting was also described by Hamilton Jenkin:

'Thus as soon as the business part of the meeting was finished, a dinner consisting of roast beef, giblet pie or other delicacies would be served by the count-house woman and her assistants in some long low room adjoining, where the trestle tables covered with rough but snow white cloths, and the clean, holystoned floor set scenes of homely festivity hard to describe.' [12]

In 1838, a special counthouse dinner at Fowey Consols, was arranged to celebrate the sale of a large quantity of lime, and was described as the 'Lime Feast'. Seventy people sat down to dine in the dining room, and a further twenty-six dined in the map room. The menu included boiled and roast beef, as well as legs of mutton. Cider was supplied, and the ninety-six guests also drank seven gallons of gin, rum and brandy! Little wonder that the mine purser began to suggest that the adventurers should look into the *'Counting House Expenses'*, and the *'Wine and Spirits Expenditure'* books.[13]

Preparation for any of these special dinners would have required a very early start for the counthouse staff. All the rooms to be used would require thorough cleaning and the laying of fires from early on. The dining room needed to be prepared; laying the trestle tables with coarse white cloths, and often using tin, copper, or pewter plates and dishes made from ore from the mine. At Botallack, for instance, the table would be set with the pewter dinner service made from tin from the mine, a set of silver decanters used at one of the royal visits, along with a 'gigantic' punch jug.

In early days, all the cooking was done over a fire in the open hearth in the kitchen. The joints of meat were turned on a spit, with potatoes and vegetables roasting in trays underneath. Meat and vegetable stews would also be prepared in cauldrons over the fire. Alternatively, a giblet pie might be baked under the ashes, on a baking stone covered by an inverted iron pot or dish. This might be followed by a dessert of apple pie, rice pudding, cheese and biscuits, or fruit.[14]

In some mines, the counthouse kitchen was 'open house' during the morning and early afternoon, and, if the weather was particularly bad, guests might be given a dish of warming soup taken from the stew. Sometimes, during the business part of the meeting, adventurers would go out to the kitchen to collect a bowl of soup, if the dinner seemed a long time coming.[15] Eventually, the business part of the meeting would end, and the counthouse women would be called on to serve the dinner.

Fig. 53 Botallack Counthouse Pewter Dinner Service
(made from Botallack Tin)
Courtesy of National Trust (Cornwall)

After the two courses had been served and consumed, the counthouse women would 'clear the board' and the drinking would begin. Meanwhile, in the kitchen, the women could begin the clearing away and washing up. In cold weather, they would have to make a hot punch ready to serve to the visitors before they went home, and this would be simmering in a cauldron over the hearth.

The end of the meeting was probably the most difficult part of the day for the counthouse women, having to enable the adventurers to get on their way, often in a less than sober state. It was only after the party had broken up and people were on their way home, that the counthouse staff could finally clear away whatever debris was left from the carousing, before they could go home. It must have been a very long day.

Henwood reports that, towards the middle of the 19th century, the money spent on these mine account meals was beginning to be limited, and the meetings were less riotous. However, some mines continued to be quite extravagant, on food at least, as this account of 1872 indicates:

'A real old-fashioned meal, - plain but good, tummels of beef and mutton, vegetables piled up like little haystacks, wholesome beer; followed by steaming punch.'

Although the mine was not identified, this particular feast was prepared, served and then eaten in terrifying circumstances. It is difficult to imagine the conditions under which the counthouse women had cooked the food, or indeed carried out any of their duties, at this particular mine:

'The manager holds that the mine will never be a success unless there is a bit of grub and a glass of punch once a quarter, but he will not expend much on the old rattle trap of an account-house. It is a land of storms, on the very edge of the cliffs, and catches the full force of the gale; while, from its windows, a magnificent sight, of wrathful sea and stern cliffs may be witnessed. Chains - passed over the roof, and secured by iron bars to the cliff - keep the frail and rocking tenement in its place. The windows were buttressed by pieces of timber, nailed to the floor and jammed diagonally against the wooden framework.' (RCG 27th Jan 1872)

Other mines, by this time, had completely phased out their sumptuous feasts. The author of the same article of 1872, having reminisced about old-style account-house dinners, was very scathing of what generally began to replace them. This was usually a more simple fare of bread and cheese, which he called a '*Captain Teague*' in honour of the mine agent who had first instigated them at the Counthouse Meeting he attended.

With the advent of limited companies taking over the cost book companies during the 1880s, the quarterly account meeting became a thing of the past. Big dinners continued to be provided at the mines for directors and shareholders, but usually now on an annual basis, or on special occasions. For example, the following was prepared by the counthouse staff at Wheal Emma, in 1899:

'Boiled leg of mutton at the head of the table, ribs of beef at the bottom, two steak pies in the middle with plain dumplings after, and apples, pears and grapes for desert, all washed down by a liberal supply of claret.' [16]

NAME	YEAR	MINE
Ann Eva	1785	Cook's Kitchen
Elizabeth Wise	1785	Cook's Kitchen
Jenny Jenkins	1815	Ailsborough Mine
Betsy West	1822-23	Dolcoath
Elizabeth Middleton	1841	Gwallon
Elizabeth Roskilly	1841	Fowey Consols
Jane Lean	1841	Fowey Consols
Elizabeth Wittington	1841+1851	Fowey Consols
Elizabeth Mill	1848-50	Wheal Agar
Mary Hosken	1849-50	Ding Dong (Gulval)
Jane Gribble	1850-52	Wheal Agar
Elizabeth Johns	1851	Carn Brea
Grace Martin	1851-8	Trumpet Consols
Betsey Nicholas	1852-54	Ding Dong (Gulval)
Hannah Mathews	1852-55	Wheal Agar
Caroline Carpenter	1855	Wheal Agar
Nanny (Ann) Cock	1856-57	Rosewarne Herland United
Jane Vine	1858-62	Trumpet Consols
E. Tippett	1859	Wheal Trerew
Matilda Grenfell Snr.	1861	Botallack
Elizabeth Johns	1861	Boswidden
Mary Peake	1863	East Brookwood Mine
Mary Runce	1864-65	East Great Work
Mary Masters	1855-63?	Carn Vivian
Elizabeth Kitto	1865-66	Godolphin Hill
Susan Jenkin	1866-71	Wheal Basset & Grylls
Susan Moyle	1871-72	Wheal Basset & Grylls
Mary Ann Goldsworthy	1871	Wheal Uny
Matilda Grenfell Jnr.	1871+1881	Botallack
Ann Williams	1876-82	Wheal Goole Pellas
Sarah Ford	1881	Wheal Maria
Alfreda Richards	1881	Devon Great Consols
Mary Tregellas	1882	Wheal Coates
Philippa Wills	1883-4	North Metal
Sophia Nicholls	1883-6	Pednandrea United Mines
Emma Trevena	1883-6	Pednandrea United Mines
Mary Bedington	1884	Wheal North Metal
Mary Jane	1885-6	Pednandrea United Mines
Betty Webb	1890-1900?	Dolcoath
Eliza Dunnell	1891	Pednandrea
Eliza Treloar	1893-94	Wheal Agar
Mary Ellen Sleeman	1893-94	Wheal Agar
Mary James	1894	Pednandrea
Elizabeth A. Cock	1894	Wheal Agar
Alice Maud Tonkin	1894	Wheal Agar
Olive Treloar	1894	Wheal Agar
A. Crocker	1895	West Wheal Francis
Stella Chenoweth	1940s-70s?	Geevor
Sally Bradford	1950-66	Great Rock
Lynne Ting	1950s	Geevor
Bessie Bennetts	1950s	Geevor

Fig. 54 Named Counthouse Women by Mine

PARISH FEAST DAYS AND SPECIAL EVENTS

One of the annual holidays was the Parish Feast Day, celebrated on or near the Saint's Day to whom the church was dedicated. Quite often, part of the celebrations would take place at the mine. Special church services would be held on the Sunday, and then, on the Monday, there would be a carnival procession, usually followed by a communal meal. At the Wendron Feast Day held at Porkellis Mine in August 1859, seven hundred miners, with their friends and families, sat down outside the counthouse to share tea and cakes, while the guests of the adventurers had refreshments inside the counthouse. This was another mammoth organisational task for the counthouse women, but no doubt they were aided and abetted by other women of the parish.

One of the other major events at the mine which would involve the counthouse staff, was the beginning of new ventures, such as the opening of a new shaft, the 'christening' of a new mine engine, or the restarting of an old one. These, too, were all-day events and involved the whole community. Generally, the counthouse and other mine buildings would be decked out in evergreen and laurel decorations, and great evergreen bowers built around the area designated for where the miners and their families would eat. Considerable numbers of important guests would be invited, including local landowners and JPs, and the parish vicar, who would perform the blessing ceremony. We have this description of the festivities that took place when the engine was re-started at Wheal Helena in 1891:

'In front of the blacksmith's shop an ox was being roasted whole, and in the account-house a whole sheep was undergoing a similar process, while a long row of boilers suspended over an open fire in the open air contained the vegetables for the dinner. The account-house, carpenter's shop, and a few other places were decorated with flags, the carpenter's shop being fitted up as a dining room, while four rows of tables were laid outside for the workmen. 150 guests partook of a champagne dinner.'

Because celebrations of this kind were of such proportions, they were beyond the capacity of the counthouse kitchen and kitchen staff alone. Frequently, some of the catering for the special guests was done at the mine manager's house, by his domestic staff, and then carried in crates and boxes to the counthouse, when ready. The food that could not be easily moved, such as the vegetables, punch etc., would be prepared at the counthouse. Catering for the miners and local people would not be done by the counthouse staff, but probably by a local butcher and licensee.

Such a day might begin with the special guests gathering for a breakfast at a tavern in a central place, and then being driven to join the local parade at some place along its route. This would include mine employees and their families, local residents, and a band. As the parade wound its way through the streets, the numbers would increase until, by the time it had reached the mine, it would have swelled to great proportions. On arrival, the dignitaries would be given a conducted tour of the new engine, or new part of the mine, by the captain and engineer. Eventually, when all was ready, the vicar would give the blessing, and the engine driver would start the new engine.

Meanwhile, the counthouse staff would have laid out the food for the special guests and, at the appropriate time, rung the mine bell to signify *'quarter of an hour to dinner on table.'*[17]

The special guests would make their way to the counthouse, where the celebrations would continue all day, with food, champagne, brandy and gin. Outside, the mine employees would be provided with a roasted ox, and plenty of beer and cider, whilst they enjoyed various sports and games.

Similar large-scale celebrations were also arranged at times of national celebrations, presumably involving the counthouse staff in much the same way. Special Christmas food was also prepared for the mine officers and staff. For example, the counthouse woman at Wheal Agar prepared '*ale and cakes*' for the mine officers for Christmas 1822.[18] At Dolcoath (in the 1890s), Betty Webb, remembers a much more elaborate affair:

'*We all looked forward to the Saturday before Christmas when Christmas dinner was eaten. On the Friday we often worked until 10 o'clock. The best tablecloths and glasses and the silver made the tables look very nice. I remember that for one Christmas dinner we cooked a boiled turkey, 3 roast geese, some chicken and roast beef and vegetables. Also we had afterwards a Christmas pudding and all kinds of fruit. There were drinks and smokes. When the men left, the women used to have their dinners. We worked hard but we enjoyed ourselves.*' [19]

FIRST AID POST AND MORGUE

From time to time, the counthouse women had to turn their hands to much more sombre occupations than preparing dinners and banquets for the mine adventurers, or the gentry of the parish and county. When there were the inevitable accidents at the mine, casualties were often brought up to the counthouse area.

Where possible, injured miners were taken home, but in some cases this was not appropriate or possible, and so the carpenter's shop and the area around the counthouse would become a first aid post or morgue. The counthouse women would administer what care they could, while waiting for the mine surgeon, which could take several hours. This would be particularly true of accidents where victims were burned or scalded, or too seriously injured to survive a long journey home on a stretcher or cart. For instance, when the boiler exploded at Boiling Well Mine in 1858, it seems that the injured were carried there. The engineer was killed outright, and nine others were seriously scalded or burned, among them two women. It was here that Mary Webster died shortly after the accident. The other woman, Alice Jones, died later in the evening, but it is not clear whether it had been possible to move her, or whether she too died at the mine.[20]

The dead were sometimes carried to the carpenter's shop, which would be cleared to become a temporary morgue. The bodies might remain there until the inquest, which was usually held the following day. Thus, the counthouse staff would be involved in the preparations for both the appropriate laying-out, and for the inquest itself. For instance, at Poldice Mine in March 1789, the cost book shows an entry of 6s 6d for a shroud for '*Enylew*', followed by a payment to Martha Higga for '*striping him*' (presumably stripping him).

OTHER TASKS

Brief mention has been made of other tasks relating to the more domestic tasks at the mine. From 1832 to 1834, 'sack washers' were employed at Wheal Comfort Mine in Carbis Bay. In 1867, Mary Peak was paid 1s for making sacks at New Trelawney Silver and Lead Mine.

Some of the later census records give an insight into other, more clerical, tasks that women and girls began to do at the mine office. Fanny Short (of St Cleer) was described as a *'mine errand girl'* in 1871, as were Elizabeth Gerry (at South Phoenix) in 1881 and Frances Waters (of Stray Park) in 1901. Alfreda Richards (of Gunnislake) was an *'office girl in a copper mine'* in 1881, while Beatrice Craze (of Illogan) and Margaret Rowe (of Camborne) were *'mine post errand girls'* in 1901. Between 1874 and 1891, Delabole Slate Quarry employed a woman to clean the office and light the fires, and also a post woman.[21] In 1881, the office woman was probably 64 year-old Mary Abbott (of Delabole) who may have been slightly mis-recorded as *'a slate quarry labourer'* (females were no longer employed on the dressing floors at this time).

RECRUITMENT, PAY AND CONDITIONS

In the latter part of the 19th century, as many of the mines became less profitable, the amount of money spent on the counthouse hospitality began to decrease. The expenditure had almost always come out of the mine's accounts and often to excess in the early days. It was not unheard of in failing mines for sick club money, or money earmarked for outstanding bills to be used to fund a final dinner for the adventurers. By the 1860s, the amount was usually closely regulated, and the number of women needed at the counthouse was much more closely scrutinised. The total numbers employed at the mine office would probably have been considerably reduced.

From the limited census information it seems that, generally, the counthouse women were older than the bal maidens on the dressing floor, with most being over 40 years old. (For instance, twenty-four of the thirty-eight counthouse women with identifiable ages in the *1861 Census* were over this age). Many were widowed, some with dependant children, or single with elderly or disabled dependants. Among the oldest were 71 year-old Ann Richards and 73 year-old Sarah Goldsworthy, both of Camborne, 72 year-old Mary Hosking, of Connor Downs and 71 year-old Jane Williams of Treskerby. These were all working in 1881. One of the youngest was 12 year-old Elizabeth Martin from Lower Dimson, who was working with her mother, in 1851. In some cases, it seems, that girls went on to inherit the post from their mothers, as with Matilda Grenfell who was recorded as counthouse woman for Botallack in 1871 and 1881, apparently taking over from her mother, also called Matilda, sometime after 1861. It seems that the offer of this type of work was often viewed as a charitable act on behalf of the mine adventurers, and was given to women perceived to be in the most need.

Fig. 55 Counthouse Staff (South Condurrow?) c. 1890
from only known surviving photocopy
Courtesy of Cornwall Federation of Women's Institutes

Many counthouse women became a respected and long-term presence at the mine. Ann Williams, at Wheal Goole Pellas (West Providence) in Towednack, was employed between 1876 and 1882, and possibly longer. During that time she worked 24 days per month (i.e. full-time) and was never absent. One of the longest-serving counthouse women was Ann Richards of Park Bracket, Camborne who was recorded in the *1841, 1851* and *1861 Census* records.

The general rate of pay for senior full-time counthouse women in the mid 19th century appears to be about £1 per month, or 1s per day. This had increased to about £1 5s by the turn of the century. This was a significantly higher rate of pay than for ore dressing; however, not all worked full-time. Mary Masters, who was counthouse woman at Carn Vivian was being paid 5s per month throughout 1856 and into 1857, indicating a very regular, but part-time, pattern of employment.

When mines ran into difficulty, counthouse women were also among those who remained unpaid, or were laid off. For instance, in 1874, when Boscaswell Downs Mine was failing, counthouse cleaners were among those listed as not receiving their wages.

Counthouse women continued to be employed at the mines, long after their sisters on the dressing floor had gone, and as late as the 1950s women were still employed there. However, their daily tasks must have been very different from their counterparts a century before, with quarterly account meetings replaced by the Annual General Meeting, tighter accountability of the hospitality budget, and labour-saving devices for use in the kitchen and office. Gone were the days when the mine would provide a sumptuous meal. However, Cornish ranges were often still in use in the kitchens of the counthouses, and visitors could leave their Cornish pasty on arrival, and find it warmed through and ready for them when they returned to the kitchen at the end of a cold and damp mine inspection. Stella Trenoweth was one of these latter-day counthouse women, working at Geevor in the 1950s. Her day began at 7 am with the cleaning of the offices, before the mining staff arrived. She was then responsible for morning and afternoon teas, and serving a cooked meal for the directors at lunchtime. Even at this time, there was no water laid on at the counthouse, so she remembers having to collect the water for cooking and cleaning from the leat.[22] Another 20th century counthouse woman, was Sally Bradford, who worked at Great Rock Iron Mine in Hennock from the end of the Second World War until its closure in 1966.[23]

Our last words on counthouse women, perhaps, should come from Levant Mine. In a lengthy traditional song about the various personalities associated with the mine, two verses were dedicated to the counthouse women. The sentiments expressed indicate that although they were the sort of women not to be trifled with, but they must also have had a sense of humour or the men would not have dared to have made up the verses: [24]

'Then next comes Cappen Fanny
And also Cappen Grace;
Among the other Cappens
They too must have their place

They cook the beef and mutton
And serve the bread and cheese,
They do not care a button
Whether they vex or please.'

FOOTNOTES

1. Bottrell, W *Traditions and Hearthside Stories of West Cornwall* (1870) (repr. Newcastle 1973) p.70.
2. WB 31st October 1889.
3. Pryor (1973) p. 50.
4. Greeves (2006) p. 9; Newman (1940) p. 112.
5. Noall (1982) p. 6.
6. Buckley (2007) p. 76.
7. Henwood (1857) pp. 70, 72 + 84.
8. Leifchild (1855) p. 52.
9. Henwood (1857) pp. 10 + 22.
10. Williams (1862).
11. CT 7th July 1880.
12. Hamilton Jenkin (1948) p. 194.
13. Diaries of William Pease (CRO: X 715/4).
14. Hamilton Jenkin (1948) p. 194.
15. Cornish Telegraph 7th July 1880.
19. Troon WI (1952) pp. 18-19.
20. WB 12th Feb 1858, Boiling Well Broadsheet (CRO: X 106/21).
21. Jenkin (1888) pp. 40-41.
22. *Women and Mining* Geevor Oral History Project 2004
23. Brooks (2004) p. 91.
24. Corin (1997) p. 22.

Chapter 9

BAL MAIDENS - THE COST

During the 18th and 19th century, bal maidens would most frequently work from their early or mid-teens for five or six years before marriage, but could well have worked for up to ten or twelve years at the mines, or more. Although a few may have worked for a comparatively short time or intermittently, generally these young women were severely disadvantaged by their lack of schooling, and also had to live with the medical consequences of their demanding work for the rest of their lives.

EDUCATION

Even though formal full-time schooling was not provided by the state until after 1876, the school movement had been growing in momentum in Cornwall from the early nineteenth century. Prior to 1800, it seems that bal maidens would not have had much opportunity for any type of schooling. From about 1800, 'dame schools' began to open, and, from about 1840, schools run by the church or other educational charities were established in most sizeable towns or villages. This gave the opportunity for a handful of children from working families to obtain some very basic education. Children could generally attend for about a penny a week. Within mining families education was usually highly valued, so miners would often struggle to send at least one child to school. However, this was dependent on the money being available and, with large families and intermittent earnings, the chances of any child from the mining community receiving continuous education remained very small, especially among the girls.

Sometimes, philanthropic mine managers provided some basic education for the mining children. As early as 1811, Wheal Alfred Mine, being a Quaker concern, was providing a Sunday School for over 250 mine girls and boys.[1] By 1842, some mines, such as Wheal Friendship and Wheal Betsey (in Devon) were providing day school education for the children of their employees. Others provided places at a local school for a levy on the miner's wages (as at North Roskear). In 1841, there were twenty-seven day schools open in the central mining district, of which nineteen were co-educational. In the eight girls' schools, the teaching (unfortunately) was described as *'scarcely passing the boundary of the merest elements'*.[2] Because of the great value placed on education, however, much informal teaching was done within the mining community, and many taught themselves. For instance, during the 1830s, William Murrish, *'The Miner of Perranzabuloe'*, who was self-taught, went on to teach the children in the hamlet where he lived to read and write.[3]

In the same era, ex-bal maiden Susan Robins (née Wills) recalled how her education at home surpassed that of her schooling:

'I only went to a little dame's school for a short time, but I never wrote a line there in my life, and my father taught us children to read and to write with a bit of burnt stick.' [4]

Bal maiden Patty Tremellin, having had the benefit of some schooling paid for by an aunt before she went to work at the mines, went on to teach the young children of Wrestling Green from her sick bed in her later years, between 1833 to 1837.[5] (Her story is told more fully in Chapter 12.) Any schooling that the girls did receive, however, was severely disrupted when they started work at the mines. Continued attendance at day school was no longer possible, as mines did not generally provide schooling during the day for their young employees. In 1864, though, the Kinnaird commissioners were impressed with the exceptional provision at North Roskear Mine:

'Many of the girls are being taught to write by the clerk of the mine, under the auspices of the manager, who gives prizes monthly for the best copybook, and best reading.'

Those girls who went to the mines as young as 7 or 8 years old, would have had virtually no education at all. However, those who went at the average age of 10 or 11 may have received up to four or five years of schooling at best. Once at the mine, the only opportunities to continue with some education would be to attend one of the local Sunday Schools, or be taught by someone in their family or local community. Of the mining parishes surveyed in 1841, only 25% of the bal maidens under 18 years old attended Sunday School, but this varied from parish to parish. St Just had by far the lowest attendance of only 8%, and the St Agnes area and West Devon had the highest at 36% and 29% respectively. The level of attendance for the girls was approximately twice that for the boys. When asked, one of the most common reasons given for non-attendance by girls at Sunday School was the lack of suitable clothes for them to wear, presumably only having their working clothes and maybe some other very old clothes to change into while these were being laundered.

At the Sunday Schools, girls were taught the basics of reading and writing, usually through Bible teaching, and 'a little sewing'. In 1841, bal maidens attended Sunday School, on average, until 17 or 18 years old. This was longer than the boys, who tended to leave at about 15 or 16 years. It was commented that the girls who attended Sunday School commonly achieved a higher level of education, and developed a keener understanding of its importance than the boys. In 1841, 35% of bal maidens could 'read a little' compared with 17% of boys, but very few wrote their names on the data collecting sheets (0.2% compared with 10% of boys). This trend was echoed at a later stage of life, when very few bal maidens signed their names on the marriage register. Barham suggested caution in interpreting the attainments of these young people, and despite being described as being able to *'read a little'* he said: *'many read so badly that no pleasure or interest can be derived by themselves from reading'*. By 1855, however, the number of children who could read and write had risen dramatically to about 80%, at least in Wheal Basset Mine:

'It was stated that in mines in the parish of Gwennap, about eighteen out of forty of the children could not read or write; that on mines in the parish of Redruth, at least 20% of the children could not read or write; and that on Wheal Basset Mine, out of two hundred and four children employed, forty eight could not read or write.' (WB 10th Aug 1855)

Although in some parishes evening classes were also available, in addition to Sunday School, it seems that girls did not normally attend them. These classes were far more expensive than the Day or Sunday Schools, sometimes costing 3d per week plus a candle. Presumably it was not considered appropriate to invest this much money in the education of girls.

The benefit that bal maidens would have gained from their limited education was often lost through lack of sustained learning. In 1841, when schoolteachers were asked about the effect of early removal from school, they replied:

'What little they have learned is soon forgotten'; 'education is not continued long enough to fix in the mind what may have been acquired'; and 'they have not learnt to read with ease...and they soon give it up altogether'.

Most Victorian commentators placed much store on the ability of girls and women to manage the domestic chores in the home. Of all the concerns about the well-being of bal maidens at the mine, it is this area of neglect that they seemed to lament the most. In 1836, Dr. Richard Lanyon remarked: *'We may observe how desirable it is that the wives and daughters of miners should be better acquainted with culinary and other domestic affairs'.*[6] Only four years later, the *1842 Royal Commission* concluded:

'The slenderness of the stock of domestic knowledge possessed by the females employed in the mine is attested by all parties. When they come to be wives and mothers, the consequences are very injurious to the husband and children.'

Thus these young women, denied the opportunity of education and achievement for themselves, were also then blamed, in part, for the subsequent ill health of their husbands and families.

From 1876, schooling was compulsory for all children under fourteen, and so, by the 1880s, most young women coming to work at the mine had received some degree of basic education. Suddenly the scene changed. When visiting a copper mine in the Carn Brea area in 1880, Rideing remarked that all the young girls could write, and spent much of their spare time reading. He described how they eagerly spent their pocket money, as soon as they were paid, on penny instalments of popular fiction.[7] For generations, the vast majority of the girls and women who had worked at the mines had never been able to read or write. This was the end of a long dark era.

PHYSICAL HEALTH AND MORTALITY

With growing public concern during the 19th century for the plight of miners, from about 1830 onwards, much was researched and written about the health of men and boys working underground. In contrast, virtually nothing was written about the health of surface workers or, more particularly, about the health of the women and girls. There is one recorded experiment involving the working conditions of women and girls, but the results were then applied, not to their situation, but to improve the working conditions of the men and boys underground.[8]

The most detailed information on the health of bal maidens in the 19th century comes from the *Royal Commission Reports* of 1842 and 1864. The *1842 Report* includes interviews with nineteen girls or women who were working at the mines, in which there are indications of their general state of health. These interviews were published in full in an appendix to the report.

In the 19th century, illness was rife, not just among the mining communities, but among the population as a whole, due to poor housing, diet and sanitation and almost non-existent healthcare for the poorer classes. It is difficult to assess how much ill-health was due to the general living environment of the bal maidens, and how much to their working environment. However, some trends do emerge from these reports.

Neurological or Skeletal Problems

The unnatural and demanding postures of many of the tasks undertaken by the bal maidens, along with their repetitive nature, took their toll. In addition to the physical strain on the structure of the body, these girls and women were also exposed to extremes of weather, many working with no shelter at all, or, at best, working in an unheated shed open to the elements. This in itself could exacerbate arthritic and rheumatic complaints. The *1842 Royal Commission* comments on the effect of these damp working conditions:

'Some of the girls are liable to get wet, especially in the feet in their employments, and all are so in coming to the mines. No provision is ever made for the change of shoes or stockings under these circumstances and the liability to injurious chill is consequently great, particularly to those (a large majority of the whole class) whose labour gives little or no exercise to the lower limbs.'

Spalling was carried out for the most part in a semi-stooping posture, whilst wielding a long-handled hammer weighing three pounds, for hours at a time. In 1841, 17 year-old Christina Pascoe, working at Consolidated Mines, had to be taken off spalling because of pains in her back, and shortness of breath. She was moved under cover to work in the cobbing shed. Elizabeth Hocking, also 17 years old, working at Charlestown Mines, found spalling by far the hardest work on the dressing floor. She suffered pains in her limbs and her back, which continued even when she had stopped work and had laid down.

Neither Barham (1841) nor Kinnaird (1864), respectively, considered that picking and washing, the tasks done by the very youngest children, would cause health problems in themselves. However, they recognised that, when the children were exposed to bad weather, they could then be at risk:

'The work is in itself but little laborious but there is much exposure to cold from the openness of the sheds and the wetness of the mineral and the posture constrained, the lower limbs having little or no exercise.'

'This employment [picking by young children]*, when carried on under cover is not found to be prejudicial to their health.'* (Kinnaird 1864 p. xxv)

Those who had to carry out those tasks sometimes felt otherwise. 14 year-old Mary Verran, a picker at Consolidated Mines, did find picking hard and complained of pain in her back and side towards the end of the morning session. The dinner break seemed to give her a chance to recuperate, and she usually felt less discomfort in the afternoon. Some of the girls who operated the new mechanical jiggers, which required moving the sieves up and down in their boxes by means of a long lever, also complained of pains in the back.

From about 1840, cobbing and bucking were usually carried out under shelters, or in sheds, giving the girls and women a little more protection from the weather. Even then, their legs and feet were vulnerable to severe chilling from the accumulated debris around their ankles. In 1841, Christina Pascoe, having been moved from spalling to the cobbing sheds, found her legs became very cold, especially when the ore-stuff was wet. She also described how the rain came into the sheds, so that their feet were soaked, even if the ore-stuff was dry. Of all the tasks on the dressing floor, bucking was generally considered the most physically demanding task:

'The less robust are usually obliged to relinquish it after a short time, and many apparently strong girls are unable to continue at it. Pain in the back and side is the most frequent complaint. Giddiness and faintness now and then occur.'

Only three 'bucking girls' were interviewed for the *1842 Royal Commission*, and all had some difficulty when carrying out this task. 18 year-old Elizabeth Larkeek, a bucker at Tresavean, described getting pains in her left arm, especially in damp weather. 19 year-old Sally Fall, at Gwennap, reported pains in her side. Most severely, 17 year-old Jane Sandow from Wheal Gorland did not have the strength to continue at the bucking table, and had to be moved to work in the cobbing shed.

One of the other most strenuous and demanding tasks on the dressing floors, for the women and girls, was barrowing. When barrowing, two girls would carry a very heavy weight between them. Each hand barrow was constructed to hold 1.5 cwt of ore, but the total weight could exceed this by a considerable amount, as it did not account for the weight of the barrow itself, or for the weight of water held in the ore, if it was wet. 14 year-old Martha Buckingham, at Consolidated Mines, complained of back pain after barrowing all day. In his report of 1842, Charles Barham seemed to imply that this employment had the most potential for serious injury, and had this comment to make about the bal maidens who carried barrows at sampling:

'The latter have, during their turn, by far the harder work (carrying usually about 1.5 cwt). It is hard work and is often complained of as causing pain in various parts, and not infrequently, occasioning more permanent injury from sudden strains or falls.'

He reported that the bal maidens, despite the many very heavy and strenuous tasks they had to perform, were remarkably free from physical deformation or serious orthopaedic problem. This is at odds with the observations of a visitor to Fowey Consols. Having observed that the girls who filled the buddle strips might shovel as much as fifteen tons of tin-stuff in a day, the following query was raised:

'...it was often wondered...why they should choose this heavy work which often caused deformation in the shoulders by the continuous use of the shovel'[9]

Interestingly, there is a common understanding that bal maidens (especially cobbers and buckers) regularly suffered permanent damage to their left hands, due to misdirected blows from the hammers. For instance, 19 year-old Mary Ann Harris of Perranzabuloe was described as having her *'left fingers crooked'* when she was admitted to Bodmin Gaol in June 1851. Bruising and cuts to the fingers, and even fractures must have occurred despite wearing protective padding or gloves.

General neurological and orthopaedic complaints would probably manifest themselves years later. Christina Morom, who had been working at the Gwennap mines in the early 19th century, believed that the lumbago she suffered in mid-life had been caused by her work at the mine as a young woman. Two of the girls interviewed in 1841 thought that the chronic pain from which they suffered had begun when they had strained themselves lifting too heavy a weight at the mine.

Fig. 56 Spalling Floor, Pednandrea 1858
Courtesy of Paddy Bradley

Respiratory and Circulatory Problems

Apart from the cold, damp environment on the dressing floor potentially causing problems with muscles and joints, there was also the risk of aggravating or triggering respiratory disease. This in turn could also be affected by high levels of dust in the atmosphere. This was particularly acute in dry weather, especially in proximity to the stamps or crushers, and in the cobbing and bucking sheds.

In 1839, Samuel Moyle carried out some interesting experiments in the bucking shed of one of the copper mines. He discovered that 4.5 grains of copper was deposited on an area one foot square per day, when the bucking house was in full use. This compared with just over half a grain per day, when only one person was working there. The results of this experiment were then used to illustrate the potentially hazardous levels of dust below ground, and to indicate the pressing need for improved ventilation down the mines.[10] Despite these findings, there is no evidence that there was any attempt to reduce the levels of dust pollution for the women and girls working in the bucking sheds. However, at this time, mechanical crushers were already beginning to perform the tasks which the bucking girls had previously done, so that they were gradually being replaced. It was subsequently observed, in 1842, that the amount of dust created by the mechanical crushers, brought in to replace the buckers, was even greater than when the breaking was done by hand:

'The working of this machine is attended with the suspension in the air of a great quantity of mineral dust, often of a very suffocating nature when inhaled cursorily, but producing serious ill effects with the lungs exposed to it during many successive days.'

In the report, it is observed that it was usually boys who attended this machine, and that they were the ones affected most by the dust. There is no indication as to how much the other workers on the dressing floors were affected by this pollution of the air. However, John Rowe made the following observation in 1993:

'When copper-ores were crushed dry (as opposed to wet stamps with tin) this must have increased the incidence of silicosis and ensured that many women and girls died of 'consumptions' and 'declines' as well as men.' [11]

Of the very small sample of girls interviewed in 1841, four reported respiratory problems. Eliza Allen, aged 20 years, of Wheal Anna Francis, was only able to earn half her normal wages due to breathlessness and weakness. Anna Wasley, also 20 years old, working at the Cakes and Ale Mine, complained that she had been suffering shortness of breath, on exertion, for about twelve months. Sally Fall, 19 years old, working at the Gwennap Mines, described various symptoms, including shortness of breath, since *'over-straining herself'* some ten months previously. (A Sarah Faull of the same age was recorded as a patient at the Truro Infirmary about six weeks after this interview took place.) Christina Pascoe, 17 years old, *'fell into a decline'*, her breath getting very short, when she worked outside as a spalling maid at Consolidated Mines. She was subsequently moved to work under cover in the cobbing sheds.

During the 19th century, the proportion of deaths from consumption was very high in the population as a whole, but was higher in the mining communities than elsewhere. It was not generally accepted, in 1842, that this condition was either aggravated by, or brought on by, work on the dressing floor. In the *1842 Royal Commission*, Barham sits on the fence on this issue:

> 'There is reason to believe that consumption is more frequent than in the non-mining districts. Whether it is more frequent among those members of miners families who are engaged in surface labour at the mines…remain [sic] in doubt.'

Pepper, however, in 1862, had something stronger to say about the prevalence and seriousness of consumption among bal maidens:

> 'It is unnecessary to add, that 'consumption' here is scarcely less fatal with these young women than with the underground workmen.' (Pepper 1862 p. 270)

Barham commented on *'acute conditions'*, which could suddenly carry bal maidens off, but he did not specify what they were. In 1857, George Henwood made a somewhat bleak (but probably exaggerated) statement on this matter:

> *'These poor girls* [bal maidens] *remain from the early age we have mentioned, until they either get married off to some of the miners, or die of consumption, which carries off hundreds annually.'* (Henwood 1857 p. 120)

Retrospectively, we would recognise active or passive smoking as a further danger to the bal maidens' health. Commentators report on the prevalence of smoking, especially among those who worked underground, but it was by no means confined to them alone. Celia Fiennes, when travelling through St Austell in 1699, wrote:

> *'I was much pleased with my supper, but not the custom of the country, which is a universal smoking, men, women and children have all their pipes of tobacco in their mouths and so sit round the fire smoking.'* [12]

There is no evidence that there was smoking on the dressing floor while the girls and women were working, but they would be almost certainly exposed to the effects of tobacco either directly, or indirectly in the home, or when socialising.

There are few reports of bal maidens with major problems of the circulatory system, but minor problems were probably common. For instance, Murriel Sara records that bal maidens commonly suffered badly from chilblains, Minnie Andrews described the terrible pain in her hands due to exposure to cold water at the frames, and a Troon bal maiden of the 1870s recalled *'I have cried scores of times with wonders in my fingers and toes'*. [13]

Digestive Problems

Due to the extreme poverty experienced in Cornwall, from the end of the 18th century, almost to the end of the 19th, most mining families survived on very limited and poor quality food. When, in 1841, the mining agent at Trethellan Copper Mine reported that more than half the boys and girls brought *'fish and potatoes'*, or *'stew with a small amount of meat in it'* for their dinner and that in most cases they *'had as much as they could eat'*, one of his colleagues had a different view. He described how some of the girls were ashamed of their meagre repast and hid away to eat it. This same colleague also believed that some of the girls fainted for lack of food.

In times of hardship, when wheat prices were high, the only available cereals were barley or pillas, often grown by the miners themselves. The 'hoggan', made from barley, became the staple diet. These were often the only food brought to the mine by the bal maidens. Digestive problems were rife, particularly in older girls and women, and much of this was put down either to the prevalence of barley bread in the diet, or poor food preparation. Barham also suggested that many suffered in this way due to resorting to stimulants such as teas in order to give them the energy to continue their demanding work which, without food, would cause further digestive problems. He also comments on the uncomfortable and rushed circumstances under which food was often eaten at the mine, as being a contributory factor.

In relatively good financial times, the indigestible hoggan or fuggan was replaced with the pasty. Even on this more digestible and balanced diet, the bal maidens did not always receive enough sustenance to support their very hard, prolonged labour. (Throughout the 18th and 19th century, the bal maidens wage was only the equivalent of between £12 and £30 per week at 2005 prices). In 1841, 17 year-old Grace Bowden and 11 year-old Martha Williams took a pasty each for their dinner at Trethellan Mine. However, they had often eaten some by mid-morning, usually secretly, in order to allay their hunger pangs, leaving precious little to sustain them for the rest of the day.

In addition to digestive problems caused by diet and lack of food, working in dusty conditions, especially with lead ore or near arsenic fumes, could also affect the digestive system. Bowel complaints had been common at Wheal Vor when arsenic fumes were discharged right into the mine centre. The lack of facilities for bal maidens to wash their hands before eating, and wearing contaminated clothing, also aggravated these types of complaint.[14]

In 1841, seventeen year-old Fanny Francis, working at United Mines, suffered from dyspepsia, and Jane Sandow working at Wheal Gorland, suffered from *'gastrodynia'*. Elizabeth Curnow (24 years old), a cobber at Consolidated Mines, described how, about twice a year, she lost all her strength and her appetite. She generally found that the harder she worked, the less appetite she had. She had only been able to work at the mine for two days during the previous two months because of this ill health.

'Women's Problems'

Problems of this nature were rarely discussed in polite Victorian society, so there is a shroud of secrecy around the issue. However, the Commissioners of the *1842 Report* saw fit to break silence and the mine surgeon at Wheal Vor reported that *'Females suffer from amenorrhea and dysmenorrea when they labour'* and the mine agent at the same mine said *'ammorrhoea and chorosis are very frequent, and are commonly severe and sometimes fatal.'*

This total suppression of periods, or their irregularity, and the associated anaemia, may either have been due to severe malnutrition or to exposure to harmful toxins, such as the mundic waters, at the mines. The agent at Wheal Vor ascribed these symptoms to *'the exposure of the young women to the stream of warm water, especially in framing.'*

These serious conditions were probably not unique to Wheal Vor, but remained largely unreported. They would have immediate consequences on the general health of these young women in the prime of their lives. Not only would their reproductive health be affected in the short term, but possibly in the long term as well. Even more tragically, it seemed that there was an unseen army of girls whose premature deaths were just passed over unnoticed in the already high mortality rates in the mining parishes. However, these deaths from anaemia and related illnesses, if brought on by exposure to toxic discharges, should have been entirely preventable by modifications in the way the bal maidens performed their tasks.

Sight and Hearing

Although there is no direct documented evidence of these types of problem arising from ore dressing, bal maidens who were spalling, cobbing, or bucking, must have been in continual danger of damage to the eyes from flying shards. Similarly, those working close to the stamps or crushers, and those in the large bucking or cobbing sheds, must have been exposed to levels of noise which were potentially damaging.

There are indications of the sort of noise levels generated on the dressing floors. At Dolcoath Mine, in the mid-1850s, we are told *'sixty maidens worked in a row in a great cobbing house known as 'The Roarer', roaring and resounding with noise'*. At Wheal Kitty in St Agnes, there was so much noise on the dressing floor that the mine bell could not be heard above it. It was the responsibility of one of the girls to watch for the bell to ring, and then call 'Bell-ho' to her companions, assuming they could hear her.[15] An indication of the level of noise generated by the stamps is given in this passage from the novel 'Deep Down' by Ballantyne:

'Those who have delicate nerves would do well to keep as far as possible from the stamps of a tin mine! They are fearful things these stamps; iron in spirit as well as in body, they go on for ever - night and day.' (Ballantyne 1897 p. 197)

Two accounts, from 1858 and the 1890s, also graphically illustrate this point:

'It may be imagined, that the noise produced by such a number of heads, alternately falling, when the stamps are at work, is deafening to any person standing near them; and in the distance, it resembles the roaring of a heavy surf on the sea-beach.' [16]

'I have been here [Camborne] *on a week-day, when the stamps were at work, and the noise was simply terrific. I have never heard anything to equal it. Not only is it impossible to hear or be heard speaking, but the mind seems almost stunned by the clamour.'* [17]

A more modern account, confirming how noisy the environment was around the ore-dressing machinery, comes from one of the women who worked on the picking belt at Geevor during the Second World War:

'The washer and crusher were very noisy, and we couldn't hear ourselves speak. We had to lip read and make up our own sign language.' [18]

She also described how, on occasion, small pieces of 'spar' would fly up from the picking belt into their eyes. When this occurred, they would have to report to the First Aid post to have the piece removed. No doubt this would be an even more common occurrence in the cobbing and bucking sheds, where here too the women and girls wore no protection over their eyes.

Toxicity and Poisoning

The women and girls were sometimes dealing with, or working near, toxic materials, such as arsenic, lead, and uranium, but there seems to have been little acknowledgement by the mine management of the potentially dangerous nature of these elements. No particular precautions seem to have been taken to avoid contamination. Neither are there specific records of individual bal maidens whose ill-health was attributed to toxic exposures.

There is some indication that the 'mundic waters' (waste from the dressing floors, containing copper, iron, and arsenic) made some of those working on the floors quite ill. In 1841, 21 year-old Jane Jewell was unable to continue to work at Consols Mine, after working there for only two weeks. The agent at Wheal Vor believed that the warm 'mundic water' at the frames may have been responsible for the gynaecological problems of some of the bal maidens at that mine.

The detrimental effect of arsenic fumes on the countryside, and also on individuals, seems to have been commonly acknowledged. For instance, the night captain at Dolcoath in 1823 describes the working conditions when the arsenic calciner was at work, and the wind blowing the fumes back over the dressing floors: *'O the infernal Burning House smoke, I'm almost choked with it….I've been choked with poison.'* [19]

Similarly, the chief agent at Wheal Vor described how, in former times, the arsenic calciner flue discharged into the centre of the mine when the whole place filled with suffocating fumes and *'bowel complaints were very frequent'*. Later, in 1864, symptoms of arsenic poisoning of wounds were recognised and described in the *Kinnaird Commission* as *'gatherings and blotches of the skin'*. Possibly, some of the women and girls interviewed by Barham in 1842 were suffering from this type of contamination, including Fanny Francis who suffered from skin eruptions. However, Barham had not considered working at the arsenic calciners to be dangerous:

'Furnaces employ very few hands, and these are chiefly adults, neither is their exposure to heat or effluvia at all materially detrimental.'

The problem of arsenic vapour falling back onto the dressing floors on a still day (before the construction of the long 'lambreths' or flues to carry fumes away) was deftly described by a chemist giving evidence of arsenic fume damage from the arsenic works in Perranwell, in 1850;

'Two stacks, however high, were of little use on a still day, the vapour issuing from them was fifty or sixty times heavier than the air, and fell to the ground in a very short time.' [20]

By the time Baring Gould wrote his *Book of Cornwall* in 1899, however, there was an increased awareness of the dangers of arsenic, although the most primitive of precautions were still being taken. He wrote:

'*Arsenic dust has a tendency to produce sore places about the mouth, the ankles and the wrists. More over, if allowed to settle in any of the folds of the flesh it produces a nasty raw....Unhappily, in spite of all precautions, the work at the arsenic mine and manufactory is prejudicial to health. For the last three years, out of every 100 deaths among persons of all ages in the parish of Calstock, 26 have been due to diseases of the respiratory organs, but out of every 100 employees at the arsenic works who died or have become disabled, 83 deaths have been due to respiratory diseases.*' (Baring Gould 1899 p.110)

Lead was another source of potential toxicity. No particular precautions were taken to protect workers at the lead mines and smelters from lead poisoning. The first official investigation and government enquiry into lead poisoning did not take place until they had ceased production in Devon and Cornwall. Legislation enacted to protect workers in 1886 applied mostly to factory workers. However, even if the dangers were not acknowledged nationally until the 1880s, it was probably common knowledge that lead was toxic among those who worked with it. In '*The Uncommercial Traveller*' by Charles Dickens, published in 1869, which contains apparently factual accounts of visits to some of the poverty stricken areas of Britain and Ireland, an elderly Irish woman says of young women who worked at the 'lead mills' in East London:

'*Tis lead poisoned she is, sur, and some of them gets lead poisoned soon, some of them gets lead poisoned later, and some, but not many, niver, and 'tis all according to the constitooshun, sur, and some constitushuns is strong, and some is weak; and her constitushun is lead poisoned* [sic].' [21]

Nor were lead poisoning cases unusual. A total of 30,000 cases were reported from the lead mines of Utah State between 1875-1900, and many women and girls who worked with lead paints at the Staffordshire Potteries were also affected in this way.[22] From this, we might assume, even in the absence of documentary evidence, that lead poisoning was an occupational hazard for the bal maidens at the lead smelters and possibly at the mines in Cornwall and Devon. Unfortunately, there is very little information about their work in general, let alone detailed information on health issues. Unlike the tin and copper mines, there were no first hand interviews or examinations of any of female lead dressers recorded in the *1842* or *1864 Commissions*. However, in writing about the health of the lead miners and dressers of the Pennines, where women and girls were not employed from 1840, Burt makes the following observation:

'*The failure of all but the largest mines to provide adequate changing, washing and drying facilities before the late 19th century also undoubtedly increased the risks of non-ferrous poisoning from prolonged exposure to contaminated clothing and surface grime. This was a particular problem for workers in lead mines and applied with equal force to both miners and dressers.*' [23]

Other parts of the *1842 Royal Commission* relating to conditions in other mining areas, make very little reference to the dangers of working with lead. At Leadhills Mine in Scotland, the mine surgeon acknowledged that men working at the lead-smelting mills '*suffered a little from colic pains*' and recorded three deaths from inflammation of the brain, five from inflammation of the stomach or bowels, one from gout, three from convulsions and one from paralysis, out of a total of 130 deaths in a six-year period between 1835 and 1841.[24]

Lead poisoning can take two forms - acute and chronic, the acute form sometimes being fatal. Symptoms can include colic and digestive upsets, anaemia, convulsions, paralysis, gout, and blindness. In females, the reproductive capacity is particularly vulnerable, including healthy foetal development. In a study in the potteries of North Staffordshire (1904), those women that had worked with lead paints before marriage, and those which had worked with them after marriage, had three and four times more miscarriages respectively than the control group who had not. In an earlier study of a similar group in 1896, of a total of seventy-seven married women, only thirty-six had given birth to live children, whereas there had been twenty-one still births, ninety miscarriages, and fifteen women were childless. Of the one hundred and one children born, forty had died in the early years, with most of these deaths attributed to convulsions.[25] Disruption of the gynaecological functions was recognised:

'A considerable number of women working in lead processes suffer from amenorrhea, and often from periods of menorrhagia and dysmenhorrhea, which as a rule, is the more striking symptom.'[26]

By the mid-1880s, lead was understood to be taken into the body by several key routes: by inhalation of dust, absorption through the skin, and ingestion of contaminated food. At the lead smelters and mines in the South West, there had been every opportunity for the women and girls to be at risk. Those at smelters would have been exposed to the acrid fumes of the furnaces. With these women and girls having no proper washing facilities, often eating in contaminated areas, and having no means of washing work clothes each day, the risk of poisoning may have been cumulative. Even if the effects of lead on the bal maidens at the mines was nowhere near as severe as on the pottery workers in Staffordshire, it still seems possible that some may have experienced considerable ill health, and a detrimental effect on their ability to conceive and give birth to healthy children.

It seems almost inconceivable from our privileged position of Health and Safety Directives and a Welfare State that men, women, and children, should ever have taken up occupations with such known risks. Perhaps the curt remarks of the Irishwoman's daughter in East London (to Dickens) give us an insight into the desperate choices facing poor families prior to the 20th century:

'The woman's married daughter had by this time come down from her room on the floor above. She herself had been to the lead mills very early that morning to be 'took on', but had not succeeded. She had four children; and her husband a water-side labourer. She knew all about the sufferings of the unfortunate invalid, and all about the lead poisoning, and how the symptoms came on, and how they grew, - having often seen them. The very smell when you stood inside the door of the works was enough to knock you down, she said; yet she was going back again to get 'took on'. What could she do? Better be ulcerated and paralysed for eighteen pence a day, while it lasted, than see the children starve.'[27]

Parasitism

In the 1890s, underground miners began to be affected by hookworm, which affected their breathing and caused anaemia, and had probably been contracted from employees returning from abroad. The condition was well known, for instance, in the Sicilian Sulphur Mines. It was spread by the unsanitary conditions underground, and it is believed that this parasite had been around in the Cornish Mines since the 1850s. The symptoms mirrored other miners' complaints, such as miners' consumption or anaemia, so often went undiagnosed. It was first identified in 1894 at Dolcoath, where almost every underground worker was infected. The disease became commonly known as 'Dolcoath Anaemia'. By 1903, it had *'obtained a firm hold in Cornish Mines'*. In that year, it was eventually diagnosed as ankylostomiasis.[28] None of the identified cases was fatal.

There are no particular reports of the condition being contracted by bal maidens on the dressing floors, but they would certainly be at risk from infection, either from members of their own families working underground, or due to the lack of sanitary arrangements at surface. As with the underground miners, infection among the general community, including the bal maidens, may have gone unnoticed and the symptoms ascribed to something else.

In the *1842 Royal Commission*, Barham expresses concern at the risk of malaria (ague or marsh fever) for those workers employed at stamps and stream works, especially those situated in warm sheltered valleys on the coast. However, while he doesn't report any actual cases, this disease had certainly been rife in low lying areas of Britain for many centuries, and it seems that miners were no stranger to it in Cornwall. This slightly less virulent disease than the form known in the tropics (but still sometimes fatal) could be passed from infected mosquitoes to humans where there were stagnant pools of warm water, as in the mines or at surface.

General Physical Health

It is hard to contemplate the shock to the system of the first days at work for these bal maidens. Whatever physical labour they had done before (possibly with the exception of those who had worked in the fields), it would hardly prepare them for the nine to twelve hours that would face them at the mines. It is especially difficult to imagine how very young girls faced this ordeal. Susan Robins (nee Wills) recalled how she was so tired when she first began working that she used to say she was unwell and go home. She was only six or seven years old at the time.[29]

Most of the information on health and injury comes to us from a very small sample of bal maidens who were interviewed for the *1842 Royal Commission*. The same report also gives a glimpse of the general health of bal maidens at one of the larger mines. A table showing causes of absenteeism at the Charlestown Mines in 1841 demonstrates a range of general ailments. The most frequent reason (seventeen reports) given for girls not attending work was headaches, but there were also twelve reports of various digestive upsets, and four reports of various fevers and colds. Forty-one incidents of absenteeism were reported for the year, in a workforce of 181 girls, totalling just over 800 days. This averages out at about four and a half days per person per year.

From time to time, the census records refer to bal maidens who were sick or in hospital. For instance, Mary Ann John (16 yrs old) was with Sarah Faull as a patient in the Cornwall Royal Infirmary in Truro in 1841, and Mary Ann Coad from Perranzabuloe was a patient there in 1851. In 1891, Mary Jane Lawrence and Mary Ann Harris were both patients in the Redruth Women's Hospital.

Many commentators remark on the healthy appearance of the women and children who work above ground at the mine. When James Boswell visited Poldice Mine in 1792, he made the following observations:

'I was surprised to see the miners look so well, even when just come out of the pits, and the men, women and children employed in beating and sorting and otherwise preparing the ore and stone seemed active and cheerful.' [30]

In 1841, Barham favourably compared the appearance of bal maidens with boys who work underground, and with those women and girls who worked in the safety fuse factories. He remarked:

'Whatever the average duration of life...it is difficult to find anywhere a class of girls and young women more free from malformation, distortion or infirmity.'

At Devon Great Consols, the following report was made to the *1864 Kinnaird Commission*:

'The appearance of the girls employed in the dressing floors at Devon Consols is sufficient an indication that whatever may be said of the miner, their employment cannot be deemed injurious. They look the picture of robust health.'

This was to prompt the commissioner to draw the following conclusion (without any interviews with the bal maidens themselves having been conducted):

'Though breaking ore is laborious, it does not appear to be an injurious occupation, as the women are remarkably healthy.'

However, it was recognised that their healthy appearance may mask underlying problems, or be due to the fact that only those in good health could work, and that at least some may be languishing from serious complaints at home:

'It seems probable that the ruddiness of hue imparted by constant exposure to fresh air, may have given to these boys and girls an appearance of health to a certain extent deceptive. Moreover, as their ailments are, for the most part of rather acute character, they prevent those who are suffering from them from coming to work...but some of these acute disorders prove rapidly fatal and greater numbers pass into incurable structural changes.'

What ill health bal maidens suffered was very often blamed on themselves. For instance, suggestions were made that digestive problems were caused by lack of personal hygiene, the crude preparation of food, or the wrong diet, and that a range of other problems may have been brought on by wearing inappropriate clothing.

Women and girls sometimes continued to labour at the mines, regardless of major health problems. This is illustrated by an elderly woman, working at Carn Brea, despite being well over 60 years old. She continued to do very active work even though she was subject to epileptic fits at least twice a week, and had been so afflicted for the forty years she had continued to work on the dressing floors (Fig. 58).[31]

Mortality Rates

The 1842 Commissioners looked at mortality rates for females in mining and non-mining parishes. As not all the females in the mining parishes were working, or had worked, at the mines, the figures do not necessarily show the direct effect of a mining occupation on longevity. However, the figures show a clear effect of living in the mining parishes compared to rural areas. In the non-mining parishes, of all females who died in a two-year period, 48% were under 30 years of age, but, in mining parishes, it was even higher at 57%. Similarly, in non-mining parishes, 33% of the females who died in that time had survived to over 60 years of age, but, in the mining parishes, the corresponding figure was only 28%.

Infant and child mortality was also higher in the mining parishes. Deaths of children under ten years old accounted for between 36% and 45% of the total in Illogan, Gwennap and Redruth. This compared with 30% to 35% in Mabe, Mylor, St Mary's, and Penzance. With poor nutrition, and women often working at the mine for a considerable proportion of their pregnancies, it is hardly surprising that their children had a lower survival rate. The following is an account of one bal maiden who continued to work at the mine until the day of her baby's delivery, with a tragic outcome:

'An inquest was held on Monday touching the death of a female infant, the daughter of Elizabeth Boase. It appeared that the woman Boase worked at Wheal Harmony and about three months ago she confesses to being enceinte. Boase confessed to having delivered herself near the hedge in Treleigh Lane (near Redruth) and that while doing so she lost her senses and lay upon the child for a considerable time; when she came to herself, she found the child was still under her, and she took it up in her cloak and apron and carried it home. Boase admitted that the child was born as she was returning from her work.' (WB 30th July 1841)

Parish	Under 30 years	30-59 years	Over 60 years
Non-mining parishes: Mabe, Mylor, St Mary's, Penzance	47.5	19.4	33.1
Mining parishes: Illogan, Gwennap, Redruth	56.6	15.8	27.6

(From CEC 1842 Table 3)

Fig. 57 Percentage of Female Deaths by Age in Selected Parishes 1838-40
(from CEC Table 3)

EXPLOITATION AND ABUSE AT WORK

This is also a topic barely aired in the Victorian documentation, but we have indications that the women and girls were on occasion exploited or abused, either physically, emotionally or even sexually. Because of the hierarchy on the dressing floors, it would be very easy for the men (dressing floor labourers as well as the captains or agents) to take advantage of the girls or women in various ways, without them having any real recourse to justice.

At a very simple level, there were opportunities for surface labourers or captains to express some degree of favouritism. This might manifest itself in giving special tasks to a selected bal maiden, or enabling her to do her job more efficiently or effectively. For instance, the men working at the Polpuff Glass Mine during the First World War were quite open about the preferential treatment given to some of the young women by the trammers. Favoured individuals, especially those which the trammers 'fancied', would have better quality ore delivered to their part of the picking table. Conversely, those they disliked would be given the worst. This would immediately affect the length of the working day for each woman or girl, as they were on task work and could not leave until they had filled a given number of boxes with ore.[32]

A daughter of a bal maiden at Devon Consuls described how, in the mid-19th century, the women and girls were paid by the number of trays of washed and spalled rock they cobbed and sorted in a day. These trays were supplied by men and boys from the washing tables. There was opportunity for men to supply poor quality ore to them, as they were paid by the number of trays they packed, not by the ore content. There were often altercations between the men and the women over this issue.[33]

At another level, women and girls were sometimes bullied and subjected to verbal abuse. Minnie Andrews, the '*last bal maiden*', gave an insight into this world, when she described her work at one of the tin stream works. She told of how the manager would not tolerate any distractions:

'*You wouldn't look your head off from what you was doing, the old fool would have a stick aimed at ee, or something thrown at ee. Oh, he's some demon, he was, an old thing, he was. He'd thraw a stick at ee.*' [34]

Another Troon bal maiden remembered a young girl being bullied by the surface captain at West Wheal Seton, in about 1875:

'*I well remember once a girl [picker] going for a drink of water, which was kept in a tin pitcher, when the man who was looking after the girls thought she was going to drink too often, he picked up the pitcher and threw the contents over her, saying*' *have 'ee had enough now?*' [35]

Sexual exploitation and abuse was not unheard of either. The story of Patty Tremellin, with her three illegitimate pregnancies, resulting from liaisons established through her work at the mine, hints at this darker side of mine work. She comments:

'*Those mines are bad places for boys and girls, for there is nothing but sin to be heard or witnessed all the day long, when the agents are out of the way.*'

Implicit here is that all may have been sweetness and light when the mine captains, inspectors, and visitors came around, but, in her experience, when just left to the supervision of the surface captain, conversation could become rather unsavoury. She clearly states that her problems were associated with the influences of working at the mine, and at least once (possibly twice, as the text is not clear) she served time in Bodmin Jail for refusing to divulge the name of her illegitimate child.[36]

It seems that some men working at the mines considered that the bal maidens could be sexually exploited, as a matter of course. The night and day shift captains at Dolcoath in 1822 and 1823 did not seem unduly surprised by the behaviour of one of the principal timber men. It was reported that after he had finished a particularly dangerous and difficult job he demanded *'a three weeks round among the women after he had finished'*. Later he was recorded as complaining that he *'had not yet had his fortnight round the women.'* This sort of attitude was obviously tolerated as the captains commented that *'one week should be enough'*. [37]

Another 'young bal girl' (unnamed) was brought before the Truro County Court in June of 1868, charged with the theft of some drapery goods from a shop. In the course of the hearing, it transpired that she had an illegitimate child, and had no financial provision, and that the father was one of the agents at the mine where she worked. The judge indicated that he would like to see the person responsible for this before him, and also any others who abused their employees in this way. Within a week or two of these remarks, Mary Harvey accused Samuel Scaddon, the surface captain at Wheal Vor where she worked, of raping her. The case went to the summer assizes where the judge decreed that a rape charge *'was easy to make and difficult to refute'*. He instructed the jury to be guided by the demeanour of the girl. He made much of the point that, although she admitted that Scaddon had taken liberties before, she had not made any previous complaint. Not unsurprisingly for the time, the case was thrown out.[38]

A newspaper report of 1897 describes a court case involving a bal maiden from Dolcoath who had also given birth to an illegitimate child, the father being a miner. The man had promised to marry her, but, days before the birth, he had fled to America, and stayed there for over a year. The man, in his defence, argued that the bal maiden, being 10 years older, should have 'known better' than to fall pregnant. The judge found in favour of the woman, and ordered the miner to pay weekly maintenance.[39] In the 1*842 Royal Commission*, there is only one account of a sexual attack on a bal maiden, and this was by a group of male workers, and is possibly the most serious recorded:

'In the Central District...a party of thirty miners are said to have taken a woman violently into the fields and to have subjected her to all the outrage which licentious brutality could suggest.'

No further details are given as to the outcome of the case, or the consequences for this poor woman.

MENTAL HEALTH AND TRAUMATIC STRESS

There is very little information about the mental health of bal maidens. A small number of ex-bal maidens feature in the list of patients at the County 'Lunatic Asylum' in the Census records. There were five in 1851, four in 1861 and 1871, and eight in 1891. Patty Tremellin became very suicidal at the time of her second pregnancy, and there is this very sad account of a deserted bal maiden who became so depressed that she tried to take not just her own life, but the lives of her children as well:

'Many times I have gone to the wash tray without breakfast, and my two dear children have had to stay until I came home without any food in the house. I have cried myself to sleep many a night. One night I lost heart, so I took my children to a water shaft at Basset Mines, with the intention of drowning them and myself; but the captain of the mine saw me just in time.' [40]

The outcome of this particular story was encouraging, because, although her husband never returned, the woman received a one pound charitable donation from the mine where her husband was working in Australia, which enabled her to continue to provide for her family.

As well as experiencing desertions, or the stress of living apart when husbands migrated to find work, bal maidens were not strangers to death, either sudden or lingering. Most mining families would know what it was to lose a loved one through a tragic accident at the mine. All mining families would also have watched someone die a lingering death from miners' consumption or a related disease. Bereavements of this kind were so common that questions as to how these women and children faced their daily mine work after these 'mine-related' losses were never asked. There is no indication that any support was given to these girls or young women to help them cope with the trauma and memories of what they had seen or felt. One young woman who was so overwhelmed by what she had experienced was to be found in Helston Workhouse in the 1870s. It was understood that she had left her family home in the Helston area when her father remarried, to take up work at a mine in Devon. She was subsequently returned to her home parish workhouse in a state of profound mental disturbance. It was believed that she had witnessed the death of her fiancé at the mine. In the Workhouse, she lapsed between beautiful singing of hymns and fits of depression when she would cry such things as *'Take him up, take him up, he's dashed to pieces – pick up his fingers'*. [41]

Serious accidents on the dressing floors were not very common, but, when they occurred, they would usually be witnessed by a good number of people. Invariably, among the witnesses were the bal maidens, and very often they were the key witnesses when inquests were being held.

One cold January morning in 1830, Jane Goyne had gone with her cousin Elizabeth to get warm in the boiler house at United Hills Mine. On arrival, the engine man had asked Elizabeth to fetch a pitcher of water for him, but Jane had offered to go instead. She had only been out of the building about thirty seconds when the engine house boiler exploded. She ran for cover and was unhurt. Of the eleven she left in the engine house, nine died, including her cousin, and the other two were seriously injured. Jane then had to give evidence at her cousin's inquest at the counthouse the following day.[42] At Ding Dong Mine in July 1873, Alice Stephens tried to avert the death of her friend, Eliza Hall, when she had jumped on the crown gear wheel. She had urgently called her to come down from the machinery, but Eliza refused, and was crushed. Alice, subsequently, was the key witness when she gave evidence at the inquest.[43] Annie Olds, one of the ore dressers at Botallack Mine, also witnessed a fatal accident in October 1893. Annie was walking home with 9 year-old Mary Dale, who had just come from school with her younger brother, when Mary ran up on the roof of the arsenic flues. Annie immediately called her off, but Mary ran up on them again. When Mary dropped out of sight Annie assumed she had run to the blacksmith's shop to shelter from the rain. Mary was not missed until the evening, and her body not found until the following day. As she had been running over the roof of the arsenic flue, it had given way; she had fallen in and suffocated. Annie was the last to see Mary alive and so was also called to give evidence at the inquest. There is no indication that these young women were given any support, either in preparation for giving evidence, or in dealing with the subsequent of effects of what they had experienced. They would just be expected to continue 'as normal' at their place of work.

ACCIDENTS AT WORK

Surface workers at the mines in Cornwall and Devon were not exposed to so many dangers as those working underground, so the number of accidents in which women and girls were involved seems comparatively few, and the accidents, on the whole, tended to be less serious. However, caution should be exercised in assessing the level of this risk. In 1842, Barham states that:

'*A great number of accidents, though for the most part slight, occur in almost every mine. No record exists by which the proportion can be ascertained in which such accidents befall children and young people.*'

Having stated that no records of minor injuries were kept, so there was no way of knowing the extent of the problem, he then goes on to assume, rather patronisingly, that:

'*The surface operations in these mines are very free from occasions of accident and such as do occur are for the most part slight, arising from strains or falls, or casual blows with tools.*'

One wonders if those who actually suffered these minor injuries thought them so trivial. In his lack of reporting any serious injuries, he also overlooked his own collected evidence of some ten reported deaths on the dressing floors in the previous two years, and also a longer history of a few, but regular, serious injuries and deaths involving bal maidens and boys over the years.

The most common injuries would be due to minor falls, wrenching of muscles and joints, and cuts and bruises from the various crushing implements. These seem to have remained unrecorded and, no doubt, were considered part of the job. Interestingly, there was an ancient Celtic belief, in Cornwall, that binding an implement which had caused an injury would help to heal the wound itself. Apparently, it was not uncommon for miners to be seen carrying a heavily bandaged pick into the mine, so presumably the sight of a bal maiden using a bandaged shovel or hammer would not be a rare sight either.[44]

However, serious accidents did happen from time to time. The most serious dangers on the dressing floors were the moving parts of the various engines and machinery, or from moving wagons. Along with the occasional exploding boiler, these were the causes the worst accidents. Unlike their counterparts in the iron mines of Shropshire or the collieries of Lancashire, women and older girls in Cornwall and Devon were not employed as 'landers' at the head of the shaft, and so unlike in these other regions, there are no reports of females falling down the shaft in the course of their work.

Machinery and Equipment

Probably the most frequent cause of serious injury and death for the girls and women at the mines was accidents involving machinery. The great engines, crushers, and stamps were generally not made very safe, probably with only cursory arrangements for blocking off the dangerous moving parts. All workers would be warned to keep well clear, and told of the terrible dangers, because, once drawn into them, there was very little hope of surviving terrible crushing injuries.

Although injuries involving these large pieces of machinery were usually fatal, some were lucky. At Wheal Agar, Redruth, on 16th April 1888, 16 year-old Rebecca Bottrell moved away from her usual place of work on the dressing floor to talk to one of the boys, when her dress caught in the gears of one of the dipper wheels. The mining accident report recorded that she was 'severely bruised', whereas the local newspaper stated that she was 'seriously crushed'. In 1892, at Dolcoath Mine, 23 year-old Annie Martin (a spaller) inadvertently leant up against the engine pillar of the stone crusher. Her hand was crushed in the crankshaft.

One of the earliest reported fatalities was in 1823, and involved a girl of just 17 years of age. The victim was Jane Buzza who lived in Kenwyn (although the newspaper recorded that she was from Gwennap):

'On Thursday last, a young woman by the name of Buzza, of Gwennap, about 17 years of age, met an untimely death in consequence of retiring to a stamp shed, in Poldice Mine, at the hour of refreshment; when by going too near the axle by which the stamps are set in motion, her clothes were caught by one of the caps, and she was drawn in between the stamps and the wall and crushed to death.' (WB 16th May 1823)

A letter from the land agent at Fowey Consols, to William Rashleigh, tells of a very serious and possibly fatal accident at Fowey Consols, which happened just weeks after the publication of the *1842 Commission Report*. It reads:

'A poor girl got her clothes entangled in the wheels of the separating machine, which revolves at a rapid rate; she was instantly drawn between the cogs and whirled around at a frightful rate till both her legs were so mangled as to pass between the wheels without any further impression being made upon them. She was carried home and a surgeon was quickly on the spot. She still survives although little hope remains of her recovery. Her parents reside in St Blazey Parish.' [45]

The first female to be recorded as injured at Levant Stamps was 'a very young girl', Grace Trembath. On 13th January 1845, she was at work at the stamps and became entangled in the machinery and dreadfully injured. It is not known if she survived.

At South Caradon Mine, in February 1862, 17 year-old Jane Husband was late arriving at the mine one morning. Instead of going straight to the tool shed to collect what she needed for her work, she hid in the jigging house to avoid being seen by the surface captain. Somehow, her dress became entangled with the coupling of the jigging machine and she was crushed to death.

On 7th July 1873, 16 year-old Eliza Jane Hall jumped up on the crown gear wheel of the winding engine at Ding Dong Mine during her dinner break. Her clothes were caught in the gearing and her leg was crushed between the wheel and pinion. Although the engine driver stopped the engine as soon as he heard her screams, she died a few hours later from her injuries. It seems from the Cost Books for Ding Dong, that Eliza had only been employed there (as a framer) for about six weeks before this terrible accident. Presumably, in that short time she had not come to appreciated just how dangerous the machinery could be.[46]

While tin streams (with less machinery) were generally less hazardous than the mine dressing floors, there were fatalities occasionally there too. On January 13th 1888, 19 year-old Jane Cock (or Cook) of Kehelland Downs was killed at the Magor Tin Stream Works, on the Red River. Her dress was caught up into the revolving shaft of the scoop wheel machinery. She was drawn into the mechanism and killed instantly. The coroner returned a verdict of accidental death.

Fig. 58 Gravestone for Ellen Vincent
Redruth Cemetery
Courtesy of Geof Purcell

In 1894, another serious accident took place at Wheal Agar, but this time, sadly, it was fatal. On the 6th January, 24 year-old Ellen Vincent (of St Day Road, Redruth) was drawn into the machinery at the stamps. She died almost immediately, and her body was then taken home on a mine wagon. It seems that she had attempted to regulate the flow of water but it was unclear as to why she had not used the usual control, but had attempted to climb up to another tap over the stamps. At the inquest, two days later, it was decided that her scarf had then been caught in the axle, and a verdict of accidental death was given. It seems Ellen may only have gone to work at the mines since her father's death in the previous year.

Reports of boys or men being caught up in machinery and receiving serious injury are rare, probably because the clothing worn by the men on the dressing floor was far more suitable and safe. The girls and women seem to be particularly vulnerable, in part due to the voluminous nature of their skirts or their loose shawls, which could so easily catch in the machinery, without the wearer even noticing. Unfortunately, the women and girls in Cornwall never wore trousers like their counterpart 'pit-brow girls' in the Lancashire collieries. This would presumably have been much safer. (It was found that females who wore skirts in the coal mines in Scotland, were also more liable to accidents than those who wore trousers).[47]

The moving parts of the stationary machinery and engines on the mine surface were not the only dangers. Sometimes the women and girls were at risk from the moving wagons. One such accident occurred at Botallack Mine in January 1872. In early January, at eight o'clock in the morning, a wagon was caught up by a gust of wind and started down the very steep incline of the tramway. It damaged railings and woodwork on its way down, but only stopped when it crashed into a shed at the bottom. Unfortunately, this was a shed in which girls were working, and three of them were injured. One, who was not named, received a cut over one eye. Another, whose surname was Ladner received a very badly bruised leg. The third, Sarah Ann Downing, was seriously injured. She suffered a compound fracture her left leg, her kneecap was cut in two, and she had a deep cut over her right eye. However, as the women and girls were not usually involved in moving wagons in the same way as they were in some of the northern collieries, there are no known accounts of fatalities where they were crushed between the wagons themselves, as were their northern counterparts.

Falls, Subsidence and Floods

One of the main causes of death underground was from falls from ladders or levels, but serious falls at surface were rare. One such serious fall did happen, in about 1841, at United Mines, when Fanny Francis, 17 years old, was barrowing. She suffered fits as a consequence.

Widow, Elizabeth (Betsy) Noy, who was 58 years old, must have been one of the older tin dressers working at Morvah Consols in St Just. On 1st August 1874, she had gone to the engine room to dry her clothes. Whilst there, she had a dizzy turn and fell to the next floor. She struck her head on the machinery below and fractured her skull, and died the following day from her injuries. The inquest, held four days later, returned a verdict of accidental death.

Fig. 59 Spalling and Loading Copper Ore-stuff Carn Brea Mine 1881

One of the other most common causes of death for underground workers was from drowning, either during flash floods, or when huge bodies of water were suddenly released when old workings were breached. At surface, in a conventional deep mine, drowning was rarely a danger, unless a worker fell unconscious into one of the many areas of shallow water. However, those working at tin streams or sea tinning could be at risk from sudden floods or storms. For instance, in St Agnes in 1812, a bal maiden working at one of the tin-streams tried to rescue her hat from a swollen stream. She fell in and was carried downstream for half a mile. Luckily she survived, but was very shaken, cut and bruised.[48] In January 1875, 9 year-old Lavinia Ellans (or Hellings) of Treswithian Downs was not so fortunate when she fell into the Red River while working as a 'frame watcher'. It seems that she had to cross the river on a single unprotected plank in the course of her work. Her body was found a quarter of a mile downstream, near Mendarva Bridge.[49]

Another major danger below surface was subsidence and, on occasion, could bring danger above ground as well. On 24th August 1858, there was a sudden rock fall at the Porkellis Moor Mine in which seven underground workers were killed. This also caused a massive subsidence on the dressing floor. It was probably caused by the falling-in of extensive slime pits, where the underground workings had come too close to the surface. It happened while the bal maidens were working, and without notice. Some of the frames fell in entirely, and others were damaged. All the women and girls who were at the frames and slime pits managed to jump clear and, amazingly, none were injured.

Boiler House Explosions

Early on Wednesday 3rd February 1830, a bitterly cold morning, several workers at the United Hills Mine at Porthtowan took shelter in the boiler house. Within a few minutes the boiler exploded. Of the eleven people there, all were severely burnt and scalded, and nine died, either instantly or within a few hours. Among them was 20 year-old Elizabeth Goyne, from Mount Hawke, St Agnes. One of the newspapers described the terrible accident:

'All the deceased were dreadfully burnt and bruised, so much so, that their persons could scarcely be recognised; some were so scorched, that the skin of their hands fell off, and when picked up, was not unlike dry leather gloves.'

A similar accident happened at Boiling Well Mine in Gwithian on 10th February 1858. It was also a wet and cold morning, so several men, women and children had gathered in the boiler house to dry themselves before beginning work at 7 a.m. The boiler exploded while they were there, and the engine driver was killed instantly. Two bal maidens, Mary Webster and Alice Jones (aged 30 and 16 years respectively) died within hours from their injuries, and another man died a few days later. Six were badly scalded or burned, but survived. A broadsheet printed at the time gives a graphic description of both Mary and Alice's plight and suffering. (Mary's husband had been killed in a mine not long before and so she left orphaned children).[50] The coroner's verdict was *'accidental death from being scalded'* for both women.

'INCONSEQUENTIAL LOSSES' AND 'INVISIBLE' ACCIDENTS

Significantly, none of the accidents recorded here appear to have generated any compensation. Historically, in common law, an employer was liable for the results not only of his or her own negligence, but also for that of his or her employees when acting within the scope of their employment. However, from 1837, it was deemed that an employer was no longer liable for an employee causing damage to another employee. In practice, this meant that the adventurers could find ways of no longer being liable for damages in almost all cases of accidents at the mines.[51] Official reports regularly implied, in the way they were worded, that the blame lay with the victim, and this is true of most reported mine accidents of the early and mid-19th century, not just applying to injuries or fatalities to females. For example, Eliza Hall died because *'in spite of warnings from other girls'* she had *'persisted in jumping onto crown wheel of the whim and riding round'.* Annie Martin had her *'hand crushed by crank of engine driving the stone breaker, she having thoughtlessly leaned up against the engine pillar',* and Jane Buzza died *'by going too near the axle by which the stamps are set in motion'*. There was no acknowledgement that the mine adventurers had any responsibility to ensure employees could not have access to dangerous moving parts of machinery.

Eventually, some degree of safety consciousness and sense of responsibility toward young and vulnerable employees began to surface in the public mind during the 1870s. This may be illustrated by the comments of the coroner on the tragic drowning of Lavinia Ellans in January 1875:

'...as it was supposed that the deceased, in crossing the river on a plank, must have slipped her foot and fell into the stream, they strongly recommended that a rail should be attached to the plank for protection.'

However, mining companies were not legally liable for employees' safety until 1879, and even then to a very limited degree. When Jane Cock died at the Magor Tin Works in 1888, after she was drawn into the water wheel, the Mining Journal correspondent remarked:

'That despite the company 'being exonerated from all blame' the event seemed 'to point to the necessity of some good guard being provided for such machinery...a very slight protection often suffices to prevent such a [sic] event as this; and in factories the law secures that this shall be provided.' (MJ 21st Jan 1888 p. 75)

As late as December 1896, when 8 year-old Ada Harris died from falling into an unfenced arsenic flue at East Pool, as she was not an employee, the company did not have to pay any compensation. Children were expected to behave with adult concepts of responsibility and danger, and youngsters who forgot the warnings and played on or near moving machinery and were injured, where viewed with very little sympathy.

This cavalier attitude to life and limb is indicated by the casual way in which accidents involving women or girls were reported, or sometimes not reported at all. Women, when injured, or even killed, were not always given the dignity of identification in public reports, assuming they found their way into reports in the first place. In contrast, men and boys are named almost without exception. Of the seven deaths mentioned in this chapter which should have been reported, only two seem to have come to the notice of the Inspector of Mines. The accidents to Mary Webster and Alice Jones (1858), Jane Husband (1862), Sarah Ann Downing (1872), and Ellen Vincent (1894) do not seem to appear in the Inspector's records.

Under-reporting of accidents was general. In the *1842 Royal Commission*, there is a summary of 75 fatal accidents which had occurred in mines in Cornwall and West Devon between 1839 and 1841, and ten of these fatalities related to surface workers. Five had been killed in a boiler explosion at Consols, three died when they were entangled in machinery at Tresavean, Fowey Consols and Balleswidden, and two were involved in unspecified accidents at Restormel and East Polberro Consols. It is probable that a considerable proportion of these fatalities were female, and yet, other than being a statistic in this table, we have no further information about these terrible accidents or who was involved.

Barham believed that the fatality figures for 1839 to 1841 were under-reported by about 25%, so even discounting the five fatalities due to a boiler explosion as atypical, this suggests about thirty fatalities on the dressing floor per decade, or three hundred per century. If this figure is anywhere near accurate, it illustrates the severity of the under-reporting of serious accidents. An added complication is that the tin streams were not subject to mining legislation (as they did not involve underground work) so that accidents there were not usually reported to the mine inspectors. Of the two fatal accidents at tin streams described in this chapter, neither would have appeared in the annual mine statistics. However in 1875, Le Neve felt strongly enough to write a report about one of them (Lavinia Ellans), calling for such accidents to be included.

After considerable research, only fifteen serious or fatal accidents involving females have been identified so far, covering a period of fifty years. This reflects a similar under-reporting of mining accidents in the Llanelli area, where a colliery agent, in 1841, recalled *'about 24 fatal accidents at one works'* in a period of 25 years, whereas *'published sources between 1816 and 1841, give no indication that so many fatalities could have occurred in a single colliery.'* [52] (Similarly, Richard Fynes also noted serious under recording of deaths in coal mines in Northumberland and Durham during the 1880's).[53]

MAKING MINES SAFER

In 1842, as a result of his findings in the mines of Cornwall and West Devon, Barham made strong recommendations to the government, which would have significantly improved the working environment for all workers, including the bal maidens. These changes included:

1. No child under nine to work at the mines.
2. No child under thirteen years old to work more than eight hours per day.
3. Food at the mines: 'hoggans' to be discouraged; a place for employees to warm food and prepare a hot drink to be made available, and with a minimum of 45 minutes for the dinner break.
4. A place to be provided to change and dry wet shoes and stockings.
5. More holidays to be provided and more task work to be made available.
6. Mine management to sponsor evening classes for their young employees plus day schools for the miners' younger children (with an appropriate deductions in miners' pay).

These recommendations, if put into practice, would have improved the educational opportunities, and health and safety for all bal maidens working at the metalliferous mines. In the event, none of these recommendations were implemented, and the legislation enacted as a result of this report was applied to the collieries only. It was to be another thirty years or more (1872) before similar recommendations would bring significant improvements to the circumstances of the bal maidens of Cornwall and Devon. It was to be more than thirty-five years before mine managers were made more liable for safety of their workers (from 1879), and, even then, only partially. By the time appropriate levels of protection were achieved for all employees, women and girls were no longer working at these mines.

FOOTNOTES

1. Hamilton Jenkin (1951) p. 161.
2. CEC esp. pp. 53-96, Tables 3, 9, 21, 25, & Evidence Nos. 21, 28, 33, 46, 47, 56, 61, 75, 85-86, 89, 103.
3. Tyacke, W. Davis *William Murrish, The Miner Of Perranzabuloe* (Hamilton Adams 1866) p. 33.
4. WB Oct 31st 1935, Oct 29th 1936.
5. Tremellin (1841) p. 7.
6. Lanyon (1836) p. 45.
7. Rideing (1881) p. 812.
8. Moyle (1839) p. 57.
9. Harris (1974) p. 74 note 13.
10. Moyle (1839) p. 57.
11. Rowe (1993) p. 26.
12. Chope (1967) p. 124.
13. Sara (1970) p. 43; Brooke (1967); Troon WI (1952).
14. Burt (1984) p. 80.
15. MJ 15th Feb 1879; Barton (1968) p. 56.
16. Henderson (1858) p. 197.
17. Harper, Charles *From Paddington to Penzance* (Catto & Windus 1893) p. 247.
18. Personal corresp. (PL/LM 2003).
19. Buckley (2007) p. 40.
20. Barton, D. B. 'Arsenic Production in West Cornwall' in *Essays in Cornish Mining 2* (D. Bradford Barton 1970) p. 106.
21. Dickens, Charles *The Uncommercial Traveller* (1869) Chap. 32.
22. International Network for the History of Occupational and Environmental Prevention (4th Dec. 1999) p. 1.
23. Burt (1984) p. 191.
24. CEC: for Lanark and Dumfries: Joseph Fletcher (1842) p. 13.
25. Harrison (1989) pp. 184-5.
26. Legge & Goadby *Lead Poisoning and Lead Absorption Symptoms* (Arnold 1912) p. 36.
27. Dickens, op cit.
28. MJ 25th Apr 1903; 2nd Apr 1904.
29. WB Oct 31st 1935, Oct 29th 1936.
30. Jaggard, Edwin 'James Boswell's Journey Through Cornwall 1792' *RIC Jour.* (2004) p. 23.
31. Rideing (1881) p. 809.
32. Personal corresp. (JT/LM 2002).
33. Paige, R. T. *The Tamar Valley at Work* (DART 1982).
34. Brooke (1967).
35. Troon WI (1952) p. 22.
36. Bodmin Quarter Sessions (CRO: QS1 12/300); Tremellin (1841) p. 70.
37. Buckley (2007) p.55.
38. Cornubian 12th June 1868.
39. Cornubian 4th June 1897.
40. Payton (1984) p. 200.
41. Pascoe, Charlotte Champion *Walks about St Hilary* (Rogers & Rogers 1879) p. 34.
42. United Hills Explosion Broadsheet (CRO: X 106/10).
43. Vivian (1990) p. 10.
44. Bird, Sheila *Tales of Old Cornwall* (Countryside Books 1992) p. 105.
45. William Rashleigh Letters (24th Dec 1842) (CRO: R/5335/30).
46. Vivian (1993) p. 10.
47. King, Lillian *Sair, Sair Work; Women and Mining in Scotland* (Windfall 2001) p. 53.
48. WB 13th Nov. 1812.
49. Le Neve, Dr. C. Report Part 2...Mines Classed Under Metalliferous Mines Reg. Act (CRO: CA/B43/26) p. 7.
50. Boiling Well Explosion Broadsheet (CRO:X 106/21).
51. Williams, J. E. *The Derbyshire Miners* (Allen & Unwin, 1962) p. 458-459.
52. Symons, M. V. *Coal Mining in the Llanelli Area Vol. 1: 16th Century to 1829* (Llanelli Borough Council 1979) p. 339.
53. Fynes, Richard *The Miners of Northumberland and Durham* (Davis 1986) pp. 160-1.

Chapter 10

MINE CLOSURES: THE END OF THE ROAD OR A NEW LIFE?

In order to understand the enormous changes that confronted bal maidens when the mines closed or became mechanised, it is necessary to appreciate the comparative economic and social freedom which their mine work provided. Working at the mines gave bal maidens a degree of independence and sense of personal identity which was denied many other working-class women of their time. As with many manual jobs, the work was hard, dirty, poorly paid and often done at the expense of their health and education. Despite all this, there were advantages of this type of labour over the other alternatives available to them, such as working as farm labourers or domestic servants.[1] It seems that mine work was generally better paid and not quite as seasonal as farm work. In the novel *'Norah Lang, Mine Girl'*, after the mine closed and Norah lost her job as an ore dresser, she considered going to hoe turnips as a very inferior job.[2] In common with domestic service, the farm-labouring hours were invariably longer than those at the mine, resulting in much less free time. Both of these occupations usually entailed 'living in' which brought the double disadvantage of less freedom and almost non-existent wages, once board and lodging had been deducted from the pay.

Another advantage of mine work was the companionship and bonding that occurred between the women and girls as they worked together. A particular type of team relationship developed on the dressing floors, where many different tasks had to be co-ordinated to ensure smooth flow of the processes. Girls and women were often called off one task to another, to assist girls already working there, if a bottleneck was building up at one of the stages in the operation. The girls, therefore, needed to be adaptable in what they were able to do, as well as flexible about who they could work with. The almost collegiate nature of the bal maidens relationships was expressed in the way in which they gathered together to travel to and from work, more often than not forming their own spontaneous choirs, and singing complex harmonies on the way.

In the earlier years, bal maidens were also able to have some control over their own lives in the commonly accepted practice of 'keeping company'. Young people would sometimes establish sexual relationships without marrying in the first instance, choosing to remain with their own families. This arrangement would be considered an unofficial betrothal. In this way, they could both continue to contribute to the economy of their own family whilst, hopefully, being able to save towards their own future home. They would usually then marry when a child was on the way, and when the bal maiden could no longer work at the mine, due to her condition. While still living at home, in the slightly better economic times, older bal maidens probably contributed more to the family budget than they actually cost the household, as well as being able to save for their own home. In this situation, both the families and the couples benefited. Conversely, in hard times, the system would not work well, as the bal maiden would not have enough to pay her way and save any money.

Long before a bal maiden started saving for her own home and family, she would have been acutely aware of the way in which her few shillings a week bolstered the family economy. In a mining family consisting of seven people, in the Gwennap area in 1841, two sisters contributed to the family income by working at the mine. The eldest, 21 years old, contributed about one sixth of the family income, thus subsidising the other members, and the youngest, just 12 years old, contributed two shillings.[3] In good times, a bal maiden's earnings, however meagre, might enable small luxuries, such as sending a sibling to school, or paying for a visit from a doctor. In hard times, it could mean the difference between hunger and having enough food, and between being cold or having coal on the fire. Either way, the bal maiden would normally feel that her work and earnings had played a significant part in the economy of her own family over the years, and she would also expect to make a considerable contribution to her own marital home before her earning days ended with the arrival of the first children.

From this, it is possible to picture young women who were part of a very distinct working group within their communities, tightly bonded, and having some sort of financial independence, even if their hard earned money was used entirely to support the family's basic needs. They would also be marked out as a group by virtue of their patterns of spare time, and those not courting would band together for jaunts to the Saturday markets, or the special seasonal fairs. This psychological sense of financial independence, along with social freedom in terms of free time, seems to have led to a real sense of self-worth. This was often indicated by the various ways in which bal maidens stated their individuality, mostly through what they chose to wear, both at the mine and elsewhere.

Each bal maiden, therefore, must have had to make considerable psychological adjustment if her employment suddenly and unexpectedly ended. With wide-scale closures of mines happening repeatedly in the history of Cornwall many a dream must have been shattered. Each would have to find her own way through the dramatic change in roles, and startling reduction in independence.

THE BEGINNING OF THE END

This process became a stark and final reality for whole communities of women and girls when the mines began to close *en masse* from about 1867. It has been estimated that, between 1861 and 1900, over 26% of Cornish women between the ages of 15 and 24 emigrated overseas, and over 35% migrated to other counties in the UK. Many of these would have been bal maidens. It was only then, when the numbers of people affected was so vast, with poverty and hunger driving people to desperation, that the needs of these women in their changing roles were actually publicly acknowledged and addressed. Particular charities and schemes were set up during these difficult years, for instance in 1867, 1876 and 1879, to try and meet some of their needs.

As the tasks for which the women and girls were responsible became mechanised or the mines began to close, what options were there for these women and girls who lost their jobs? The simplest solution might be for the family unit to absorb the financial shock and rely entirely on the male breadwinners. However, invariably the men were also being thrown out of work. There was rarely any slack with which to re-adjust the family budgets. Finding home-based alternative occupations for the women and girls, such as dressmaking or food production, was occasionally an option, but with whole communities having reduced incomes, there was very little money for purchasing these extra goods or services. Often, the trades and home-based industries within the community also went out of business.

A few statistics illustrate the sudden reduction in employment in the mines of Cornwall from 1867 onwards. In a matter of months, the number of females employed at Botallack had been reduced by 40%. In Chacewater, 144 children had been put out of work, and over 300 children had lost their jobs at Dolcoath.[4] In some families, it had been the children who were the only breadwinners, and even work for them was at a premium. In March 1867, ninety mines were wound up at the Stannary Courts. In an eighteen month period during 1866 and 1867 Balleswidden, Carn Brea, Wendron Consols, Great Wheal Busy, South Wheal Tolgus Mines, Wheal Reeth, and United Mines all closed, along with many other smaller mines, and more than 11,000 were thrown out of work.[5]

At the same time as these dramatic job losses, the prices of basic commodities had increased so that the buying power of the miner's meagre wages had been reduced to one half. As a result, whole mining communities were becoming destitute. Extreme hardship had been caused not only by high corn prices, but by the scarcity and high price of cotton due to the American Civil War. This meant that mining families were not only unable to buy bread, but unable to afford replacement bedding or clothing. The vicar of Sithney and Breage wrote in April 1867:

'The clothing of the miners is nearly worn out, and sad to relate, many of them have had no under linen for sometime. Although the want of clothing is great, still the craving of hunger seems to throw this want into the background. The average gettings of the majority of the miners for the last twelve months has been from twenty five to thirty shillings per month. Many cases have come before us where families have been without bread for some days, and they have had to subsist on a bare supply of barley bread and boiled turnips.' (RCG 12th Dec 1867)

A County Distress Fund was set up in 1867, with smaller district committees responsible for administration in different areas. In December 1867, reports to the District Fund indicated widespread deprivation. Across the mining parishes, over seven hundred families were in receipt of help from the fund - most earning less than 2s per head per week, the amount considered necessary to buy flour for one person. In the Helston district, at this time, it was estimated that one third of the mining population, over 1,000 families, were in need of clothing. In the east of the county, when local magistrates visited cottages in the Tywardreath area, they found that forty families did not possess a single blanket, while forty others had scarcely any bedding at all. Miners were going underground with no breakfast and only a slice of barley bread for 'croust'. It was reported that some bal maidens in the Truro went to work two days in a row having had only fried turnips to eat.

The most immediate relief was given in the form of food, blankets and clothing, with the County Distress Fund giving grants to District Sub-Committees for clothing and bedding, and for setting up soup kitchens. For instance, the Relief Committee in Chacewater collected and distributed about £35 worth of vouchers for bread, flour, and clothing, while soup kitchens were set up in Tywardreath in January and February 1868.[6]

History was to repeat itself from 1876 to 1879, when the conditions in the mining parishes were described as *'positively appalling'*. In 1876, a Miners' Relief Fund was set up by Rev. H. J. A. Fothergill, the curate of Sithney, one of the parishes worst affected at that time. In the same year, kitchens were set up at Blowing House Hill at Wrestling Green to provide soup, at 1d per quart on three days a week, for destitute china clay workers. In 1879, the County Distress Fund aimed to provide clothing and bedding, and 'aid in sickness' to those who were most destitute. In January of that year, a Wesleyan Methodist Relief Fund for the Cornwall District had been set up nationally. In the first instance, grants of £10 were made to Helston and Camborne, £5 each to Marazion, St Just, Hayle, and Newlyn East, and £2 to St Austell.[7] Soup kitchens were also set up in Truro, Penryn, Bodmin, Falmouth and Camborne. This fund enabled men and women who had been laid off from the mines to be employed on various road schemes (including building the new road in Perranporth, using mine waste for the foundations). Women were also paid 1s or 1s 3d per day to clean or help redecorate many of the chapels. In addition, £500 was set aside for assisted passages to Canada. By March 1880, the fund had raised nearly £9,000 from Methodists all over the world. (After 1881, its work continued in a lower key for emergency purposes, until the 1930s).[8]

In addition to supplying emergency provisions, the County Relief Committee also tried to find more permanent solutions. Particular attention was paid to finding alternative employment, and an assortment of schemes was devised for young bal maidens who had lost their jobs. Various local initiatives were taken, like this one by a local mine manager:

'Capt. N. Climo, formerly manager of Camborne Vean, has taken a plot of ground a little below Penponds viaduct to erect some machinery for untinning [sic] slimes, a quantity of which he has purchased on Camborne Vean old sett. This will give employment to many little ones resident in Baripper and Gwinnear, who now have to travel three or four miles to Dolcoath and adjacent mines.' (WB 12 Jan 1880)

While mines closed across Cornwall and Devon at this time, the central mining area around Carn Brea was slightly less affected. This was because some of the largest mines continued in production, and was also due to the expansion of the tin streams. During the next fifteen years or so, bal maidens continued to move into the Carn Brea area (usually with their families, but sometimes independently) for work. Between 20 and 30% of the bal maidens recorded in the *1871* and *1881 Census* for Redruth, Illogan and Camborne had been born outside these parishes. By 1891, the mines and tin streams in this area also began laying people off, and this in-migration seems to have eased off a little.

Some migration to find work at other mines within the South West was still possible, up until about 1876. Workers could sometimes find work at the China Clay Pits or at the copper and arsenic mines in the Tamar valley, some of which were still expanding in terms of production into the early 1870s. However, these local initiatives and transfers within the mining industry were destined to be only a temporary measure, There was another wave of mine closures from 1893, with women and girls among those laid off. In the seven years from 1893, 3,500 surface workers lost their jobs (many from the tin stream works).

The final major wave of closures which involved bal maidens happened in the winter of 1920-21. Nearly 4,500 employees were thrown out of work, mostly in the Carn Brea area, of whom 83 were women and 25 were girls. Relief Committees were again in action by March 1921, to support destitute mine workers. This time £300 was set aside for wages, and £100 for food and clothing. The parishes of Redruth, Camborne, and Illogan received £30 each, and other parishes could apply for £10 grants.[9] Only a handful of mines (mostly tin) remained open in Cornwall beyond this date.

THE WORKHOUSE

The ultimate fear was to end up in an institution, and for some, the fear of the workhouse became a reality. In each census year, about thirty bal maidens were to be found resident across the Union Workhouses of Cornwall, as well as a handful described as *'pauper bal maidens'* (ex-bal maidens now dependent on parish relief). The greatest numbers were always recorded at the Illogan Workhouse in Barncoose. Interestingly, the *1871 Census* gives the tasks allocated to inmates there. Of the seventeen former bal maidens recorded, four were allocated to housework, two to the laundry (one of whom was blind), two to the scullery, one to *'cutting bread'*, one to picking oakum, one was working in the nursery and one in the hospital. Some twenty years later, in 1891, there were twenty-three *'former tin mine labourers'* recorded in the same place, this time noted just by their initials. With the exception of one widow, all of these women were single. Their ages ranged from 16 to 70 years old, with over half between 20 and 45. In the following year, there were still similar numbers of ex-bal maidens in residence.[10]

ALTERNATIVE EMPLOYMENT

Out-of-work bal maidens would usually only be able to find alternative work in new industries, or in those which were expanding. The main avenue in the Carn Brea area, during the 1890s, appears to be at the various safety fuse works. Whereas the number of females employed in this work remained at about eighty in the 1870s and 1880s, the number had risen to over two hundred by 1901. Bal maidens Annie Glanville of Lower Penponds, Lavinia Wallace of Kehelland, Laura Richards and Mary Sims of Dolcoath Row, and Annie Trengrove of Brea were among those who found work in this way by 1901. Mrs. Gay, who recalled her days at the tin streams in the 1870s, also left tin dressing for the fuse factory in 1877.[11]

A few new job opportunities also arose in the St Day area, in 1881, when a velveteen factory was opened in Little Beside. The enterprise employed about forty women and girls, but this too had closed by the end of the century.[12]

MAKING MAIDS OUT OF BAL MAIDS

Another alternative for the redundant mine women and girls was to find local employment in the service industry. There was a huge increase in the number of people employed as domestic servants during the latter part of the nineteenth century, and most of them were girls and women. Much of this increase of available work appears to be among the ranks of artisans and trades people who, in wanting to emulate the upper classes, found that inexperienced servants could be hired relatively cheaply via charitable institutions, prisons, or direct from the workhouse:

'Artisan and trades people were the usual customers at the workhouses and the charitable institutions; when they went away empty handed it was more likely to be because of a shortage of supply, not because of the price.' [13]

With precious few jobs available in the mining industry, this expanding market of domestic service seemed to be one of the most obvious outlets for the surplus female mine workforce in Cornwall. Projects and schemes were set up across the mining parishes to find domestic work for ex-bal maidens, such as happened in the parish of St Day during 1878:

'The recent reductions of surface hands at many of the mines have compelled numbers of the bal girls to try domestic service; though clumsy at first, they are generally painstaking and honest.' (MJ 23rd Mar 1878)

A similar scheme for placing the young women in service, was adopted in Redruth:

'The distress in the neighbourhood of Redruth is caused in a great measure by a number of girls and boys being thrown out of employment by a curtailment of operations at the various tin streams. An effort is being made to provide clothing for the girls, and to place them in families to be trained as domestic servants.' (WB 24th Feb 1879)

Fig. 60 Ex-Bal Maiden
Marah Goninan
'In Service' 1891
Courtesy of John Saunders

One of the bal maidens who found work in service within the county was Marah Goninan. In 1881, at the age of 13, she was working as a tin stream labourer, near Connor Downs, with her older sister Catherine. By 1891, she was working as a servant on a farm in the parish of Crowan (Fig. 60).[14] Similarly, Mary Ann Pill, who had been working at one of the lead mines in the parish of Perranzabuloe, in 1871, had become a cook to the household of John Henry Bawden (a Bank Manager) at Upper Lemon Villas in Kenwyn, by 1881.

With limited opportunities of finding domestic work within the county, schemes were also developed for finding work outside Cornwall. For instance, in December 1867, a hotelier from Oldham had written to the County Distress Fund suggesting that girls from the mines could be sent north where there was a shortage of domestic servants, and a training scheme was suggested in order to prepare them for this type of work.[15] In 1896, bal maidens from Redruth were also being placed in domestic service outside the county. The difficulties faced by bal maidens, in trying to adapt to a very different living and working environment, are captured in the following two newspaper extracts. The first is a conversation reportedly between two ex-bal maidens, one who continued in service, and one who left after a few weeks:

'I put some working men in the drawing room and called them 'Sir', and, when they told me I had made a mistake, left a gentleman who called standing on the doorstep, telling him to wait there, for Master was engaged, and then forgot to mention a word about it when master was disengaged. Another day, I asked the missus what I should take up the soup in as I couldn't see any basins, and she said in the soup plates; so out I goes and takes up the soup in the vegetable dishes.' (Cornishman 22nd Aug 1879)

The second is from a report made to one of the District Relief Funds:

'The Redruth Ladies' Committee had applications from all over the county and outside the county for general servants, many asking for respectable girls, and stating they were quite prepared to teach them. They had been able to send away three women. The Rev. H. Oxland said that they had sent some women away from Illogan; but up to that morning six of them had returned. One, a woman of 28, for whom a situation in a good family in Fowey was found, came to him as pale as a ghost, and said that she was sorry to say she had 'taken fear' and could not go, adding that she had never been in a train, and was afraid for her life.' (WB 19th Mar 1896)

It seems that some women managed to make the transition from bal maiden to servant, and then were happy with their new life:

'Some few, who from time to time have done so and who have fortunately got into places where pains have been taken to instruct them in their duties, would now on no account exchange their present position for mine work: on the contrary, they affirm they are much more comfortable indoors, out of the wet and cold....Mine girls when they settle in service, are generally trustworthy and honest; but they are fond of liberty and require plenty of patience to make them good servants. At times they are inclined to be uncouth, and steadily resist any fancied infringement of their right; but this is often more than made up by their other sterling qualities.' (WB 19th Mar 1896)

When the various schemes were set up to encourage bal maidens to take up employment as domestic servants, certain geographic areas appear to have been targeted. When Deacon analysed the *1891 Census* looking for Cornish-born females, he found an amazing 17,757 in Devon, 10,005 in London and Middlesex, and 4,439 in Lancashire, many of whom were in service. Of the 17,500 found in Devon, the greater proportion were in domestic service in the Plymouth area.[16]

It is highly probable that a proportion of these women and girls had been bal maidens, and had taken these posts when they were thrown out of work as the mines closed. Mary Hannah Reynolds may well have been one of these. When she was 13 years old, in the *1861 Census*, she was recorded as working at the mine. At the time she was living at Polwheveral, near Constantine, and was probably working at Wheal Vyvian Copper Mine. By 1864, when Mary Hannah was 16 years old, the mine closed. The next record of Mary shows that she was living in Croydon at the time of her marriage in 1873, where her family believe she was working as a domestic servant. Although it is not known how or when she came to Croydon, she may well have been one of the many bal maidens encouraged to go into service in London.

Although many remained where they were and made new lives in their adopted homes, there were some who found this impossible, and returned to Cornwall. Mary Hannah Reynolds was one of those. By 1881, she had returned home to Constantine, but she was deserted by her husband, and raised her two sons on her own. She experienced great poverty and hardship, living in a 'one up, one down' cottage, with no water or other services, until her death in 1935 at the age of 86 years. During her years in service, there had been no opportunity to make provision for her own future.[17]

'BETTER THE NOR' THAN OVERSEA'

Whether by their own initiative, moving with their families, or being placed by charitable schemes, the most likely outcome of mine closures for bal maidens was migration out of the South West area altogether. Large numbers moved either within this country or went abroad. In some mining parishes, up to three-quarters of the young people moved in a period of some twenty years, leaving the places they left behind almost like ghost towns.

Many of the redundant mine workers and their families felt that, if they had to move, they would rather stay in this country than go abroad. A common saying among them was 'better the nor' than oversea'. Even in the 18th and 19th century, whenever there were desperate food shortages or major mine closures, there had been various waves of internal migration out of Cornwall, to the various other mines in Britain. In the early days, migration had been mostly to the metalliferous mines, where the skills learnt at the Cornish mines were most transferable. For instance, considerable numbers of Cornish miners went to the lead and silver mines in mid Wales or to copper mines in Ireland in the 1830s and 1840s, and took not just their mining skills, but methods as well. Cornish mining communities sprung up at places like Llynwernog and Cwmystwyth in Cardiganshire, Llanfyrnach in Pembrokeshire, and Allihies in Co. Cork. As was the Cornish practice, women and girls were employed on the dressing floors at some of these mines, but it is not clear how many, if any, were Cornish born bal maidens.[18]

By the time of the mass exodus from the mines in Cornwall from 1867, mining jobs (mostly in the collieries, but some at iron mines) were being offered in many different places in Britain, as well as Ireland. Advertisements offering opportunities at the mines in other parts of the UK were often placed in Cornish newspapers, or displayed on flyers or billboards in the main towns such as Redruth and Truro. Sometimes, agents from these companies would travel to Cornwall and hold public meetings to attract would-be employees. This was especially true of the coal mines, and, for the first time, Cornish miners started to work in appreciable numbers in the collieries of the North and Wales, as well as in the 'hard-rock' (metalliferous) mines. These advertisements are from this time:

'About a dozen miners wanted for Ironstone Mining at Grosmont, Yorkshire. Constant work.' (WB 6th Oct 1865)

'During the last fortnight, Messrs. Brown and Howatson, from Glasgow, representing the coal and iron masters of that city, have been engaging miners to proceed to Scotland, and already 300 have contracted. The liberal terms offered viz. 4s a day, certain for 12 months, and free transit, have proved attractive.' (WB 2nd Nov 1866)

Some miners and their families travelled north to work in the iron mines of Shropshire or Furness. Others found work, sometimes strike-breaking, in the coalfields of South Wales, Staffordshire, Lanarkshire, Co. Durham, Northumberland, Yorkshire and Lancashire. Around 1872, bal maiden Mary Ann Kitto (of Stoke Climsland) travelled with her husband to Dreghorn in Scotland for him to take up work at the collieries there. Within a few years, however, they had moved south to Burnley, where Mary Ann died of typhus fever in 1877.[19] In 1851, 31 year-old widow Charity Gundry was working at a mine in St Blazey to support herself and her five daughters. She then married miner Edward Bailey in 1865 and, by 1871, the whole family had all moved to Llantrisant in South Wales, where Edward was working in the iron mines. Charity's daughters Grace, Amelia and Selina (who had also been copper dressers, back in Cornwall in 1861) appear also to have married and settled in the Merthyr Tydfil area. Charity died in Llantrisant in 1881.[20] Mary Ann Northey (née Johns) and her daughter Mary Jane travelled from St Blazey to Northumberland, via the Tamar copper mines. Both had been copper dressers in their younger days; Mary Ann in St Blazey in 1841, and Mary Jane in Tavistock (probably at Devon Great Consols) in 1861. In 1865, Mary Ann's husband had been offered work at a coal mine in Cramlington, Northumberland, and so the family moved north. Tragically, after only three weeks at work William was killed by a rock fall.[21] The family somehow managed to scrape a living in Cramlington for several years. Daughter Mary Jane married Nicholas Down in 1871 and moved south into County Durham This is where her mother, Mary Ann, died in 1883.

Many of the mining areas to which the Cornish miners went also had a tradition of women working at surface. In Shropshire, women and girls were employed seasonally to pick out haematite from the heaps of weathered ore-stuff. In Lancashire, for example at Wigan, St Helens and Burnley, young women pushed full coal wagons around the floors from the pit-head to the screens. In Lancashire and Yorkshire, they also picked out rubbish after the coal had been graded at the screen. In the Staffordshire collieries, they even landed the kibbles as they arrived at surface. In these areas they were known as '*pit-brow lasses*'.

Fig. 61 Mountain Mine Engine House Allihies 2007

In these mines and collieries, it seems wives and children of local miners were probably given first priority over the Cornish, for any available jobs. So far, there is no record of Cornish bal maidens working at these tasks. For those families who had been strike-breaking, it would be unlikely that the local women would welcome the Cornish bal maidens at the bank, pit-head, or screens, to work with them. With increasing middle-class abhorrence at women and girls working at mines at this time, and increasing mechanisation of the jobs which the remaining women did, there was little hope that these migrant bal maidens would find work on the dressing floors or picking belts again. So, as bal maidens made plans to move, whether with their families, their husbands, or independently, they knew that their economic role was going to change, and they would need to look for jobs outside the mining industry.

At least one Cornish bal maiden ended up at Allihies in County Cork. Jane Boyns Eddy, who had been born in St Just and was working at the copper mines in Pendeen in 1861, had moved with her father (a copper mine agent) to the copper mines in Allihies, South-West Ireland by 1865 (Fig. 61). Here, the Cornish families lived in the *'Cornish Village'* on the side of the mountain, just below the mine, and quite separate from the local community (Fig. 62). It is not known if Jane continued to dress ore here. Back in 1842, it had been reported that there were 130 girls working at Allihies, with the mines under the supervision of Cornish mine captains. Almost certainly, 11 year-old Jane Frewhella (originally Trewhella?), who worked the bellows at the mine forge in 1841, was of Cornish extraction.[22]

Fig. 62 Cornish Village and Counthouse Allihies 2007

The early 1870s were a time of great expansion of the textile industry in Yorkshire and Lancashire. Advertisements were regularly placed in newspapers in Cornwall for workers for the newly opened cotton and woollen mills. Here was the opportunity for secure employment, and many jumped at the chance:

'Since 1868, between Chacewater, Gwennap and Redruth 2,750 persons have removed their homes in Cornwall to the North of England. In Burnley alone, there are about eight new factories about to be opened, each of these will absorb about 800. At Bacup there are two more factories waiting for hands. At Skipton, Oldham and others places Cornish hands are in great request, at from 8s to 25s per week. It is evident that for young women and children to work at the mines for 4d and 6d per day is simply a waste of time and opportunity of doing better. One family, for instance, reports having been half starved in Cornwall upon 48s per month at the stamps, burning houses and night duty at the arsenic works, where in Burnley they now obtain from 50 to 55s per week, work regular hours, and are always sheltered from the wet and cold.' (WB 5th Oct 1871)

In September 1872, agents from the cotton mills visited Lostwithiel, encouraging people to take up this type of work. Seventy people left Lostwithiel by train that month to take up the offer:

'There is great advantage in the north for people who have large families, as the children earn several pence per day, and are sent to school certain times in the week.' (WB 19th Sept 1872)

Although most, but not all, of the jobs available at the mills in Lancashire and Yorkshire were for girls and women, there were other jobs outside this industry available for the men. Some work was offered at the Yorkshire and Lancashire coal mines, but also Cornish miners were highly valued for their skills in building tunnels for the ever-expanding railway network. In the 1870s, there were many tunnels being built through the Pennines, including the famous tunnel under Whernside. Once again, advertisements appeared in the Cornish press:

'Midland Railway; Settle to Carlisle Contract No. 1 Blaemoor Tunnel. Wanted, now and in the course of a few months, upwards of 500 miners for the above tunnel, in gritstone and limestone. The works are dry and there is good air. Ample accommodation close to the works in healthily situated huts. Applications for huts and for further particulars, apply to John Ashwell, Contractor, Ingleton.' (WB 15th June 1871)

With work available in these areas for both men and women, Cornish families would still have the opportunity of a multiple wage, and ex-bal maidens would still be able to earn their own keep. The connection between the Cornish men working on the railway and Cornish women working in the mills can be seen in several census entries for Skipton in 1881. 20 year-old Mary Lord, born in St Just, had married a railway mason and was working as a cotton weaver. Whether she was an ex-bal maiden, we do not know. Ellen Rule had been working at the mines in Camborne in 1871, probably at Condurrow, at the age of 14, but, by the age of 23, she was a thread polisher in Skipton, where she was lodging with railway workers. Whether she had travelled with her family from Cornwall to take up work at the mills, or whether she had made the journey on her own, we do not know, but she, too, had made use of this Cornish connection with the Yorkshire railway navvies.

These bal maidens who went to work at the cotton mills found themselves employed in slightly more comfortable circumstances than at the mine. However, they were still faced with all the inherent dangers of working long hours in a very noisy and dusty atmosphere. Also they still had to be very careful to avoid injury from the largely unprotected machinery with which they worked. How many bal maidens from Cornwall took up this sort of work is unknown.

TO FAR AWAY PLACES

From about 1840 onwards, travellers returning from their journeys, and miners writing home, told wonderful stories of fortunes to be won in far-off places. As copper and gold were discovered in Australia, advertisements placed in local newspapers encouraged emigration, and very cheap passages were offered to people with skills relevant to mining. In the 1840s, a company was formed in London to work a seam of lead on land called Glen Osmond, belonging to Osmond Gilles, in South Australia. A Captain Pascoe set out from Cornwall with ten miners and their families to work the lead mine in Cornish fashion. On arrival, the girls in the party, who were 10 or 11 years old, were employed to wash and sort the ore.[23] However, this custom of employing females at the mines did not continue long in South Australia.

Because of the predominance of single men in these early mining settlements, there was a great need of women to undertake various domestic tasks. Men were therefore encouraged not just to take their families, but also to take unmarried sisters or female relatives. A significant number of unaccompanied girls and women must also have migrated. Twenty were recorded in 1837, but this number was to increase over the years.

In addition to the 'Labour Office' in the port of Adelaide, a special hostel was opened for *'single unprotected women'*.[24] How many of these were ex-bal maidens is unknown, as previous occupations of the women were not often recorded. Only eight women who applied for assisted passage to New South Wales, between 1837 and 1877, were described as mine workers.[25] The earliest recorded bal maidens to travel out to Australia were Jane and Suckey Fletcher, both from Wheal Burton, who emigrated to Australia in 1839. Whether they travelled with other family members or to meet boyfriends who were already there, we do not know.[26]

Later, as more gold, silver, and copper was discovered around the world, there became a wide range of destinations - North and South America, Italy, Sardinia, and South Africa for instance – both to work in the mines and also to 'open up' the land to agriculture and settlement. Many Cornish left during the 1850s, not always out of necessity but due to the attraction of the 'Gold Rush', and many a bal maiden must have been lured away too. Further waves of migration were generally from necessity, especially in 1867, between 1876 and 1879, and again in the mid 1890s. The following advertisements for New Zealand and Nova Scotia are typical of what would appear each week in the Cornish Press:

'Assisted passages: a few miners having grown-up daughters, farm labourers, single females, miners able to do farm work as well, carpenters, shepherds, smiths, masons and others, may obtain assisted passages to New Zealand by applying to Mr. W. Wade, Redruth. NB. Emigrants paying their own passage to New Zealand will be taken for £15, and to New York by steam for £5. 5s' (WB 19th June 1863)

'Miners, mechanics, and labourers to work on railroads, at the coal mines and at the gold mines, will find constant employment at high wages. A great demand for female servants. For further particulars, apply John S. De Wolf and Co., 1 Tower Chambers, Liverpool, emigration agents for Nova Scotia.' (WB 30th Mar 1866)

Although passenger lists rarely indicate the status or occupation of women and girls, it is commonly understood that the majority of wives or girlfriends travelling out to places such as Moonta and Wallaroo had been mine workers.[27] How many single unattached bal maidens travelled with their brothers or cousins in search of adventure is hard to tell. However, many ex-bal maidens married in order to travel with their partners, often at short notice, when decisions were made quickly to take up jobs overseas. 20 year-old Mary Ann Hooper, an ore dresser living at Illogan Highway married John Teague (alias Tyack), a miner, on 16th July 1854. By October 1854, they had arrived in South Australia, and made their way, in the first instance to Moonta. Similarly, 17 year-old Ann Snell, a copper ore dresser in Gunnislake in 1851, married William Sleeman, a miner from Callington, in May 1854 and they emigrated to the Buningyong very soon afterwards.[28]

Alternatively, marriages to fiancés were often arranged to take place almost immediately at the port of disembarkation. For instance, Redruth copper dresser Sarah Seller (also known as Salley) married John Hicks in 1857 in Melbourne, only three days after her arrival there. John had sailed three years previously, with her brother. Sarah subsequently settled in Victoria.[29] Similarly, Mary Bennetts Rowe arrived in South Africa at Christmas 1885 and was married in the New Year of 1886.

First settlements in the mining areas were generally tents and hurriedly-made shelters. If considerable amounts of ore were found, permanent mining towns were established, with the usual array of community facilities. Few females went out with their men-folk to these early mining camps, but there were exceptions. Mary Hallock Foote, the artist and novelist, and the wife of a mining engineer, discovered that, at New Almaden Quicksilver Mine in California in 1876, there were two quite separate mining camps, one for the Cornish, and one for the Mexican miners. They were both squalid affairs, turning into dust bowls in the dry season, and with no sanitation. Despite the desperate conditions, many of the Cornish miners had their wives with them.[30] In most mining areas, there had probably always been a difference between the 'official' lack of female employment at the mines and the 'unofficial' reality, where women and children were used as needed. Certainly, a sketch by S. T. Gill (drawn at Bendigo in 1852) clearly shows the multi-tasking mother of a mining family clutching a baby in one arm, while rocking the gold dressing cradle with the other. A few feet away, her toddler is holding a small spade full of undressed ore ready to refill the cradle as it empties (Fig. 63).

Fig. 63 "Zealous Gold Diggers, Bendigo 1852", S. T. Gill
Courtesy of National Library of Australia[31]

Most women and girls, however, emigrated to established ore fields where settled mining communities were already built. These already had some of the luxuries of modern living such as schools, stores, medical services, churches and chapels. Once there, they met an entirely different economic framework from the mining communities of Cornwall.

On arrival, ex-bal maidens would generally find that they were not needed for ore dressing. In some cases, as with gold, which is found in almost pure form, there was little dressing to be done. Where ore dressing was required, it was increasingly done by machinery. Alternatively, where ore needed hand-dressing, there was usually no shortage of indigenous labour. For instance, in California in 1849, some miners were employing fifty or sixty Native Americans at their gold diggings.[32]

There seemed, also, to be an expectation that, in their new (and hopefully more prosperous) life, women and girls would be saved the 'indignity' of working at the mine. This type of manual labour was generally considered undesirable and, in some of the colonies, it was even made illegal for women to take up employment at the mines (as in Queensland).[33] Occasionally, it seems they would be needed, and would help with the mining processes in an emergency, but the general expectation was that this would only be a temporary measure. The only known report of children being employed was at Glen Osmond Mine in South Australia, in the very early days, where it was reported that:

'A number of boys and girls were busy washing and cleaning ore'. (The Australia 22nd Jan 1847)

In the early years in the mining camps and settlements, there was a dramatic gender imbalance, and a chronic shortage of people with the skills to attend to the domestic life. Any unmarried woman in the mining camps and settlements would not only be eagerly sought after to provide domestic comfort and succour for the single miner, but would soon also be prevailed upon either to open a boarding house or a store, or to cook, wash, mend, sew, or nurse the sick, for the wider mining community. Likewise, any woman with a basic education would be encouraged to teach. Consequently, the female's prime contribution to the economy of the mining family lay, not in the mining skills she may have brought, but in her domestic, caring and teaching skills, such as they were. Having been used to her own financial independence, here was the new economic opportunity. When Zanjani writes about the role of women in the American mining communities, she remarks:

'Since gold rush days, running boarding houses had been a leading occupation for entrepreneurial mining camp women, both married and single. They provided a service much appreciated by the miners and prospectors tired of their own cooking, their own housekeeping, and their own company. A woman who arrives in a new mining camp was likely to be importuned to open a boarding house or at least to cook meals. Like most working women of the period, the boarding house keeper laboured long and hard - one woman recalled that her day's work began when she prepared breakfast at seven and continued without respite until well into the evening.' [34]

When silver was discovered at Caribou, Colorado in 1869, 60% of the initial mining population came from Cornwall. New arrivals stayed with friends and relatives, or at boarding houses run by Cornish women. These women often lent money to other miners, especially to enable them to bring their families to join them.[36] Ex- bal maiden Caroline Rodda ran a very successful boarding house in New Jersey. On the other side of the world, when Ruth Hopkins investigated the roles taken by Cornish women in Victoria, Australia, she found that they included running small stores, dressmaking, or running boarding houses or hotels.[35]

Ann Gribble (née Bawden) was a former bal maiden who eventually was to run a general store in Blackwood, Victoria. In 1841, at the age of 13 years, she had been working at a mine in the Camborne area. In 1852, she married miner Charles Gribble, and followed him out to Ballarat, two years later. Within a year or two, they had moved to nearby

Blackwood, where Charles and his brother continued their success as gold miners. Ann soon opened a store in Red Hill. Sadly, Charles died in 1887 (when Ann was only 46 years old). Subsequently, she continued to run the store, assisted by her daughter Jane, until about 1908. Ann died in 1925, at the age of 97 years. She was buried next to her sister Susan Dunn, who had also been a bal maiden in her younger years, back in Cornwall. Susan had married a cousin of Ann's husband (also a miner). She had sailed for Australia in 1858, and seems to have followed Ann and Charles out to Blackwood. Susan died in 1918, aged 83 years.[37]

Although the bal maidens' role in society overseas had changed dramatically, their skills from the dressing floors were still useful. They could play their part when it came to the heavy manual labour involved in the construction of buildings or clearing land, as this comment from South Australia illustrates:

'Wives usually gave a hand, and some of them could use a shovel as skilfully as a man. Usually these were bal maidens who had worked as ore-dressers at mines in Cornwall.'[38]

Fig. 64 Ex-Bal Maiden Ann Gribble (née Bawden)
Courtesy of Ian Gribble

Fig. 65 Ex-Bal Maiden Susan Dunn (née Bawden)
Courtesy of Bev Bennie

It is very difficult to trace individual bal maidens from their work at their mines in Cornwall, into their new lives overseas. One of the few whom it has been possible to follow is Lavinia Rowe (née Terrill). When she married James Rowe of Camborne in 1845, she was described as a *'miner'*. She was probably employed at Dolcoath, where her husband worked. By 1859, James's four brothers were already working a gold claim, called 'Mosquito', near Fryer's Creek in Victoria, Australia. Because of James's mining skills, they requested him to go out and join them. As a result, Lavinia travelled out to Australia with her husband and their eight children, sailing from Liverpool to Melbourne on the 'Black Eagle'. They went directly to the Fryer's Town mine, near Castlemaine. The mine was relatively successful and the brothers eventually became mine owners, known as 'Rowe Bros.' By the late 1880s, however, the gold rush was in decline and the government was making land available in areas near the river Murray. The Rowe family decided this would be the best future for them, so three of their children applied for adjacent blocks. They moved to Yalca in 1876, where they were required to build houses, and then clear the allotted acres and bring them into cultivation within certain time limits. Sadly, James was already in decline from 'miner's pthisis' and was never to enjoy this new home, as he died in 1879, aged 58 years, whilst still in Fryer's Town. The widowed Lavinia joined her three children, initially working under hard and primitive conditions to clear the land. They built up a prosperous farm, calling it Pendarvis, and it continued in the family until 1908. It was here that Lavinia spent her final years. She died unexpectedly in 1895, at the age of 71, whilst away from home, visiting a married daughter in South Australia. She never returned to Cornwall, and her body was taken back to Fryer's Town, so that she could be buried with her husband. A fine headstone still marks the grave.[39]

Another bal maiden who emigrated to Victoria, Australia was Catherine Hellyar (née Davey) from Cusgarne in Gwennap. When she was about 20 years old (in 1841), she and her sister Elizabeth were employed dressing copper at the United Mines, and it is likely that they had been working at the mines for some years. In 1842, Catherine married miner Henry Gray, and, by 1851, they had moved to Rose Hill in Lanlivery, where she was widowed in the same year. In 1852, she married stone mason George Hellyar, a widower with three children, one of whom was just a few months old. Catherine had her first child in 1853. In 1854, the combined family migrated to Victoria. Catherine gave birth to her second child while still on board ship at Portland, Victoria, presumably after a very difficult birth, as it was two days after everyone else had disembarked! Sadly, this child died at just three months old. Catherine subsequently settled at Port Fairy, and had another five children. Her husband George died when the youngest was only one year old. She subsequently remarried. After an eventful but far from easy life, Catherine died in Glen Thompson in 1907, aged 85 years.[40]

Tasmania was the destination for bal maidens Grace and Ann Thomas. They were from a mining family in Cusvey, Gwennap and both had been working at the mines in 1841. The following year, when they were 13 and 15 years old respectively, they sailed with their parents on the '*St. Charles Napier*' to Hobart. This was where they were to spend the rest of their lives. Here their parents found work as groom and housekeeper, presumably at a large house. In 1846, Grace married mariner, John Rice, but, by 1879, she had been widowed and left with four children. She subsequently remarried and eventually had a total of fourteen children. She died in 1890, at her sister Anne's home, at the age of 62. Ex-bal maiden Ann had married John Fry Wheatley around 1845 and also had fourteen children. Ann died in 1917, aged 89 years.[41]

Another Lavinia who had been a bal maiden, and who also made a new life in Australia, was Lavinia Magor from Salem in the parish of Kenwyn. She was born in 1836, and was an ore dresser at the time of her marriage, in 1855, to John Symons, a miner working at Wheal Busy. It is highly probable that Lavinia was also working at Wheal Busy, and this is how John and she had met. Their first son John was born in 1856, and they sailed on the *'Marion'* for South Australia, arriving in 1857. Her husband John took up work at the copper mines in Burra, and they later moved to Moonta. Eventually, from 1874, they took up farming. They had nine more children, and their eldest, John, was to become Mayor of Moonta in 1890.[42] On her 90th birthday, she was described in this way:

'Mrs. Symons, who is highly esteemed among a large circle of friends, enjoys remarkably good health for a lady of her advanced age, has a cheerful disposition, and alert mental powers, and can converse in interesting strain upon incidents of the distant past'. (South Australian 22nd Jan 1847)

Fig.66 Ex-Bal Maiden Mary Bennetts Harry (née Rowe) and Family c. 1914
Courtesy of Harry Trembath

Mary Bennetts Rowe also was believed to be a bal maiden who went to make a new life overseas, her destination being South Africa. Born in 1876 in St Just, as a young girl she had lived with her family on Trewellard Hill, and probably worked as a tin dresser at Carnyorth Mine, just outside St Just. Her 'young man', William Thomas Harry, had left for South Africa to work in the gold mines on the Rand, probably in the 1890s, when many mines were closing on the St Just area. He became an underground mine captain. Mary subsequently travelled out to South Africa in December 1885, and married William at Durlaston in January 1886. Tragically, as happened all too frequently, her husband's health was seriously damaged by the very sharp dust created by the mining drills, and they had to return to Cornwall. Mary travelled back first, and then William followed. He took up work at Wheal Cock, and Levant, and then finally worked a tin stream on Carnyorth Moor. During this time, Mary had seven children. The eldest, William, was to become a well-known mining engineer, and another son, Raymond, wrote the book 'Mine under the Sea', featuring himself as Jack Penhale. Mary's husband, William, eventually died in 1917, when she was 41 years old, after many years of ill health. Mary continued to live in Carnnyorth Terrace, St Just and died in 1967, aged 91. She is buried in Pendeen Cemetery.[43]

Fig. 67 Ex-Bal Maiden Caroline Adams
(née Benbow)
Courtesy of Peter Benbow

Fig. 68 Ex-Bal Maiden Caroline Rodda
(née Riddle)
Courtesy of Anne Stephens

The 19th century journeys overseas often turned out to be as difficult, dangerous and unpredictable as the destinations themselves. For instance, bal maiden Caroline Benbow's journey to New Zealand almost ended in tragedy - twice! Caroline had been born in Croft Row, Carharrack in 1858, and her father had died when she was only one year old. Consequently, she and her sisters were soon working at the mines. In November 1878, Caroline sailed from Plymouth on the '*Piako*' bound for Lyttlelton, New Zealand. A serious fire broke out on board when they were 180 miles off the South American coast. The passengers were rescued by another ship and taken to Pernambuco (Recife) Brazil, but could not land there due to a smallpox outbreak. Instead, they were taken to Coconut Island, seven miles up river. For nine weeks, supplies were brought to them from Pernambuco, These passengers eventually arrived in Lyttlelton in March 1879 after a journey of 145 days, and having lost most of their belongings on the way. For a short while, Caroline lived in Hook, but in 1881 she married timber-man Samuel Adams in Waimate. They subsequently had five children. She died in 1935, aged 77 years.[44]

Another bal maiden who survived a treacherous sea was Caroline Rodda (née Riddle). Born in Redruth in about 1836, Caroline lived in Sandow's Row, and was working at the mines in 1851, along with one of her sisters. In 1861, she was employed at 'pottery' (probably the crucible factory at Pednandrea), and was still working there in 1871. By this time, she was the only sibling left at home supporting her widowed mother; her brothers having migrated to the Pennsylvania coalfields. However, later in that year, she and her mother sailed to New York to join them. They had a long and rough crossing, and the family story relates that Caroline was found by one of the seamen clinging on to the privy door, hanging out over the ocean! On arrival in Pennsylvania she met and married Edward Rodda, a miner from Camborne, and they later had two daughters. They moved to New Jersey, where it was found that Edward was suffering from miner's lung. In order to support her family, Caroline took in boarders and became a seamstress, while her daughters worked at a silk mill. By the time Edward died in 1896, Caroline was the owner of a busy boarding house. Through continued hard work, Caroline was able to buy a new property in 1902. She died in 1929 (in her early nineties) one week after visiting the local tax office. She had tripped over the railway line on the way home and just picked herself up and taken herself home to bed![45] Another ex-bal maiden who also migrated to Pennsylvania, but eventually moved to New Jersey was Mary Jane Down (née Northey). However, her journey also took in Northumberland, Michigan and New York, before she and her family finally settled in New Jersey.

A bal maiden who was destined to travel right across America, to the lead mining region of Nevada was Eliza Jane Paull. She was born in 1848 in Illogan and was working at the mine by the time she was 13 years old. In 1867, she married miner Alfred Argall. Alfred was probably mining overseas by 1871, but it seems he came home in 1873 to take Eliza and their children to New Jersey, via Liverpool and New York. Subsequently they moved on to the lead mining area of Grass Valley, where Eliza spent the rest of her life.

A particularly widely-travelled bal maiden was Mary Richards of St Blazey. Working at the copper mines in 1861, she married Thomas Eslick in the following year. By 1870, they had migrated to Almaden Township, San Jose County, California. She had not been there very long when Thomas died. She subsequently married another miner, Fred Argall, in 1875. They then made the long journey from California to Newtown in New South Wales, where they settled. Mary died there in 1922.[46]

Another America-bound bal maiden was Elizabeth Jane Penna, who was born in the village of Rose in the parish of Perranzabuloe, in 1831. She was a lead ore dresser in 1851 (probably at nearby Wheal Hope). She subsequently married miner Philip Penna (from the same village) and they left for the coal mines of County Durham, when the local mines closed. In 1881, they migrated from there to the coalfields in Brazil, Kentucky. Philip and his brothers were highly successful and eventually founded the Templeton Coal Company. Over the years, hard work had transformed them from a poverty-stricken mining family, travelling the world to find work, into highly respected mine owners and coal traders.[47]

In contrast, many a bal maiden's dream of making a new life or finding a fortune on the gold, silver or copper fields overseas came to nothing, due to failing ventures, sickness, accident or even death. Some returned home very quickly, due to homesickness, failing health, or having lost their partner. Even for those migrants who were able to stay in their new country of abode, there was rarely the opportunity to remain in one place for long. The vagaries of mining enterprise often meant that mines were quickly worked out, or became uneconomic. Better returns were often promised elsewhere, and so families would be on the move. Mary Ann Teague (née Hooper), who had emigrated with her husband to Moonta in 1854, only stayed there for a short while, during which time their first child was born. Soon afterwards, they made a long wagon trek across Victoria, with her brother-in-law and his family, to Campbell's Creek, Castlemaine, where they eventually settled for good. While there, she gave birth to another ten children. Sadly Mary Ann died in 1872, at the early age of 38 years old.[48]

The independent spirit of the bal maiden also lived on, even when fortunes let them down thousands of miles from their native Cornwall. While some women returned home on the premature death of a partner, others made the best of it on the other side of the world. As with their sisters at home in Cornwall, they resorted to the well-tried economic expedients for the independent widow: laundering, dressmaking, midwifery or taking in lodgers. At Moonta Mine, for instance, widows of miners were provided with a basic 'laundry kit' consisting of a mangle and a sort of industrial iron, a long wooden container filled with stone. With this basic equipment, they would charge other miners a few pennies for their laundry (for example, two pence per six items passed through the mangle), and therefore support themselves and any family they had. They were expected to return the laundry equipment when it was no longer needed, for instance, when their children were old enough to support themselves and their mother.[49]

Despite the prevailing attitude against women working at the mines in the late 19th and early 20th centuries, there are now stories emerging of women who actually involved themselves in mine prospecting and mine management in the New World and elsewhere. Sally Zanjani, in her book *'A Mine of her Own'*, tells the story of over one hundred women who were involved in mining in the USA between 1850 and 1950, some in conjunction with other employments, and others for whom prospecting became their total world.[50] Similarly, in *'The Adventures of Pioneer Women in New Zealand'*, Sarah Ell records the story of 'Little Biddy of Buller' (Bridget Goodwin 1813-1899) who was part of a three-person gold prospecting team in Buller in the mid 19th century.[51] Although none of these stories have a proven Cornish bal maiden connection, one can only surmise that, among the thousands of mining women who emigrated from Cornwall and Devon, there must have been a few who tried their hand at mining and prospecting in their own right. We can glimpse a little of what their lives may have been like from the biography of Ellen Jack. Ellen was not Cornish, but was born in Nottinghamshire in 1842. She had married an American sea captain, but embarked on a career as a gold prospector and miner around 1870, after she was widowed. She almost perished in the snows on her long journey over the Rockies, and she slept on a sofa in the office of the only hotel in Gunnison, when she first arrived. For a few weeks, she rented a 'cot' in another woman's tent. Then, she saved up to buy her own housing lot and tent. She lived in the tent with only a bed and several crates for furniture until she eventually found enough gold to pay for building a log cabin. She then set up the tent as a paying bathhouse for the other miners.[52]

A few stories have emerged of Cornish women being involved in mining enterprise overseas. Mary Buzza was mining full-time at Red Streak, Creswick and another enterprising Cornish woman, Mary Porlock, brought mining machinery with her on board ship from Cornwall. She sold this machinery on arrival and then entered into a partnership to supply machinery to the mines in Ballarat. Similarly, at Bendigo, a Mrs. Leggo and her sister-in-law, Mrs. Rowe, dug briefly for gold with one of their husbands, and were quite successful. They buried the gold under the floor of their tent and then sat on top of it to keep it safe, making plans at how they would spend it.[53]

One Cornish bal maiden who was almost as adventurous as Ellen Jack was Sidwell Woolcock. She had travelled out to Australia with her family as a young woman. She met and married a son of a Norwegian sea captain, and together they became 'hawkers' (travelling sales people), supplying basic requisites to miners in the outback of New South Wales and Victoria. Eventually, they opened a remote wayside trading post and hotel. At this time, Sidwell was shown ore samples and was the first person to identify them as being rich in copper. This was how copper came to be discovered at Cobar. Her story is told more fully in the final chapter.

FOOTNOTES

1. Schwartz (1999) p.14.
2. Hocking (1886) pp. 94, 99.
3. CEC (1842) p. 84.
4. Rowe (1993) p. 319.
5. RCG 18th Apr + 12th Dec 1867.
6. RCG 28th Nov 1867; WB 23rd Jan + 8th Feb 1868.
7. WB 3rd Mar 1879.
8. Tangye, Michael 'The Wesleyan Methodist Relief Fund for the Cornwall District 1879' *Old Cornwall* Vol. 7 (1967-73) pp. 185-90.
9. Cornubian 24th Mar 1921 p. 2.
10. Redruth Union Indoor Relief List 1892 (CRO: PU Redruth 124).
11. Troon WI (1952) p. 22.
12. Mills, Joseph; Annear, Paul *The Book of St Day* (Halsgrove 2003) p. 123.
13. Prochaska, F. K. *Women and Philanthropy in 19th Cent. England* (Clarendon, 1980) p. 88.
14. Personal correspondence (JSA/LM 2002)
15. RCG 12th Dec 1867.
16. Deacon (1998) p. 96.
17. Personal correspondence (IJ/LM 2002).
18. Personal correspondence (PC/LM 2001).
19. Personal correspondence (JH/LM 2006).
20. Personal correspondence (SH/LM 2007).
21. Personal correspondence (DH/LM 2008).
22. Williams, R. A. 'The Beerhaven Copper Mines' *British Mining* No. 42 (NMRS 1991)
23. Auhl & Martleet (ed.) *Australia's Earliest Mining Era: South Australia 1841-1851; Paintings by S. T. Gill* (Axiom 1988) p. 26.
24. Barton (1968) p. 73.
25. Lay, Patricia *One and All, The Cornish in New South Wales* (Heritage 2000) Table 2.5.
26. Payton (1984) pp. 12-14.
27. Personal correspondence (RJ/LM2001).
28. Personal correspondence (JE/LM 2002).
29. Personal correspondence (WH/LM 2007).
30. Rodman, Paul (Ed.) *A Victorian Gentlewoman in the Far West* (Huntingdon, 1972) p. 103.
31. National Library of Australia (ref. nla pic-an 7518147-v)
32. Rowe (1974) p. 99.
33. Personal correspondence (JW/LM 2001).
34. Zanjani (1997) p. 29.
35. Hopkins, Ruth *Cousin Jack, Man for All Times* (Hopkins,1994) p. 189.
36. Pettem, Silvia.'Go West Young Man' *Cornish World* (April 2000) p. 13.
37. Gribble, I. *A Flash in the Pan – A History of Camborne Gribbles* (Gribble 2008).
38. Pryor (1973) p. 65.
39. Personal correspondence (LM/LM 2002).
40. Personal correspondence (JH/LM 2006).
41. Personal correspondence (HW/LM 2006).
42. Personal correspondence (JL/LM 2002).
43. Personal correspondence (HT/LM 2002).
44. Benbow, Peter 'Caroline Benbow Bal-Maiden' *Carn Brea Newsletter* No 54 (June 2005) pp. 4-6.
45. Personal correspondence (AS/LM 2006)
46. Argall, Ian *Argall Worldwide Website* (www.argallfamilyworldwide.co.uk.)
47. Glanville, Roger *Rose: The Story of a Village and Its People* (2004) pp. 151-3.
48. Personal correspondence (AC/LM 2002).
49. Personal correspondence (RB/LM 2001); (GB/LM 2002).
50. Zanjani (1997).
51. Ell, Sarah *The Adventures of Pioneer Women of New Zealand* (Bush 1992) pp. 179-184.
52. Jack, Ellen *The Fate of a Fairy; Seventy Years in the Far West* (Donahue 1910) p. 108.
53. Hopkins (1994) op cit p. 188.

Chapter 11

MYTH AND REALITY

No exact figures are available for the total numbers of girls and women who worked at the mines in Cornwall and Devon from 1720 to 1920. Conservative estimates are that somewhere between sixty and eighty thousand females may have worked at the mines over this period of just over two hundred years.

Of this huge army, we have precious few personal details at all. Almost no personal writings or diaries survive, and only a handful of photographs, drawings and independent records. It is rare to find a record of the personal feelings or reflections of these women and girls - they seem to be almost entirely lost. The nearest to personal reflections that we have are records of interviews with a handful of girls and one woman for the *1842 Royal Commission*, the retrospective glance at the life of Patty Tremellin, probably based on the short journal she wrote, and a total of about twenty-five interviews recorded of women who worked in the mines of Troon and Camborne (c.1880-1900), at Polpuff Glass Mine (WWI), and at Geevor and Great Rock (WWII).

On the other hand, we do have records of how observers perceived them, mostly from the pen of the wealthy and privileged. They included travellers, contemporary writers or artists, who usually viewed them briefly or from afar. Then there were those who often had regular contact, but for various reasons may have wished to perpetuate a certain kind of image, such as the mine managers and surgeons, or clergy.

THE MYTHS

Outsiders writing about the mining communities could be over-sentimental, patronising or unrealistic about either the general subservience or well-being of the mining community, as shown in this *West Briton* report of a festival in Wendron:

'From the church a procession formed, comprising agents and persons employed at the mine, with their families, and, preceded by the Porkellis Band, they marched to the account house, where tables were laid and nearly 700 persons sat down. A happier party can scarcely be imagined - there sat the miner with his goodly wife and healthy children - the fine muscular sumpman - the intelligent tributer, and the bold, tutwork man, with many a fair 'bal girl', and those who constitute the stamps pair - and all looked grateful and pleased, and even the babe seemed to enjoy the festival by crowing in its mother's arms.' (WB 2nd Sept 1859)

Some writers who tried to describe the mining communities fell into the age-old trap of needing to discern the 'deserving' from the 'undeserving' poor. This resulted in judgements about lifestyle, and how people chose to spend their earnings, meagre though they might be. Generally condemned is the perceived over-consumption of alcohol and tobacco, and the lack of money spent on good food. Consistently, the women, and bal maidens in particular, come in for criticism for their 'squandering' of hard-earned money on their appearance. Mine captains would certainly have an interest in portraying bal maidens as being extravagant or irresponsible with their earnings, when questions of adequate pay were raised. In 1841, one of the clergy in Camborne remarked: *'The young women are more expensive in their dress than desirable'*, and he had heard of *'clubs among them for the purpose of procuring more showy articles of dress than they could individually afford to purchase, lots being cast to determine whose property they should be.'* [1] Similarly, in 1849, a writer in the West Briton observed:

'The miners as a class, sacrifice to a great extent their domestic comforts to their inordinate love of dress. This failing has long characterised them, but within the last few years it has greatly increased....To see the miners, both men and women, at church on Sunday, or enjoying themselves at a fair at Redruth, one would not suppose that there was much distress of any kind among them. Most of the men are attired in fine broad cloth, whilst women parade their finery. But many...emerge from holes and dens more resembling pig-sties than human abodes.' (WB 14th Dec 1849)

Such judgements continued until comparatively recently. This 20th century author, writing about the late 1860s, still observed their budgeting priorities with a critical eye:

'The mining population of Cornwall had never been noted for its thrift or abstinence. Pay-day, feast and famine had customarily alternated with regularity throughout their working lives and now, in spite of, or perhaps because of the privations during the 60's and 70's, this improvident way of life was maintained. Money that would have been better directed towards the feeding of large families continued to find its way into beer-shop and brothel or into the dextrous pocket of Johnny-come-fortnightly. The Sabbath silk dresses and fine black coats of bal-maidens and their mates caught the eye of many a visitor otherwise appalled by conditions which, in this period of economic decline, revived the county's old name of 'West Barbary'.' [2]

Also prevailing in the writing and reporting of the mid-19th century onwards was the idea that the proper, and safe, place for girls and women was in the home doing, or learning, their 'wifely' and 'motherly' duties. Here are George Henwood's views in 1858:

'Their being so long from home, renders them wholly unfit to perform and attend to those domestic duties which should constitute the comfort and charm of every home, particularly that of the working man.' (MJ 1858 p. 36)

Several interviewed for the *1842 Royal Commission* lamented the lack of domestic skill, and, in one case, also made a judgement about bal maidens being too much *'out and about'* rather than in their *'rightful place'*:

'In alluding to domestic economy, we may observe how desirable it is that the wives and daughters of miners should be better acquainted with culinary and other domestic affairs. Being employed from their girlhood the entire day at the mine, little time or opportunity remains for them to acquire knowledge of matters of so much importance to the health and happiness of those with whom they become connected.'

'Very slight knowledge of culinary work possessed by the young women leads to a coarse preparation of food.'

'I have visited at least a thousand houses of miners at St Agnes and here [St Just] and I find the females taken from the mines very deficient in skill in domestic work. Unable to make or mend they are not much inclined to stay at home.'

Fig. 69 Sketch of Bal Maidens entitled 'The Three Graces'
Seymour c. 1870
Courtesy of Mining Communications Ltd

At the time of the 1841 mine inspections, and later in the 1850s when Leifchild and George Henwood were describing life at the mines, Victorian Britain had been shocked by the revelation that women and girls were working at the mines, and, of course, in the north of England, Scotland and Wales, had actually been working down the mines. The dismay was not so much to do with the hard and demeaning labour - long hard hours of agricultural and factory labour were still the norm - as with the supposed 'moral degradation' of females working in such close proximity to boys and men.[3]

They were horrified that the two sexes should even mix, let alone that the girls might be exposed, as they perceived it, to rough language and habits. Even worse, in the north, where women and girls were working underground, the boys or men worked with the minimum of clothes, or occasionally none. They overlooked the fact that the few who may have seen the exposed male form were almost certainly wives, daughters and sisters, seeing nothing more than they were used to in their overcrowded homes. They also thought (mostly unfoundedly) that the girls and women laboured 'semi-naked' as well. All this was viewed as the most horrific scandal, and a terrible corruption of the female mind. Although women and girls had not been known to go down the mines in the South West, the concern for their 'moral welfare' was still strongly expressed. In 1858, Henwood again comments:

'Whilst at their work, and under the supervision of the master dresser, all goes tolerably well, save coarse joking, and that continual association we so much complain of; at meal times, and on going to and from their work, it is almost impossible to prevent that conversation and rude behaviour we so much wish to see prevented....The indiscriminate association, in their employment, of the sexes naturally begets a want of modesty and delicacy, so important in the formation of character.'

Despite their concern for the moral exploitation of bal maidens by their association with the opposite sex at the mine, some of the same 19th century writers then go to great lengths to feature the girls as unrealistically naïve and innocent. Just as they are often portrayed as untouched by the physical grime and dirt of the mine, they are sometimes seen as untainted by the perceived 'moral' grime and dirt of their working environment. We are continually treated to romanticised pictures of bal maidens at their tasks. Lucy Fitzgerald, travelling in Cornwall in 1825, described bal maidens in this way when writing to her relative, Lady Sophia Fitzgerald:

'The little girls washing and picking out the best parts, the bigger ones beating it with hammers all the time, thirty nine in a row, was a very pretty thing. They were, all singing hymns which sounded so beautiful, and they looked so blooming and healthy from being so much in the air.' [4]

One suspects that other Victorian visitors to the mines either viewed the dressing floors from a distance, passed relatively cleanly-dressed maids on the way to and from work, were only introduced to bal maidens who had been sent to wash and change into their best aprons, or just over-sentimentalised the picture:

'They give quite a picturesque aspect to the Cornish mining scene, and although they have to handle stones, wheel barrows, manage machinery and work among vessels and streams of water they usually present a very clean and neat appearance. Their boots are nearly always blackened and polished, their large sun bonnets and short print dresses are seldom either soiled or torn, and altogether they afford such an example of tidiness as is well worthy of imitation, even by some whose employment is of a domestic nature.' [5]

In 1855, they were described in much the same way:

'How happy and healthy they look compared to children in coal pits and colliery work! There they sit, doing all manner of mining mysteries, and delighting in them too. Hark! The whole set are singing a hymn, and singing it in parts too! How well the girls take their parts!' (Leifchild 1855 p. 164)

He was not the only one to compare the bal maidens' work favourably with other possible employments open to girls and women. In the *1842 Royal Commission*, Barham described work at the mines as more healthy for girls than working at the local fuse works, and the following was written about bal maidens working at East Pool as late as 1895:

'The spalling of the ore was done mainly by women, for whom the breaking of stones sounds a rough employment. But it does not seem so to look at it. It was a blithe company that wielded the long-handled hammers and cracked the dull red rock into fragments whose fractured surface revealed the lustrous metal within. The women looked gay under the bright sunshine in their picturesque hoods, aprons, and gloves, all white, and some wore nosegays. They laughed, sang, and chatted merrily. There was none of the un-intermittent, machine like drudgery of the factory nor its close atmosphere.' (WB 12th Sept 1895)

It seems that some people went a step further in assuming that the outdoor life as experienced by the surface workers was an insurance against ill-health in later life. Some educated and privileged people actually believed that they had been deprived of the benefits of working outdoors in this way in their youth, and looked upon the bal maidens and boys with some degree of envy. This extraordinary attitude of believing this work was the 'grand panacea' comes over strongly in these words written about the Red River tin streams in 1877:

'We could not but think that these boys and girls will, in after life, bless their parents for sending them to work on the Red River, as they are trained by a rigorous discipline to be as hardy as the Spartan...so that no climate or hardships can afterwards affect them; and have we not many time wished we had two years experience on this river. To sickness and indisposition we should then be strangers, as it cannot be any other than the grand panacea'. (RCG 12th October 1877 p. 7)

Another myth is the oft-repeated picture of the obedient bal maiden, born into a life of poverty and hard work, but knowing her place in society. She is the one who loyally plays out her role as reliable and honest labourer, and faithful, loving wife and mother. Leifchild, to illustrate this, records the words of the hymn that he reports bal maidens used to sing. These are two of the verses:

'O Lord! We mining children raise
A grateful song to Thee;
Thou wilt accept the feeblest praise
From all that bend the knee'.

'O give us grace to do thy will,
What ere that will may be,
To labour daily, praising still,
Loving and serving Thee.'

When the Rev. John Buller wrote about bal maidens in 1842, just at the time that the *Royal Commission* was made public, he too mythologised the bal maiden into the one who either struggled under terrible burdens of poverty and responsibility, or was vain and self-indulgent:

'Under the sheds of these mines the stranger may observe many females, toiling like slaves, from morn to night, to gain a hard-earned pittance. One, with the virtuous object of ministering to the wants of an aged and worn-out parent: others, not infrequently to gratify their vanity, and display their goodly figure in a costly dress on the approaching holiday.' (Buller 1842 p. 55)

Victorian novelists also portrayed pictures of purity and innocence:

'At night they [bal maidens] *returned in little companies, singing very sweetly as they passed homeward through the lighted streets. On Sundays, or when choirs and Sunday Schools had their outings, they went gaily dressed'.* [6]

Hand in hand with this subservient obedient image of the bal maiden is the picture that they were virginal and sexually naïve. Dr. Lanyon, a mine surgeon, described them in this way:

'In chastity, it may be said, they [bal maidens] *are not excelled by any, not withstanding the constant intercourse which daily takes place in their work, among the sexes, we may aver, that the mine girl is as much to be admired for her virtue.'* (Lanyon 1838 p. 39)

In the same vein, in 1864 a reporter in Tavistock believed the bal maidens at Devon Great Consuls could do no wrong (whereas those over the border in Cornwall could):

'If all accounts be true, the 'bal girls' of many a mine in Cornwall might well take a lesson from the females employed at Devon Consols. Among hundreds of men, young women, boys and girls, the writer in the course of three days never saw an improper action, nor heard an improper word.' (Tavistock Gazette 23rd Dec 1864 p. 5)

The mythology of the bal maiden, then, is complex and contradictory. A saying, still current in Cornwall, certainly reflects some of this: *'Bal maidens were famous for the whiteness of their aprons and the foulness of their language.'*

THE REALITY

How strange that no one noticed the contradictions in the public myths of the working bal maidens. On the one hand, they were tainted and corrupted by an unsuitable working environment and lack of training for domestic life; on the other hand demure, sweet, obedient, hardworking and pure. Sharron Schwartz summarised this when she described 19th century commentators as seeking to *'trivialize, moralize, criticize, condemn, champion or romanticize'* them.

In the first instance, the dressing floors were not the clean and tidy places readers of some Victorian descriptions might be led to believe. However, despite the dirty working environment, it seems that bal maidens, on the whole, had enough pride to dislike being seen looking dirty and unkempt. Captain Bennetts, one of the Red River tin stream captains, indicated that there was more than one reason that the women and girls were generally fastidious in going to work in clean boots. His father would sack anyone with dirty shoes for *'wasting tin'*! [7]

Bal maidens sometimes refused to have their pictures taken, or covered their faces. Most pictures that survive from the 1860s and 1870s indicate that they had not been photographed while actually working. They have invariably changed into their clean aprons, and seem to have had a wash and brush up, or, more likely, had been photographed before the day's work began. Hence, despite the grime, visitors were often surprised at how neat and clean the girls looked, as in this description of Morwellham Quay:

'The dress of the women, of whom a great number are employed on the different works here, was when we visited, mostly white; and, although some of their occupations are of a nature in which we could hardly expect much neatness, they all appeared quite clean, their light dresses frequently contrasting strongly with their sombre employments.' (Hearder 1841 p. 55)

The female author of the article in the *Ladies Journal* of 1872 was very taken with their neat and clean appearance too, but somewhat oblivious to the impracticalities and dangers of their bulky costume:

'She wears a clean print dress, cut very short, stout shoes well covering the feet, a white canvas apron with bib or stomacher, and canvas sleeves to protect her arms. On her head is perched a sensible sun bonnet...always kept scrupulously clean....Round her ankles, to save them from the inadvertent blows from the ore when swept from the table, the Bal maiden swathes strips of flannel, which she mostly removes when work is done. There cannot on the whole be a more practical costume....On washing her hands and throwing off the coarse apron...the Bal maiden is as neat and clean as if she never handled copper ore or hammer.'

Contemporary photos and drawings show that, although there was a basic dress for bal maidens, the women and girls found all sorts of creative ways of expressing their individuality, despite a limited budget. (This was much to the despair of Victorian commentators, who felt their money should be spent elsewhere.) For instance, unusual collars, bows, and other decorations were added to blouses and dresses, especially around the neckline. Flowers and bows were added to straw bonnets, and simple but attractive jewellery was sometimes worn. When Princess Victoria visited Botallack Mine in July 1865, we are told that the bal maidens were dressed in their best attire and *'Johnny Fortnight took care, by supplying the poor mine girls with the latest fashions'*.[8] Shortly after, she also visited Devon Great Consols, where she was so taken by the dress of the bal maidens that she asked if she could take one of their ribbons! She, at least, did not feel that their dress was frivolous.

Reading between the lines, however, are the signs of a rebellious nature and wildness, independence and ability, courage and determination, and, most importantly, individual personality. For instance, not all the bal maidens' music was sweet and reverent hymns! It is generally believed that much traditional Cornish music was lost when Methodist conservatism outlawed it and replaced it with the hymns of John and Charles Wesley. Folk songs and working chants, which may have told us much about the bal maidens way of life and their attitudes, have not generally survived. However, here is a sample of one of their songs that has. It must have been the 19th century equivalent of teenage pop music:[9]

> *I can buddy* [buddle] *and I can rock* [spall],
> *And I can walk like a man.*
> *I can lobby* [toze] *and shaky* [riddle],
> *And please the Old Jan* [surface captain?].

The youngsters, in particular, must have been regularly playing pranks. Mrs. Gay, who had worked at tin streams as a child, remembered being sent home for throwing stones at the *'flushet'* (sluice).[10]

Despite the Victorian anxiety about the roughness and coarseness of the bal maidens' occupation, there is very little evidence of them generally being unruly. However, at least one newspaper report indicated that some were well able to look after their own interests. In February 1819, a ship was wrecked off the north coast of Cornwall, not far from Padstow. It seems that news had spread around the neighbourhood that plunder from the shipwreck had been secreted in the sand dunes of St Minver. A group of local young women went searching and discovered a large box of figs. Just as they discovered this prize, a group of bal maidens came along on their way home from Pentire Glaze Mine, which was about a mile away. It is not clear whether the bal maidens were the ones that had hidden the figs in the first place and therefore considered themselves the rightful owners, or whether they just felt that, with their superior strength or numbers, they could claim them for themselves. Whatever the situation, a major scrap ensued, which lasted over two hours, and resulted in minor injuries and torn clothes. Eventually, the bal maidens won, and presumably carried off their prize.[11] These were not weak and feeble young girls if they could sustain a two-hour fight after a day's labour at the mine.

There are occasions when bal maidens certainly seem to be able to 'fight their own corner'. In July 1823, the day captain at Dolcoath recorded that Grace Harvey had come to the Account House about her grievance over her non-payment. It seems there was a disagreement as to which of two men owed her money (possibly the surface captain and the mine purser), but she was not willing to let the matter go.[12] In another account, a bal maiden had picked up her 'boss' and '*thraw'd'n in the kieve*' (a large barrel).[13] We do not know what had transpired to cause her to act in this way, but she was obviously well able to look after herself!

Inevitably, some bal maidens found themselves on the wrong side of the law, or very near it! A Mr. Bellamy of Wedlake in Peter Tavy, recalled how he and a colleague would take a two-wheeled cart to fetch lime from Morwhellham Quay in the late 19th century. They would leave early in the morning to avoid queues at the kilns, but they would have to pass bal maidens on their way to Devon Great Consols Mine. They would be forced to give the women and girls a lift, even though the horses could hardly carry the load. If they refused, the 'maidens' would pull out the tip-iron, and upset the cart![14] In 1823, a group of North Roskear bal maidens were lucky not to be charged with theft. On an April evening in 1823, they were seen at Dolcoath Mine by the night Captain and the burning house assistant. One girl was acting as sentry, while two others were trying to carry an anvil away from the cobbing and bucking house in a hand barrow. Another girl was carrying an anvil under her cloak! All three ran off empty handed. The Captain recorded in the 'Night Book' that he would report this attempted theft to the North Roskear purser, so that the offenders could be spaled (fined). From the same ledgers, we learn that bal maiden 'Eudy' (no other details were given) was convicted of theft on 16th Jan 1823, that the '*South Valley maidens*' had supposedly stolen a piece of whim rope in August 1823, and that Jenny Stone (charge hand on the dressing floors) was spaled 5s for fraudulent recording of the number of days worked by the bal maidens under her.[15]

Not many bal maidens, though, found themselves in serious trouble. Patty Tremellin (whose story appears more fully in Chapter 12) was held twice in Bodmin Jail in the 1830s, either for debt or for withholding the name of the father of her illegitimate children.[16] Despite the financial difficulties faced by many bal maidens, in addition to Patty, only one is identifiable as in the Debtors Gaol between 1831 and 1853. Two were recorded in the Census in 1861 and one in 1871. Five were recorded in the Gaol Registers between 1868 and 1879; they were 41 year-old Catherine Kemp of Gwithian (owing £1 in 1868), 34 year-old Emily Berryman of St Ives, 31 year-old Martha Eslick of Kenwyn and 40 year-old Elizabeth Williams of Camborne (owing 16s 9d, £3 and £1 respectively in 1869), and 18 year-old Mary Ann Tonkin of Gulval (owing £1 in 1871). Very few bal maidens seem to have been sentenced for anything other than civil offences (debt or not declaring the father of an illegitimate child). Mary Ann George (of Crowan) and Christina Park (of Illogan) were recorded as in Bodmin Gaol in the *1851 Census*, but we have no details of the offence. In the same year, Mary Ann Harris was sent to the Bodmin Bridewell for 3 months for attempting to obtain goods by fraud, and copper dresser Emily Berryman (who was later sent to Bodmin for debt) was sentenced to 2 months for stealing a cotton gown.[17]

Minor misdemeanours at the workhouse often resulted in bal maidens being sent up to Bodmin Gaol for short periods of time. For instance, 19 year-old bal maiden, Mary Holman, was referred from '*Perranzabuloe Poorhouse*' to Bodmin Gaol in 1829 for 2 months for breaking the Poorhouse windows.[18] Similarly at Redruth Workhouse in 1892, when Mary Ann Sawle and Harriet Ann Moyle had been fighting, Mary was cautioned and Harriet was sent to prison for seven days. In the same year, bal maiden Mary Jane Chard was received from Bodmin Gaol, but her offence was not recorded.[19] When bal maiden Elizabeth Jane Hill of Gunnislake was admitted to Tavistock Union Workhouse in March

1886, she was described as *'vagrant'*. One can only imagine the possible circumstances and story which led to her plight.[20]

Sometimes a more objective view of the demeanour and behaviour of the bal maidens appears to come from the pen of the mining professionals of the 19th century, especially with regards to their home lives. In 1841, the agent at Wheal Vor comments that there was some swearing by the women and girls on the dressing floor, but that they were generally well behaved and honest. Some commentators thought there had been improved behaviour and industriousness throughout the mining communities during the 19th century, which they accorded to the increasing influence of the non-conformist churches, especially Methodism. As already mentioned, many bal maidens had very strong links with the church and chapels of their communities and this was especially so by the mid 19th century. The Redruth Union Workhouse documents between 1892 and 1894 record the religious allegiance for fifty-seven of the sixty bal maidens admitted. Thirteen gave the established church as their faith; the remaining forty-four gave the various strands of Methodism (the Wesleyans predominating). Closely connected with the expansion of non-conformism, some believed that membership of Temperance and Abstinence Societies had significantly improved the quality of life for many mining families. The Collector of the Poor Rate in Redruth in 1841 reported that: *'I have noticed a decided improvement in the living of the mining lasses with these last thirty years.'*

Several reporters to the *1842 Royal Commission* also had a different view on the domestic competence of bal maidens. One mine agent reported that *'the young women employed in the mines make generally very careful, cleanly wives when they get steady husbands'*.

Barham himself then concluded that bal maidens made able household managers:

'Their hearts are in their homes and they are for the most part tender mothers and industrious wives. Indeed the laborious occupations to which they have been inured make household duties appear comparatively light.'

A decade later, in 1851, John Taylor makes the following observation about the abilities of bal maidens, not just in managing the domestic aspect of the home, but in having a very sound economic instinct:

'I may observe that they are strong and healthy, active, well-formed girls, and make for the most part, very good wives, generally contriving to hold the reigns of power in their own hands, ruling their husbands and finances with a good deal of tact and discretion: for be it known, that the whole earnings or gettings are generally entrusted to the wife's care; and, like a good Chancellor of the Exchequer, she lays out the surplus to the best possible advantage.' [21]

Looking at marriage and baptismal registers, and alternative reports, we are also given a very different picture of the sexual standards of the bal maidens. Most girls continued working at the mines until their marriage, usually between about the ages of 18 and 22 years, but with some marrying as early as 17. They invariably married into other mining families, and often within the extended family, sometimes cousins.

Amid the prevailing myths, of either sexual innocence or complete corruption among bal maidens, one lone voice in the *1842 Report* mentions the ancient Cornish custom of 'keeping company'. This was an arrangement by which a young couple entered into a sexual relationship prior to marriage, but with the understanding that the relationship was binding and that marriage would ensue. There is mention of this as early as 1810, when Joseph Farington visited Cornwall:

'The men and women marry at a very early age, and generally signs of connexion make it necessary for the credit of the female. But when this sign does appear the men are very faithful; and [when] a marriage has been solemnised there is no after reproach.' [22]

Sabine Baring Gould made the same observation:

'The Cornish woman will sometimes have a baby before she is legally married, it is only an old custom of the county, though less deeply rooted than the corresponding custom in Wales.' [23]

Similarly, in the 1820s and 1830s, Patty Tremellin speaks of:

'Keeping myself from all company, until I went to work at the mine, when I gave myself to company again.' [24]

How this system of betrothal worked, and the way in which it had fairly general acceptance in Cornwall, is made clear in this article in the Morning Chronicle in 1849:

'It really seems, in many places, to be taken as a matter of course that a young woman will be found with child before she is married. Indeed, I have reason to believe that in an immense number of cases young people come to a distinct understanding with each other to cohabit illicitly until the woman becomes pregnant, the man promising to 'make an honest woman of her' as soon as that takes place. This they find more convenient than marrying at once, in as much as the girl may be of service for herself, and the man elsewhere employed all the time...living better on their separate earnings than they could do in a house of their own.' [25]

This custom of 'keeping company' led the agent at Charlestown in 1841 to observe that, although pregnancy before marriage was not unusual, illegitimacy and single parenthood was rare, as most couples subsequently married before the birth of their first child. Certainly, marriage and baptismal registers bear this out as a fairly common practice throughout Cornwall. Similarly, the surface captain at Levant Mine remarked: *'More, I think, of those who have been married from this mine, have proved to have been in the family way when married than not.'*

It does seem, though, that with the influence of Methodism, in its various forms, in Cornwall in the 19th century, an alternative moral climate developed, where it was considered that sex outside of the marriage bond was unthinkable. Those of active Methodist persuasion and more mature years would be members of a class meeting and probably also an 'in-band' class, where their everyday behaviour was open to close scrutiny. Not only would other members observe them, and feel free to comment on their behaviour, but each member was expected to use the 'in-band' meeting as a confidential confessional. The story that Patty Tremellin tells illustrates these conflicts very well. It seems she engaged in sexual liaisons with the usual expectations of marriage, became pregnant, and was then deserted. In the case of at least one pregnancy, she felt the need to keep the identification of the father secret, even though it resulted in her going to jail. Later, looking back from her new Methodist perspective, she saw her behaviour as shameful, and believed she had committed the most grievous of sins, not just once, but three times. It would be easy to make assumptions about two moral codes operating side by side, one for the churched and one for the un-churched. Parish registers, however, show that this is probably too simplistic an interpretation.

In the 19th century then, it seems that bal maidens were not necessarily sexually naïve, but nor were they necessarily promiscuous. The traditional economic expedient was for some betrothed couples to indulge in sexual relationships, but to continue, for a while, to live separately in the parental home. This custom meant that some bal maidens were sexually experienced at marriage, but probably having had a stable and monogamous relationship prior to matrimony. As in the case with Patty, pregnancy did not always result in marriage, but a newspaper reporter in 1893 had this to say about bal maidens who were single mothers:

'Personally I know of many cases of mine girls who have illegitimate children; and except they lack husbands, they live irreproachable lives.' (Cornishman 5th Jan 1893)

Despite the common custom of 'keeping company' and the possible risk of abandonment, very few bal maidens seem to have been left to raise children on their own. Between 1851 and 1891, of all the thousands of bal maidens at the mines, only a handful were recorded as single parents in the census records. For instance, in 1861, there were twelve in the workhouse, one was in Bodmin Gaol (with her child) for an unpaid debt, and six were supporting themselves and their child by working at the mine. The Redruth Union Admission and Discharge Book for 1892-95 only records eight single bal maidens in three years, who subsequently gave birth there. Of all the Calstock admissions to Tavistock Workhouse between 1880 and 1886, only eight were described as bal maidens, just four of whom were pregnant. Sadly, in June 1880 one of them (Christina Moon of Gunnislake) died five days after giving birth to her child.[26] Some illegitimate children, of course, may have just been 'absorbed' into the extended family and passed off as siblings or cousins, so would not appear as a statistic. Also, those who suffered miscarriages or still births in the workhouse would not be identifiable.

Glimpses of how bal maidens were viewed by society in general can be gained from contemporary literature. In the novel *'Norah Lang, the Mine Girl'* by Salome Hocking (written in 1886), we are given the impression that mine girls were generally 'looked down on' by the rest of society. When Norah applied to work at the mine in order to earn money to support herself and her family we are told:

'It was a hard struggle for Norah to decide to work at a mine, for though only a miner's daughter, she had always been greatly respected in the village in which they lived, and envied by not a few; and she knew that being a mine girl she should fall in the estimation of a certain class of people.' (Hocking, Salome p. 13)

The same book sets about challenging these judgements as unfair, suggesting that mine girls could rise above this social stigma. Norah rails against an accusation that she has ambitions above her station:

'Why should I not keep down to my own level? Norah Lang, the mine girl, has no right to expect to be treated like a gentleman farmer's daughter. I have no right to learn music or read poetry. I had better keep to household, and knitting stockings!' (p. 49)

Fig. 70 Frontispiece from 'Norah Lang, the Mine Girl' by Salome Hocking

More concrete indications of this social stigma come from census material, which invariably shows that, while the sons of mine agents or professional people often worked at the mine, the daughters certainly did not. There were exceptions to this, where women or girls worked in an administrative capacity. For instance, Gussie Retallack, the daughter of the mine manager at Polpuff Glass Mine, was the tally checker. Occasionally women, such as Hettie Julian, a surface captain's daughter who worked in the clay pits during the First World War, actually took over jobs previously done by men.[27]

The idea that being a bal maiden was socially unacceptable seems to date mostly from the late 19th century, and is still present in the communal memory in Cornwall today. Most present-day descendants of bal maidens express great pride in their forebears and what they achieved, but this pride is sometimes tempered with a little doubt. *'It was nothing to be ashamed of, was it?'* is a comment frequently heard, as if answering an expected criticism before it is made. There is still a concern that some families may feel it demeaning to be shown to have bal maiden ancestors. One correspondent wrote:

'I can remember my grandmother telling me how her parents used to impress on her how important it was not to take a job in the mines, and how it would be better to take a job in service, because the bal maidens were reputed to be 'fast'.' [28]

And what did bal maidens think of their life and work? Because of the lack of first-hand records, it is hard to know. What glimpses we have are, not surprisingly, contradictory. At the very beginning of the industrial employment era, it seems that women and girls chose to take up new employment opportunities at the mines rather than go into service, and some even gave up their jobs as domestic servants to go there. In 1736, the Rev. William Borlase of Ludgvan laments that his household was:

'Under the great necessity for a servant, no woman to be hired here in this parish for friendship nor money, being employed about copper.' [29]

The allure of work at the mine is also depicted in the novel *'Tales of a Tin Mine'* by Silas Hocking. Lucy Penarth who works as a barmaid in her father's kiddlywink (tavern) announces:

'...that she would no longer serve drink at his bar, and that she would go to the mine as other girls did, and earn her living.'[30]

Certainly, in the *1842 Commission Report*, the general consensus appears to be that the young people who worked at the mines generally did so in good spirits:

'The air of the children and young persons employed at the surface is cheerful and alert, and a disposition to make the most of the intervals of labour in sports of various kinds is generally evinced. Even when labour is excessively prolonged, it is rare to perceive any external sign that the flow of spirits has dried up.'

Of the girls and women interviewed, two had taken up work at the mine in preference to their previous employments, one from straw bonnet making and the other from domestic service. The former had to leave her job due to ill health, but found mine work was better. The latter preferred the relative freedom of working at the mine, compared to working as a live-in servant. During the late 19th century, when various schemes were set up to place out-of-work bal maidens into service, many found it was not for them:

'Everything was so strange to me, it seemed to me I was a regular gawk: I couldn't understand half they meant for me to do. I made awful mistakes. After that (thinks I) I'd better start [hand in one's notice] *for I shall never get on. And I did start.'* (Cornishman 22nd Aug 1879)

When John Tonkin interviewed the women who had worked at Polpuff Glass Mine during the First World War, he found that, with the exception of one person, they all looked back with some sort of pride and affection for their time there, even though it had been gruelling and hard. Sixty years on, they still had amazing memories of each other, indicating the close friendships which developed between these working women. Similar memories were shared by the surviving women who had worked on the picking belts at Geevor in the Second World War.[31]

Not all the bal maidens enjoyed their work, had good memories, or preferred it to other employment. Patty Tremellin saw her work as a bal maiden as the cause of her misfortunes, and called the mines a *'devilish place'*. She subsequently advised young girls not to go there. When the visitor to Dolcoath in 1893 asked some spalling girls how much they earned, they refused to tell him. He also described an occasion when the girls refused to pose for a photograph, and, under duress, only posed in such a way that their features were not visible (fig. 71). These actions, he concluded, were because the women had a *'rooted dislike for their calling'*. For some, the opportunity to find alternative employment was embraced with great relief:

'Some few, who from time to time have done so and who have fortunately got into places where pains have been taken to instruct them in their duties, would now on no account exchange their present position for mine work: on the contrary, they affirm they are much more comfortable indoors, out of the wet and cold, but all they can say on the matter will not induce some of their companions to follow their example.'

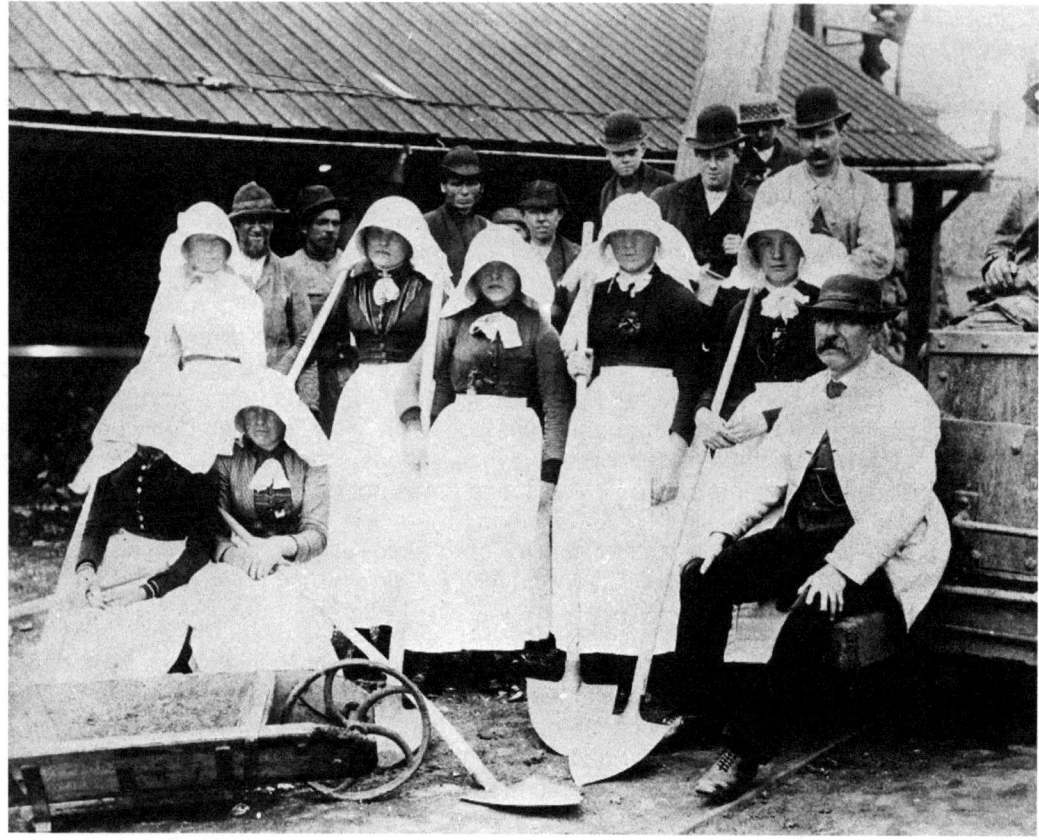

Fig. 71 Dolcoath Bal Maidens c. 1890
Courtesy of Cornwall Centre Collection

Traditionally, the bal maidens were sometimes looked on as very feminine, possibly fragile, creatures. The real bal maidens behind the myths were capable, hardworking and down to earth. They had to be (and generally were) physically and mentally tough. The visitor to Dolcoath in 1893 made the following observations about the spalling girls there:

'Only exceptionally strong girls and women can do this work, and so dexterous do they become that they can usually do more work than men who may be occasionally employed with them.'

It was nothing to them to be carrying weights, adopting postures, or performing repetitive actions, which would be banned under current Health and Safety regulations, and which would be totally beyond the capability of many people today. Those that survived the vigorous demands of the work must have had remarkable strength and resilience.

Rideing, on visiting Carn Brea in 1881, was amazed at the strength of an elderly woman he saw filling a wagon with copper ore. He likened her ability to *'the willing vigor of a young man'* and *'much more activity than the average navvy'*. It was little wonder that these women made good prospective partners for those who would try their chance at pioneering in new lands. One commentator described bal maidens as *'strong like men'*.[32]

When there were accidents at the mines, the women and girls, where appropriate, would be involved in rescue operations, alongside the men, using their physical strength and stamina. In August 1899, two men at West Wheal Basset Mine were trapped behind a fall of thousands of tons of rock at the mouth of one of the tunnels. The only hope of rescue was to sink a new shaft down to the level in which they were trapped. From a contemporary newspaper report, it seems that the bal maidens were involved in the rescue over several days. Although details are not recorded, the bal maidens almost certainly helped barrow away the spoil as it was brought to surface, probably working shifts, day and night. These actions caught the attention of national newspaper reporters:

'It is not generally known beyond the boundaries of Cornwall that hundreds of peculiarly dressed, but attractive and clean looking girls are daily engaged in the breaking the stones of ore which are brought to surface. Many of them are as strong as men, as indeed they need to be to work the livelong day in a big shed open in the front and at the sides, subject to exposure and the strain of continuous labour in a stooping posture....No milk-and-water misses these, as you would think if you saw how they relish their potato pasties for dinner or their 'figgy hoggan'.' (Cornubian 25th Aug 1899 + WMN 12th Aug 1899)

As well as their general physical strength, it seems that bal maidens, on the whole, did not lack intelligence either. As early as 1825, John Taylor, one of the leading mining entrepreneurs in Cornwall, remarked on the innate ability of the average Cornish miner:

'Education is much sought after among miners, and that its benefits are improved as much as the means will admit, and even far beyond what would have been expected from the new opportunities at present afforded them. Miners in general are a superior class of men, and, in the deep mines particularly, the constant exercise of judgment and thought which is necessary, produces a proportionate degree of intelligence.' [33]

Fig. 72 Re-created Scene of Women Dressing Clay, Carloggas c. 1905
Courtesy of China Clay Country Park Mining & Heritage Centre

It was within this context, where mining families often strove to improve their lot by education, that so many bal maidens were raised. The story of William Murrish in the 'Miner of Perranzabuloe' illustrates the great care with which adults attempted to improve not just their reading and writing skills, but their general knowledge as well. Those who could, avidly read any scrap of printed material they could find, and they just as eagerly shared their new-found skills with the children and young people around them. This hunger for knowledge among bal maidens is illustrated by their attendance of Sunday School up to the upper age limit of 18 years old. We also catch some of that desire to learn from Rideing's account of bal maidens at the Carn Brea Copper Mine:

'At the mill we found large numbers of young girls, ...all neatly clothed and intelligent, even pert in manner. They can all write, and the literature much sort after and devoured in spare time - penny instalments after work.' (Rideing 1881 p. 812)

It seems that bal maidens rarely became rich unless by a fortunate marriage. Because of such low levels of pay compared to the cost of living, bal maidens were never in a position to make a real living, let alone a fortune, from their work. Those that remained single and had to support themselves, and those who had to support ailing or disabled relatives, were in real difficulty. Many found themselves in debt, like Patty Tremmellin who ended up in debtors' prison.

Many watched a widowed parent also struggle to provide for the family. The mother of Mary Jane Richards (of Porkellis) collected shellfish. Ellen Nicholls' 76 year-old mother broke roadstone in Poldice, and Jane and Eliza Craze's mother sold '*small things*' in Camborne. It seems that the chance of marriage was significantly reduced for those bal maidens who had to support parents or siblings. Older spinster bal maidens with widowed mothers or invalid siblings were common, whereas unmarried men with these responsibilities were rare. Quite often in these struggling families, several, if not all, of the daughters remained single, such as Amelia, Ann and Mary Bennetts, and Hannah, Jane and Mary Williams supporting their 60 and 77 year-old mothers respectively, in 1861. For many, it seems that the death of their father meant the end of their hopes for marriage, and the requirement to become the main breadwinners in the family.

In reality then, the bal maidens did not fit the mythical images easily. As a group they were neither sweet, innocent and ineffective; nor were they brazen and brash. Summarising the innate abilities of bal maidens, in terms of strength, courage, wit and intelligence, Hamilton Jenkin describes them as:

'*...forming a class of workwomen to themselves. A class as a whole, shrewd, honest, respectable and hardworking. Though sometimes rough in speech and generally plain spoken enough in repartee, as anyone who addressed them disrespectfully soon found, their work brought no demoralization of character.*' [34]

SKILLS, LEADERSHIP, RESPONSIBILITY AND STEREOTYPES

It was usually assumed that the women and girls were working at the mines as a 'temporary measure', and that their jobs were, at very least, a useful money-earner between going to school and getting married. At most, it was seen to be a vital short-term addition to the family budget. As a result there was no proper structure for progression, increased responsibility, and earning capacity, as there was for the boys and men, other than a simple increment of wages depending on age. The mine or works management did not offer any, and the women and girls, and their families, did not expect any. The boys could graduate from the dressing floor, if they remained healthy and were industrious, until they eventually become fully-fledged miners. From then, they had the opportunity of becoming tributers or specialised artisans like engine drivers, blacksmiths, or carpenters. If they were lucky, they could possibly become mine captains, agents, or even owners. The girls and women could only graduate from washing and picking to cobbing, bucking or barrowing, and then marriage.

Despite the lack of structure and opportunity, the bal maidens often showed the ability to organise themselves. In several known instances, they took industrial action in protest at working conditions or pay. The earliest record is of bal maidens on strike in 1806 at Wheal

Friendship. They also went out on strike at Devon Great Consols in 1850, Balleswidden in 1857, Wheal Basset in 1871, Dolcoath, Pendeen and Ding Dong Mine in 1872, West Seaton in 1877, and Devon Great Consols again in 1878. However, they were invariably the losers in these confrontations, and were either replaced by other workers, or forced to accept increased hours or reduced pay. A rare exception to this was a round of pay strikes in the Central Mining District in 1880. Another occasion when management capitulated was after bal maidens and boys walked out at Phoenix United Mine in August 1882, due to having to work more hours (in the pay-day week) for no extra wages.

Apart from their informal mobilisation into action groups, there was probably an informal, or sometimes formal, working hierarchy among women and girls. For instance, Jenny Stone, seems to have been responsible for a group of bal maidens at Dolcoath in 1823, keeping a record of the number of days worked to the day captains.[35] In 1836, Kitty Grigg and Ann Brook seem to have had some seniority over other women and girls carrying clay out onto to the moors for drying at Goonvean Clay Pits. They were either the sub-contractors who were paid for the work that was done by the group, who they effectively employed, or they were the leaders of a group of women or girls who presented themselves for employment, and they were the women who received payment on behalf of the whole group. Much later, in 1918, Mary Higgins was responsible for the women and girls at Polpuff Mine as the 'shift boss'. At the same mine, 18 year-old Gussie Retallack (daughter of the surface captain) was the tally checker.[36] At some mines, one senior woman was appointed by the surface captain to oversee the very complex task of the re-sorting and redistribution of ores ready for sampling. As this was a particularly complicated task, this person must have been multi-skilled, and also an accepted appointee from the point of view of the labour force.

Evidence to the *1842 Royal Commission* indicates women and girls of mixed ages sometimes working at similar tasks. This may indicate a senior woman or girl responsible for smaller working groups, for instance, to oversee the very young girls or boys at each picking table. One such woman may have been Hannah Lance (a 67 year-old widow) who was described as *'overseeing mine girls'* at Wheal Rose (St. Agnes) in the *1871 Census*.

There were also women or girls who were singled out for making preparations in the dinner sheds for 'croust'. At North Roskear Mine, in 1864, there were six such women responsible for dinner at each of the six separate dining sheds for the surface workers:

'Half an hour before the bell rings for the hands to leave work, one of the girls for each house goes in, prepares the fire, boils the kettle, makes the tea, puts the pasties in the oven etc, so that when the bell rings and the dressers go in, they can sit down to a warm meal at once.' (Kinnaird 1864 p. 80)

Two decades later Minnie Andrews was given similar responsibilities in the dining shed at Tincroft Betty Adit:

'I used to go in the dinner-house and cook, not cook, used to get their food ready and the hot and things; used to put their pasties and things in the oven and warm them again and they come in twelve o'clock and get the tea, get their tea ready, and then I used to tell them when it was turn for them to bring their tea. Now I used to say 'You must bring your tea, whose turn is it? You ought know, I ain't got no tea here', so they bring their tea, like that, and they'd have a good cup of tea and then we used to go on like that.' [37]

One of the most colourful 'dinner ladies' was Jenefer Terrill, who was in charge of the dinner house at Dolcoath from the 1860 until about 1910. She, and possibly another woman, were described in the 1952 Troon W.I. Scrapbook in this way:

'I remember old Jenefer, with very white hair always covered with a heavy black chenille net; a voluminous dress, skirt which touch the ground, white apron, and grey woollen shawl. A pasty is a pasty, but it is surprising how pasties can differ one from another in looks. Jenefer knew them all'.

'A story goes in Troon that an old dinner-woman at one of the mines sometimes had as many as a hundred pasties to warm. If anyone claimed the wrong pasty she would pounce; "That idna thy pasty. I know thy mother's pasties like my awn cheeld [child].*" Any attempt to question her decision would be in vain and her last words would not always be complimentary to the pasty.'* (Troon WI 1952 p. 6a)

Although the stereotype of women's and girls' tasks at the mine was limited to the dressing floor or the counthouse, there were a substantial number who broke the mould! Some became wagoners, transporting ore or clay from the mines and pits to the ports or railways for export, such as Ann Key and Nancy Phillips (probably at Wheal Prosper) and Grace Briney (at Treskerby). Grace Briney, it seems, had never been a bal maiden as such. She began at the mines as a driver for the horses at the whim; she then went on to landing kibbles, a highly dangerous job requiring great strength, and usually the unique preserve of the stronger men. Another woman who was not afraid of taking on the men's tasks at the mine was Sally Satterley, at Eyelsbarrow Mine in the mid 19th century.[38]

Some women achieved considerable skill and experience in a more professional way in their work at the mines. One of these was a Miss Beckerleg who worked as assistant to the assayer at Dolcoath for many years. Her story is told more fully in the next chapter, but she was known as having as much knowledge about tin as the mine officers.

In very exceptional cases, it seems that women achieved major management roles, against the expectation of their time. Lydia Taylor was manger of Wheal Lovell Mine from about 1840 until 1845, and may also have been involved in the management of Wheal Towan. In the clay mining areas, Phillipa Lovering, Rebecca Martin and Sara Michell were among several who became clay merchants on the death of their husbands. They were not 'sleeping partners', but took a full, active interest in their businesses, and were quite capable of forming new policies and taking steps to expand their empires. A Miss Lidgey is also believed to have managed Magdalen Mine in Ponsanooth early in the 20th century.

The tasks which were allocated to the bal maidens on the dressing floors at the mines in the 18th and for the first half of the 19th century were many and varied. In the course of her working life, the 'average' bal maiden would have learnt to pick and sort ore, and probably carried out a variety of dressing processes which required not only strength, but dexterity, care, and an eye for detail. In 1855, George Henwood had this to say about the skill necessary to dress tin ore:

'A large amount of dexterity, to be acquired by practise alone, is necessary in tin dressing, the ore, as I before observed, being exceedingly difficult of separation from certain matrices.' (Henwood 1855 p. 14)

Sorting, and separating the 'values' from the waste at all stages of the process required considerable skill, but most especially at picking, buddling and framing. However, this was not to say that the separation stages requiring physical strength: spalling, cobbing and bucking required none. As trained geologists and experienced miners will affirm, there are particular fracture lines and shatter points at which ore will part more easily from the rock in which it is set. This requires a practised and trained eye. The late John Gurney captures this concept in describing a woman spalling, in his poem '*Bal-Maidens*':

> '*Even now I see her…aiming at the weak spot
> of the stone…still shattering…thirty tons a week.
> …battering on, half-covered by the rockdust of the floors
> eternally returning with the same mechanical precision*' [39]

In some respects, the women and girls working at the tin and copper mines would be learning quite different skills. Leifchild remarked that copper and tin mining were different trades, and that the skills of one were not necessarily transferable to the other:

'*The one class of dressers are quite incapable of performing the work of the other*; '*Tin men are not copperers*' [sic] *as the Cornish miners say.*' (Leifchild 1855 p. 228)

While these comments may have been made with reference to the miners and captains, it does not seem to have been so true of the women dressers. The women and girls frequently moved from one mine to another for work, which would invariably involve learning slightly different techniques, and sometimes moving between tin, lead or copper mines, and facing entirely new types of work. Some would be processing more than one mineral at a time, such as Ann Paull of Silverwell, Jane Berryman of Kirley, and Grace Rogers of Truck's Lodge, all of whom were dressing tin and copper. In 1881, Nancy Tamblyn of Newlyn East was recorded as dressing '*iron and blende* [zinc].' A little after this time, Minnie Andrews, the '*Last Bal Maiden*', worked at four different mines, sometimes picking copper, and sometimes working at the racking frames in a tin mine.

For those women and girls who were employed at very small mines, they would almost certainly be expected to be multi-skilled, being called on to perform a selection of the dressing tasks in turn. As early as 1809, Sarah Davies, employed at Wheal Union & Owlcombe Beam Nine in Devon, both picked and bucked copper ore, and worked at the tin frames.[40] At East Wheal Russell in 1856, their eight or ten bal maidens were employed to both cob and buck the lead ore. It seems that they alternated between these two processes, being paid 8d per day for the former and 1s per day for the latter. At Carn Vivian, the two or three bal maidens employed between 1860 and 1862 would spend several days (dispersed through the month) bucking lead ore instead of '*dressing*', when they would be paid by the barrow rather than by the day.

Often, the tasks that required the most skill were mechanised first, and gradually the bal maidens were taken away from the complex tasks to the simpler ones, so becoming more and more de-skilled. In their final years, it seems that the bal maidens were restricted to the physical spalling of ore, serving the buddles, overseeing racking frames (which were eventually almost totally automated), or barrowing ore. The communal memory generally seems to associate the bal maidens' work with what appears to be comparatively simple, but physically demanding and repetitive actions.

Changes in the way these women and girls were described subtly reflected this change in perception. For instance, in the *1841* and *1851 Census* records, the bal maidens were often referred to as 'dressing ore', or 'ore dressers', with the adult male workers on the dressing floors described as 'surface labourers'. In the *1861 Census,* a change in language is noticeable, with 'mine woman', 'mine girl' or 'mine labourer' becoming more common. By 1891, the nomenclature often become reversed, with the females described as 'mine labourers', and the men as the 'ore dressers'. The memory of a multi-skilled, talented, and experienced workforce of girls and women seems to have been superseded by these later perceptions of unrelenting physical labour. This seems to have resulted in a rather sad under-valuing of the abilities and achievements of both these latter day women and the earlier bal maidens.

Perhaps the words of John Gurney re-capture some of the real spirit of these labouring women and girls:

> *'A rough and callous beauty in their forms,*
> *rag-handkerchief tied up above*
> *the soul's fierce sunlight.'* [41]

FOOTNOTES

1. Throughout this chapter material has been drawn from the *1842 Royal Commission into the Employment of Women and Young People* [CEC], especially pp. 57-113, Table 17, Evid. Nos. 5, 6, 36, 56, 86, 96, 104.
2. Barton, R. *Life in Cornwall in the Late 19th Century* (Bradford Barton 1972) p. 8.
3. Schwartz (1999); (2000) p. 77; Burke (1986).
4. Barton (1968) p. 56.
5. Chamber's (1853) p. 37.
6. Burke (1986) p. 187.
7. Troon WI (1852) p. 23.
8. Ballantyne (1897) p. 65.
9. James (1972) p. 242.
10. Troon WI (1952) p. 21
11. WB 5th Feb. 1819.
12. Buckley (2007) p. 54, Lowenac MS F.146 (A. L. Thomas Collection, Camborne School of Mines).
13. Tangye, Richard *Redruth and Its People* (1988) p. 53.
14. Greeves (2006).
15. Buckley (2007) pp. 52-55, 129.
16. Bodmin Debtors Goal Admissions Book (CRO: AD 1676/1/1 No. 6605); Tremellin (1841) p. 12.
17. County Debtors Gaol Admissions Register (CRO: AD 1676/5/1 & 2, Nos. 5322, 5332, 5303, 5412, 5640, 5790).
18. Bridewell Admissions Register (CRO: AD 1676/1/1 & 2, Nos. 5844, 9670).
19. Redruth Union Masters Report Book 1892-95 (CRO: PU Redruth 99).
20. Tavistock Workhouse Admissions (DRO: PLU Tavistock).
21. Lewis (1997) p. 91.
22. Gray, Todd *Cornwall, Travellers Tales* (Mint Press, 2000) p. 94.
23. Baring Gould, Sabine *Book of Devon* p. 22.
24. Tremellin (1841) p. 12.
25. Razelle (1973) p. 33.
26. Redruth Union Admission and Discharge Book 1892-1895 (CRO: PU Redruth 146); Tavistock Union Admissions, Births and Deaths Registers (DRO: PLU 21 and 23).
27. Personal corresp. (JT/LM 2002).
28. Personal corresp. (AS/LM 2003).
29. CRO Borlase MSS.
30. Hocking, Silas *Tales of a Tin Mine* (Horace Marshall 1898) p. 23-4.
31. Geevor Oral History Project.
32. Rideing (1881) pp. 808; Tangye (1988) p. 53.
33. Burt (1977) p. 69.
34. Hamilton Jenkin (1948) pp. 237-8.
35. Buckley (2007) p. 55, 129.
36. Personal Correspondence JT/LM 2002.
37. Brooke (1967).
38. Cornish Magazine (1886) p. 125; Greeves (2006) p. 9.
39. Gurney, John *The Bal-Maiden* (courtesy of Sally Gurney).
40. Greeves, (2006) p. 9.
41. Gurney, John 'The Bal-Maiden' *Cornish Review* (Summer 1972) No. 21 p. 8

Chapter 12

BAL MAIDENS - THE REAL PEOPLE

LYDIA TAYLOR: Mine Manager

Mrs. Lydia Taylor is the only known 19th century female manager of a tin mine, in West Devon or Cornwall. She was manager at Wheal Lovell Tin Mine, Wendron, from at least 1840 until 1845. It was situated on what is now the Manhay Estate, east of Crahan Farm.[1] Her co-adventurer was Christopher Wallis, but he does not appear to have taken an active part in managing the mine. This was possibly Christopher Wallis Popham, who was owner of Tresarno Mine nearby, and grandson and heir of Christopher Wallis, a Helston solicitor. Wheal Lovell appears to have been an amalgamation of Commellack, Mengearne and Treguntis Mines.

Lydia was born around 1800. It seems that she had been married at least twice, as she had son John and daughter Charlotte both with the surname Cowper. She appears to have been the estranged wife of Alexander Taylor of West Lodge, Enfield, who subsequently went overseas. She had been responsible for managing the mine at Wheal Lovell and lived in the counthouse there, where she was involved with the day to day management. At the time of the *1841 Census*, Thomas Jones was her mine agent, and James Philp, the clerk. Thereafter, she employed Captain William Kite as purser, and other agents were: Captain J. Crease (1840), Captain Hannibal Perry (1841-44) and Captain Richard Kendall (1844-45). There was also a storekeeper. On this particular mine, tin was found in pockets or chimneys, and the three most productive lodes were Quoin (Coin) Work, Middle Work and North Lode. Cape's and Goblet Lode were also being worked in about 1842. Lydia's Shaft, in the main part of the mine, was named after Mrs. Taylor.

There is little information about the overall production of the mine. Lydia sold £4,402 worth of black tin in 1841. There were probably no dressing floors at Wheal Lovell, as such. Subsequent mines in the area, in 1871, took their tin to be stamped at Glebe, Wood or Treloquithack Stamps, a few miles away. It may be that this was the case, also, with Wheal Lovell. There were two accidents recorded at Wheal Lovell; one in July 1840 and another in December 1842, one of which was a fatality.[2] In 1843, Lydia sold just over 130 tons of tin-stuff at auction, indicating that the ore had not been stamped before sale. In April 1844, Lydia negotiated to buy one of Wheal Montague's engines. Treleaven described her as *'Cornwall's only woman mine manager'*, and records how she sent some of her men, with Mr. West, her engineer, to move the engine. Treleaven did not allow them to proceed, as he knew nothing of the arrangement nor whether any payment had been made. Eventually, in May 1844, William Kite, the purser for Wheal Lovell, removed the engine after John Williams Jnr. of Burncoose had stood surety for the £455.[3] This was probably the engine for the new work on the west part of the sett, where they subsequently failed to find sufficient amounts of tin.

After considerable investment in this failed venture, the mine ran into difficulties. There were cases brought against Captain Kite by James Cliff, a tributer working on Coin Lode, and Hannibal Perry, one of the agents, to the Vice-Wardens Court in Bodmin in August 1844, for non-payment of wages. In the second case, at least, the court ruled against the mine, and ordered the outstanding £36 12s to be paid by 1st October. On 19th October 1844, Lydia mortgaged Wheal Lovell to John Williams Jnr. and brothers, along with another mine at Port Towan, St Agnes. Operations at Wheal Lovell appear to have stopped about this time and the mine was eventually sold to William Carne of Falmouth in 1846 for £7,000. In 1870, at East Wheal Lovell, a later mine in the same area, it was found that, instead of the expected good tin lode running through the sett, they were in fact mining a vertical cylinder of tin which ran for only seventy fathoms.[4] As this was often the pattern of the tin deposits in the area, it may well have been that Lydia experienced the same sort of situation at Wheal Lovell, so that the return on this limited deposit of tin did not cover their expenditure.

As records have only been found for Wheal Lovell from 1840 until 1845, it is not known when Lydia Taylor first took over the management of the mine. She also had interests in a mine at Porth Towan, probably South Towan Mine, where her son was an absentee manager. From about 1840, he was serving in the army in Canada. Although Christopher Wallis mostly acted on behalf of John Cowper, Lydia seems to have dealt with some of the administration in his absence.[5] Significantly, in the mid 1840s, this mine was also known as Wheal Lydia.

GRACE BRINEY: Equal among Men

Fig. 73 Grace Briney c. 75 yrs
Courtesy of Redruth Old Cornwall Society

Grace (or Gracey) Briney is the only known woman kibble lander. She worked at one of the mines in the Redruth area, but it is not known which one, in the latter part of the 18th Century, and the early part of the 19th. Kibble landing was generally considered too hard and dangerous for women, and involved landing the large iron bucket full of ore-stuff, as it came to surface. This was usually done by a man on a landing platform, using an iron hook to haul in the kibble. It required strength, coordination, and great care, to avoid the kibble swinging back over the shaft, taking the lander with it. In 1886, this task was described as follows:

'Landing the kibble when it came to the surface...was a somewhat difficult task, and a very comfortless and exposed one, without shelter from wind and rain. It was accomplished by seizing the mouth of the kibble with an iron pot hook, and drawing it off the mouth of the shaft on to a landing stage. Difficult and dangerous though it was for a man to accomplish, in one instance, and I think the only one known, a woman attended to this duty.' (Cornwall Magazine 1886 p. 125)

Grace's real name was Grace Huchens (Hichens or Hitchins), and she was born in 1778 in Gwennap. It seems that she had been raised in the workhouse, and at a very young age was sent as a pauper to work at one of the copper mines in Redruth. She was apprenticed to Capt. A. Treneer, and her job was to drive the horse at the whim which raised the kibble from underground.[6] From an early age, she would have watched how to land the kibble, and her ability to control the whim horse at that moment would also have been crucial.

As a young girl she became pregnant, but nothing is known of the circumstances, or what happened to the child. Subsequently, she is described as having a change of personality, and from then on usually wore a mixture of what was considered masculine and feminine attire. It may be at this time that she became a kibble lander. However, as a young woman she was renowned for her ability to wrestle, fight, run, and do heavy work. She was obviously a colourful and well-known figure throughout West Cornwall, and there are several surviving descriptions of her. Generally her outer clothing was consistent with that worn by the male surface labourers at the mine, and, as kibble lander, she would have been considered, presumably, part of the male surface labouring team:

'Her dress consisted of a man's high hat, known among her fellow workers as a 'long sliver' 'bell toppe', and more recently 'Par stack'; a blue clawed hammer coat (so called from the shape of its tails) having a thick, deep collar.'

'Her feet were encased in coarse blue worsted stocking and thick rough boots, a short skirt with woollen or printed apron, a man's jacket and a man's hat completed her attire, while she generally carried in her hand a good cart whip.'

'She dressed in the very unfeminine costume of a blue cloth coat with gilt buttons, a high hat, petticoats, stockings, and shoes - a style of dress from which she never departed for the last 35 years.'

She obviously had bought her own horse and cart, and was later employed as a wagoner, transporting tin or copper from the mines in Redruth for shipping from Devoran or Portreath. Her odd attire would contribute to her safety in journeying with her cart up and down the county. For many years, she lived in the east end of Redruth at East Turnpike Hill in a single room, and on pay day was a regular drinker at the local miners' pub the 'Pick and Gadd' Inn, in Treskerby. It was the Treskerby mines for which she worked.[7] She also sold fish at the weekly market in Redruth.

In her latter years, she continued selling fish, as well as dealing in mazzards (cherries) and other fruit. Passmore Edwards recalled that, as a child, he used to carry strawberries, which his father had grown, to sell to Gracey at her stall in Redruth market. She bought cherries from the Bere Alston area in season and, it seems, sold them throughout the west of Cornwall. As a trader, she must have been a formidable woman:

'Rugged, but not altogether unpleasing, with a rough voice, she ruled those who came in contact with a rod of iron. Her journeyings as a wholesale purveyor of fruit took her from the Tamar to Penzance, especially in the cherry or mazzard season. Indeed, her influence with the proprietors of the mazzard gardens seemed unlimited. Only in the towns she approved of could mazzards be had, and again in towns in which the retail dealers had offended her, she retaliated by keeping mazzards from the districts.'[8]

After an accident when she was 75 years old, she walked with the aid of crutches, and was dependent, in part, on parish relief. However, even just a few weeks before she died, she had travelled fifty miles to St Dominic, near the Devon border, to buy cherries for the Redruth Mazzard Fair. She died in Redruth on 18th October 1869, aged 91 years, and was buried at Redruth Parish Church on 21st October 1869.[9]

REBECCA MARTIN: 'Clay Baron'

Rebecca Julyard was born in St Austell in 1799. She subsequently married John Martin, who had been heavily involved in the development of the major clay works in the St Austell area from about 1835. Together, they lived in Blowing House, St Austell. John died in 1844, and Rebecca took over the responsibility for the running of their various businesses. It seems that she inherited considerable holdings in the Cornwall China Stone and Clay Co., which failed in 1848, but, at the same time, she was one of the five independent producers who controlled over one third of the china clay output in Cornwall.

In 1849, she seemed to be instrumental in pushing for an agreement between producers to regulate china clay prices, and to put an end to the practice of allowing purchasers to accumulate enormous debts.[10] Steam engines were introduced relatively late into the clay works, from 1837, so, as Rebecca was selling an old steam engine at Little Treviscoe in 1851, her works had presumably been among the first to install this technology.

By 1852, Rebecca appears to have been in partnership with John Lovering when Carclaze Tin Mine was taken over, with a view to exploiting the mine for china clay. In the final month of entries in the cost book for the tin mining enterprise (January 1852), she received a payment of £7. 7s. 6d. (three months at 52s 6d per month).

In 1858, Rebecca was managing at least six works: Carvear, Screeda, Lansallson, Huel Virgin, Mellangoose, Little Treviscoe, and possibly North Goonbarrow as well. The clay produced from these works in that year totalled 6,900 tons, and it was used for paper and bleaching as well as pottery.[11] At some stage before 1860, she began to show an interest in the clay works opening on the southern fringe of Dartmoor, and leased a sett at Cholwichtown.[12] In 1862, she also took over the lease for Lee Moor Clay, Brick and Tile Works. Interestingly, in the *1861 Census*, Rebecca is recorded as blind, so presumably these later transactions must have been carried out despite considerable disability.

Although she had three sons, William Langdon, Thomas and Edward, all of whom were involved in the clay business, it seems that during her lifetime she held the control of the family ventures. She died in 1863, at the age of 64, only one year after taking out the extended lease on Lee Moor, which was to provide a secure future for her sons and their descendants. Rebecca was described in this way:

'She was a lady of great determination and, in spite of her small size, was more than a match for her sons or any other clay producers. Her reputation for forthrightness did not enhance her popularity amongst her rivals, but they respected her nevertheless because she was honest and fair in her dealings with them.' [13]

What businessman or woman could want for a better epitaph?

PATTY TREMELLIN: A Hard, Short Life

Of all the stories in this chapter, this is possibly the most poignant. A tiny book, no more than three inches by four and a half, published in 1841, tells the retrospective story of Patty, who died in 1837 at the age of 33. The book is called *'Patty Tremellin: the Life of a Cornish Mine Girl Written by Herself'*.[14] At first glance it appears to be written as a fictitious 'improving novel', to be an inspiration and warning to other young women, sometimes in the first person, sometimes in the third. However, the book carries much irrelevant detail, and has a distinct lack of flow and structure, indicating that it was probably based on real life, rather than being a constructed novel. Subsequent research of parish registers of Redruth, St Mewan, St Ewe and St Austell supports the general framework of the story, and almost certainly identifies the central character as Patty (Patience, also known as Martha) Tremelling (Tremellyn, Tremelline or Tremellin). It seems that the book was written after her death, based on a journal she began to write during her illness, and on conversations she had with the author of the book. We do not know who the author was, but it may possibly be the minister who had been pastor to Patty in her final years.

Patty states that she was born in Redruth in 1804, a daughter of a mining family. Her parents were almost certainly Francis and Martha Tremelling, and her baptism was recorded at St Uny Parish Church on 18th March 1804. Her parents appear to have come from the St Ewe and St Austell area. When she was 2 years old she was taken to Penzance, to be looked after by an aunt. Her aunt and uncle ran a shop in the town, and were probably childless. Unlike her own parents, they were able to afford to send Patty to school. Patty first went to a school where she did 'reading and sewing', then went on to the 'writing school', which she attended until she was 8 years old. She then was taken out of school to help her uncle in his shop, but was sent to evening classes instead. By this time, she had presumably acquired the reading and writing skills that she was to use to good effect in later years.

Suddenly, when she was about 9 years old, the happiness and stability that she had known in Penzance was shattered. The aunt, whom Patty thought of as 'mother', became seriously ill. Over the next few years she was shuffled amongst her own family, who had moved to the St Austell area by 1812, her invalid aunt in Penzance, and yet another aunt. Eventually, the beloved aunt in Penzance died, and Patty went back to her parents again, to look after her ever-increasing number of siblings. Her mother sometimes went out to work at the mine, but was often too ill to go. When she was ill, Patty nursed her as well. When she was 16 years old Patty also went to work at the mine, but still had to carry out the household chores at home. We are not told where Patty and her family worked, but it was at some distance, adding about an hour's travelling time each way to the working day. Patty described their family circumstances in this way:

'My father's wages at that time were small, my mother very ill, our family large, and corn dear, so that both my father and mother had to go to work without meat. Many days we had nothing but boiled greens to make use of. I had three miles to go to work every morning, and all the work of the house to do after my return at night, as my poor mother was laid up of cancer.'

Worse was yet to come, when they were all thrown out of work because the mine closed. (This may have been Wheal Hewas, which closed in 1822). Patty went to Truro to find work, and started going to 'the dancing rooms' until ten or eleven o'clock at night, probably, with other girls from the mine:

'I became deeply attached to a young man...who had often promised marriage. Soon after he deserted me, and I was left to bewail my condition and lament my fall. When near my confinement my father ordered me to leave his house; but I got a place to go, with a very sober woman, about half a mile from our house.'

Patty subsequently had three illegitimate babies. After the birth of her first child, her health began to decline. She was obviously suffering from a progressively degenerative disease which caused haemorrhaging. Despite being the mother of young children, and her declining health, she was twice committed to Bodmin Jail. The sequence of these events as described in the book is largely supported by formal records, but with a few time discrepancies and one slight difference in detail. It seems that Patty was in her mid twenties when she gave birth to her first child. This seems to have been Richard Bray Tremellen, who was baptised at St Austell Parish Church on 6th June 1830, and recorded as the son of Patience Tremellen. After the birth, Patty went back home, where she was bedridden for nine months. When she was eventually 'better', she went back to work at the mines. She then became pregnant again. During this second pregnancy, Patty became suicidal, and even went to the mine shaft with the intentions of throwing herself down it:

'I was struck with trembling whilst standing on the brink of the shaft, and I seemed to be on the verge of hell.'

It was at this time that a bal maiden friend, who was a Methodist, began to help and support her. When her second confinement was near, Patty went to live with two elderly people nearby, doing a little sewing to support herself. William Thomas was probably born in the summer of 1831, when Patty was 27 years old, but he was not baptised until 1834. She put the child out to nurse so that she could go back to the mines to support them both. Subsequently, she became ill again and could not work. She was committed to the County Gaol in Bodmin on October 5th 1831; her book records that it was for a small debt, but the admissions register states for *'disobeying an order of bastardy to satisfy the parish of St Ewe'* (i.e. not naming the father of her child). She was sentenced to three months imprisonment or was to pay a £1 0s 10d fine. It was possibly this fine that was described as the *'small debt'*. The register gives her description: height 5' 3", grey eyes, brown hair, oval face with pale pockmarked complexion. Her behaviour was described as orderly.[15] When she was discharged on 13th December 1831, she returned home to her family in St Austell:

'After my return home I kept myself from all company until I went to work at the mine, when I gave myself to company again. The third time I brought myself to shame.'

Patty's third child, John Francis, was baptised on 29th April 1832 at St Ewe Parish Church, where he was recorded as *'bastard child of Martha Tremelling (servant)'*. Once again she was committed to jail for refusing to divulge the name of the father of her child. An entry in the Bodmin Quarter Sessions of 1833 reads:

'2nd July: Martha Tremellen, St Ewe. For refusing to name father. To remain in custody.' [16]

She was very ill in jail and suffered a major haemorrhage, so obtaining early release on health grounds. During this time, she had increasing contact with the Methodist community, and her faith began to deepen. It seems that it was after her return from jail the second time that she began to write the journal, which is quoted in the book. However, after release, in November 1833, she was again ill. She was never to regain her health. On 30th September 1834, her middle child William was baptised at St Ewe Parish Church, at the age of *'almost three years old'*, where he is described as *'bastard of Martha Tremelline, servant'*.

Patty was bedridden from 1835, but began instructing the young children of the neighbourhood in reading and needlework, and in her faith. Her bedroom was her schoolroom. She was able to support herself by doing some needlework, rather than enter the workhouse. Eventually, she died, on 10th October 1837, aged 33 years. An entry in the St Austell Parish Church burial register simply reads:

'12th October 1837: Martha Tremellen aged 33 of Wrestling Downs, bed lier [sic] *for 3 years.'*

Her death is among the first recorded with the General Register Office for England and Wales, as the legal requirement had only been made a few weeks before. Her death certificate, issued on the 4th November, in the sub-district of St Austell, reads:

'October 10: Martha Tremellen 33 years spinster'

The cause of death is described as consumption, and Patty's mother, Martha, was the informant who had been present, as the book describes, at her death.

It seems that Patty took little pleasure from her years as working as a bal maiden, and looked back on the mine as an *'evil place'*. She considered that it was this working environment that had been the corrupting influence in her life, encouraging her to the dance floors. Some of her final words recorded in the book, to her young sister, were:

'I...beg of you, not to give your mind to dress, it is a very great snare; and to avoid the dancing room, it is often the first step to the ruin of young women....Those mines are bad places for boys and girls, for there is nothing but sin to be heard or witnessed all the day long, when the agents are out of the way.'

It was, however, her friends from that same mining environment that had supported her, and encouraged her in her darkest moments. It was bal maiden friends, one in particular, who had shared their faith with her, so that Patty was able to 'shine' in those last difficult years of her life.

It seems probable that all three of Patty's sons emigrated. It is thought that Francis migrated to India (and died there), and that John went to South America. William appears to have travelled to America, firstly to mines in the Lake Superior area, and then moving to Pennsylvania. It is believed that descendants of Patty's still live in that area today.[17]

MARTHA BUCKINGHAM: Copper Ore Picker

Martha Buckingham, who was born in 1827, was one of the ore dressers who gave evidence to the *1842 Royal Commission on the Employment of Women and Children at the Mines*. Hers was the most detailed interview recorded, and gives considerable insight into her life, both at home and at work.[18]

She was interviewed in May 1841 at the Consolidated Mines, by the mine surgeon, Dr. Charles Barham, author of the report. At that time, Martha was just 14 years old. She had been working at the Consolidated Mines in Gwennap, for about four years, working mostly at the picking table, but occasionally she was called on to barrow, riddle, or spall. Of all the tasks she did, she found barrowing the hardest job of all, and sometimes had to do it all day (presumably at sampling). She said that it gave her back pain. At Consolidated Mines, ore picking was normally done under a shed with a roof but no sides. In winter, this afforded virtually no shelter from the wind and rain, and Martha's feet were often cold and wet. As she only had one pair of shoes, and, having no dry shoes to change into, she reported that she sometimes caught cold.

Martha lived at Bissoe Bridge, which was about three miles walk from the mine. She normally got up at about 4 a.m. and prepared her own breakfast, and would leave home at 5.30 a.m. to start work at 7 a.m. In the evening, she would finish work at 5.30 p.m. and arrive home about 7 p.m. When she arrived home, she would have supper, and then go to bed between 9.30 and 10 p.m., giving her about six and a half hour's sleep. However, for a week or fortnight in every month (at sampling), she would start work an hour earlier at 6 a.m. and not finish until 8 p.m. She admitted how tired she was at these times, with a fourteen hour working day, and about six hours sleep. When sampling was over, the women and girls were allowed one whole day at home to recover, but they were not paid overtime for this extra work. Martha said that work was usually available continuously during the winter months, but, due to water shortages, it was not always available during the summer.

At Consolidated Mines, the bal maidens were allowed an hour for dinner. Martha would take a pasty or hoggan, which could be warmed in the dry when the weather was cold. The girls ate together in the dinner shed. They did not have a mid-morning break, but by 9 or 10 a.m. they were usually already hungry, and would often take a bite or two of their pasties while still working, and when the surface captain wasn't looking!

Martha was one of seven children, and her mother was widowed. Many years previously, her father had gone to Scotland to work, leaving the family in Cornwall. He had been sending money to support his family, but, unfortunately, he died there when she was 6 years old. Her older brothers and sisters went to work at the mine to support the family, and, in due time, she was sent to the mine to work as well. She had one younger sibling not yet working. One of her brothers, who normally worked at Poldice Mine, about five miles away, was chronically ill. She attended the local Methodist Sunday School, and was learning to read and spell. This family appears to be the family of Delia Buckingham of Bissoe, as described in the *1841 Census*, although Martha and her 30 year-old sister Mary were not described as working at the mine, whereas her brothers were. The youngest child of the family was only 2 years old at this time.

When interviewed by Charles Barham for the *1842 Royal Commission*, Martha described having *'overheated her blood'* from carrying too much at the mine, and that she was continuing to *'break out'*. The mine surgeon reported that she was generally healthy, despite a *'cough and papulous eruption'*.

SUSAN WILLS: A Hungry Bal Maiden in the 'Hungry Forties'

Susan Wills was born in St. Agnes on 28th October 1835, and as a child lived in the Trevellas Coombe area. Although she was the daughter of a mine captain (Benjamin Wills), starvation was never very far away during the hungry years of the 1840s, with thirteen in the family to be fed. By 1842, at the age of six, she was already working at the mine. Despite the poverty of her early years, Susan survived to celebrate her 100th and 101st birthdays. She was interviewed on both occasions and some of her memories recorded:

Fig. 74 Susan Robins (née Wills) on her 100^{tth} Birthday
Courtesy of West Briton

'My father was a miner. He only earned 15s per week, and yet he reared a family….I had time to go to school for a short time, but I never wrote a line, and my father taught me to write with a bit of burnt stick. We had very little to eat in those days….Bread and swedes we lived on chiefly, and sometimes we had pilchards when the farmers went to St Agnes to fetch fish to manure their land. They let us go behind their cart and pick up any fish that were shaken off into the road.

I went to work when I was six. About twenty of us, boys and girls, 'dressed' tin at works near St. Agnes Beacon. I left home every morning at six, walked three miles to work, and trudged home again, at six in the evening. Long hours were they, with never a thought of a holiday. Our wages were two and a half pence a day, and if we happened to be a few minutes late or dawdled at work we were 'docked' a quarter.

Before setting out, however, we were not allowed to waste our time so as a whole family we would sit around the kitchen table at four in the morning, knitting the striped stockings which nearly everyone then used to wear. We worked by the light of a tallow candle, and were paid a penny for every once of wool we knitted.' (WB 31st Oct 1935 & 29th Oct 1936)

It seems that the family later moved to the Devon border, presumably for work. Susan was married at Stoke Damerel Church in 1860, to a dockyard worker named Robins. She subsequently had eight children. At 100 and 101 years old she was living with two surviving daughters at Minions, and was still sprightly and alert.

THOMASINE PILL: 'Better the North'

Thomasine Pill (an ancestor of the author) was born in Cocks, a small hamlet in the parish of Perranzabuloe, in 1837, and was the third daughter of copper miner, Robert Pill. Although she had a few years in school, by the time she was 14 years old she had followed her older sisters to work at the mine. They were probably working at the Perran St George Copper Mine out on Cligga Head, which employed about 500 people in the 1850s. All of her brothers or sisters who were over the age of 7 years were working as ore dressers at surface, or below ground with their father. Thomasine continued to work at the mine until her marriage, at the age of 19, to John Bawden, who was also a miner.

After marriage, as was the norm, it seems she did not work at the mine again. She had eleven children, ten of whom survived into adulthood, and all of whom went to the local lead mines to work as soon as they were old enough. In 1875, however, when the mines closed in the parish, Thomasine's husband, John, and some of her sons found work in the Durham coalfields. This was probably offered to them by visiting agents from the northern coalfields, who were looking for non-union Cornish miners to strike-break. They were offering reasonable wages, a one-year contract, accommodation and free travel to miners and their families. The starving Cornish miners would not be happy with this situation but the common saying was *'Better the North than Oversea'*, which was the only other option to find work. So, Thomasine and the family up-rooted, with the exception of the eldest daughter who went into service locally, and moved to Sunniside in Weardale. It seems that Thomasine was pregnant when they made this move, as her last child was born there, soon after. Despite the annual contracts, the Cornish miners were in fact free to go after only six months. Understandable animosity from the local miners often forced the Cornish on, and, in a short time, it seems that Thomasine and her family had moved again.

They moved to the Furness area of Lancashire, where Thomasine already had relatives working. Her widowed mother had travelled there with Thomasine's brother and family some years before. Thomasine's husband, John, and their sons found work at the iron mines at Stank, just outside Barrow in Furness, and they moved into one of the new terraced houses, built especially for the miners, at Roose. This community was known as 'Little Cornwall', and some descendants of those Cornish miners still live there today. Thomasine's husband, John, died very suddenly in March 1883, when Thomasine was only 46 years old, after they had been in Roose for seven years. Thomasine's elder children had left home, or were about to marry, by this time, but she had three children of school age still at home. She resorted to the tried and tested means of supporting herself and her family, relied on by countless generations of miners' widows before her - she rented out a room, and she took in other people's laundry. This first expedient may have had more long-term consequences than she envisaged, as two of her three daughters still at home married two of the lodgers.

Meanwhile, history was to repeat itself, and, by 1888, the mines at Stank closed, so the Cornish miners once again had to move on to find work. Although most of her sons left, Thomasine, at the age of 51, did not go with them this time. She stayed in Roose with two of her married daughters, whose husbands had been offered work in the Vickers Shipyards. Thomasine ended her days in Roose, dying, in November 1906, at the age of

69 years. She is buried in the windswept cemetery in Barrow, overlooking the Irish Sea, a long way from her Cornish home.[19]

LORETTA COON: A Brave Young Woman

Loretta was born in August 1857 at Kilhalland, Tywardreath, and was the daughter of John and Elizabeth Coon. In 1861, while Loretta (Lauretta) was still at home, her father and two sisters were recorded as working at a copper mine, and were almost certainly employed at Fowey Consuls. Sometime before 1871, the family had moved from Kilhalland to St Cleer. This was probably because of the closure of Fowey Consuls in 1867. They went to live in the mining community of Common Moor, where Loretta and her brother, who was four years her senior, both followed their father to the mines. Sadly, by 1871 their father had died, Loretta, at 15 years old, was dressing copper ore, and her brother was mining underground. Most of the other young women living at Common Moor were also bal maidens, including 17 year-old Mary Truscott, and Ann and Christiana Goldsworthy, who were 25 and 34 years old respectively. This little group of women probably made their way to and from the mine together. Perhaps Loretta and Mary would have been particular friends, being of a similar age. Loretta almost certainly continued to work at the mine until her marriage in 1874, and it is there that she probably met her future husband.

Loretta was married at St Cleer Church in August 1874, nine days before her eighteenth birthday, according to her birth certificate, although she was recorded as being fully 18 years old in the marriage register. She married 21 year-old Thomas James Wilton, who was an ex-miner. He was already probably blind at the time of his marriage, and he was working at the local village shop in St Cleer. Although the exact circumstances of him losing his sight are unknown, it is thought that he had been blinded in a mine accident, probably by a delayed or accidental explosion.

It is not known whether Loretta and Thomas had been courting before the accident which blinded him, or if their courtship developed afterwards. Either way, Loretta married him before her eighteenth birthday, her widowed mother presumably giving parental consent, as she was a minor.

Fig. 75 Loretta Wilton (née Coon) with her Husband Thomas, Common Moor c 1910
Courtesy of Edna Collins

Loretta subsequently helped Thomas to run the general shop in St Cleer. They also had fourteen children, although four of the girls tragically died in their first 2 years, and one of the boys at 12 years old. The surviving sons helped Loretta and Thomas with a local coal round in the village. Loretta died in 1926, aged 69, and was buried in the churchyard at St Cleer. Her husband, Thomas, died only a few months later and is buried with her.[20]

THE OLD WOMAN AT CARN: Work or the Workhouse?

When American, William Rideing, and his friends, visited the Carn Brea Copper Mine in 1881, they encountered an elderly woman loading wagons with ore-stuff ready to be taken to the copper crusher. William was so startled by her that he wrote a graphic description of her appearance:

'Picking our way through the purplish mud and stones below Karn [sic], we discovered a little old woman labouring over a pile of unmilled copper ore. We had to look twice before we could assure ourselves of her sex: not only was her dress perplexing, but there was an unreality and weirdness in her person. She was very small, almost dwarfish, with bent shoulders and wrinkled hands and face, her skin had the texture of parchment, and was curiously mottled blue, her hair was thin and wiry.'

She was wearing petticoats which ended above the ankle, and which were stained purple with the hue of the copper. Her legs were covered in woollen wraps, and she was wearing substantial shoes. They watched as she loaded the wagon with ore, using her Cornish shovel, and they noticed the ease and strength with which she moved, despite her age:

'She seemed very old, but her eyes had a shrewd and penetrating quickness, and her movements were utterly without decrepitude. Indeed, she applied herself to her work with the willing vigor of a strong young man. Shovelful after shovelful was thrown in with an easy muscular swing, and with much more activity than the average "navvy" ever exhibits.'

They engaged her in conversation about her age, and the heavy nature of her work. She replied:

'Deed, sir, I don't know how old I am, but I've been at it this forty years. I'm not young any longer, that's sure....No use being tired; when you are tired, there's the workhouse for you.'

When they asked her if she had a husband, she explained that she had never married, and that, since being pushed down stairs by her employer at the age of 24, when she was in domestic service, she had suffered regular fits:

'No, sir; nobody would ever have me, nobody would have me or go with me, as I was always subject to fits – terrible they are. I still have them once or twice a week sometimes.'

Eventually, when she had almost filled the wagon, two other younger bal maidens joined her to help. Then, together with two of the surface labourers, the three women pushed the wagon to the crushers. One of the party visiting with Rideing was an artist, and apparently drew a picture of the scene (Fig. 57). By her own admission, this woman must have been at least 64 years old.[21]

ELIZABETH ASHTON: Assayer and Smelter

The story of Elizabeth Ashton is a remarkable one, and features only our second woman not born in Cornwall. We do not know Elizabeth's maiden name, but she was born in Aylesbury in either 1845 or 1846. Unusually, in her early twenties, she trained as a chemist (probably in London) and this must have been where she met her husband-to-be, Edward Ashton, who was also a trained chemist.

It is not known exactly when Elizabeth and Edward were married, but, after completing his training in 1866, Edward moved from London to St Ives. Together with his brother, Nicholas, he opened chemist's shops in Hayle and St Just; both including a photography studio. It seems Elizabeth remained in London until 1867, when their daughter Minnie was born, but she then followed her husband down to Cornwall. By 1871, the three had also opened a shop in St Ives. They were to run this shop for many years, whereas the first two shops had closed by 1880.

In July 1883, Nicholas Ashton, Elizabeth's brother in law, leased the derelict Wheal Fanny Adela Mine at Carrick Gladden, between Carbis Bay and Lelant, calling it by its original name, Hawke's Point Mine. This mine had been closed since about 1871, but had previously been mined for tin, copper, lead and nickel-silver. The building of the St Ives Railway had resulted in the excavation of a cutting at Hawke's Point, and this revealed some of the old copper lodes. Under the supervision of a Mr. Barry Lord, the Ashtons re-opened the mine.[22] Originally, 19 men were employed, and some quantities of copper and cobalt were extracted. There were high hopes in the St Ives area at the time, that the revival of this mine would provide much-needed employment in the area, but this was not to be. Hamilton Jenkin was uncertain of the exact location of this mine, but believed the workings ran under the headland at Carrack Gladden, adjoining the railway. A surviving sketch map shows Big Ben Tin, Cobalt and Copper and Ashton's Caunter Lodes.[23] To what extent the Ashtons expected to make a commercial venture out of the mine, and how much they intended it just to supply essential elements for their pharmacy and photography business, is not clear. The detailed outcome of this early venture is unknown, but it seems that no great fortune was made by anyone. An ex-miner from Hawke's Point Mine had remarked: *'There was too much of everything and too little of anything ever to make a keenly bal.'*

However, during the subsequent fifteen to twenty years, the three Ashtons continued to run the mine themselves, extracting cobalt, nickel and peacock copper, presumably for use in their chemist and photography business. Together, they dressed, assayed and refined these ores in a small smelting house on top of the cliffs at Hawke's Point, where they were frequently observed working at their furnace all through the night. The ores were separated and the copper dressed in the normal way. The mixed cobalt and nickel ore was probably left in the open air for up to a year so that the cobalt component would oxidise. When this process was complete, the weathered ore would be sieved and crushed to a powder, ready to be burnt in the furnace. After a light roasting, nickel could be run off. Further roasting then reduced the oxidised cobalt to pure cobalt.

During these years of work at the mine and smelter, Elizabeth also carried out most of the dispensing at their chemist shop opposite the Market House in St Ives, and, latterly, ran a 'picnic site', known as *'Grannie Ashton's Tea Gardens'*, from their cottage on Hawke's Point. A visitor described the picnic grounds in 1885:

'Hawke's Point just had the cottage, a round thatched summerhouse, a picnic room, used principally on Bank Holidays, few people going on other days, except private parties. A large studio faced the sea, the view from this studio was exquisite'. [24]

Elizabeth was described as *'quite as good a chemist as her husband'* and *'she had knowledge of most things'*. She was also well-known for her healing powers, ascribing them to the *'magnetic'* qualities of her hands. It is said that a magnet could be deflected when near her, but bearing in mind her years of working with cobalt, which has ferromagnetic properties, this may not be such an unreasonable suggestion. She first started offering massage in about 1875, and, even in her old age, many people still went to 'Little Granny Ashton' in the hopes of finding relief from a whole range of ailments of the muscles and joints. She could also dowse for water, and is said to have found water locally where mining engineers and geologists had failed.[25]

In 1893, Elizabeth was among those who helped to look after the survivors of the ship 'Cintra', which had been wrecked in a gale. Around 1905, when she was about 60 years old, it seems that Elizabeth grew tired of the amount of time and energy that the three were investing in the mine, and the consequent dressing and smelting of the ores, and so she took matters into her own hands. Reputedly, she went down to the workings on her own one evening, and pulled out some of the pit props, causing the roof to fall in, effectively closing the mine.[26]

Both Elizabeth and her husband, Edward, survived into their nineties, with Elizabeth outliving her husband by just twelve months. She died in May 1934, and was buried in Lelant Churchyard. There was a very large attendance at her Requiem Mass at the local Catholic Church. She had long since become quite a local personality!

SIDWELL KRUGE: and the Discovery of the Cobar Copper Field

Sidwell was the daughter of copper miner Ephraim Woolcock and Elizabeth Willoughby, who were married in Illogan in 1821. They lived at Nancekuke Gate, on the outskirts of St Agnes, and subsequently had six children. Sidwell was the fourth, and was born about 1827. Her mother died when she was just 4 years old, and her father remarried two years later. He died when Sidwell was 15 years old, and then her step-mother remarried. Consequently, Sidwell and her youngest sister Mary Ann were both living independently on Illogan Downs, and working at the mines by 1851. Some of their brothers and sisters emigrated to Australia in 1848 or 1849, at first going to Burra and then settling in Armagh, near Clare. Sidwell and Mary followed their family out, where Sidwell helped to look after the children of her married sister, Emily. During this time, she met Henry Kruge, the son of a Norwegian sea captain, and they were married on 19th June 1858 at St Barnabas Church in Clare.

The two of them then embarked on the nomadic life of 'hawking', basically running a mobile general store from their bullock-drawn wagon, travelling the river valleys of Victoria, South Australia, and New South Wales. At some time in the 1860s, they settled in a place in New South Wales that was halfway between the River Murray and Bourke, calling it Gilgunnia. As Henry was skilled in the carpentry and the smithing trades, it was an ideal spot to open a trading post, smithy and workshop, and subsequently a hotel which they named the 'Gilgunnia'. In due course, a small settlement grew up around them, and they opened a post office in their store, with Henry becoming the postmaster.

Meanwhile, they had also acquired the lease of six hundred acres of land and had started to keep livestock. In 1869, there were severe droughts, and the Kruges had to travel with their livestock nearer the Murray River, to Priory Station, in order to find water. Here, they met up with three well diggers, Charles Campbell, and Thomas Hartman, both Danes, and George Gibb from Scotland. Whilst being cut off by floods in the area, some aborigines had helped these three young men find their way through and had led them to their Kubbur waterhole, an old aboriginal sacred place. While camping there, they noticed the unusual blue-green rock in the sides of the water hole. Not knowing what it was, as they were only familiar with gold ore, they took a sample. When they met Sidwell and Henry at Priory Station, they showed them the ore which they had not been able to identify. Despite her relatively tender years as a bal maiden in Cornwall, Sidwell immediately recognised the ore as a form of copper carbonate (probably malachite). They all returned to Gilgunnia, where Henry heated the ore in a crucible to smelt it and poured the molten metal into a sandy groove in the ground. They were able to confirm Sidwell's identification of the ore. The three young men then departed for Bourke, to register a mining claim for the Kubbur area. This was the beginning of what was to become one of the largest copper mining areas in Australia, known as Cobar.

Fig. 76 Sidwell Kruge (née Woolcock) with Husband Henry c. 1885
Courtesy of John Symons

Fig. 77 Gravestone for Sidwell Kruge (Dean) at Cobar
Courtesy of John Symons

Henry and Sidwell did not become involved in the opening up of the mines as such, but continued to run their store and hotel at Gilgunnia. A nephew took over the store and Post Office in 1886, leaving Sidwell and Henry to run the hotel, but Henry died, suddenly, two years later. Sidwell remarried in 1889, her second husband being James William Dean, also a hawker. Subsequently, there were problems with the management of the Post Office, and James left Gilgunnia about 1893. Sidwell continued running the hotel until 1908, probably with assistance from her nephew and his wife. She then sold the hotel and land, and went to live with her niece in Cobar. She died on 17th April 1913, and was buried in the Methodist section of Cobar Cemetery.

As a mark of Sidwell's involvement in the discovery of copper at Cobar, the adventurers of the Cobar Copper Company presented her with a gold brooch with word '*Regards*' set in diamonds! The date of this presentation is unknown, but was probably after 1885, when the Cobar Copper Company was making good profits. The Stele monument was erected in Cobar in 1969 to commemorate the part Campbell, Hartman and Gibb played in the founding of both the mining industry and the township, but no mention is made on it of Sidwell and Henry Kruge. Today, however, there is a commemorative display, telling their story, in the Great Cobar Heritage Centre.[27] Henry and Sidwell are honoured as the founders of the township of Gilgunnia.

LIFE AT THE BUDDLES AND STRIPS

The Troon Women's Institute Scrapbook of 1952 records the memories of women who had worked at the mines in their younger days. This is how Mrs. Collins recalled her time at working at the strips at Wheal Grenville, probably around 1890:

'*I started work at Wheal Grenville when I was eleven. We girls started at seven every morning and worked until half past five. Whit Mondays and Midsummer days we started at five to leave off at eleven but then sometimes it was nearly twelve before we could leave work. I can remember hurrying home to wash and change and have dinner in time to walk with the schools.*

We worked very hard. Sometimes I must have lifted hundred weights in a day. The buddles used to fill up and had to be cleaned out three times a day. They had to be cleaned out about half past nine, then again before dinner and again in the afternoon. Four men cleaned out the buddles. They wheeled the head to me in a wheelbarrow and I had to return it to the buddle again for another washing. That was done three times, then it had to be taken to the packing house. I liked a sharp shovel, the sharper the better. I used to take mine to the men to be sharpened.

Sometimes we had to help the men. We filled the kieves with water from the launder and then carried a kieve of water across to the men, as much as two of us could lift.

I started work for 1s 6d per week. When I was seventeen I had 18s per month. I left and went into service because that was not enough money.'[28]

MISS BICKERLEG: In the Sampling Room

In the *Troon WI Scrapbook*, there is also what is possibly a unique description of what occurred in the sampling room at Dolcoath, in the early 1880s. The daughter of the mine assayer remembered the scene clearly:

'This was a large room, which had a huge fireplace at one end. All round were shelves and a long table filled the centre. Square pieces of thick white paper almost like parchment, each about a foot square, were arranged on the shelves and the table. These each held a sample of tin ore with the name and working position in the mine of the man who had submitted it, to be smelted to find the value of tin. Each one had to be separately smelted in a container shaped like a flower pot made of earthenware, greyish green in colour, glazed and specially treated to be resistant to the terrific heat needed to separate the tin from the other materials. These containers were known as crucibles.'

She then recalls her father's assistant, a Miss Bickerleg, who she described as always wearing a black dress, well covered with a large white apron and a 'bal maiden's' gook to protect her hair. This is how she remembered her work:

'Carefully brushing every scrap of tin from the crucible onto a very small pair of brass scales, the size of a child's toy, she would say 'We must be very careful about this, my dear, as it means the men's living'. Instead of using, as might have been expected, a brush - she used a hare's foot explaining that it was so fine no tin would be held in it, to cause any waste. The tin was then placed in an envelope with the weight, value of the sample and the man's name and working position written on it, to correspond with the paper square.'

As yet, it has not been possible to identify this woman. However, she was obviously held in high respect, as this concluding remark observes: *'Miss Bickerleg had the reputation, among the men with whom she worked, of 'knowing as much about tin as they did'.'* [29]

BETTY: A Counthouse Maid

Mrs Betty Webb was another whose memories were recorded in the *Troon Scrapbook*.[30] She had been one of the Counthouse women at Dolcoath, probably in the 1890s. This is how she remembered her work:

'Four women worked at Dolcoath Count House when I was there. Their work was similar to any person in service. Each person had her own job. There was a cook and a girl to help on the kitchen. The others cleaned the rooms of the Managers and the Clerks, and the bathrooms. On Mondays the towels and tablecloths were washed and ironed. Every day we cooked lunch for the Captains and the Clerks.

On 'Sist' days the men had part of their pay that was on the first fortnight every month. Then we cooked a special roast dinner. Full pay came once a month and then a big dinner was cooked for the Managers and Clerks and the underground shift Bosses and the Surface Captains.

However, all the women worked hard. We all looked forward to the Saturday before Christmas when Christmas dinner was eaten. On the Friday we often worked until 10 o'clock. The best tablecloths and glasses and the silver made the tables look very nice. I remember that for one Christmas dinner we cooked a boiled turkey, 3 roast geese, some chicken and roast beef and vegetables. Also we had afterwards a Christmas pudding and all kinds of fruit. There were drinks and smokes. When the men left, the women used to have their dinners. We worked hard but we enjoyed ourselves.'

HETTIE JULIAN AND THE DAVIS SISTERS: Working at the Monitors

During the First World War, some women took over the tasks of men in the 'clay bottoms' of the Clay Pits. By this time, all the pits were very deep, and, at most works, the clay was removed by the hydraulic method. This involved men loosening the sides of the clay pits by explosives, and then the broken clay matrix being washed out of the clay pit sides by directing water through narrow hose nozzles at pressure. The hoses were usually held on a wooden frame, and directed by an operator by means of a lever arrangement. These hoses became known as 'monitors' due to their lizard-like appearance. The liquid clay 'wash' was channelled into gullies and eventually pumped up from the quarry to the separating and settling tanks.

Fig. 78 May and Jane Davis
Rocks Clay Works

It was this task of handling the hoses which was done by the women. During the course of their shift, the women would need to keep moving the jet of water over the 'washing face' in order to obtain an even sample and to 'advance' the face safely. At regular periods, the position of the hoses and frames would need to be moved in order to work on another part of the face of the clay.

Three of the women who carried out this work were May and Jane Davis, and Hettie Julian. The Davis sisters worked at Rocks Clay Works under Captain Fred Pinch. They were two of four women working in pairs on six-hour shifts. Although they were expected to work in all weathers, apparently they were given slightly favoured treatment, compared to the men, by the captain, and were told *'when ice forms on your oilers* [oilskins]*, you can leave the bottoms for a warm up'!* Fig. 79 shows three of these women operating the monitors from a wooden platform, forming a bridge over the liquid clay,.

Hettie Julian was the daughter of Captain Jack Julian (also known as Capt. Guts!) of Bluebarrow Clay Works. She was selected specifically to work at Bluebarrow, when they were short handed during the First World War, because the family lived in a house on site, and so no special provision needed to be made for a female employee! Like the Davis sisters, she too worked 'on the hose' in those wartime years. Her father was in his mid-sixties at the time, and, if there was a problem with the pumps at the pit overnight, she would go to sort it out, so that her father was not disturbed. This involved going out into the vast clay pit with a lantern, whatever the weather, and climbing down into the pump shaft. Once there, and having secured her lighting, she had to use an enormous spanner to undo sixteen two-inch nuts on the air seal door. Having loosened the nuts, she would then have to swing open the steel door (which weighed three hundred pounds) by its chain. She then had to remove any obstructions very quickly from the valve below, as, once this air seal was broken, the shaft would very rapidly fill with water. She then had to do this all in reverse and find her way back home safely.[31]

Fig. 79 Women Working at the Monitors Rocks Clay Works First World War
(including May and Jane Davis)
Figs 78 & 79 Courtesy of China Clay Country Park Mining & Heritage Centre

PHYLLIS THOMAS: On the Picking Belt

This is the first-hand account of Phyllis Lockett (née Thomas), who worked at the tin picking belt at Geevor Mine during the Second World War. Sadly Phyllis died only a few months after she wrote these words:

'During the Second World War seven of us worked on the picking belt at Geevor Tin Mine, while the men were away. We were all single, except for one who was a widow. Our job was to remove as much of the waste from the tin-bearing ore as possible, before it went to the crushers. We all lived in the village of Pendeen. When we started we had no real training; we were just shown what to do by the supervisor.

The hooter sounded at Geevor at 8 o'clock to start work; at 12 o'clock for dinner time, at 1 o'clock to be back at work, and at 5 o'clock to finish for the day. It also sounded at the New Year and any other special occasion. Our normal working day, then, was eight hours, but we had to work late if the plant broke down. We worked a full day Monday to Friday, and then Saturday mornings as well.

The seven of us who worked on the picking belt all changed places every hour so that we all took it in turns at the different jobs, including lifting off the large granite stones. Some were very big and could not go down the chute, so they were thrown on the floor to be broken up by the foreman. If a stone got jammed in the washer chute we had to run around shutting down the plant, and then start it all up again when it was clear. The ore-stuff had first come through the washer, so we always had our fingers in water. The other smaller pieces of granite which we picked out were put on another conveyor belt, to be disposed of. This ore was carried to another house where it was delivered down chute into waiting trucks. This was then on to the crushers.

Fig. 80 The Late Phyllis Lockett (née Taylor), Geevor Picking Belt 2004
Courtesy of Ann Donnithorne & Fiona Young

Sometimes we had to work until 11 p.m. if there had been a breakdown, so that all the tin was gone from the main bunkers for the night-shift men to have room in their bin. We had plenty of other jobs to go to while the fitter was mending the machinery. One was to clean the tin sacks. This was done on the tin floors, and we used to beat the bags on an iron stand and then pick off the pieces of string. Another job was to get in the bunker and clear out all the tin that had been left in the corners and shovel it through the square holes out to the shaking tables.

The washer and crusher were very noisy, and we couldn't hear ourselves speak. We used to lip read and made up our own sign language. The working conditions were also very dirty. However, we worked undercover, in sheds, so that we were able to work despite weather conditions. Sometimes small pieces of spar would fly up into our eyes, and we would have to go to the first aid post to have it taken out.

There was a canteen at Weatherhead, and we used to have pasties from there, which we ordered early, if we didn't go home for lunch. Sometimes we brought our own lunch. We had our own little tearoom and took it in turns making tea. We took our tea breaks two at a time. We wore our own clothes and shoes to work, and some of us brought clogs, as they lasted longer. We were paid weekly.

Although working on the picking belt was hard work, we all got on well and we all enjoyed ourselves.' [32]

Richard Lawry, who was the person responsible for overseeing the machinery on the picking belt at this time, remembered that, for the war effort, the normal three shifts at Geevor were reduced to two, with these women working the daytime rota. He had been responsible for showing Phyllis, and the other women, how to distinguish the ore-bearing rock and remove the waste. Like her, he also described the noise on the belts as *'unbearable'*. It was hard work indeed! [33]

MRS. MINNIE ANDREWS: The Last Bal Maiden?

Minnie Andrews was born in Camborne in 1874. She was interviewed by a journalist from the Cornishman newspaper in April 1967, and a few weeks later by Justin Brooke. It was believed she was one of the last surviving bal maidens, if not *the* last, in Cornwall, who had worked on the traditional dressing floors. She was then in her early nineties, and, when asked about her days at the mines, she could still give a very clear account of her experiences. [34]

She was born in a house adjacent to the square in Beacon, on the outskirts of Camborne. She was possibly the daughter of William Symonds Harris, a tin miner from Marazion, and Mary Ann, who was born in Crowan. Even before she began work, she was familiar with work at the mine, as, from the age of 5, she used to carry dinner to her father at Carn Camborne, just over the road from her home. He subsequently suffered ill-health, and, when Minnie was about 9 years old, he became too ill to carry on mining. It was then that she was sent to join other girls from the village already working on the dressing floors at West Wheal Francis. She remembered having to leave home very early to walk across the moors to start work at 7 a.m. She recalled that they were allowed twenty minutes for crowst and half an hour for dinner.

She first worked at the racking frames, and remembered how difficult it was. She had to learn how to keep the channels of the frame unblocked. She worked long hours and described how desperately cold and painful her hands became:

'I was turt [taught] to the frames and cleaning the holes and getting the water to run, and taking out gravels out from the holes; it did choke up the holes, you know, they things. Oh, I worked awful hours, mister, because I been dying with the cold, my hands, no wonder they go dead, I didn't, they don't go dead, my lor'.'

After learning to rack, she sometimes had to fill the buddles. These she filled twice a day, while the young men would empty them out when the ores had separated out. At first, she was earning fourteen shillings per month. By the time she was 18 years old, she was earning eighteen shillings per month, but that year the mine closed, and she had to find alternative employment. She went to work at Betty Adit, Tincroft.

She worked at several different mines over the years, depending on the availability of work, and the wages offered. She said that the girls and women would often move to work at another mine if the rates offered were better. Wages also increased with age, but the most she ever earned was twenty-two shillings per month. She commented several times that she often worked harder than the men, presumably meaning the surface labourers, who actually earned much more.

At some stage, Minnie worked picking copper at Carn Camborne, where her father had worked. While there, she worked with an elderly lady, possibly a widow, called Anna Sincock. Their task was to remove the 'deads', leaving the better ore in the strip ready for washing and dressing. Over time, she also worked at Dolcoath, as well as at several tin streams, including Old's and Rodda's. She did not like working at Dick Old's, as he was so abusive:

'I worked down Dick Hole/Old's streams. And then I worked down to Rodda's streams, down by the adit. That's the only streams I worked. They two. Dick Old. You wouldn't look your head off from what you was doing, the old fool would have a stick aimed at 'ee, or something thrown at 'ee. Oh, he's some demon, he was, an old thing, he was. He'd thraw a stick at 'ee.'

Coming from a very poor family, Minnie only had one hessian work apron, unlike some of the other bal maidens who had one apron to work in, and a better one, possibly of cotton or linen, to wear for best, and to and from work. Instead, she would try to wash her hessian one as white as she could. It seemed to be a matter of pride to look as smart as possible. She also described the hand cloths they used to wear to protect their hands:

'We wore a towser. I used to come home in the evenings and wash my towser. I never had but one, I was too poor to buy the rest, I tell you true; I never bought but one. I had to wash un every so often, and he was white, he was lovely, he was, he wasn't a white stuff, he's like the hessian bags you do see, and you try wash em' white, come white lovely. And I used to go Monday mornings with a clean towser on, clean hand-clothes; we put hand-clothes on our hands, 'cause we was proud, we didn't want to soil our hands.'

Minnie wore *'a sun bonnet'* at work, and she described how some women covered their faces with the bottom edges, just leaving the eyes uncovered:

'I had a sun-bonnet. Could be pinned round here [round her neck]. *When I worked West Frances* [there was a woman who] *used to pin the bonnet in round, that nobody shouldn't see her face, hardly, or just leave her eyes showing.'*

For most of the time as an adult, Minnie worked at Tincroft. Here, as one of the more senior, and obviously more reliable, girls, it was her job to go to the women's shed to get ready for dinner time. She would be responsible for making the tea and warming the pasties and organising the tea rota for about a dozen other women and girls:

'I used to go in the dinner-house…to get their food ready and the hot water and things; used to put their pasties and things in the oven and warm them again and they come in twelve o'clock and…get their tea ready, and then I used to tell them when it was turn for them to bring their tea. Now I used to say 'You must bring your tea, whose turn is it?'

Fig. 81 Minnie Andrews 1967
Courtesy of Cornish Telegraph

She remembered that when she was about 14 years old, they journeyed to work from Beacon to Tincroft during the blizzards of 1891 by walking over the tops of the hedges. Once there, they still had to work, despite the appalling weather conditions. Another story she told was of some of the other girls from Beacon being persuaded to go underground, which was normally considered very unlucky. Minnie refused to go with them. They were caught and the man who took them down was severely reprimanded by the mine captain! When working at Brea Tin Streams, she remembered going to the Brea Inn for *'a quick penny glass of porter'* with some of the other women and girls for a treat on pay day, but added *'but I never liked the stuff!'*

Eventually, Minnie married a miner from Tincroft, and, as was the custom, gave up her work at the mines. She continued to live in the village of Beacon all her life. She raised one son and two daughters, and was widowed for the last seventeen years of her life. Sadly, she died within a year of these two fascinating interviews. Her last days were spent at Barncoose Hospital, and she was buried at the cemetery in Troon in March 1968.[35]

What a precious record these two interviews are, preserving Minnie's memories of a lost age, giving us insights into the real lives of the bal maidens, the language in which they spoke, and the words and expressions which they used. It seems a world away from the rather pristine and sentimental pictures that the Victorian visitor to the mines would give us. Here, along with the other stories, we can begin to glimpse the rough, tough, real world of the bal maiden. The rest we can only surmise.

FOOTNOTES

1. Brooke Mine Index (CRO X 745/40).
2. MJ 24th Dec 1842 p. 415.
3. Treleaven Letters in Brooke (1980) p. 31.
4. WB 18th May 1844; WB 30th Aug 1844; Porth Towan Lease (CRO: M 1375 + 1377); RCG 9th July 1870.
5. WB 12th May 184; WB 18th May 1844.
6. Tangye (1988) p. 50.
7. Cornubian 31st May 1895 p. 4; Mitchell p. 169.
8. Best, R. S. *Life and Good Works of J. P. Edwards* (Dyllansow Truran 1981) p. 32.
9. WB 2nd Nov 1869.
10. Barton, R. (1966) p. 86.
11. Barton, R. (1966) p. 90, 98.
12. Wade, E. A. *The Redlake Tramway & China Clay Works* (Twelveheads 2004) p. 13).
13. Barton, R. (1966) p. 98.
14. Tremellin (1841).
15. Bridewell Admissions Book (CRO: AD 1676/1/2 Entry No. 6605).
16. Bodmin Quarter Sessions (CRO: QS1 12/300).
17. Personal correspondence (TT/LM 2005).
18. CEC (1842) Evidence No. 86.
19. Mayers, Lynne *Miners, Midwives and Mathematicians* (2000).
20. Private correspondence (EC/LM 2001).
21. Rideing (1881) pp. 808-812.
22. Western Echo 19th May 1928; Cornishman 26th July 1883.
23. Hamilton Jenkin (1978) *St Ives* p. 38; Chellow Collection (CRO: CH 27/10).
24. 'Carbis Bay; After the Mines Closed' *St Ives Archives Study Centre News* (Spring 2004) p. 8.
25. St Ives Times 4th May 1934.
26. Hamilton Jenkin (1978) *St Ives* p. 38.
27. Personal corresp. (JS/LM2002 + 2004).
28. Troon WI (1952) pp. 16-17.
29. Troon WI (1952) pp. 13-15.
30. Troon WI (1952) pp. 18-19.
31. Personal correspondence (JT/LM2002).
32. Personal correspondence (PL/LM J2003).
33. Lawry, Richard Nicholas *Scrapbook of Memories of a Pendeen Man: My Early Life* p. 23.
34. Cornishman 6th Apr 1967; Brooke (1967).
35. WB 7th March 1968.

GLOSSARY

Account house; *see* **counthouse**.
Adventurer; shareholder in a cost book mine.
Anker; small barrel.
Attle; waste rock.
Beetal; mallet used for splitting slates.
Beetle; *see* **beetal**.
Benefication; medieval term for ore dressing.
Bing ore; lead ore reduced to small hazelnut-sized pieces after 'cobbing'. A term more commonly used in the Pennines.
Blende; zinc ore.
Boxes; tables where ore is picked.
Bucking; method of breaking cobbed copper or lead ore down to fine granules and powder.
Bucking hammer; short-handled hammer with a flat face for bucking ore.
Bucking plate; cast iron anvil on which ores are bucked.
Buddle; rectangular or round apparatus for separating fine ores from waste.
Buddling; one of the sedimentation techniques for separating ore from waste.
Burning house; *see* **calciner**.
Calciner; furnace for roasting ore to remove arsenic.
Captain; mine overseer, origin of word uncertain. In Cornish mines, captains were sometimes given separate areas of responsibility, i.e. underground captain, surface captain etc.
Casserite; tin oxide.
Casualties; *see* **leavings**.
Chimming; tozing with the kieve at a 45 degree angle.
Cobbing; method of breaking medium grade copper or lead ore into small pieces, to separate waste.
Cobbing hammer; short-handled hammer, with slightly pointed end, for cobbing ore.
Core; one shift at the mine.
Cost book; accounts ledger for mine or clay works.
Counthouse; mine office.
Cover; a reservoir for holding tin slimes.
Crazing mill; mill used in early days of Cornish mining for grinding stamped ore into fine grains. Originally hand powered, then water or horse driven.
Crib; midday meal at the mine.
Crib bag; a rough linen drawstring bag used by mine workers for holding a pasty or hoggan for dinner. Usually made out of flour bag material.
Crib house; dinner shed at mine or clay pit.
Croust; mid morning break.
Deads; waste material.
Dilluing; similar to hand jigging, but using fine hair sieve to wash fine ore or tin-stuff under water.
Doles; piles of crushed ore, usually two or three feet high with flat summits, laid out ready for sampling.
Dradge or drage; *see* **dredge**.
Drags; settling pits for separating mica and sand from china clay.
Dredge; stony ore of low value.
Dresser; *see* **grass captain**.
Fire-setting; method by which ore-bearing rock is dislodged from a rock face by building fire at its base, and then cracking it with cold water. (Pre explosives era).
Foul tin; tin-stuff or mixed material before dressing.

Frame; large rectangular frame, built on the slant which is used to separate very fine tin particles from fine waste, by running water across it.
Framing; the finest sedimentation technique to separate tin ore from waste using ragging frame.
Fuggan; *see* **hoggan.**
Gangue; medium grade copper ore.
Garboldi; *see* **garribaldi.**
Garribaldi; bodice worn by bal maidens.
Gollibolder; dialect for **garribaldi.**
Gook; felt or cotton bonnet with wide brim and edge falling over shoulders.
Grass; surface of the mine.
Grass captain; supervisor of dressing floor. Occasionally 'Dresser' or 'Materials Man'
Halvans; poor copper ore-stuff separated after the first washings, and often reprocessed.
Halvings, *see* **halvans.**
Han(n)aways; *see* **halvans.**
Hennaways; *see* **halvans.**
Hoggan; coarse savoury barley bread. Fuggan is the sweet version with raisins.
Huggan; *see* **hoggan.**
Hures; copper ore-stuff.
Hutch; a shelter without sides, a water reservoir, or a wooden box for holding tin slimes.
Hutch work; *see* **jigging.**
Jack; zinc ore.
Jigging; sieving fine copper or tin-stuff under water, in order to raise light waste to the top. Initially done by hand, but eventually mechanised.
Karer; a sieve.
Kibble; large iron or steel bucket for bringing ore up from mine.
Kieve; vat or large barrel for washing ore.
Kitty bags; leg protectors worn by bucking girls, probably made of tarred canvas.
Knits; small particles of lead ore.
Knock-bark; lead ore reduced to pea sized pieces (equivalent to bucked copper ore).
Knocking; part of the dressing procedure for lead ore where ore is reduced to small pieces, equivalent to cobbing in copper dressing.
Lappior; old name for boys and girls who worked at the buddles.
Launder; wooden gully through which water was delivered to machinery at the mine.
Leavings; poor tin or copper ore left after the first washings, often reprocessed.
Limp; semi-circular flat board used for skimming off waste from sedimented ore in the kieve. Originally made of wood, sometimes shod with iron on the circular edge. Latterly made of iron.
Loobs; tin slime or sludge containing mineral.
Materials man; *see* **grass captain.**
Monitor; the high pressure hose pipe used for washing out clay at the clay pits, named after its particular configuration on the wooden support frame.
Mundic; iron pyrites, arsenic or sulphur waste from tin ore copper dressing.
Niflin; traditional Cornish meal made from dried cod.
Orthoclase; *see* **potash felspar.**
Parcel; a measured heap of ore, dressed and ready for sale.
Peasy; lead rich sediment obtained from the kieve.
Picking rough; copper hures which after sieving were sent to the picking table to be sorted.
Pillas; barley like grain that will grow on very poor soils, commonly grown in Cornwall up to the beginning of the 20th century.
Potash felspar; important constituent of glass.
Prill; piece of pure ore.
Racking; *see* **framing.**
Racking frame; *see* **frame.**
Recking; *see* **framing.**
Reeders; towers of china clay blocks set out to dry, or the reed hurdles that covered them.

Rill; inner part of dole assayed at sampling.
Shaft small; the finest copper hures which pass through the sieve on riddling and were sent straight to the bucking table.
Shambles; place where waste from the mine is taken.
Shed; long side-less shelter under which the cobbers or buckers work.
Shoad; *see* **shode**
Shode; rock containing tin ore.
Sist; *see* **subsistence**.
Slimes; fine mud containing metallic ore.
Smitham; lead ore sediment obtained after its final washings.
Soap rock clay; soapstone.
Spalling; breaking of larger rock pieces from the mine into suitable size for the stamps (tin) or for the crushers or cobbing (copper).
Spalling hammer; long-handled, blunt-ended hammer for breaking large lumps of rock.
Stamps; ore crushing machines for tin, originally water powered, latterly steam or electrically powered.
Stanking widths; puddling framed tin with the feet, to raise any remaining water to the surface.
Strake; wooden trough in which copper ore is placed for washing and sorting.
Streke; *see* **strake**.
Strips; sedimentation areas for collecting the tin-stuff that had passed through the gratings at the tin stamps, where material was tossed, with a shovel, against the flow of water to separate out the waste.
Subsist; *see* **subsistence**.
Subsistence; half wages paid ahead of time, where need was demonstrated.
Summer saving; china clay left to dry in sun pans over the summer months.
Sun-rising houses; houses built overnight on common land, in order to gain tenancy. A chimney had to be built, and a fire lit, before dawn.
Surface captain; *see* **grass captain**.
Surface labourer; male manual labourers on the dressing floors who carried out the heaviest tasks such as kibble landing, wheal-barrowing and ragging.
Tailings; worthless portions of ore washings.
Terloobing; *see* **tozing**.
Thumblebeans; *see* **thumblebinds**.
Thumblebinds; leg protectors, made by twisting straw into ropes around the thumb.
Ticketing; selling of ore.
Tossing; *see* **tozing**.
Towrag; traditional Cornish meal made from dried cod.
Towser; the hessian working apron worn by bal maidens at the mine.
Towzing; *see* **tozing**.
Tozing; settling fine tin ore in kieves by knocking the side of barrel, manually or mechanically, until the fine ore settled at the bottom.
Train oil; oil from pilchards, and used for rush lights. Usually stored in large earthenware pots outside the home.
Travelling iron; gouge used in the quarries for marking slates prior to shaping them.
Tribute; typically Cornish system of employment at the mines, where a team accepts work at a given rate for ore raised from a prescribed area in the mine.
Trunking; part of the tin dressing process, separating slimes ready for framing.
Venturer; *see* **adventurer**.
White granite; china stone.
Winter saving; china clay left to dry in sun pans over the winter months.
Yard of cardboard; bal maidens' headwear made from fabric covered cardboard placed on top of head and tied with a second piece of fabric under the chin.

REFERENCES

Agricola, Georgius. (1556) *De Re Metallica,* H. & L. Hoover (Ed.) (repr. Dover, 1950).
Baker, Helen. (1951) 'Clay Works, Castle an Dinas', in *Cornwall Federation of Women's Institutes Nancledra Scrapbook.*
Ball Clay Heritage Society. (2003)*The Ball Clays of Devon and Cornwall.*
Ballantyne, R. M. (1897) *Deep Down* (Ward Lock).
Barham, Charles. (1842) *The Employment of Children and Young People in the Mines of Cornwall and Devonshire,* Winstanley, Ian (Ed.) (Pics Publishing 1999; www.cmhrc.co.uk/site/literature/royalcommissionreports/).
Bartlett, Stephen. (1994) *The Mines and Mining Men of Menheniot* (Twelveheads).
Barton, D. B. (1961) *A History of Copper Mining in Cornwall and Devon* (Truro Bookshop).
――――― (1968) *Essays in Cornish Mining History Vol. 1* (Bradford Barton).
――――― (1970) *Newham, Calenick and Treyrew, the Genesis of Reverberatory Tin Smelting* in Essays in Cornish Mining Vol. 2 (Bradford Barton 1970) pp 85-100.
――――― (1971) *The Mines and Mine Railways of East Cornwall and West Devon* (Bradford Barton).
――――― (1989) *A History of Tin Mining and Smelting in Cornwall* (Cornwall Books).
Barton, Rita. M. (1966) *The Cornish China Clay Industry* (Bradford Barton).
Beare, Thomas. (1586) *The Bailiff of Blackmoor,* J. A. Buckley (Ed.) (repr. Penhellick 1994).
Boase, Henry. (1819) 'On the Tin Ore of Botallack and Levant', *Trans. Royal. Soc. Cornwall* Vol. 2 p. 383.
Booker, Frank. (1971) *Industrial Archaeology of the Tamar Valley* (David & Charles).
――――― (1974) *Industrial Archaeology of the Tamar Valley* (David & Charles).
――――― (1971) *Morwhellam* (Dartington Amenity Research Trust).
Borlase, William. (1758) *Natural History of Cornwall.*
Borne, F. W. (1872) *The King's Son or A Memoir of Billy Bray* (Bible Christian Book-Room).
Bottrell, W. (1870) *Traditions and Hearthside Stories of West Cornwall* (repr. Newcastle 1973).
BPP 1799 HM Government Report for the Committee appointed to enquire into the state of the Copper Mines and Copper Trade of this Kingdom (London).
BPP 1857 62.87-91, *Select Committee on the Rating of Mines.*
BPP 1864 70.192-207, *Epitome of Evidence to Lord Kinnaird's Commission Appointed to Inquire into the Condition of All Mines in Great Britain.*
Brooke, Justin. (1967) *Transcript of Interview with Mrs. Minnie Andrews.*
――――― (1978) 'Stannary Tales', *British Mining* No. 8 p. 20.
――――― (1980) *Stannary Tales* (Twelveheads).
――――― (1994) *The Tin Streams of Wendron* (Twelveheads).
Brooks, Tony. (2004) *Great Rock: Devon's Metal Last Mine* (Cornish Hillside).
Broughton D. G. (1971) 'A Land Half Made', *Kingston Geol. Rev.* No. 2 Vol. 1. (6).
Buckley, Allen. (2007) *Princes of the Working Valley* (Truran).
Buckley, J. A. (1990) *A History of South Crofty Mine* (Dyllansow Truran).
――――― (1988) *The Cornish Mining Industry: A Brief History* (Tor Mark).
Buller, Rev. John. (1842) *A Statistical Account of the Parish of St Just in Penwith* (fasc. Dyllansow Truran 1983).
Burke, Gill. (1986) 'The Decline of the Independent Bal Maiden' in Angela V. John, (Ed.) *Unequal Opportunities. Women's Employment in England 1800-1918* (Blackwell).
Burritt, Elihu. (1865) *A Walk from London to Land's End and Back* (Sampson).
Burt, Roger. (1977) *John Taylor, Mining Entrepreneur 1779-1863* (Moorland).
――――― (1982) *British Ore Preparation Techniques in the 18th and 19th Centuries* (De Archeolkogische Pers).
――――― (1984) *The British Lead Mining Industry* (Dyllansow Truran).
――――― (1969) (Ed.) *Cornish Mining; Essays on the Organisation of Cornish Mines and the Cornish Mining Economy* (David & Charles).
Burt, Roger; Wilkie, Ian. (1984) 'Manganese Mining in the South West of England', *Jour. Trevithick Soc.* No. 11 pp. 18-40.
Carpenter, Frank. (1993) 'China Clay Workers', *Old Cornwall* Vol. 11 No. 5 p. 211.
Chamber's. (Ed.) (1853) 'The Mines and Miners of Cornwall' in *Chamber's Repository.*
Clark, Stafford. (1995) *Mining and Quarrying in the Teign Valley* (Orchard).
Claughton, Peter. (1994) 'Silver-Lead, A Restricted Resource', *PDMHS* Bull. Vol. 12 (3) pp. 54-9.
Collins, J. H. (1878) *The Hensbarrow Granite District* (fasc. Cornish Hillside 1992).
Corin, John. (1997) *Levant, a Champion Cornish Mine* (Trevithick Soc.).

Cunnack, Richard John. (1845) *The Cunnack Manuscript,* Justin Brooke (Ed.) (Trevithick Soc. 1993).
Darlington, John. (1878) 'On the Dressing of Ores' in *Ure's Dictionary of Arts, Manufactures, and Mines* (repr. Dragonwheel 2002).
De la Beche, H. T. (1839) *Geol. Report on Cornwall, Devon and Somerset* (Longmans).
Deacon, Bernard. (1998) 'A Forgotten Stream' *Cornish Studies* No. 6 (Exeter) pp. 96-117.
Earl, Bryan. (1994) *Cornish Mining* (Cornish Hillside).
——— (1996) *The Cornish Arsenic Industry* (Penhellick).
Esquiros, Alphonse. (1865) *Cornwall and Its Coasts* (Chapman & Hall).
Fiennes, Celia. (1699) *The Journeys of Celia Fiennes*, Christopher Morris (Ed.) (Cresset Press 1949).
Furze, Sidney. (1936) 'Tin Dressing', *Roy. Cornwall. Polytech. Soc. Rep.* pp. 21-22.
Gerrard, Sandy. (2000) *The Early British Tin Industry* (Tempus).
Gill, Michael. (1994) 'New Needs, New Technologies; the 18th Century Dressing and Smelting of Lead in the 18th Century Britain', in P. Benoit (Ed.) *Mines et Metallurgie* (Lyons: Programme Rhone-Alps No 21)
Goodridge, J. C. (1964) 'Devon Great Consols; A Study of Victorian Mining Enterprise', *Trans. Devon. Assoc.* No. 96.
Greeves, Tom. (2006) 'Women, Tinworks and Mines', *Dartmoor Mag.* No. 83 pp. 8-10.
Hamilton Jenkin, A. K. (1948) *The Cornish Miner* (Allen & Unwin).
——— (1951) *News from Cornwall* (Westway).
——— (1967) *Mines and Miners of Cornwall ; Part 13; The Lizard, Falmouth, Mevagissey* (Truro).
——— (1976) *Mines and Miners of Cornwall; Part 15; Calstock, Callington and Launceston* (Forge).
——— (1978) *Mines and Miners of Cornwall Part 1; St. Ives* (Forge).
——— (1978) *Mines and Miners of Cornwall Part 2; St. Agnes and Perranporth* (Forge).
——— (1979) *Mines and Miners of Cornwall Part 3; Redruth* (Forge).
——— (2005) *Mines of Devon* (Landmark Collectors Library).
Harris, T. R. (1974) *Dolcoath: Queen of Cornish Mines* (Trevithick Soc.).
Harrison, Barbara. (1989) 'Some of Them Gets Lead Poisoned', *Soc. Hist. of Med.* Vol. 2 pp 171-195.
Hatchett, Charles. (1796) *The Hatchett Diary*, Arthur Raistrick Ed. (Bradford Barton 1967).
Henderson, James. (1858) 'On Methods Generally Adopted in Cornwall in Dressing Tin and Copper Ores', *Proc. Inst. Civil Eng.* Vol. 18 pp. 195-220.
Henwood, George. (1855) 'Four Lectures on Geology and Mining: 2. Observations on Certain Tin Works in the County of Cornwall', *MJ.* p. 11.
——— (1855) 'Four Lectures on Geology and Mining: 4. On the Manipulation of the Ores of Devon and Cornwall to Render them Marketable', *MJ* p. 8.
——— (1857-8) *Cornwall's Mines and Miners*, Roger Burt (Ed.) (Bradford Barton 1972).
——— (1858) 'The Bal Maiden' *MJ.* Vol. 16 p. 36.
Henwood, W. J. (1826) 'On the Manipulation to which the Ores of Tin and Copper are Subjected in the Central District of Cornwall', *Geol. Soc. Cornwall* Vol. 4 pp. 145-165.
——— (1838) 'Cornish Mining Statistics', *MJ. Review (MJ Suppl* .No. 4 Vol 4, 30th Apr 1838).
——— (1843) *Metalliferous Deposits of Cornwall and Devon* (London).
Hocking, Salome. (1886) *Norah Lang, the Mine Girl* (Crombie).
Honor, Charles Garton. (1869) *Fish, Tin, Copper* (Lister).
Hooson, W. (1747) *The Miners Dictionary* (transcr. IMM 1979).
Hudson, Kenneth. (1959) *The History of English China Clays* (David & Charles).
Hunt, Robert. (1884) *British Mining* (Lockwood).
——— (1887) *A Historical Sketch of British Mining* (repr. EP Publishing 1999).
J. H. (Mine Engine Driver). (1871-1908) *Reminiscences of Old Times,* transcr. M. J. Groombridge, (CRO DDX 152/11 1955).
James, C. C. (1972) *History of Gwennap* (Private Publication).
Jenkin, John. (1888) *Delabole Slate Quarry; a Sketch by a Workman on the Quarry* (Everleigh).
Joseph, Peter. (1999) *Mining Accidents in the St. Just District 1831-1914* (Trevithick Soc.).
Ladies Journal (1872) *The Work done by Women in the British Isles; the Balmaiden*, Vol. 2 No. 29.
Langsworthy, David. (2002) *The Bal-Maidens and Children on the Dressing Floors of Levant Mine* (Private Publication).
Lanyon, Richard. (1838) 'On Various Diseases of Miners, their Causes and the Best Practical Means of Remedying Them', *Roy. Cornwall Polytech. Soc.* Vol. 1 pp. 35-53.
——— (1841) 'Statistics of Camborne' *Roy. Cornwall Polytech. Soc.* Vol. 9 pp. 99-119.
Leifchild, J. R. S. (1855) *Cornwall, It's Mines and Miners* (Longmanns).
Lemon, Sir Charles. (1838) 'The Statistics of the Copper Mines of Cornwall', in R. Burt (Ed.) *Cornish Mining; Essays on the Organisation of Cornish Mines and the Cornish Mining Economy* (David & Charles 1969).
Lewis, G. R. (1965)*The Stannaries* (Bradford Barton).
Lewis, Jim. (1997) *A Richly Yielding Piece of Ground, The Story of Fowey Consols* (Cornish Hillside).

Lowry, Henry Dawson. (1927) *Wheal Darkness* (Hutchinson).
Messenger, Michael. (2001) *Caradon and Looe; The Canal, Railways and Mines* (Twelveheads).
Meyerstein, E. W. (1907) *A Key to Cornish Mining* (The Mining Journal).
Mid Wales Mining Museum. (1981) *How a Lead Mine is Worked at Surface.*
——— (1981) *A History of Mining in Mid Wales.*
Michell, F. B. (1978) 'Ore Dressing in Cornwall', *Jour. Trevithick Soc.* No. 6 pp. 25-52.
——— (1980) 'The Development of the Copper Mining Industry in Cornwall and the Industrial Revolution', *Camborne School of Mines Jour.* pp. 45-53.
Morrison, T. A. (1980) *Cornwall's Central Mines: The Northern District 1810-1895* (Hodge).
——— (1983) *Cornwall's Central Mines: The Southern District 1810-1895* (Hodge).
Moyle, Samuel. (1839) 'On the Ventilation of Mines', *RIC Jour.* (Oct) p. 57.
Murchison, J. H. (1854) *British Mines* (Mann).
Muspratt, Sheridan (1886) (Ed.). *Chemistry; Theoretical, Practical and Analytical, as Applied to the Arts and Manufactures* (Mackenzie).
Nash, Henry John. (1933) *Essays on Mining and Kindred Subjects* (Search).
Newman, Thomas. (1940) *The History of Coryton* (Cassell).
Noall, Cyril. (1972) *Botallack* (Dyllansow Truran).
——— (1973) *The St. Just Mining District* (Bradford Barton).
——— (1982) *The St. Ives Mining District Vol. 1* (Dyllansow Truran).
——— (1993) *The St. Ives Mining District Vol. 2* (Dyllansow Truran).
Norwood, Stephany. (1991) *Balmaidens; a Study of Victorian Female Workers in the West Country,* B. Ed (Hons.)Thesis, Wolverhampton Polytechnic.
Payton, Philip J. (1984) *The Cornish Miner in Australia* (Dyllansow Truran).
Penny Magazine. (1835) *Notes of a Journey to the Mines of Cornwall and Wales,* No. 220 (5th September).
Pepper, John Henry. (1862) *The Playbook of Metals* (Routeledge)
Pococke, Dr. Richard. (1750) 'Travels through England 1750' in Chope, R. Pearse, *Early Tours in Devon and Cornwall* (David & Charles 1967).
Pryce, W. (1778) *Minerologia Cornubensis*, D. B. Barton (Ed.) (repr. Bradford Barton 1972).
Pryor, Oswald. (1973) *Australia's Little Cornwall* (Rigby).
Raistrick, Arthur. (1939) 'Ore Dressing in the 18th and Early 19th Centuries', *Mine and Quarry Eng.* pp. 161-6.
Razelle, P. E.; Wainright, R. W. (1973) *The Victorian Working Class: Selections from Letters to the Morning Chronicle 1849-50* (Frank Cass).
Rideing, William H. (1881) 'In Cornwall with an Umbrella', *Harper's New Monthly Mag.* No. 378 (Nov) Vol. 63 pp. 801-22.
Rowe, John. (1974)*The Hard-Rock Men; Cornish Immigrants and the North American Mining Frontier* (Barnes & Noble).
——— (1993) *Cornwall in the Age of the Industrial Revolution* (Cornish Hillside).
Salmon, H. C. *Mines of the Sixties,* G. W. Hall (Ed.) (Griffin 2000).
Sara, Muriel. (1970) *Cornwall Remembered* (Private Publication).
Schwartz, Sharron P. (1999) 'In Defence of Customary Rights', *Cornish Studies* No. 7 (Exeter) pp. 9-31.
——— (2000) 'No Place for a Woman: Gender at Work in Cornwall's Metalliferous Mining Industry', *Cornish Studies* No. 8 (Exeter) pp. 68-96.
Schwartz, Sharron P.; Parker, Roger. (2001) *Tin Mines and Miners of Lanner* (Halsgrove).
Simonin, L. (1868) *Mines and Miners or Underground Life* trans. W. H. Bristow.
Spargo, Thomas. (1864) *Mines of Cornwall and Devon.*
——— (1865) *Mines of Cornwall and Devon.*
——— (1868) *Mines of Cornwall and Devon.*
Stanier, Peter. (1998) *Mines of Cornwall and Devon* (Twelveheads).
Stewart, R. J. (2003) *Devon Great Consols* (Tamar Mining Press).
Stocker, H. M. (1852) 'An Essay on the China Stone and China Clays of Cornwall', *Roy. Cornwall. Polytech. Soc.* p. 77.
Taylor, Charles D. (1873) 'Tin Stream Works at Restronguet Creek', *Proc. Mech. Eng.* p. 155.
Taylor, Christopher. (1988) 'The Story of Devon Great Consols Mine 1844-1901', *Tamar Jour.* 10.
Taylor, Rev. Isaac. (1829) *The Mine* (Harris).
Taylor, John. (1814) 'On the Economy of the Mines of Cornwall and Devon', *Trans. Geol. Soc.* 12 pp. 309-27.
——— (1831) 'Notices of Some More Improvements in the Dressing of Ores', *Quart. Mining Rev.* No. 11. pp. 82-7.
Terrell, Ernest. (1920) 'The Hemerdon Wolfram-Tin', *Mining Mag.* No. 22 (Feb) pp. 75-87.
Thomas, R. (1819) *A Survey of the Mining District from Chacewater to Camborne* (London).
Thurlow, Charles. (1996) *China Clay* (Tor Mark).
Todd, A. C.; Laws, Peter. (1972) *Industrial Archaeology of Cornwall* (David & Charles).

Todd, Arthur Cecil. (1967) *The Cornish Miner in America* (Bradford Barton).
────── (1977) *The Search for Silver, Cornish Miners in Mexico 1824-1947* (Lodenek).
Toll, R. W. (1938) 'The Arsenic Industry in the Tavistock District of Devon', *Sands, Clays and Minerals* (Apr) p. 224.
────── (1953) 'Arsenic in West Devon and East Cornwall' *Mining Mag.* p. 84.
────── (1958) 'Manganese in West Devon' *Mining Mag.* p. 17-19.
Tredinick, R. (1857) *A Review of Cornish and Devon Mining Enterprise, 1850-6*.
Tremellin, Patty. (1841) *Patty Tremellin; The Life of a Cornish Mine Girl* (Wright & Albright).
Troon Women's Institute. (1952) *Troon Scrap-Book; Women and Girls on the Mines and 'Streams'* (Camborne School of Mines Library).
Turner, John T. F. (1864) *A Familiar Description of the Old Delabole Slate Quarries* (Stonehouse).
Ure. (1839) *Dictionary of Arts, Manufactures and Mining*.
────── (1856) *Dictionary of Arts, Manufactures and Mining*.
────── (1878) *Dictionary of Arts, Manufactures and Mining*.
Varcoe, Philip. (1978) *China Clay: The Early Years* (Francis Antony).
Vivian, John. (1993) *Tales of Cornish Miners* (Tor Mark).
Von Arx, R. (1991) 'A Glimpse at Cape Cornwall Mine', *British Mining* Vol. 43.
Waller, William. (1698) *An Essay on the Value of the Mines Late of Sir Carberry Price*.
Watson, Joseph Yelloly. (1843) *A Compendium of British Mining with Statistical Notices of the Principal Mines in Cornwall* (London).
White, Walter. (1861) *A Londoner's Walk to the Lands End and a trip to the Scilly Isles* (Chapman & Hall).
Williams, J. (1862) *Cornwall and Devon Mining Directory 1862* (Kent).
Willies, Lynn. (1982) *Lead and Lead Mining* (Shire).
Zanjani, Sally. (1997) *A Mine of Her Own - Women Prospectors in the American West 1850-1950* (Nebraska UP).

COST BOOKS

Agar, Wheal (CRO: TL 96).
Basset, Wheal CB (CRO: X 316/1.
Bloomdale China Clay (CRO: AD 79).
Botallack 1816-21 (RIC: ICA 1/7).
Calstock Smelter Treasury Accounts 1702-8 (TNA: 30 Edward I (1302-3), 32-33 Edward 1 (1304-5) and 34 Edward I (1306) E101 260/22, 260/26 and 260/30.
Carclaze (CRO: MT 339; WM: 1989.1712).
Carn Vivian (CRO: STA 46/1, 2 + 5).
Caudledown, South CB (RIC: ICA 1/9).
Coates, Wheal (St. Agnes Museum).
Cocke, Wheal (RIC: V).
Cook's Kitchen (CRO: TEM 55).
Crenver (CRO: AD 1583/11/68).
Ding Dong (CRO: RG 93 + 245).
Dolcoath (CRO: TEM 62).
Goole Pellas, Wheal Day Labourers Book (RIC: V10).
Goonvean (WM: 1988.233 + 237).
Gunheath (RIC: 1/8).
Lady Bertha Dressing CB (CRO: STA 13/24).
Lovell, East Wheal (CRO: STA 230/10).
Maiden, Wheal (CRO: TL 93).
Newham Smelter Cash Book 1703-5 (RIC: ISC), Petty Cash Book + Receipt Book 1704 (RIC).
Ninestones China Clay, Lower (WM: 316.1).
Pednandrea (RIC: V32).
Poldice (CRO: X 475/4, 15 + 17).
Pool Adit (CRO: J 1784).
Porthilly, North (CRO: STA 204/1).
Prussia, Wheal Receiving Book 1879-82 (RIC: V76).
Rosewarne Herland (RIC: V110).
St Just Mine (CRO: STA 141/14 + RG 244).
Towan, Wheal (CRO: TL 96/6).
Trelawney Silver and Lead Mine, New (CRO: STA 259/5)
Trevanion Clay Day Book (CRO: STA 283/4).
Trumpet Consols (RIC: V 121).
Unity Wood, Wheal (CRO: TL 97).

NEWSPAPER REPORTS AND MINING JOURNAL REFERENCES

Agar, Wheal (CT 24th May 1888; WB 8th Jan, WB + RCG 11th Jan 1894).
Balleswidden (WB 4th + 11th Dec 1857, 22nd Jan 1858).
Basset, West Wheal (RCG 6th Jan 1872).
Boiling Well Mine (WB 12th Feb 1858; MJ 20th Feb 1858 p. 128).
Boscaswell Downs (RCG 11th + 30th Apr 1874).
Boscean (WB 23rd Feb 1855).
Botallack (WB 4th Mar 1864; CT 5th Jan 1872, 5th + 23rd Jan 1879; Cornishman 12th Nov 1893).
Camborne mines (RCG 30th Jan + 27th Feb 1880).
Caradon, South (WB 28th Feb 1862 p. 39).
Condurrow (WB 8th Feb 1867).
Condurrow, South (WB 3rd June 1878; RCG 2nd April 1895).
Ding Dong (RCG 8th June 1872).
Dolcoath (RCG 23rd Sept 1871; 30th Jan + 27th Feb 1880).
Helena, Wheal (WB 29th Oct 1891).
Levant (WB 24th Jan 1845; MJ 1st Feb 1845).
Magor Tin Stream Works (WB 16th Jan 1888; Cornishman 19th Jan 1888).
Morvah Consols (RCG 8th Aug 1874 p. 4).
Owles, Wheal (WB 23rd Feb 1855; 20th June 1856).
Pendeen (CT 5th June 1872).
Phoenix United (WB 10th Aug 1882).
Polgooth (WB 2nd July 1847).
Porkellis (MJ 28th Aug 1858; WB 2nd Sept 1859).
Red River Tin Streams (WB 14th Jan 1875 p. 5; RCG 12th Oct 1877 p. 7).
Relubbus Tin Stream (RCG 12th Aug 1881).
St. Austell area clay works (WB 8th + 20th Jan 1881).
Spearn Consols (RCG 13th Aug 1870).
United Hills (WB 19th Jan 1949).

GENERAL INDEX

Bold numbers indicate illustrations

A
'Abraham, the tinner' 4, 42, 93
accidents: 186-91, 231
   arsenic flues 31,185
   explosions 30, 189-90
   falls 31, 188-9
   floods 189
   machinery 186-8
   subsidence 189
Adams, L. 62
Africa 4
Agricola, Georgius 6
America 4,178 *see* migration
American Civil War 197
Angerstein, R. R. 8, 23
antimony 146
arsenic 131, 132-5, **133**
arsenic toxicity, *see* toxicity
arsenic works 135, 177
assaying 2, 88, 107, 234, 251-2, 255
Austen, J. T. 27
Australia 153, *see* migration
average working life 31, 129, 167

B
Baker, Helen 119
Ballantyne, R. M. 62, 176
ball clay 126
Barham, Charles 20, 168, 170, 171, 173, 174, 177,
   179, 181, 186, 191, 192, 225, 246, 247
Baring Gould, Sabine 177-8, 226
barrowing **83**, 86, 101, 106, **107**, 171, 246
Bawden, John (Truro) 200
Beare, Thomas 4
Bedford, Duke of 54
Bell, Henry Adolphus 125
Bennetts, Capt. B. (Camborne) 29, 110, 222
Black Death 135
blown tin 95
Borlase, Rev. William 36, 228
Boswell, James 180
Boulton & Watt 20
Boundyn, James (Wh. Prosper) 119
brick cleaning 2, 89
Briton & Brayley 99
Buller, Rev. John 221
bullying 182
Bray, Billy 26

C
calcining 12, 133-4,
Carew 7
Carne, William (Falmouth) 239
celebrations 34-5, 70, 160-61, 254, 255

china clay:
   dressing **118, 120, 231**
   drying 118
   history 115-17
   managers 123-4
   monitors **256, 257**
   scraping, *see* dressing
China Clay Works 2, 22, 35, 115-26, 198, 256
circulatory problems 172-4
Cliff, James (Wheal Lovell) 240
Climo, Capt. N. 198
clothing, *see* dress
Clymo Jr, Capt. Peter 26
coal mining 3, 12, 191, 203, 247
cobalt 131, 251
Cockin, John (Cook's Kitchen) 154
compensation 190-1
consumption 173-4, 246
copper:
   dressing, *see* ore dressing
   mining history 1-15, 73-74
   ore 73,81, 252-3
Cornwall County Gaol 171-2, 224, 226, 244-5
Cornwall County Lunatic Asylum 184
cost book system 12, 121
counthouse 2, 151-2, **154, 163, 204,** 255
courtship & marriage 13, 31, **69,** 70, 195-6, 225-7, 232
Cowper, John and Charlotte 239
Crease, Capt. J. (Wheal Lovell) 239
Crushers 11, 13, 84, 137, 173
Cullum & Co., William (Fowey Consols) 26
Cunnack, Richard J. 108

D
Dale, Mary (St. Just) 31, 185
Darlington, John vi, 69, 75, 79, 84
De La Beche, H. T. 10, 81, 84
Dickens, Charles 178, 179
diet, *see* food
dinner ladies 233-4, 260
digestive problems 174-5
disability & special needs 29-30
domestic service 200-202, 229
dress **59,** 61-67, **63, 64, 65,** 68, 123, 129, 186,
   188, 218, 220, 222-3, **231,** 241, 259-60
dressing, *see* ore dressing
drift mining 92

E
earnings, *see* wages
education 12, 167-9, 231, 246, 247
employment: **3,** 14
   ages 27, **28**-9, 126

illegal 12, 29
equipment, *see* ore dressing
Esquiros, Alphonse 66, 116, 122, 133
exploitation + abuse 128, 182-4

F
fairs & markets 61, 68, 70
Fiennes, Celia 7, 174
fines 39, 224
fire-setting 4
first aid 161, 176, 258
food 48-50, 54-55, 58,59, 60, 154-61, 174-5, 255, 258
food shortages 43, 197-8, 247
Foote, Mary Hallock 207
Fothergill, Rev. H. J. A. 198
Frue Vanners 13, 112
Fuller's Earth 15, 146
furnace, reverbatory 6

G
general store 208, 252
German mining 5
Gold 131, **207,** 214, 215
Gurney, John 46, 235, 236
gynaecological problems 175-6, 179

H
Harris, Ada (East Pool) **31,**191
Harris, John xi
Hatchett, Charles 74
health 169-82
hearing problems 29, 176
Henderson, James vi, 79, **79, 80,** 82, **82, 83,** 84, **85,** 101, **105,** 133
Henwood, George 48, 87, 131, 154, 155, 174, 218, 219, 234
Henwood, William J. *preface,* 9, 15, 20, 84
Hocking, Salome 227, see *Norah Lang*
Hocking, Silas 228-9
Holman & Son, Messrs 32
home life 58-60, 243
Hopkins, Ruth 208
horse whim 88,108, 234, 241
hospitals 38, 39, 173, 180
hours of work & holidays 32-35, 70
housing 53-57, **54, 55,** 207, 208
Hunt, Robert 10, 116, 133

I
iron 15, **145,** 146-7, 235

J
Jack. Ellen 214
Jenkin, William 35, 108
Jewell, Henry (Trumpet Consols)108
job security 31-2
Jones, Thomas (Wheal Lovell) 239
Julian, Capt. Jack 256
Jutsam, John (Shaw) 94

K
keeping company, *see* courtship
Kendall, Capt. Richard (Wheal Lovell) 239
kibble raising & landing 2, 88, 240
Kinnaird Commission (1864) 37, 46, 49, 60, 61, 168, 170, 181
Kite, Capt. William (Wheal Lovell) 239
Knuckey, Philip (Menheniot) 30

L
Lanyon, Dr. Richard 17, 28, 169, 221
lappiors 1-2, 85
Lawry, Richard (Geevor) 113, 258
lead:
  dressing, *see* ore dressing
  mine history 135-9
  ores 131, 132, 136,
  poisoning, *see* toxicity
  smelting 5, 135-6, 140, 178
  toxicity 178-9
leadership 232-4
legislation:
  Elementary Education Acts 12, 29
  Employment Acts 44, 235
  Enclosure Acts 54,74
  Factory and Workshop Acts 12, 29, 112
  Metalliferous Mines Reg. Act 12, 29
  Truck Act 41
Leifchild, J. R. S. 21, 154, 219, 235
Lemon, Sir Charles 15, 20
Lillicrap, Mabel (Carloggas) **231**
Lord, Mary (St. Just) 205
Lovering, John 35, 124, 242

M
Majendie, A. 125
malaria 179
manganese 8, 27, 37, 141-3
manganese mills 34, 142, **143**
mental health 184-5
Methodism 198, 223, 226
micaceous haematite **145,** 146
migration 12, 202-19
  Australasia 205, **207,** 208-11, **209, 212**-3, 214, 252-4, **253**
  Canada 198
  NE England 202, 204-5, 247
  NW England 203, 204-5, 247
  SE England 201
  SW England 201
  Ireland 202, **203, 204**
  Scotland 202
  S. Africa 206, **211**-2
  USA 207-8, **212,** 213, 214, 245
  Wales 202, 203
Mills, Mary 66
mine:
  account meeting 156-7
  adventurers 9, 26, 35, 38, 44, 50, 89
  closures 89, 111-13, 196-9,
  coinage **40,** 41

molybdenum 132
morgue 161
mortality rates 181-**2**
moss gathering 2
Moyle, Samuel 173
Mundic, *see* arsenic
Murchison, John Henry 43, 81
Murrish, William (Perranzabuloe) 167, 213
Music 68-9, 164, 221, 223

N

neurological problems 170-2
nickel 251
Norah Lang, the Mine Girl 69, 70, 195, 226, 227-**8**

O

ore dressing 75-86, **76, 96,** 98-106, 128-9, 136-9,
    bucking **8,** 10, 36-7, 64, 69, 74, 77, **83**-4, 138,
        171-2, 173, 176
    buddling 77, 85-6, 8, 101, **102,** 108, 138, 142, 171,
        254, 258
    chimming 103
    cobbing **8,** 37, 65, 74, 77, 78, **82**-3, 138, 171-2,
        173, 176
    dilluing 103
    dollying 138
    equipment 13, 48, **78,** 79, 81, 82, 84, 86, 101,
        138-9
    floors 74-5, 97, 99
    framing, **45,** 46, 104-5, **105,** 106, 108, 139, 259
    griddling, *see* riddling
    jigging 10, 76, 84-**5,** 103-4, 137, 138, 142,
        170-1
    mixed ores 131-2, 235
    packing 103
    picking 37, 43, **80,** 81-2, 99, **113,** 131-3, **137**-8,
        140, 142, 170, 176, 257-8, **258,** 259
    racking, *see* framing
    riddling 37, 77, 79-80, **83,** 247
    serving the buddles, *see* buddling
    sieving, *see* riddling
    spalling 37, 38, **47,** 78-9, **79,** 99-100, **100,** 137,
        170, **172, 189,** 230, 250
    stanking 105
    tozing 98, 102-**3**
    trunking 98, 104, 140
    washing 5, 6, 77, **80**-1, 99, 135, 137, 170, 176
orthoclase (potash feldspar) vi, 15, 126-9

P

pack horses, donkeys 147
parasitism 179
parish relief 27, 28, 116, 199
Pascoe, Capt. (Glen Osmond) 205
pay day 30, 40
Penrose, Mr. M. G. (Dolcoath) 44
Pepper, John Henry 174
Perry, Capt. Hannibal (Wheal Lovell) 239, 240
pewter 95, **157**
Philp, James (Wheal Lovell) 239
pig club 56

Pococke, Dr. Richard 8, 125
Poisoning, *see* toxicity
Polper, John 93
potash feldspar, *see* orthoclase
pregnancy & childbirth 178-9, 181, 182-3, 226,
    244-5
Pryce, William vi, 1, 8, 38, 74, 82, 85, 94, 97, 103,
    104, 108, 134, 136,
pumps, hand 2, 118-19, **120**
pumps, mechanical 256

R

Rashleigh, William 187
relief funds and committees 197-8, 200-02
Remfry, Henry (Blackwater)27
respiratory problems 172-4
Rideing, William 87, 169, 230, 231, 250
recruitment 26-31, 122, 152

S

safety fuse factories 181, 199
sampling 87-8, 107, 171
sampling day 156
sanitation 50, 57-58,
Sara, Muriel 1, 47, 64, 108, 174
Schwartz, Sharron *preface*, 27, 65, 222
seasonality, *see* weather
sea tinning 94-5
second streaming, *see* tin streams
setting day 155
sewing 2, 140, 154, 168
Seymour Jr, George 62, **63,** 66, **69, 153, 154, 219**
sexual abuse 183
shiny ore **145,** 146
shode mining 91
sick club 38
sieving cinders 7, 111
sieving tan bark 136
sight problems 29, 176
silver 5, 6, 131, 140-2
Simonin **59,** 61
Sincock, William 26
skeletal problems 170-2, 246
Skerry, George 32
skills 234-6
slate 22, 146-8
smelting 5, 251-2
Smythe, Customer Thomas 5
soapstone 125-6
social life 60, 67-70,
Spackman, Mr. 20
Spargo, Thomas 16
stamps *see tin stamps*
stannaries 5, 93
statistics 15-23, **21,123,** 139-40, 141, 142
Stephens, David (Gwithian) 94
Stocker, H. M. 123
strikes 43-4, 233
Strode, William (Plympton St Mary) 94
Sunday School 67, 167, 168, 169, 231, 246
Surfe, Benjamin (Bottle Hill) 94

Swete, Rev. John 46, 74

T
tallying 36, 147, 233
Taylor, Alexander 239
Taylor, John 10, 26, 84, 225, 231
technology; effect on employment 10-15, **14,** 69, 84, 89, 98, 104
Thomas, Herbert 99
Thriscott, Thomas 124
tin:
  dressing, *see* ore dressing
  mine history 2-15, 95-7, 112-14
  ores 93,
  smelting 6, 110-11
  stamps 97, 101, 108, 112, 176
  trading 4
tin streams 7, 29, 47, 48, 66, 69, 108-110, 187, 223, 259
tin works 91-2, 93, 94
toxicity **133,** 134-5, 175-6, 176-9, 177-8,
tramming, *see* wagoning
Tremellin, Richard, William & Francis 244
Treneer, Capt. A. (Redruth) 241
TREPOLPEN 119
Trevillian, Capt. Thomas (Herodsfoot) 27
tribute system 25-6, 43, 52, 53, 46, 47, 137, 146
truck system 41

U
unions & industrial relations 43-45, 203, 232-3, 247
uranium 146

V
velveteen factory 199

W
wages 35-38, 42, 43, 61, 121, 135-6, 148, 154, 163, 175, 196, 223, 240, 254, 258
wagoning 2, 86, 119, 140, **189,** 234, 250
Waller, William 40
Wallis, Christopher 19, 239
Warner, Rev. Richard 125
waste picking 89, 110, 134, 135, 144, 146
weather 32, 97, 118, **121,** 122, 129, 170-2, 260
weeding 2, 108
White, Walter 118
Williams, James (Cook's Kitchen) 154
Williams John 41, 239, 240
Williams, William (St Austell) 119
Wills, Capt. Benjamin (Trevellas) 247
wolfram 15, 131-2, 143-5, **144**
workhouse 29, 30, 134, 199, 224-5, 226, 241
women managers 2, 124-5, 234, 239-40, 242
World War I vi, 2, 14, 113, 117, 119, 126, 135, 144, 145, 182, 229, 256
World War II vi, 2, 14, 113, 117, 119, 146, 164, 176, 257-8
Wynneslond, Henry 94

Z
Zanjani, Sally 208, 214
zinc 131, 132, 138, 141, 235

MINE INDEX

Bold numbers indicate illustrations

A

Agar, Wheal (Illogan) iii, 37, 39, 40, 41, 154, 159, 161, 186, 188, 269, 270
Alfred, Wheal (Phillack) 167
Ailsborough, see Eylesbarrow
Angarrack Tin Smelter (Phillack) 111
Anna Francis, Wheal (Kea) 173

B

Baddern, Great Wheal (Kea) 131
Balleswidden (St Just) 26, 43, 49, 109, 112, 191, 233, 270
Balmynheer (Wendron) 1
Basset & Grylls (Wendron) 159
Basset, West Wheal (Illogan) 13, 39, 112, 231, 270
Basset, Wheal (Illogan) 30, 43-44, 58, 101, **102**, 168, 269
Bere Alston Lead Mines 5
Betsey, Wheal (Mary Tavy) 138, 167
Birch Tor (N. Bovey) 32
Bloomdale China Clay (St Stephen) **121**, 122, 269
Bluebarrow (Bunny) China Clay (St Austell) 119, 124, 256
Blue Hills (St Agnes) 134
Boiling Well Mine (Phillack) 30, 132, 161, 190, 270
Boscaswell Downs (St Just) 42, 163, 270
Boscean (St Just) 32, 270
Bosorn & Bollowell (St Just) 156
Boswidden (St Just) 32, 159
Botallack (St Just) 12, 31, 39, 66, **152**, 155, **157**, 159, 162, 185, 188, 197, 223, 269, 270
Bottle Hill (Plympton) 94
Brea Tin Streams (Illogan) 260
Brook Mine (Buckfastleigh) 58
British Silver & Lead, see Penrose Consols
Brookwood, East (Buckfastleigh) 159
Budnick Consols (Perranzabuloe) 42, 141
Bullen Garden (Camborne) 73
Bunny China Clay, see Bluebarrow
Burton, Wheal (St Agnes) 206
Busy, Great Wheal (Kenwyn) 112, 197

C

Caharrack (Gwennap) 18
Cakes & Ale (Gwennap) 173
Calenick Tin Smelter (Truro) 111
Calstock Lead Smelter 5, 35, 39, 135-6, 269
Camborne Mines 270
Camborne Vean 198
Cape Cornwall (St Just) 99
Caradon, East (Linkinhorne) 49
Caradon, South (St Cleer) 39, 187, 270
Carclaze China Clay (St Austell) 124, 242, 269
Carnclaze Slate Caverns (Liskeard) 147

Carbeen China Clay (St Austell) 124
Cargoll (Newlyn East) 136, 141
Carloggas China Clay (St Austell) 115, 117, 231
Carloggas China Clay, South (St Austell) 117
Carn Brea (Illogan) 30, 159, 169, 197, 230, 250
Carn Camborne (Camborne) 31, 82, 259
Carnon Mines (Perranworthal) 48
Carnon Tin Streams (Perranworthal) 48, 94
Carvear China Clay (Par) 242
Carn Vivian (Warleggan) 37, 39, 41, 140, 159, 163, 235, 269
Castle an Dinas China Clay (Nancledra) 119, 123
Caudledown China Clay Works (St Austell) 124-5
Caudledown China Clay, South (St Austell) 122, 269
Charlestown Mines (St Austell) 26, 99, 105, 170, 180
China Stone Clay Co. (St Austell) 242
Chiverton Mines (Perranzabuloe) 32
Chiverton, West (Perranzabuloe) 136, 141
Chyandour Tin Smelter (Penzance) 111
Clifford Amalgamated (Gwennap) 110
Coates, Wheal (St Agnes) 34, 39, 133, 159, 269
Cobar Copper Field, Australia 253-4
Cocke, Wheal (St Agnes) 32, 36, 269
Comfort, Wheal (St Ives) 39, 154
Condurrow (Camborne) 11, 34, 270
Condurrow, South (Camborne) 112, 163, 270
Cook's Kitchen (Illogan) 18, 36, 44, 73, 88, 89, 154, 159, 269
Consolidated or Consols (Gwennap) 18, 37, 41, 48, 79, 82, 70, 171, 173, 175, 191, 246
Cornubian, Old (Perranzabuloe) 136, 138
Coryton Manganese (Coryton) 37, 154
Creegbrawse (Kenwyn) 141
Crenver, Wheal (Crowan) 18, 269
Crinnis, Great (St Austell) 141
Crinnis Moor Tin Streams (St Austell) 109
Crofty, East Wheal (Illogan) 18, 41, 87
Crowndale, Wheal (Tavistock) 10, 84
Cuccold Tin Works (Plympton) 94

D

Darley Ford Tin Stream (Linkinhorne) 109
Dartmoor mines 48
Delabole Slate Quarry (St Teath) 27, 146-8, 162
Devon Great Consols (Tavistock) 19, 29, 34, 43, 44, 54, 66, 69, 74, 77, 81, 89, 134, 159, 181, 223, 224, 233
Ding Dong Mine (Gulval) 44, 109, 159, 185, 187, 221, 233
Dippertown Manganese (Marystow) 142
Dolcoath (Camborne) i, 9, 12, 13, 18, 19, 32, 33, 35, 38, 39, 41, 43, 44, 45, 46, 47-8, 49, 50, 62, 64, 66, 73, 74, 78, 82, 87, 89, 99, 104, 107, 109, 112, 113, 159, 161, 176, 177, 179, 183, 184, 187, 197, 213, 224, 230, 233, 234, 254, 269, 270

Drakewalls (Calstock) 32, 109
Dudnance, Wheal (Illogan) 8

E
Emma, Wheal (Tavistock) 158
Eylesbarrow (Dartmoor) 154, 159, 234
Exmouth, South Wheal (Hennock) 39, 140
Exmouth, Wheal (Christow) 138
Exwick Manganese Mill 142

F
Falmouth & Sperries (Kenwyn) 142
Fanny Adela, Wheal (Lelant) 251
Fortune, West Wheal (Perranzabuloe) 41
Fowey Consols (Tywardreath) 18, 26, 27, 36, 38, 48, 74, 79, 82, 153, 156, 159, 171, 187, 191, 249
Frances, West Wheal (Illogan) 107, 112,1 59, 259
Frances, South Wheal (Illogan) 106
Frank Mills (Christow) 136, 140
Friendship, Wheal (Mary Tavy) 9, 14, 19, 48, 60, 74, 84, 135, 167, 233

G
Gawton (Tavistock) 134
Geevor (St Just) vi, 15, 49, 65, 113, 159, 163, 176, 217, 229, 257-8
Gew Graze Soapstone Works (Mullion) 125-6
Godolphin (Breage) 18, 19, 153, 159
Golden, East Wheal (Perranzabuloe) 40
Goole Pellas, Wheal (Towednack) 159, 163, 169
Goonbarrow China Clay, North (St Austell) 242
Goonbarrow China Clay, West (St Austell) 124
Goonvean China Clay (St Stephens) 121, 233, 269
Gorland, Wheal (St Day) 83, 171, 175
Gother's China Clay (St Mewan) 119
Great Orme Copper Mines (N. Wales) 2
Great Rock Iron (Hennock) i, 14, 145-6, 159, 164, 217
Greensplat China Clay (St Austell) 122
Grenville, Wheal (Camborne) 106, 254
Gunheath China Clay (St Austell) 122, 269
Gunnislake Clitters (Calstock) 74, 143
Gunnislake, Old (Calstock) 74
Gwallon (St Hilary) 153

H
Harmony, Wheal (Redruth) 182
Hawke's Point (Lelant) 251-2
Helena, Wheal (St Hilary) 159, 270
Hemerdon Wolfram (Plympton) 14, 144-5
Henry Clay Works, Wheal (St Austell) 122
Herodsfoot Mine (Lanreath) 27
Hewas, Great (St Mewan) 155,
Hewas, Wheal (St Mewan) 243
Hexworthy Tin (Hexworthy) 30, 95
W. J. Hocking's Tin Streams 109
Hogstor Manganese (Chillaton) 142
Hope, Wheal (Perrranzabuloe) 40

J
Jewell, Wheal (Mary Tavy) 9, 74
Josiah, Wheal (Tavistock) **54**

K
King Edward (Camborne) 99
Kitty, Wheal (St Agnes) 19, 176
Kutna Hora Silver Mine (Prague) 6

L
Lady Bertha (Buckland Monachorum) 19, 135, 140, 269
Lanescot (Tywardreath) 18, 136
Lansallson China Clay (Carthew) 242
Lee Moor China Clay (Shaugh Prior) 116, 125, 242
Levant (St Just) 32, 41, 164, 187, 270
Lewtrenchard Manganese Mine 142
Lovell, Wheal (Wendron) 234, 239-40
Luxulyan China Clay (Luxulyan) 124
Lydia, Wheal (Porthtowan) 240

M
Magdalen (Ponsanooth) 234
Magor Tin Stream (Illogan) 187, 190, 270
Maiden, Wheal (Gwennap) 18, 154, 269
Maria, Wheal (Crowan) 153, 159
Mary, Wheal (Lelant) 26
Mary Ann, Wheal (Menheniot) 15, 136, 143-4
Mellangoose China Clay (Indian Queens) 242
Metal, North (Sithney) 159
Mexico, Huel (St Agnes) 141
Mines Royal 3, 7, 73, 135, 136
Monkston Manganese (Brentor) 142
Morvah Consols (Morvah) 189, 270
Morwellham Quay (Tavistock) 34, 143, 222
Mountain Mine (Allihies) 203, 204

N
Newham Tin Smelter (Truro) 7, 30, 35, 111, 146, 269
Newton & Prince of Wales (St Mellion) 141
Newton St Cyres Manganese 8, 141, 142
Ninestones China Clay, Lower (Carthew) 37, 121, 124, 269

O
Okel Tor (Calstock) 134
Old's Tin Streams 259
Onslow, Great (St Breward) 140
Owlacombe Beam (Ashburton) 134, 235
Owles, Wheal (St Just) 32, 35, 270

P
Pednandrea (Redruth) 39,42,159,174,269
Pembroke (Par) 141
Pendeen (St Just) 44,233,270
Penhalls (St Agnes) 12,134
Penrose Consols (Sithney) 141
Pentire Glaze (St Minver) 223
Pentuan Tin Streams (St Austell) 94
Perran St George (Perranzabuloe) 247
Phoenix United (Linkinhorne) 44, 233, 270

MINE INDEX

Point Lead Smelter (Feock) 140
Polberro (St Agnes) 95
Polberro, East (St Agnes) 191
Poldice (St Day) 73, 88, 109, 161, 180, 187, 269
Polgooth (St Stephen) 18, 95, 98
Polpuff Glass Mine, see Tresayse
Pool Adit (Illogan) 7, 36, 270
Pool, East (Illogan) 31, **47,** 97, 99
Porkellis (Wendron) 160, 189, 270
Porthilly, North (St Minver) 37, 140, 269
Porth Towan 240
Prosper China Clay Quarry, Wheal (Roche) 119, 234
Prosper, Wheal (Lydford) 92
Providence, Wheal 112
Prussia, Wheal (Redruth) 42, 154, 269

R

Ramsdown (Marystow) 142
Red River Tin Streams 34, 69, 108, 109, 189, 220, 270
Reeth, Wheal (Lelant) 110, 197
Relistian (Gwinnear) 73
Relubbus Tin Stream (St Hilary) 108, 270
Reskadinnick Tin Stream (Camborne) 109
Restormel (Lostwithiel) 191
Retallack, Great (Newlyn East) 40, 141
Rocks China Clay (Bugle) **256, 257**
Rodda's Tin Stream 259
Rose, East Wheal (Newlyn East) 140
Rose, Wheal (St. Agnes) 233
Rosewall Hill (Towednack) 96
Rosewarne Herland (Gwinnear) 159
Rosewarne United (Gwinnear) 141, 269
Roskear, North (Camborne) 29, 49, 167, 168, 233
Ruddle Pit 124
Russell, East Wheal (Tavistock) 26, 37, 80
Ruthers (St Columb) 142

S

St Agnes Bal 7
St Austell china clay works 32, 116, 270
St Austell tin streams 93
St. Ives Consols **45,** 66, 112,
St Just Mine 154, 269
Screeda (St Austell) 119, 242
Seton (Seaton), West Wheal (Camborne) 44, **107,** 183, 233
Seton (Seaton), Wheal (Camborne) 19
Shillamill Manganese Mill (Tavistock) 142
Silverbrook (Ilsington) **139**
Slimeford Manganese Mill (Calstock) 142
Sparnon, Wheal (Redruth) 97
Spearn Consols (St Just) 32, 270
Stents China Clay 124

T

Tamar Lead, South (Bere Ferris) 140
Tamar mines 9, 19, 41, 136
Teign Valley mines 9, 19, 136
Terras, South (St Stephen) 146

Tincroft (Illogan) 18, 35, 44, 89, **100,** 101, 112, 233, 259
Tolgus Downs (Redruth) 73
Tolgus, South Wheal (Redruth) 197
Tolvadden Stamps (Illogan) 97, 99
Towan, South Wheal (Porthtowan) 240
Towan, Wheal (Porthtowan) 36, 82, 269
Treamble Iron (Perranzabuloe) 14, 145
Tregoning Hill China Clay (Breage) 115
Trehane, Wheal (Menheniot) 30
Trelawny (Menheniot) 26, 136
Trelawney, New (Menheniot) 37, 140, 162, 269
Trerew, Wheal (Crantock) 159
Tresavean (Gwennap) 18, 27, 37, 53, 79, 84, 171, 191
Tresayse Orthoclase Mine (Roche) vi,15, 126-9, **127, 128,** 182, 217, 228, 229, 233
Treskerby (Gwennap) 88, 234
Trethellan (Gwennap) 84, 174, 175
Trethosa China Clay (St Stephen) 116
Trevanion China Clay (Bugle) **121,** 122, 269
Trevaunance Tin Streams (St Agnes) 7
Treverbyn China Clay, Great (St Austell) 14, 119, **120**
Treviscoe China Clay, Little (St Austell) 119, 242
Trewavas (Breage) 140
Treyew Tin Smelter (Truro) 111
Trumpet Consols (Wendron) 108, 159, 269

U

Union, Wheal (Devon) 41,133, 235
United Hills (Porthtowan) 185,189, 270
United Mines (St Day) 18, 82, 84,104,156,175,189, 197
Unity Wood, Wheal (Gwennap) 133, 269
Uny, Wheal (Redruth) 36, 39, 159
Upton Pyne Manganese 8, 141

V

Varcoes 129
Virgin China Clay, Huel (Gwennap) 242
Virgin, Wheal (Gwennap) 18
Virgin, West Wheal (Gwennap) 18
Vitifer (Chagford) 95
Vor Flow, Wheal (Helston) 108, 175, 184
Vor, Great Wheal (Breage) 19
Vor, Wheal (Breage) 18, 19, 32, 40, 95, 101, 104, 134, 177
Vyvian, Wheal (Constantine) 27, 201

W

Weir Quay Lead Smelter (Bere Ferris) 140
Wendron Consols (Wendron) 197
Wendron Tin Streams 93
West of England China Clay 116
White Works (Princetown) 95
Widden, Wheal (Gwennap) 108
Work, Great (Breage) 19, 95, 159
Wotter China Clay (Shaugh Prior) 116

Y

Yondertown Clay Works 124

BAL MAIDEN INDEX

Bold numbers indicate illustrations

A

Abbott, Mary (Delabole) 162
Adams, Caroline (Australia) 212-3, **212**
Allen, Eliza (Trescoe) 173
Allen, Sarah Jane (Camborne) 30
Andrew, Annie (Illogan) 129
Andrews, Minnie (Beacon) vi, 31, 32, 36, 38, 47, 49, 61, 64, 82, 105, 174, 183, 233, 235, 258-61, **260**
Angove, Sylvia (St Just) 114
Annear, Jane (Poldice) 88
Argall, Eliza Jane (USA) 213
Argall, Mary (USA) 213
Ashton, Elizabeth (Hawke's Point) 251-2

B

Bailey, Charity (St Blazey) 203
Barkle, Mary (Tavistock) 80
Bastin, Mary (Twelveheads) 31
Bate, Matilda (Calstock) 136
Bawden, Ann (Camborne) 208, **209**
Bawden, Grace (Breage) 29
Bawden, Nancy (Menheniot) 144
Bawden, Susan (Camborne) 208, **209**
Bawden, Thomasine (Perranzabuloe) 248-9
Beard, Barbara (Par) **120**
Bedington, Mary (North Metal) 159
Benbow, Caroline (Carharrack) 212-3, **212**
Bennett, Margaret (Illogan) 107
Bennetts, Amelia, Ann & Maryann (Camborne) 232
Bennetts, Bessie (Geevor) 159
Berryman, Emily (Lelant) 224
Berryman, Jane (Gwennap) 235
Bickerleg, Miss (Camborne) 107, 234, 254
Blewett, Ketura (Camborne) 88
Boase, Elizabeth (Redruth) 182
Bottrell, Rebecca (Redruth) 186
Bownde, Rachel (Dartmoor) 94
Boundy, Elizabeth (Mary Tavy) 134
Boundyn, Catherine (Wh. Prosper) 119
Bowden, Grace (Gwennap) 59, 61,174
Bradeley, Elizabeth & Isabella (Dartmoor) 93, 94
Bradford, Sally (Dartmoor) 159, 164
Bray, Mary Ann (Wheal Henry) 122
Brewer, Audrey (Par) **120**
Briney, Grace (Redruth) 27, 88, 234, **240**, 241-3
Brook, Ann (St Austell) 121, 233
Browne, Matilda (Dartmoor) 94
Buckingham, Martha & Mary (Bissoe) 82, 171, 246-7
Buller, Mary (Fowey Consols) 79
Butson, Christian (Kenwyn) 28
Buzza, Jane (Gwennap, Kenwyn) 187, 190
Buzza, Mary (Australia) 215

C

Cadwell sisters (Illogan) 31
Carkeek, Elizabeth (Tresavean) 84
Carpenter, Caroline (Wheal Agar) 159
Carter, Jane (Trumpet Consols) 108
Carvolth, Miss (Redruth) 67
Chapple sisters (Carn Brea) 31
Chard, Mary Jane (Illogan) 224
Chellow, Sarah (Ludgvan) 31
Chenoweth, Stella (Geevor) 159
Coad, Mary Ann (Kenwyn) 180
Cock, Ann (Nanny) (Rosewarne) 159
Cock, Elizabeth A. (Wheal Agar) 159
Cock, Jane (Phillack) 187,190-1
Cole, Joanna (Calstock) 136
Collins, Cora (St Just) 114
Collins, Mrs. (Troon) 106, 254
Coom, Caroline (Fowey Consols) 63, 82
Coombe, Blanch (Crowan) 30
Coon, Lorreta (St Cleer) **249**
Craze, Beatrice (Illogan) 162
Craze, Jane & Eliza (Camborne) 232
Craze sisters (Camborne) 30
Crips, Martha (Newham) 87, 111
Crocker, A. (W. Wheal Frances) 159
Curnow, Elizabeth (Consolidated) 64, 136, 175
Curnow, Mary (Lelant) 111
Cutard, Isabelle (Calstock) 107, 136

D

Dalley, Mrs (Troon) 47
Datson, Eliza (Wheal Widden) 135
Davey, Catherine (Gwennap) 210
Davey, Cecilia (Kea) 133
Davey, Elizabeth (St Austell) 105
Davis, Hannah (East Wheal Russell) 80
Davis, May (Rocks) **256, 257**
Davis, Jane (Rocks) **256, 257**
Davies, Sarah (Wh. Union) 41, 235
Davies, Mary & Sarah (Dartmoor) 133
De Bonn, Gunhilde (Calstock) 136
De Falling, Emma (Calstock) 136
De Milleton, Dyonis & Desiderata (Calstock) 136
De Suthecon, Mattillid (Calstock) 136
Dolberre, Elizabeth (Dartmoor) 94
Dodd, Mary Ann (Peter Tavy) 85
Down, Mary Jane (Tavistock) 203, 213
Downing, Sarah Ann (Botallack) 188, 191
Dunn, Susan (Australia) 208, **209**
Dunnell, Eliza (Pednandrea) 159

E

Easterbrook, Mary Ann (Mary Tavy) 134
Eddy, Jane Boyns (St Just) 204

Ellans, Lavinia (Kehelland) 189, 190-1
Eselby, Jane (Bere Ferris) 140
Eslick, Martha (Kenwyn) 224
Eslick, Mary (St Blazey) 213
Eva, Ann (Cook's Kitchen) 159

F
Fall, Sally (Gwennap) 84, 171, 173
Faull, Sarah (Gwennap) 173, 180
Fisher, Elizabeth (Wheal Henry) 122
Fletcher, Jane & Sukey (Wh. Burton) 206
Floyd, Elizabeth Jane (Mary Tavy) 134
Ford, Sarah (Tavistock) 153, 159
Foy, Elizabeth (Porkellis) 105
Francis, Fanny (United Mines) 67, 68, 175, 189
Frewhella, Jane (Allihies) 204

G
Gay, Mrs (Troon) 199, 223
Gerry, Elizabeth (Calstock) 162
George, Mary Ann (Crowan) 224
Gilbert, Grace (St Agnes) 134
Glanville, Annie (Penponds) 199
Gliddon, Hannah (Stowford) 30
Goldsworthy, Mary Ann (Wheal Uny) 159
Goldsworthy, Sarah (Camborne) 162
Goninan, Marah & Catherine (Connor Downs) **200**
Goyne, Elizabeth & Jane (Porthtowan) 185,190
Grenfell, Matilda (St Just) 159, 162,
Gribbel, Elizabeth (Cook's Kitchen) 154
Gribble, Ann (Australia) 208, **209**
Gribble, Jane (Wheal Agar) 159
Gribben, Ann (Wheal Coates) 34, 133
Grigg, Kitty (Goonvean) 121, 233
Grose, Elizabeth (Lower Ninestones) 37
Gundry, Charity, Amelia, Grace, Selina (St Blazey) 203

H
Hall, Eliza Jane (Madron) 185, 187, 190
Hamblyn, Catherine (Dartmoor) 94
Hanfforde, see Hanworthy
Hanworthy, Alice (Dartmoor) 94
Harris, Anne Maria (Roskear) 29
Harris, Mary Ann (Redruth) 224
Harris, Mary Ann (Perranzabuloe) 171, 224
Harry, Mary Bennetts (St Just) 206, **211**
Harvey, Grace (Dolcoath) 223
Harvey, Mary (Wheal Vor) 183
Harvey, Jane & Mary Ann (E. Wh. Russell) 80
Head, Alice (Buckfastleigh) 58
Heathorne sisters (Penponds) 30
Hellings, Lavinia, see Ellans
Hellyar, Catherine (Gwennap) 210
Hendra, Mary (Gwinnear) 29
Hicks, Salley (Australia) 206
Higga, Mary (Poldice) 159
Higgins, Ellen (Perranzabuloe) 43
Higgins, Mary (Perranzabuloe) 233
Higman, Mary (Luxulyan) 128
Hill, Elizabeth Jane (Calstock) 224
Hill, Elizabeth (New Trelawney) 140

Hocking, Elizabeth (Charlestown) 99, 105, 170
Holman, Mary (Perranzabuloe) 224
Holn, Sara of (Holne) 94
Hooper, Mary Ann (Illogan) 206, 215
Hooper, Amelia (Germoe) 117
Hooper, Ellen (Germoe) 116
Hosken, Mary (Ding Dong) 159
Hosking, Mary (Connor Downs) 162
Howerd, Elizabeth (Bere Ferris) 80
Hughes, Olive (Par) **120**
Husband, Jane (S. Caradon) 187, 191
Hutchens, Grace (Redruth) see Briney, Grace

I
Ivey, Mary (Crowan) 30

J
Jackman, Mrs (Tavistock) 135
Jacob, Jenepher (Barbellingey) 117, 124
James, Elizabeth (St Just) 104
James, Margaret (St Just) 104
James, Mary (Pednandrea) 159
James, Mary Ann (St Just) 104
Jane, Mary (Pednandrea) 159
Jarvis, Charlotte & Eliza (Newlyn East) 145
Jeffery, Alice (Poldice) 88
Jeffery, Eliza,Hannah & Jane (Illogan) 27
Jenkin, Emma Jane (Marazion) 110
Jenkin, Susan (Basset & Grylls) 159
Jenkins, Jenny (Ailsborough) 154, 159
Jennings sisters (Illogan) 30
Jewell, Charity (Trumpet Consols) 108
Jewell, Jane (E. Wh. Crofty) 177
John, Mary Ann (Kenwyn) 180
Johns, Elizabeth (Boswidden) 159
Johns, Elizabeth (Carn Brea) 159
Johns, Mary Ann (St Blazey) 203
Jones, Alice (Gwithian) 161, 190, 191
Jones, Elizabeth (Mary Tavy) 134
Joyce *Frontispiece*
Julian, Hettie (Bluebarrow) 119, 256
Julyard, Rebecca (St Austell) 242
Jutsam, Agnes (Dartmoor) 94

K
Kellow, Eliza (Kea) 134
Kemp, Catherine (Gwithian) 224
Kempthorne, Mary Ann (Newlyn East) 140
Key, Ann (St Dennis) 119, 234
Killow, Catherine (St Teath) 148
Kitto, Elizabeth (Breage) 152-3, 159
Kitto, Mary Ann (Stoke Climsland) 203
Knuckey, Harriet (Menheniot) 30
Kruge, Sidwell (Australia) 215, 252-4, **253**

L
Lampion, Elizabeth Ann (Newlyn East) 145
Lance, Hannah (St Agnes) 233
Lane, Elizabeth Kenwyn) 148
Larleek, Elizabeth (Tresavean) 171
Launder, Amelia (Redruth) 29

Lawrence, Mary Jane (Redruth) 180
Lawry, Ada & Amy (St Just) 154
Lean, Jane (Fowey Consols) 153, 159
Leggo, Mrs (Australia) 215
Lidgey, Miss (Lanner) 234
Lockett, Phyllis (Geevor) 65, 114, 257-8, **258**
Lovering, Phillippa (St Austell) **124**, 234
Luxton, Dorothy (Tavistock) 135
Lyne, Clarice (Dartmoor) 94

M

Magor, Lavinia (Kenwyn) 211
Manadue, Georgianna (Polvenna) 111
Martin, Ann (Poldice) 88
Martin, Annie (Dolcoath) 99, 187, 190
Martin, Elizabeth (Lower Dimson) 162
Martin, Grace (Trumpet Consols) 159
Martin, Mary Ann (Quenchwell) 140
Martin, Rebecca (St Austell) 125, 234, 242
Masters, Mary (Warleggan) 159, 163
Matthews, Hannah (Wheal Agar) 159
Matthews, Josephine (St Just) 114
Matthews, Phyllis (St Just) 114
Maunder, Emma & Irena (Mary Tavy) 134
Maynard, Elizabeth (Devon Great Consols) 29
Menadue, Georgianna (Perranzabuloe) 141
Michell, Matilda (Connor Downs) 29
Michell, Sara (St Austell) 124, 234
Michell, Sarah (Dolcoath) 87
Middleton, Elizabeth (Gwallon) 153, 159
Mill, Elizabeth (Wheal Agar) 159
Miner, Betsy (St Columb Major) 29
Minhennet, Elizabeth (Tavistock) 80
Minors, Janie (St Stephen) 146
Moon, Christine (Calstock) 226
Morcom, Ellen (St Agnes) 134
Morcom, Grace (Poldice) 89
Morom, Christina (Gwennap) 172
Moyle, Harriett Ann (Wendron) 224
Moyle, Susan (Basset & Grylls) 159

N

Nancarrow, Ann (St Agnes) 30
Nettle, Eliza (Gwennap) 134
Nicholas, Betsey (Ding Dong) 159
Nicholls, Ellen (Gwennap) 232
Nicholls, Sophia (Pednandrea) 159
Northcott, Charlotte (N. Dimson) 29
Northey, Mary Ann (St Blazey) 203
Northey, Mary Jane (Tavistock) 203, 213
Nosworthy, Alice (Dartmoor) 93, 94
Northworthi, Isabell of (Dartmoor) 94
Noy, Elizabeth (Betsey) (St Just) 189

O

Oats, Mary (Ludgvan) 109
Olds, Annie (Botallack) 185
Oppenhulle, Agnes (Calstock) 136

P

Park, Christina (Illogan) 224

Pascoe, Christina (Gwennap) 82, 170, 171, 173
Pascoe, Mary Ann (Gwennap) 135
Paull, Ann (Silverwell) 235
Paull, Eliza Jane (Illogan) 213
Peake, Mary (E. Brookwood) 159
Peak, Mary (New Trelawny) 140, 162
Pearce, Ellen & Amelia (Boscell Farm) 119
Peeps, Catherine (Liskeard) 29
Penna, Elizabeth Jane (Rose) 213
Penna, Grace (Perranzabuloe) 42-43
Penrose, Jane (Mary Tavy) 134
Phelny, Meliora (Redruth) 93
Phil, Peggy (Alambra) 105
Phillips, Elizabeth (Poldice) 89
Phillips, Mrs Mary Ann (Lee Moor) 125
Phillips, Nancy (St Austell) 119, 234
Pidwell, Harriet & Jane (Illogan) 31
Pill, Mary Ann (Perranzabuloe) 200
Pill, Thomasine (Perranzabuloe) 248-9
Poad, Georgiana (Washaway) 124
Polglase, Jean (Geevor) 114
Polmear, Ann (Carn Vivian) 140
Pomeroy, Pol (Menheniot) 144
Porlock, Mary (Australia) 215
Prouse, Bella (Geevor) 114

R

Ralph, Mary (Wheal Maiden) 154
Rede, Juliana (Dartmoor) 94
Remfry, Jane & Fanny (Blackwater) 27
Remmington, Mrs. (Tavistock) 135
Retallack, Gussie (Polpuff) 128, 228, 233
Reynolds, Mary Hannah (Constantine) 27, 201-2
Reynolds, Phillippa (Gwennap) 133
Rice, Grace (Tasmania) 210
Richard, Grace (Come to Good) 140
Richards, Alfreda (Gunnislake) 162
Richards, Ann (Camborne) 162, 163
Richards, Ann (Poldice) 88,
Richards Ann & Grace (Camborne) 27
Richards, Emily (Camborne) 107
Richards, Christiana (St Minver) 140
Richards, Francis (Devon Great Consols) 66
Richards, Laura (Dolcoath) 199
Richards, Mary (St. Blazey) 213
Richards, Mary Jane (Porkellis) 232
Rickard, Mary (Gwennap) 33
Riddle, Caroline (Redruth) 208, **212,** 213
Rimmett, Maria (Peter Tavy) 85
Roberts, Annie (East Pool) 99
Roberts, Grace (Truck's Lodge) 235
Roberts, Mary (St Just) 29
Robins, Susan (St Agnes) 28, 39, 58. 59, 60, 167, 180, **247**
Rodda, Caroline (USA) 208, **212,** 213
Rogers, Grace (Silverwell) 235
Roscorle, Mary Ann (Tresavean) 27, 53
Roskilly, Elizabeth (Fowey Consols) 153, 159
Rowe, Amelia & Kate (St Erth) 111
Rowe, Lavinia (Camborne) 2, 210
Rowe, Margaret (Camborne) 162

Rowe, Mary Bennetts (St Just) 206, **211**
Rowe, Martha (Illogan) 29
Rowe, Mrs (Australia) 215
Rule, Ellen (Camborne) 205
Runce, Mary (E. Great Work) 159

S
Sandow, Jane (Truro) 83, 84, 171
Satterley, Sally (Dartmoor) 234
Sawle, Mary Ann (Camborne) 224
Scollar, Susan (Sithney) 29
Seller, Salley (Sarah) (Redruth) 206
Short, Fanny (St Cleer) 162
Sims, Catherine (Wh. Unity Wood) 133
Sims, Mary (Dolcoath) 199
Simms, Mrs. (Troon) 44-45
Sincock, Anna (Camborne) 82
Sleeman, Ann (Australia) 206
Sleeman, Mary Ellen (Wheal Agar) 159
Sleep, Mary (Bere Ferris) 140
Sludde, Agnes (Calstock) 136
Snell, Ann (Illogan) 206
Snell, Cassandra (St Austell) **231**
Spargo, Mrs Margaret (Callington) 125
Stannon, Agnes (Dartmoor) 94
Stephen, Jane (Tideford) 146
Stephens, Alice (Madron) 185
Stevens, Ann (Newham) 111
Stone, Jenny (Dolcoath) 39, 224
Surfe, Margaret (Bottle Hill) 94
Symons, Lavinia (Australia) 211

T
Tamblyn, Nancy (Newlyn East) 235
Taylor, Lydia (Wendron) 234, 239-40, **258**
Taylor, Angelina, Elizabeth & Mary (St Cleer) 57
Teague, Mary Ann (Australia) 206, 215
Terrell, Mrs (Tavistock) 134
Terrill, Lavinia (Camborne) 2, 210
Terrill, Jenefer (Dolcoath) 234
Thomas, Ann (Gwennap) 154, 210
Thomas, Grace (Gwennap) 210
Thomas, Mary (St Agnes) 30
Thomas, Phyllis (Geevor) 257-8
Thriscott, Mrs (St Austell) 124
Ting, Lynne (Geevor) 159
Tippett, E. (Wh. Trerew) 159
Tonkin, Alice Maud (Wheal Agar) 159
Tonkin, Mary Ann (Gulval) 224
Trebble, Dolly (Hexworthy) 30
Tregoning, Caroline (Newlyn East) 140
Treloar, Eliza (Wheal Agar) 159
Treloar, Olive (Wheal Agar) 159
Tremelling, Patty (Martha) *see* Tremellin
Tremmelin, Patty (Martha) vi, 58, 68, 168, 183, 184, 217, 224, 232, 243-5

Trengrove, Annie (Brea) 199
Trenoweth, Stella (Geevor) 159
Trevena, Emma (Pednandrea) 159
Traffon, Elizabeth (Newham) 111
Trebilcock, Frances (Perranzabuloe) 43
Tregellas, Mary (Wheal Coates) 159
Trembath, Grace (Levant) 187
Trewhella, Jane (Allihies) 204
Trezise, Mary Ann (Perranzabuloe) 29
Truscott, Emily Sophia (Caudledown) 25

U
Uren, Jane (Gwennap) 83

V
Varcoe, Mary Hazel (Polpufff) 129
Verran, Mary (Gwennap) 82, 170
Vincent, Ellen (Redruth) 188, 191
Vine, Jane (Trumpet Consols) 159

W
Wallace, Lavinia (Kehelland) 199
Warne, Catherine (Perranzabuloe) 42
Warren, Elizabeth & Mary (St Just) 57
Wasley, Anna (Gwennap) 173
Waters, Eliza (Illogan) 28
Waters, Frances (Stray Park) 159
Waters, Lillie & Rita (Calstock) 134
Webb, Betty (Dolcoath) 159, 161, 255
Webster, Mary (Gwithian) 30, 161, 190, 191
West, Betsey (Kea) 154, 159
Wheatley, Ann Fry (Tasmania) 210
White, Margaret (Amalebra) 105
Whitta, Elizabeth (St Agnes) 133
Williams, Ann (Towednack) 159, 163
Williams, Eliza (Bere Ferris) 140
Williams, Hanna, Jane & Mary (Treskerby) 232
Williams, Jane (Treskerby) 162
Williams, Martha (Trethellan) 59, 174
Williams, Mary Ann (St Austell) 119
Williams, Matilda (Lanner) 33
Williams, Ruth (Bere Ferris) 140
Wills, Susan (St Agnes) 28, 39, 58, 59, 60, 167, 180, 247
Wilton, Loretta (St Cleer) **249**
Winsland, Joan (Dartmoor) 94
Wise, Elizabeth (Cook's Kitchen) 159
Wittington, Elizabeth 153, 159
Woolcock, Mary Ann (Illogan) 252
Woolcock, Sidwell (Illogan) 215, 252-4, **253**
Wrehans, Christian (Dartmoor) 93
Wyncheat, Joanna (Dartmoor) 94

Y
Yendall, Harriett (Christow) 145